D1060237

The Ultimate
COOKIE
BOOK

The Ultimate
COOKIE
BOOK

**OVER 300 DELICIOUS COOKIES, BROWNIES, BARS
AND MUFFINS TO BAKE AT HOME**

CATHERINE ATKINSON
**with recipes by Joanna Farrow
and Valerie Barrett**

Published by World Publications Group, Inc.
140 Laurel Street, East Bridgewater, MA 02333
www.wrldpub.net

Produced by Anness Publishing Ltd
Hermes House, 88–89 Blackfriars Road, London SE1 8HA
tel. 020 7401 2077; fax 020 7633 9499
www.annesspublishing.com

If you like the images in this book and would like to investigate using them for
publishing, promotions or advertising, please visit our website
www.practicalpictures.com for more information.

Publisher: Joanna Lorenz
Managing Editor: Linda Fraser
Editors: Susannah Blake and Jennifer Schofield
Production Controller: Ben Worley
Photographers: Frank Adam, Karl Adamson, Edward Allwright, Martin Brigdale,
Steve Baxter, James Duncan, John Freeman, Michelle Garrett, Nelson
Hargreaves, Amanda Heywood, David Jordan, William Lingwood, Patrick
McLeavey, Michael Michaels, Craig Robertson and Polly Wreford
Additional recipes: Liz Trigg, Patricia Lousada, Carla Capalbo,
Laura Washburn, Frances Cleary, Norma MacMillan, Christine France, Pamela
Westland, Hilaire Walden, Elizabeth Wolf-Cohen, Janice Murfitt, Carole Handslip,
Steven Wheeler, Katherine Richmond, Joanna Farrow, Judy Williams, Sue Maggs,
Carole Clements, Jacqueline Clarke, Sarah Maxwell, Sallie Morris, Lesley Mackley,
Roz Denny, Sarah Gates, Norma Miller, Maxine Clark, Shirley Gill, Judy Jackson,
Gilly Love, Janet Brinkworth, Elisabeth Lambert Ortiz and Sohelia Kimberley.
Designer: Paul Oakley

ETHICAL TRADING POLICY
Because of our ongoing ecological investment programme, you, as our customer, can have the pleasure
and reassurance of knowing that a tree is being cultivated on your behalf to naturally replace the
materials used to make the book you are holding. For further information about this scheme, go to
www.annesspublishing.com/trees

ISBN-10: 1-57215-506-X
ISBN-13: 978-1-57215-506-0
Printed and bound in Indonesia

Previously published as two separate volumes: *The New Cookie Book* and *The Great Big Cookie Book*

10 9 8 7 6 5 4 3 2 1

NOTES
Bracketed terms are intended for American readers.
For all recipes, quantities are given in both metric and imperial measures and, where appropriate,
measures are also given in standard cups and spoons. Follow one set, but not a mixture, because they
are not interchangeable.
Standard spoon and cup measures are level.
1 tsp = 5ml, 1 tbsp = 15ml, 1 cup = 250ml/8fl oz
Australian standard tablespoons are 20ml. Australian readers should
use 3 tsp in place of 1 tbsp for measuring small quantities of gelatine, flour, salt, etc.

Medium (US large) eggs are used unless otherwise stated.

Contents

The Cookie-making Tradition

No matter what age you are, there's little so enjoyable as a freshly baked cookie. They always feel like the ultimate treat, despite the fact that they're so simple to make. Cookies, in one form or another, have been around for centuries, and some of the most popular cookies today derive from these original treats.

AN AMERICAN INVENTION

The term "cookie" was first used in the United States when early Dutch settlers brought their *koekje* (little cakes) to New York. At about the same time, wood-burning and coal-fired ovens were introduced, which made baking more reliable, and the popularity of cookies and cookie-making soon spread.

Eastern European, Scandinavian and British immigrants who settled in the United States all made great contributions to the cookie-making tradition. For example, refrigerator cookies originated from German Heidesand cookies, which are made by shaping the dough into long, sausage-shaped rolls, cutting them into thin, round slices and then baking them.

In other parts of the world, the word for (and meaning of) cookie varies. In Scotland, a cookie is a sweetened bread bun that is either filled with whipped cream, or thickly iced. In Britain and France, cookies are known as "biscuits," while in the United States, the term "biscuit" is used to describe a large, soft scone.

EARLY COOKIES

There are differences in opinion about the origins of the word "biscuit," but whether it is derived from the French *cuit* or from the Latin *biscoctus*, all agree that it means twice-cooked.

Originally, cookies were double-baked. They were browned for a few minutes when the oven was at its hottest, then removed and returned to finish baking when the oven was cooling down. This time-consuming process dried out the cookies so that they kept well – essential in the days before airtight containers were available. At this time, not all cookie batters were baked; some were fried into wafers.

Rusks and ship's biscuits, which were required to keep for several months, were also baked in this way. The dough was first baked, then cooled, sliced, and dried in a gentle heat until crisp; Italian *biscotti* are still made in this way.

During the Middle Ages, improvements were made. Sugar and spices were added to biscuits, to make them more palatable and, in the late Middle Ages, it was discovered that adding beaten egg to biscuit dough made the finished cookie lighter and that ground nuts could be used instead of flour. This led to the creation of meringue, sponge and macaroon cookies.

Cookie mixtures changed significantly in the 18th and 19th centuries. The tradition of baking rusks and frying cookies virtually disappeared – although in parts of Europe, India and the Middle East some cookies are still fried today – and enriched shortcakes became very popular. These rich, buttery doughs still form the basis of many modern cookies.

Although savory cheese crackers have their origins in medieval times, plain, savory biscuits were not created until the 18th century. These later developed into salted crackers and cocktail savories for nibbling with drinks.

During the 19th century, with the availability of cheap sugar and flour and chemical raising agents such as baking soda, cookie factories were able to open up to serve the public. As the quality of factory-made cookies improved, more and more people began to buy rather than make their own cookies.

COOKIE-MAKING TODAY

In more recent years, consumers have started to turn away from foods containing artificial additives. Commercial cookies have become less popular, and there has been a resurgence in home-baking.

Time-saving kitchen devices, such as food mixers, have helped to speed up cookie-making, and the widely available range of more unusual ingredients has opened up the possibilities for the modern cook, who can make just about any cookie desired.

With the help of this book, you can learn everything you will ever need to know about cookie-making – from the basic techniques to the perfect cookie to serve with coffee, put in a lunchbox or offer as a gift.

CLASSIC COOKIES

Anzac A crunchy cookie from New Zealand, named after the Australia and New Zealand Army Corps (ANZAC). It is made with butter, light corn syrup, rolled oats and coconut.

Bath Oliver A hard, crisp savory cracker created as a health product by Dr W. Oliver of Bath, England, in 1730.

Graham cracker Also known as "sweetmeal" or "wheatmeal," this moderately sweet cookie is made with brown flour. In Britain it is known as a "digestive."

Maria Popular in Spain, this thin, plain, crisp cookie was created in England to celebrate the wedding of the Grand Duchess Maria of Austria to the Duke of Edinburgh.

Fortune Cookie During the Ming Dynasty, political resisters baked cookies containing messages detailing secret meetings and plans. The idea was revived in San Francisco in the 19th century.

Below: Modern fortune cookies contain predictions of the future.

Above: Maryland cookies are one of the most popular and well-known types of chocolate-chip cookie.

Jumble Well-known as early as the 17th century, this cookie was originally flavored with rose water, aniseed, or caraway seeds and tied into knots. The mixture is now made into S-shapes.

Petit Beurre This plain, crisp French cookie has been made in Nantes since the 1880s. It was created by Louis Lefevre-Utile and is also known as "LU" or *P'tit lu*.

Shortbread Scottish shortbread evolved from 16th-century shortcakes. The main ingredients are usually flour, sugar and butter. Petticoat tails are shortbread baked in a round shape, named after an outspread petticoat.

Snickerdoodle A Pennsylvanian Dutch speciality, this spicy cookie contains nutmeg, nuts and raisins.

Chocolate-chip Cookies These are absolute classics; two of the best known being Toll House cookies and chocolate chip Maryland cookies.

The Art of Making and Baking Cookies

Cookies are simple to make, but there is some basic know-how that will make cookie-making even easier. This chapter explains everything you will ever need to know – from basic equipment and ingredients to making, shaping and baking different types of cookie dough; decorating and storing cookies; and making pretty cookie gifts for friends and family.

Cookie Ingredients

Most cookies are made from a few basic ingredients – butter, sugar, flour and sometimes eggs and other ingredients and flavorings. To make the best cookies, always use really fresh, good quality ingredients.

BUTTER

Sweet butter is best for making cookies; it has a sweet, slightly nutty taste and a firm texture, which is particularly well-suited to cookies made using the rubbed-in, or cut-in, method.

The temperature of butter is important. For rubbed-in cookies butter should be cold and firm but not too hard; take it out of the refrigerator 5 minutes before using. To cream butter, it should be at room temperature. This is very important if you are beating by hand. If you forget to take butter out of the refrigerator in advance, soften it in the microwave on low power for 10–15 seconds.

If you need to melt butter, dice it so that it melts more quickly and evenly. Melt the butter over a very low heat to prevent it burning

and remove it from the heat when it has almost melted; the residual heat will complete the job. If you need to brush baking pans or sheets with melted butter, use sweet butter rather than salted, which tends to burn and stick.

STORING BUTTER

Butter should be stored in the refrigerator or freezer. It can absorb other flavors easily, so protect it from strong-smelling ingredients by wrapping it tightly in waxed paper, or foil. If possible, store in a separate compartment.

Salted butter can be stored in the refrigerator for about a month, but sweet butter should be used within 2 weeks. Alternatively, you can store sweet butter in the freezer and transfer it to the refrigerator 1–2 days before you need it. All butter can be frozen for up to 6 months.

Left: Sweet butter produces cookies with a wonderfully rich flavor and warm golden color.

Above: *Shortening (left) and margarine sticks (right) work well in some cookie recipes.*

OTHER FATS

Margarine This won't produce the same flavor as butter, but it is usually less expensive and can be used in the same way. Margarine sticks are better for cookie-making, although soft margarine may be used for creaming.

Shortening Made from blended vegetable oils, such as soybean and cottonseed oil, shortening is flavorless and creates light, short-textured cookies. It works well in highly flavored cookies, in which you would not taste the butter. Lard is an opaque white fat made from rendered pork fat and features in some traditional British cookie recipes.

Oil This may sometimes be used instead of solid fat. Sunflower and safflower oils are preferable, as they are light in color with a mild taste. Olive oil has a distinctive flavor but may be added to savory crackers.

SUGAR

There are many different types of sugar, all of which add their own distinctive character to cookies.

REFINED SUGARS

Produced from sugarcane and sugar beet, refined white sugar is 99.9 percent pure sucrose.

Granulated sugar This has large granules and can be used in rubbed-in mixtures or to make a crunchy cookie topping.

Superfine sugar This is the most frequently used sugar for cookie-making. It has a fine grain so is ideal for creaming with butter. It is also used for melted mixtures, meringue toppings and sprinkling over freshly baked cookies.

Confectioners' sugar This fine, powdery sugar is used to make smooth icings and fillings and for dusting cookies. It may also be added to some piped mixtures.

Soft brown sugar This is refined white sugar that has been tossed in molasses or syrup to color and flavor it; the darker the color, the more intense the flavor. It makes moister cookies than white sugar, so never substitute one for the other.

UNREFINED SUGARS

Derived from raw sugarcane, these retain some molasses. They often have a more intense flavor but tend to be less sweet than refined sugars.

Golden superfine sugar and granulated sugar These are pale gold and are used in the same way as their white counterparts.

Raw sugar This rich golden sugar has a slight toffee flavor. The grains are large, so it is only used in cookie doughs if a crunchy texture is required. It is good for sprinkling over cookies before they are baked.

Above: (Left to right) Soft brown sugar and raw sugar give cookies a slightly caramel taste.

Molasses sugar This fine-textured, moist, soft brown sugar has a molasses-like flavor.

STORING SUGAR

Sugar should always be stored in an airtight container. If white sugar forms clumps, break it up with your fingers. If brown sugar dries out and hardens, warm it in the microwave for about 1 minute.

OTHER SWEETENERS

There are many other ingredients that can be used as sweeteners.

Light corn syrup Slightly less sweet than sugar, this produces moist, sticky cookies and is often used in no-bake recipes.

Maple syrup Thinner than golden syrup, this has a distinctive flavor.

Honey Use blended honey in cookie doughs, as the flavor of milder honeys will be lost.

Malt syrup This concentrated syrup made from corn and barley has a distinctive flavor, thick consistency and dark, almost black color.

Molasses A by-product of sugar refining, molasses looks like malt syrup but has a slightly bitter taste.

Above:
Coarse-grained granular sugar is good for sprinkling.

Left: Fine-grained superfine sugar is widely used in cookie doughs.

FLOUR

Most cookie recipes use all-purpose flour, as it has a low gluten content, resulting in a crumbly texture. The grains are processed then treated with chlorine to make the flour whiter. You can also buy unbleached flour, which has a grayish color. Some flour is pre-sifted but you should sift it anyway as the contents tend to settle during storage. Flour, even of the same type and brand, may vary slightly, so always hold a few drops of liquid back in case they aren't needed.

SELF-RISING FLOUR

This flour contains raising agents that make cookies spread and rise, giving them a lighter texture. If you run out of self-rising flour, you can substitute all-purpose flour, adding 1 teaspoon baking powder to each 4 ounces/1 cup. Self-rising flour should not be kept for longer than 3 months, because raising agents gradually deteriorate.

WHOLE-WHEAT FLOUR

This flour is milled from the entire wheat kernel and contains all the nutrients and flavor of wheat. It is coarser than white flour, giving a heavier result. It absorbs more liquid than white flour, so recipes should be adjusted if whole-wheat flour is used.

Wheatmeal flour contains only 80–90 percent of the bran and wheat germ and has a finer texture and milder taste.

Left: Whole-wheat flour gives cookies a lovely taste.

NON-WHEAT FLOURS

These can be great for cookie-making, although some should be combined with wheat flour.

Potato flour This fine powder is made from potato starch and can be mixed with wheat flour to give a lighter texture to cookies.

Chestnut flour This light brown, nutty-flavored flour is made from ground chestnuts and is often sold in Italian delicatessens.

Corn meal Also known as polenta" or "maizemeal," this is bright yellow and coarse or medium ground.

Cornstarch This fine white powder is made from the middle of the maize kernel. It is often used in piped cookie mixtures to give a smooth texture.

Soy flour Made from soybeans, this has a distinctive nutty flavor. It has a high protein content. Medium- and low-fat varieties are available.

Rice flour This is made by finely grinding polished white rice and is used in many cookie recipes, to give a short, slightly crumbly texture.

Above: Rice flour is often added to shortbread to give a crumbly texture.

Left: Corn meal produces cookies with a golden color, delicious flavor and distinctive texture.

GLUTEN-FREE BAKING

Some people are allergic or intolerant to the protein gluten, which is found in both wheat and rye. Specially produced gluten-free and wheat-free flour mixtures can be used for baking, as can any of the naturally gluten-free flours such as corn meal, potato flour, rice flour and soya flour.

Above: *Baking soda and baking powder give cookies a lighter texture.*

RAISING AGENTS

Although cookies are usually made with all-purpose flour, raising agents may be added to give them a lighter texture. Raising agents make cookies spread more, so space them far apart for baking.

Raising agents react when they come in contact with water, and produce carbon dioxide bubbles that make the cookie rise during baking. Cookie doughs containing raising agents must, therefore, be shaped and baked as soon as liquid is added. Store raising agents in a dry place and use them within their use-by date, because they deteriorate with age, becoming less effective.

Baking powder This is a mixture of alkaline baking soda and an acid such as cream of tartar.

Baking soda This can be added to a cookie mixture that contains an acidic ingredient.

Right: *Eggs are widely used in cookie-making and can help to produce rich, golden cookies with a great flavor.*

EGGS

These are used to enrich cookie doughs and bind dry ingredients. They are often included in rolled doughs because they prevent the mixture from spreading too much during baking. If a recipe does not specify the size of an egg, use a large one.

For baking, eggs should be at room temperature; cold egg yolks may curdle and cold egg whites will produce less volume when whisked. Add eggs to a creamed mixture a little at a time, beating after each addition and adding 1 tablespoon sifted flour if the mixture starts to curdle. Whisk egg whites in a very clean bowl and use straight away.

BUYING AND STORING EGGS

Always check the use-by date on eggs and never buy cracked, damaged or dirty eggs. A fresh egg will have a round, plump yolk and a thick white that clings closely to the yolk. Store eggs in the refrigerator, pointed-end down. Do not store near strong-smelling foods or possible contaminants, such as raw meat; their shells are porous and can absorb odors and bacteria.

SEPARATING EGGS

Some recipes require only an egg yolk or an egg white. Egg separating devices are available from kitchenware stores, but it is easy to separate eggs by hand.

1 Tap the middle of the egg sharply against the rim of a bowl, then, holding the egg over the bowl, prize the shell apart with the tips of your thumbs.

2 Gently tip the white into the bowl, retaining the yolk in the shell. Tip the yolk into the other half-shell, letting any remaining white fall into the bowl.

Cook's Tip

You can also separate the yolk from the white by tipping the whole egg into the palm of your hand and letting the white drain into a bowl through your fingers.

FRUIT, NUTS AND SEEDS

Dried and candied fruit, and nuts and seeds can be added to cookie doughs to add flavor, color and texture, or to decorate.

DRIED FRUIT

The drying process intensifies the flavor and sweetness of the fruit. Adding dried fruit does not affect the moisture of the dough, so you can usually substitute one type of dried fruit for another in a recipe.

Vine fruit These include golden raisins, raisins and currants. Buy seedless fruit, choosing a reliable brand, or go for fruit in clear bags so that you can check its softness and color. As dried fruit ages, a white coating may develop; it is still usable, but you should never buy it in this condition. It can be kept in an airtight container for up to a year, but is best used within 6 months. Some brands are lightly tossed in oil before packing to keep the fruits separate; uncoated vine fruits may stick together and should be pulled apart before adding to cookies.

Apricots These are produced in California and other parts of the American Pacific coast, Australia, South Africa, Turkey and Iran. Some are very dry and need to be soaked in a little liquid before using; others, usually labelled ready-to-eat, have a softer texture and sweeter flavor and are generally better for cookie-making. After picking and pitting, the fruits may be treated with sulphur dioxide to retain their color and prevent mold growing.

Unsulphured apricots, which are darker in color and very sticky, are also available; they should be stored in the refrigerator.

Apples and pears Dried in rings or as halved fruit, these have a chewy texture. They are best used finely chopped and added to drop cookie mixtures.

Tropical fruits Exotic fruits, such as papaya and mango, are available dried and have an intense flavor and a vibrant color. They are often sold in strips, which can be easily chopped with a sharp knife or snipped into small pieces with a pair of scissors. Dried pineapple and dried banana are also available and make a tasty addition to cookies.

***Left:** Dried fruit, such as apricots and pears, make a delicious, healthy addition to cookies.*

***Above:** Candied ingredients, such as cherries and angelica, can be used both to flavor cookies and as decorations.*

Cranberries and sour cherries These are brightly colored and add a wonderful sweet-and-sour flavor to cookies. They make a very good addition to festive cookies.

Candied fruit Fresh fruits, such as whole pitted cherries and apricots or pieces of kiwi and pineapple, are steeped in sugar. The process retains the original bright color of the fruit. Angelica, the bright green stem of the herb, is candied in this way. Because of their pretty color, candied fruits are usually used to decorate cookies, rather than in the dough.

Candying fruit takes a long time, making the fruit expensive. Candied citrus peel is cheaper and can be bought ready-chopped. However, make sure that chopped candied peel is still soft and moist, as it can dry out quickly; it is better to buy whole pieces of candied peel and chop or slice it as required.

NUTS

These can be added to cookie mixtures or chopped and sprinkled over unbaked cookies. Always buy really fresh nuts in small quantities, then chop as necessary. Store in an airtight container, ideally in the refrigerator or freezer.

Almonds Sweet almonds are available ready-blanched, chopped, split, sliced and ground.

Brazil nuts These wedge-shaped nuts are actually a seed. Their creamy white flesh has a sweet milky taste and a high fat content. Store carefully and use within a few months. They can be grated.

Cashew nuts These kidney-shaped nuts are always sold shelled and dried. They have a sweet flavor and almost crumbly texture.

Coconut White, dense coconut flesh is made into dried unsweetened shredded, and flaked coconut. It is also possible to find sweetened shredded coconut, which is good for decorating cookies.

Below: Hazelnuts have a lovely nutty taste and can be used whole or chopped into small pieces.

Hazelnuts These are particularly good chopped and toasted, as this brings out their flavor.

Macadamia nuts Also known as "Queensland nuts," these round, white, buttery nuts are native to Australia but are now also grown in California and South America.

Peanuts Strictly speaking, these are a legume not a nut, as they grow underground. Peanuts may be used raw or roasted, but do not use salted nuts unless specified.

Pecan nuts These are rather like elongated walnuts in appearance, but with a milder, sweeter flavor.

Pine nuts These are the fruit of the stone pine, which grows in the Mediterranean. Small and cream-colored, they have an almost oily texture and aromatic flavor.

Pistachio nuts Bright green in color, these are often used for decorating cookies.

Walnuts These are well flavored with a crunchy texture. In the United States there are several types: white walnuts or butternuts, the large pale-shelled variety called "English" or "Californian," and strong-flavored, black-shelled walnuts.

SKINNING NUTS

To make skinning easier, either roast or blanch the nuts first.

To roast nuts, spread them out in a single layer on a baking sheet and roast at 350°F/Gas 4 for 10–12 minutes, until the skins split and the nuts are golden. Tip the nuts onto a clean dishtowel and rub gently to loosen and remove the skins.

To blanch nuts, place in a bowl, pour over boiling water and leave for 5 minutes. Drain, then slip them out of their skins.

SEEDS

These are a popular ingredient in wholesome cookies and savory crackers. They can be added to cookie doughs to give a crunchy texture, or sprinkled over the tops of cookies before they are baked, to give an attractive finish. Sesame and poppy seeds work particularly well because of their small size. However, larger seeds such as sunflower seeds work just as well.

Left: Sunflower and pumpkin seeds can be added to cookie doughs or sprinkled over unbaked cookies.

COOKIE FLAVORINGS

There are many flavorings that can be added to cookies. They may add a subtle or strong taste, and some can also add texture.

CHOCOLATE

From cocoa-flavored drop cookies to chocolate chip and chocolate-coated varieties, chocolate is the most popular cookie flavoring.

Bittersweet chocolate This has a bitter flavor and is the most popular chocolate for cookie-making. The degree of bitterness depends on the percentage of cocoa solids. Continental bittersweet (dark) chocolate contains a minimum of 70 percent cocoa solids, so it is ideal for very sweet, sugar-laden cookies. Semisweet chocolate contains at least 50 percent cocoa solids; the eating variety may contain as little as 25 percent. It can be chopped and added to cookie doughs, but does not melt well.

Milk chocolate This contains milk powder and a higher percentage of sugar than semisweet chocolate. It is more difficult to melt.

White chocolate This contains no cocoa solids, only cocoa butter, milk solids and sugar. Some cheaper brands use flavorings and vegetable oil in place of cocoa butter. Brands that contain more cocoa butter are best for baking and melting. White chocolate may caramelize during baking, due to its high sugar content.

Couverture This fine-quality semisweet, milk or white chocolate is used by professional cooks, and can be bought from specialist stores and by mail order. It melts beautifully and makes glossy cookie coatings.

Chocolate chips or dots
These tiny chocolate pieces melt well and are easy to work with. The milk and white versions are more stable than bars of milk and white chocolate.

Chocolate cake covering This usually contains little real chocolate and is flavored with cocoa powder. It melts well and is good for coating cookies, but has a poor flavor.

Unsweetened cocoa powder This bitter, dark powder can be added to cookie mixtures or dusted over the tops of cookies. (Drinking chocolate contains about 25 percent cocoa powder and 75 percent sugar. It is not suitable for baking.)

Complementary flavors
Chocolate can be combined with many other flavorings. The most subtle is vanilla, which often goes unnoticed, yet greatly enhances the taste and aroma of chocolate. The bitterness of coffee can offset

Above: Chocolate — in its many forms — is a popular cookie ingredient.

the sweetness of chocolate, and caramel works well, especially if the sugar is cooked until it is dark, as this helps to reduce some of its sweetness. Both mint and orange add a subtle tang to chocolate cookies, and are especially good for fillings, frostings and icings; nuts are a classic addition.

STORING CHOCOLATE

Chocolate should always be wrapped in foil and kept in a dry, cool place. In hot weather, chocolate can be kept in the refrigerator, but it may develop a whitish bloom; this is the cocoa butter rising to the surface. The chocolate will still be safe to use and won't alter the flavor of cookies, but it can affect the final texture.

SPICES AND HERBS

Adding spices to cookies is a great way to add flavor. Warm spices such as cinnamon, ginger and nutmeg are mainly used in sweet cookies, while whole spice seeds such as cumin and fennel, and ground ones such as coriander and chilli are great in crackers.

Vanilla is perhaps the spice most frequently added to sweet cookies, providing a fragrant, delicate flavor. Vanilla sugar is one of the easiest ways to add the flavoring. Pure vanilla extract, which is distilled from vanilla beans, is also a good way to add the flavor. Vanilla flavoring is a synthetic product and may not actually contain any real vanilla.

Fresh or dried herbs can be added to savory cookie doughs or sprinkled on top before baking. Some, such as rosemary,

Above: *Grated citrus rind can be added to cookie doughs to give them a lovely zesty citrus taste.*

are highly pungent and should be used sparingly. Milder herbs such as mint are good in fillings, and mint extract can be added to doughs.

Above: *Fresh mint can be added to delicately flavored cookies and fillings to give them a fresh, aromatic flavor.*

OTHER FLAVORINGS

There are also a great many cookie flavorings that do not fit into a particular category. These include grated lemon, lime or orange rind, the juice of citrus fruits, rose water, orange flower water and almond extract.

ALCOHOL

Spirits, sherry and liqueurs can be added to cookie mixtures instead of liquid such as milk. They can also be used to soak dried fruit. During baking, the alcohol will evaporate, leaving a subtle flavor. They can also be used in candied icings.

SALT

This helps to bring out the flavor in both sweet cookies and crackers, but add only the tiniest pinch, especially if using salted butter. Coarse crystals of sea salt can be used to sprinkle over savory cookies to decorate.

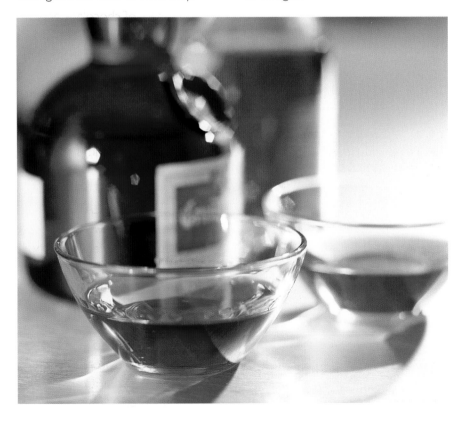

Equipment

Most cookies can be made with nothing more sophisticated than weighing scales or calibrated measuring cups, a mixing bowl, fine sieve, rolling pin, wooden spoon, baking sheet and wire rack. However, there are a few pieces of equipment that can make cookie-making even easier.

Electric gadgets can really speed up the whole cookie-making process, and more specialist equipment, such as cookie presses, shortbread molds and piping bags, can produce really professional-looking cookies.

BOWLS

Large bowls are good for mixing doughs, while medium and small heatproof bowls are good for melting butter or chocolate and beating eggs. Small and medium bowls are also useful if you need to measure out ingredients beforehand. Some people may argue that a copper or steel bowl is desirable for whisking egg whites to their maximum volume, but, for cookie-making, this really is not necessary.

Left: An electric food mixer takes the hard work out of cookie-making and can be a real time saver.

Above: A set of different sized, heatproof bowls for mixing, beating and melting ingredients is invaluable when making cookies.

ELECTRICAL APPLIANCES

Food mixers and processors are great for creaming together butter and sugar and for beating in eggs. However, if these machines are used, dry ingredients should always be folded in by hand, as it is very easy to over-mix cookie dough, which will spoil the final texture.

A food processor is particularly useful for chopping and grinding large quantities of nuts, and some come with a mini bowl specifically made for such tasks.

A hand-held electric whisk can be used for beating eggs, whisking egg whites and beating together butter and sugar, and it has the advantage that it can be used in a pan over heat. Choose one with three speeds and beaters that can be removed for easy cleaning.

SPATULAS

A flexible rubber or plastic spatula can be used to scrape every last morsel of cookie dough from the mixing bowl. They are also very useful for folding dry ingredients such as flour into a creamed or whisked mixture.

METAL SPATULAS

Round-bladed flexible metal spatulas and wide metal spatulas are essential for lifting cookies from baking sheets and can also be used for mixing liquid into cookie doughs and mixtures. Small ones are very useful for spreading cookie fillings and icing onto cookies.

WHISKS

A wire balloon whisk or hand-held rotary whisk are useful for whisking egg whites for cookies such as macaroons and for whipping cream to use in fillings. They are also good for removing lumps in icing.

Above: Flexible and wide metal spatulas make cookie-making easier.

MEASURING SPOONS, JUGS AND CUPS

A set of accurate measuring spoons is essential. Ordinary spoons vary in size, so invest in a commercially produced set. For measuring larger volumes of dry ingredients and liquids, you will need a clearly calibrated measuring cup. They are available in glass, plastic and stainless steel. Use a glass measuring cup for hot liquids; plastic may soften, and stainless steel conducts heat.

SIEVES

You should invest in a set of strong, fine sieves in at least two sizes; a large one for sifting dry ingredients such as flour, and a smaller one for dusting confectioners' sugar or unsweetened cocoa powder over baked cookies. You can also buy dredgers with a very fine mesh or tiny holes in the top for dusting with confectioners' sugar or cocoa powder, but a sieve works just as well.

Below: A set of special measuring spoons and measuring cups are essential for successful baking.

Below: A set of strong, fine-wire sieves will prove invaluable for cookie-making and last a lifetime.

Below: The flexible wires of a balloon whisk will incorporate air into everything from eggs to cream.

ROLLING PINS

These come in all shapes and sizes, some with handles and some without. Rolling pins are usually made of wood, but they are also available in marble. Mini rolling pins are sometimes available and are perfect for small children who want to help out in the kitchen. Hollow plastic rolling pins, designed to be filled with iced water, are also available. These have no special advantage over ordinary rolling pins, providing the cookie dough is sufficiently chilled before rolling out.

PASTRY BOARDS

These flat, smooth boards are good for rolling cookie dough out to an even thickness. They are made from many different materials, including wood, toughened glass and marble, which remains cool to the touch however warm the weather.

Smooth, laminated plastic kitchen surfaces provide a good alternative to a separate pastry board, but take care not to scratch the surface when using cookie cutters and sharp knives.

BAKING SHEETS

These are either entirely flat or have a lip along the length of one side; baking trays have a lip all around the edges. Baking sheets are preferable, as they allow better air movement around the cookies, but be careful when removing cookies from the oven, because they can slip off easily.

Always measure your oven before buying baking sheets, to make sure they will fit. Large sheets will allow you to bake more cookies in each batch, but there needs to be a small gap at either side and at the back of the baking sheet so that heat can circulate. Although non-stick varieties may save greasing or lining with waxed paper; crisp cookies may not crisp quite so well on them, and soft ones may spread out too much.

When buying baking sheets, always choose good-quality, heavy ones; they won't buckle in high temperatures, distort the shape of your cookies or develop hot-spots, which might cause burning. A good baking sheet can last you a lifetime. Avoid baking sheets that are very dark, as they absorb more heat, which means cookies burn more easily. Dark baking sheets are intended for other kinds of baking, such as bread-baking.

Below: Wooden rolling pins are efficient, inexpensive and very easy to clean.

Left: Baking sheets can vary greatly in size, color and quality.

PANS

These are available in many shapes and sizes, from round, square and rectangular to petal-shaped. They are used for baking cookie doughs such as shortbread and bar and brownie mixtures. The cookies should be marked into squares, bars or wedges while warm, then cut and removed from the pan when cool. If possible, use pans with a dull finish rather than shiny aluminum ones, as they will give your cookies a crispier texture.

To bake bar cookies, use a rectangular pan measuring 11 x 7 inches, or a square pan measuring 8 x 8 inches. If you do not have a pan, you can use an ovenproof glass dish. However, this will not produce such good results, and the oven temperature will have to be reduced slightly, because glass takes longer than metal to heat up, but retains more heat when removed from the oven.

WIRE RACKS

After baking, most cookies should be transferred to a wire rack to cool. The rack allows air to circulate, preventing trapped warmth turning into moisture and making the cookies soggy. Some cookies should be left on the baking sheet for a few minutes to firm up before transferring to a wire rack.

Below: Wire racks are available in all shapes and sizes.

TIMERS

These are absolutely essential for baking. Even an extra 1 or 2 minutes in the oven can result in overbaked or burned cookies. Many modern ovens are already fitted with a timer, but if you do not have an oven with a timer, it is well worth investing in one. The simplest timers have a rotating dial that registers any time up to 60 minutes. They are fairly accurate and are perfectly suitable for baking cookies. Modern, digital timers are very useful and accurate and will help ensure that your cookies are removed from the oven at exactly the right time. These small timers also have the advantage that you can take them with you if you need to go into another room while your cookies bake.

Above: Cookie dough can be pressed into pans to make squares and bars.

Above: Digital timers are inexpensive and help to ensure perfect baking.

COOKIE CUTTERS

These come in many different shapes and sizes, from the simplest plain or fluted round cutters to people-, animal-, heart- and flower-shaped ones. You will also find tiny cutters that can be used for *petits fours* and savory cocktail snacks, and multi-sided cutters that have six different shapes arranged around a cube.

For the best results, cutters should be sharp enough to give a clear, precise outline. The top side of the cutter will usually have a smooth, rounded finish for pressing down on. More intricate cutters will retain their shape better if they have a handle on them, as this helps to keep the cutter rigid.

Below: *Metal cutters are better for cookie-making than plastic ones, which can compress the cut edges.*

Below:

Pretty shortbread molds are usually carved from sycamore wood, which gives a sharp outline.

SHORTBREAD MOLDS

You can buy shortbread molds that are decorated with intricate patterns. These are perfect if you are making shortbread for a special occasion, or if you are making shortbread to offer as a gift. The molds are usually made of wood. The classic shortbread mold is traditionally engraved with a Scottish thistle motif and is usually about 7 inches in diameter.

They are simple to use; all you need to do is press the dough into the mold with the tips of your fingers, level off the surface with a metal spatula and then turn out onto a baking sheet for baking.

Above: *An aluminum cookie press comes with a choice of patterned disks to create different shapes.*

COOKIE PRESSES

Soft cookie dough can be shaped using a cookie press. The presses look like an icing syringe and work in a similar way. The dough is forced through a disk, which shapes the dough into a pretty cookie.

***Right:** Pastry bags can be filled with dough and used to make cookie shapes, or filled with icing and used to decorate baked cookies.*

PASTRY BAGS AND NOZZLES

A medium to large pastry bag and a selection of both plain and fluted nozzles is useful for piping uncooked cookie dough. Smaller pastry bags are extremely good for decorating baked cookies with icing or buttercream.

Originally, pastry bags were made of waterproof canvas, but these tended to weep and were difficult to wash; now pastry bags are made of nylon. Look for bags that are double stitched along the seams, as well as glued to avoid leakage or splitting. You can also buy disposable pastry bags, which are ideal for piping fine lines of melted chocolate or icing as decoration. (A small plastic bag with the corner snipped off makes a good substitute if you don't have a pastry bag.)

PASTRY BRUSHES

These brushes are used for glazing unbaked cookies with milk or beaten egg, or baked cookies with a thin sugar glaze. They can also be used for brushing surplus flour from rolled cookie dough and for greasing baking sheets with oil.

The best pastry brushes have natural bristles fixed in a wooden handle, although nylon bristles are sometimes considered more hygienic. Brushes that have been used for egg glazing should be rinsed in cold water before washing in hot soapy water. Flick them dry and leave to air before using again.

***Below:** A pastry brush is very useful for brushing unbaked cookies with a milk or beaten egg glaze.*

PASTRY WHEELS

These make quick work of cutting rolled dough into squares, rectangles or diamonds, although some skill is needed to create even-size cookies. They are particularly good for young children who want to help with cutting out cookie shapes. They are easy to use and do not have a sharp blade. They are available from kitchenware stores and are either made from wood or stainless steel, and have a plain or fluted blade. (A pizza cutter can be used in the same way.)

***Below:** A fluted pastry wheel gives a pretty zigzag edge to rectangular, square and diamond-shaped cookies.*

Methods of Making Cookies

There are many different ways of making cookie dough. Depending on the type of cookie you are baking, the method will vary, so it is useful to know all the techniques.

THE CREAMING METHOD

A wide variety of cookies are made using the creaming method. These include plain Shrewsbury cookies, French sablés, fork cookies, melting moments, snickerdoodles and Swiss butter cookies. The fat and sugar are creamed – or beaten – together either until just blended or, more usually, until they are well-aerated and have a light and fluffy texture. Eggs and dry ingredients are then added a little bit at a time.

The fat should be soft enough to beat easily, so remember to remove it from the refrigerator at least 30 minutes before you start mixing. Sweet butter is the best choice, but if you are going to use margarine, use the firm stick type rather than softer margarine that is sold in tubs.

The eggs should also be at room temperature, or they may curdle the creamed mixture when they are added. It is not essential to use an electric mixer or food processor for the creaming method – a wooden spoon does a perfectly good job – but it definitely makes the process easier and quicker.

Cook's Tip
Creamed mixtures have a tendency to curdle when the eggs are added. To avoid this, add the eggs a little at a time and beat well after each addition. If the mixture does curdle, beat in 1 tablespoon of the flour before adding more egg.

SWISS BUTTER COOKIES
These crisp cookies are very easy to make and delicious to eat.

Makes 24
4 ounces/½ cup sweet
  butter, softened
2 ounces/¼ cup superfine sugar
1 egg
7 ounces/1¾ cups all-purpose flour
2 tablespoons cornstarch
1 tablespoon ground almonds

1 Put the butter in a large mixing bowl and beat with an electric mixer or a wooden spoon until it is softened and creamy. Add the sugar and beat in until it is completely incorporated. Continue beating until the mixture is light, fluffy and much paler in color.

2 Beat the egg lightly with a fork. Add the egg to the butter mixture, a little at a time, beating well after each addition.

3 Sift the flour and cornstarch over the creamed ingredients. This will remove any lumps and incorporate air, making your cookies lighter. Add the ground almonds and stir together to make a soft dough.

4 Shape the dough into a ball, then flatten it slightly into a round shape – this makes it easier to roll out. Wrap the dough tightly in plastic wrap and chill for about 30 minutes, or until the dough is fairly firm. Meanwhile, preheat the oven to 350°F/Gas 4. Lightly grease two baking sheets or line them with baking parchment.

5 Roll out the dough on a lightly floured surface to ⅛ inch thick. Cut the dough into round pieces with a 3-inch plain cutter and place on the baking sheets. Bake for about 15 minutes, until golden. Leave on the baking sheets for 5 minutes, then transfer to a wire rack to cool.

THE RUBBING-IN METHOD

Many traditional cookies, such as shortbread and Graham crackers, are made by rubbing, or cutting, the fat, which can be butter, margarine, shortening or lard, into the flour. The fat should be firm and cool but not straight from the refrigerator, so leave the fat at room temperature before using. Beaten eggs, milk or water may be added to bind the mixture.

CLASSIC SHORTBREAD

These buttery cookies are cooked as a round shape, then cut into wedges.

Makes 8 wedges

6 ounces/1½ cups all-purpose flour

4 ounces/½ cup butter, diced and chilled

2 ounces/¼ cup superfine sugar, plus extra for sprinkling

1 Preheat the oven to 325°F/Gas 3. Grease a baking sheet or line it with baking parchment. Sift the flour and salt into a large bowl. Use a metal spatula to stir in the diced butter until the pieces are coated with flour. Rub them between your fingertips, lifting the mixture and then letting it drop until it looks like fine breadcrumbs. Stir in the sugar.

2 Holding the bowl firmly, gather the dough into a ball – the warmth of your hand will help bring the dough together.

3 Gently knead the dough on a lightly floured surface for about 30 seconds, until it is smooth.

4 Roll out the dough into a round shape about 6 inches in diameter and ½ inch thick. Transfer to the prepared baking sheet. Score the top deeply into eight sections, then prick a pattern with a fork. This will allow steam to escape during cooking and prevent the shortbread from rising in the middle. Chill the shortbread for 1 hour.

5 Sprinkle the top lightly and evenly with a little extra superfine sugar. Bake the shortbread for 35 minutes, or until it is a pale, golden straw color. Leave to cool on the baking sheet for 5 minutes, then transfer to a wire rack to cool.

MAKING RUBBED-IN COOKIES IN A FOOD PROCESSOR

This method of making cookies is especially useful where the cookie mixture contains a high proportion of fat.

1 Put the sifted flour and other dry ingredients, such as salt, into the food processor. Process for 4–5 seconds.

2 Sprinkle in the diced, chilled fat. Process for 10 seconds, or until the mixture resembles fine breadcrumbs.

3 Sprinkle any liquid, such as beaten egg, milk or water, over the mixture and, using the pulse button, process for just a few seconds until the mixture starts to hold together. Do not allow the cookie dough to form a ball in the food processor.

4 Remove the mixture from the food processor and form into a ball with your hands. Gently knead the dough on a lightly floured surface for a few seconds, until smooth. Wrap the dough in plastic wrap and then chill until fairly firm.

THE MELTED METHOD

Cookies such as flapjacks and gingersnaps are made by first melting the fat and sugar or syrup together. The dry ingredients are then stirred in to make a soft dough that firms as it cools. The baked cookies become crisp as they cool, so should be quickly shaped, or left on the baking sheets for a few minutes to firm up before transferring to a wire rack.

GINGERSNAPS

When baked, these spiced cookies are slightly cracked on the top.

Makes 24
2 ounces/¼ cup butter, diced
2 ounces/¼ cup light corn
   syrup
1½ ounces/3 tablespoons
   granulated sugar
4 ounces/1 cup self-rising flour
1 teaspoon ground ginger
1 teaspoon baking soda

1 Preheat the oven to 350°F/Gas 4. Lightly grease two large baking sheets. Put the butter, syrup and sugar in a heavy pan and heat gently until just melted, stirring occasionally until the ingredients are blended. Do not let the mixture boil, or some of the liquid will evaporate, altering the proportions.

2 Remove the pan from the heat and leave the mixture to cool for a few minutes. (This is particularly important if you are adding eggs, as they will cook and curdle if the mixture is too hot.) Sift the flour, ginger and baking soda over the mixture. Stir until the mixture has blended and is smooth. The raising agents will start to work right away, so shape the cookie dough and bake as soon as possible.

3 Place small spoonfuls of the mixture onto the prepared baking sheets, spacing the mounds of cookie dough far apart to allow room for the cookies to spread.

4 Bake the gingersnaps for about 10 minutes, or until they are golden brown and the top surfaces are finely cracked. Leave the cookies on the baking sheets for 2 minutes to firm up, then transfer them to a wire rack to cool and crisp.

THE WHISKED METHOD

Airy cookies or crisp, delicate cookies, such as tuiles, macaroons and *langues de chat* are made by folding the dry ingredients into a whisked mixture of eggs and sugar, or into a meringue (whisked egg whites and sugar) mixture.

TUILES

These delicate cookies are named after the French curved roof tiles, which they closely resemble if they are shaped into curls while still hot.

Makes 12
1 egg white
2 ounces/¼ cup superfine sugar
1 ounce/2 tablespoons butter, melted
   and cooled
1 ounce/¼ cup all-purpose
   flour, sifted
sliced almonds, for sprinkling
   (optional)

1 Preheat the oven to 375°F/Gas 5. Lightly grease two or three baking sheets or line them with sheets of baking parchment.

2 Put the egg whites in a large, clean, grease-free mixing bowl and whisk until stiff peaks form. Gently fold in the superfine sugar to make a stiff and glossy mixture. (It should resemble a meringue mixture.)

3 Trickle about a third of the melted butter down the side of the bowl and fold in with the same quantity of flour. Repeat until all the butter and flour are incorporated.

4 Place small spoonfuls of the mixture, at least 5 inches apart, on the prepared baking sheets, then spread out into thin round pieces using the back of a spoon. Sprinkle sliced almonds over each piece, if using.

5 Bake the tuiles for 6–7 minutes, or until the biscuits are pale beige in the middle and brown at the edges. Leave to cool on the baking sheets for a few seconds, then lift off carefully with a metal spatula and cool on a wire rack. (If you want to curl the tuiles, do this while they are still hot.)

THE ALL-IN-ONE METHOD

Some cookies are made by simply placing all the ingredients in a bowl and beating them together. Drop cookies are usually made this way. This easy method can be made even faster by using a food processor, although chunky ingredients such as dried fruit and nuts may have to be stirred in after mixing the cookie dough. It is essential that the fat is soft enough to blend easily.

RAISIN COOKIES

The natural sweetness of raisins gives these cookies extra flavor and a chewy bite.

Makes 24

5 ounces/1¼ cups all-purpose flour
½ teaspoon baking powder
pinch of salt
4 ounces/generous ½ cup superfine sugar
4 ounces/½ cup soft margarine
I egg, lightly beaten
½ teaspoon vanilla extract
5 ounces/I cup seedless raisins

I Preheat the oven to 375°F/Gas 5. Lightly grease three baking sheets or line them with baking parchment. Sift together the flour, baking powder and salt into a mixing bowl or the bowl of a food processor. Add the sugar, margarine, egg and vanilla extract.

2 Beat with a wooden spoon or blend in a food processor until combined. Stir in the raisins.

3 Drop two heaped teaspoons of the mixture about 2 inches apart onto the baking sheets. Bake the cookies for 15 minutes, or until golden brown. Leave on the baking sheets for a few minutes, then transfer to wire racks to cool.

MEASURING INGREDIENTS

Dry ingredients by weight

Electronic and balance scales generally give more accurate readings than spring scales. Spoon or pour the dry ingredients into the bowl or tray on the scales and check the reading or dial carefully.

Dry ingredients in measuring cups or spoons

To measure a dry ingredient in a spoon, scoop it up in the spoon, then level the surface using the straight edge of a knife. If you are using measuring cups, make sure you have ¼, ⅓, ½, ⅔, ¾ and I cup sizes. Where a recipe calls for a scant cup, fill the cup with the dry ingredient, level with the back of a knife, then scoop out about I tablespoon. Where a generous cup is called for, level with a knife then add about I tablespoon.

Liquids in pints or cups

Use a clear glass or plastic cup with calibrations in pints or cups. Put it on a flat surface, pour in the liquid and check the markings by bending down and looking at eye level.

Liquids in spoons

Use proper measuring spoons and carefully pour in the liquid, filling it to the brim then pouring it into the mixing bowl. Do not hold the spoon over the bowl.

Drop Cookies

These are probably the simplest cookies to make. They are called drop cookies because the dough is soft enough to drop off the spoon and onto the baking sheet. The basic mixture is often made by the creaming method where butter and sugar are beaten together until light and fluffy. Eggs are then beaten in, followed by flour, raising agents and any flavorings.

CHOCOLATE CHIP COOKIES
Created in the 1930s, these were originally called Toll House cookies.

Makes 12

4 ounces/½ cup butter, softened

4 ounces/generous ½ cup superfine sugar

1 egg, lightly beaten

1 teaspoon vanilla extract

6 ounces/1½ cups all-purpose flour

6 ounces/1 cup semisweet chocolate chips

1 Preheat the oven to 350°F/Gas 4. Lightly grease two or three large baking sheets or line them with baking parchment. Cream the butter and sugar together in a bowl with a wooden spoon or an electric mixer until pale and fluffy. Beat in the egg and vanilla extract. Sift the flour over the butter mixture and fold in with the chocolate chips.

2 Drop tablespoonfuls of the mixture onto the prepared baking sheets. (It should fall off the spoon quite easily with a sharp jerk; if not, use another spoon to scoop it off.) Leave plenty of space between the cookies to allow for spreading.

3 Flatten each cookie slightly with the back of a fork, keeping the shape as even as possible. For dropped cookies that have a soft or cakey texture when cooked, the mixture should be left very mounded on the baking sheet and not flattened; very stiff mixtures should be more widely spread. The recipe instructions should indicate this – if you are unsure, test how much the mixture spreads by baking a single cookie.

4 Bake the cookies for about 10 minutes, or until golden. Using a metal spatula, transfer to a wire rack to cool.

FLAVORING DROP COOKIES
As long as you follow the basic recipe and techniques, you can make a huge variety of drop cookies. Remember, though, that some added ingredients may alter the consistency of the dough – chopped fresh fruit, for example, may make the mixture too wet, whereas rolled oats will soak up moisture, making the cookies dry and crumbly.

Chocolate Substitute 1 tablespoon cocoa powder (unsweetened) for the same quantity of flour. For a chunkier texture, use coarsely chopped chocolate instead of chocolate chips. You can use milk chocolate or chocolate chips instead of the semisweet chocolate chips in the recipe on this page.

Mocha Use coffee extract instead of vanilla extract.

Macadamia nut or hazelnut Add whole or coarsely chopped nuts instead of the chocolate chips. Alternatively, as nuts and chocolate are a classic combination, use 3 ounces/½ cup of each.

Dried fruit In place of the chocolate chips, add chopped dried fruit, such as raisins, golden raisins, apricots, candied cherries, or a mixture of candied tropical fruit, such as pineapple, mango and papaya. Add fruit juice or milk instead of vanilla extract.

MELTED DROP COOKIES

Thin, crisp cookies, such as tuiles, florentines and brandy snaps, require the butter and sugar or syrup to be melted together first to start the caramelization process prior to baking. Such cookies usually contain little flour, which helps them spread on the baking sheet – so make sure they have plenty of room.

BRANDY SNAPS

These classic melted drop cookies have a wonderful brittle texture. They melt in the mouth to release a sweet, almost caramelized flavor.

Makes 12–14

3 ounces/6 tablespoons butter,
diced
3 ounces/scant ½ cup superfine
sugar
3 tablespoons light corn syrup
3 ounces/⅔ cup all-purpose flour
1 teaspoon ground ginger
3 tablespoons brandy
1 tablespoon lemon juice

1 Preheat the oven to 375°F/Gas 5. Lightly grease several baking sheets or line them with baking parchment. Put the butter, sugar and syrup in a heavy pan. Heat gently over a low heat, stirring occasionally until the mixture has melted and becomes smooth.

2 Remove the pan from the heat. Leave the mixture to cool for a few minutes, or the flour will start to cook when it is added.

3 Sift together the flour and ginger and stir into the butter mixture with the brandy and lemon juice. Leave for a further 1–2 minutes to allow the flour to absorb some of the moisture.

4 Drop teaspoonfuls of the mixture at 1½-inch intervals onto the baking sheets. Do not attempt to cook any more than three or four on each sheet as they will need plenty of room to spread.

5 Bake, one sheet at a time, for about 8–10 minutes, or until the cookies turn bubbly, lacy in texture and golden brown. Remove the brandy snaps from the oven and leave for about 15 seconds to firm up slightly before attempting to move them.

6 Loosen the brandy snaps from the baking sheet one at a time using a metal spatula, and shape before cooling on a wire rack.

SHAPING UP

Some melted drop cookies need to be reshaped or neatened before, part-way through or after cooking.

Tuiles Named after the curved roof tiles in France, these may be round but are usually slightly elongated. Drop heaped teaspoonfuls of the mixture on greased or lined baking sheets, then spread each into an oval, measuring 4 x 2 inches.

Florentines The mixture often spreads out further than the fruit and nuts. Remove from the oven 2 minutes before the end of cooking time and press back the edges into a neat shape with a metal spatula to create perfect round shapes; return to the oven.

Glass cookies After baking, trim these thin, delicate cookies into shape by pressing a round metal cookie cutter, slightly smaller than the baked cookie, into each, then pull away or break off the excess.

SHAPING MELTED DROP COOKIES

Melted drop cookies are pliable enough to be shaped into curls, rolls or baskets when they are warm. As they cool, the cookies become crisp and hard, retaining their shape.

MAKING CURLS

Tuiles are usually curled after baking. They make a pretty accompaniment to serve with desserts. Remove the cookies from the oven, lift off the baking sheet and drape over a lightly oiled rolling pin, gently curling them around. Leave them to cool and crisp before removing.

MAKING ROLLS

These tightly rolled, wand-shaped cookies are great for serving as an accompaniment to any dessert. Cigarette Russes are a classic example of a rolled cookie.

1 Shape small spoonfuls of tuile mixture into 3 x 2 inch rectangles on greased or lined baking sheets, spacing them far apart, and bake at 375°F/Gas 5 for 6–7 minutes.

2 Carefully lift off the cookies and place upside down on a flat surface. Wind each cookie tightly around a greased wooden spoon handle.

3 Cool slightly until firm, then ease the cookies off the handles and place them on a wire rack to cool completely. Brandy snaps can be shaped in the same way, but do not turn upside down before rolling them up.

MAKING BASKETS

You can use either large brandy snaps or tuiles to make little bowl-shaped containers for desserts such as ice cream, sorbet, fresh fruit or mousse.

1 Bake heaped tablespoonfuls of brandy snap mixture or spread heaped teaspoonfuls of tuile mixture into 4½-inch pieces on a large baking sheet.

2 Once cooked, leave the cookies to cool for a few seconds, then lift from the baking sheet. Mold over lightly greased, upturned ramekin dishes, pressing the edges into soft folds with your fingers.

3 If you do not have suitable ramekins, then small bowls, cups or even small oranges can be used to produce a similar effect. If you use oranges to create the basic basket shape, then remember to pat the base flat before the cookie sets, so that the baskets will be stable and stand upright. Lift off once set.

Variation

To make chocolate brandy snaps, use 2½ ounces/9 tablespoons all-purpose flour and 2 tablespoons cocoa powder (unsweetened). You can always omit the ground ginger, if you prefer.

FORTUNE COOKIES

Originally forming part of an ancient Chinese tradition, these are little folded cookies made from tuile mixture. They contain short messages that predict the future, and they provide lots of fun for children and adults alike.

1 Spread out teaspoonfuls of tuile mixture to 3-inch round pieces on greased or lined baking sheets and bake until the edges are just turning brown.

2 Working quickly so that the cookies do not cool before they are folded, lift the cookies off the sheets with a metal spatula. Lay a folded paper fortune message in the center and fold the cookie in half. Bend in half again over the edge of a bowl.

3 Leave the cookies to cool and harden, then lift them off the bowl and store in an airtight container.

Rolled Cookies

A cookie dough that is rolled and cut may be a creamed, melted or rubbed-in mixture, but it must have the right consistency. If the dough is too dry, it will crack and crumble; too wet and it may stick when rolling and spread during baking.

SIMPLE ALMOND COOKIES
The addition of almonds gives these cookies a delicious crunch.

Makes 24
4 ounces/½ cup butter, softened
2 ounces/¼ cup superfine sugar
I egg, lightly beaten
I tablespoon ground almonds
7 ounces/I¾ cups all-purpose flour
2 tablespoons cornstarch

I Preheat the oven to 350°F/Gas 4. Lightly grease two baking sheets or line them with baking parchment. Beat the butter and sugar together until creamy. Gradually add the egg, beating well after each addition, then beat in the almonds. Sift over the flour and cornstarch and mix to a soft dough.

2 Lightly knead the dough on a floured surface for a few seconds, until smooth. Do not overwork the dough, or the butter will start to melt and the gluten will "develop", giving the cookies a tough texture.

3 Shape the dough into a ball then flatten slightly into a round shape – this makes it easier when you begin to roll it out. Put in plastic wrap to prevent the dough from drying out and chill for about 30 minutes, or until firm, but make sure it is not too stiff to roll. If you are making a large amount of cookie dough, divide it into pieces so that you will be able to handle it more easily when rolling.

4 On a floured surface, roll out the dough lightly and evenly in one direction only to a thickness of about ⅛ inch. Roll from the center to the far edge but not actually over the edge. Always roll away from you and rotate the cookie dough occasionally to prevent it from sticking and also to make sure it is evenly rolled. Avoid pulling the dough as you roll or rotate it, otherwise it may become misshapen when baked.

5 Stamp out 2½-inch round pieces using a fluted cookie cutter, or use another similar-size shape. Gather up the scraps and re-roll to make more cookies.

6 Transfer the cookies to the prepared baking sheets using a metal spatula. Rolled out cookies should not spread as much as drop cookies during baking, but you should still leave a space of at least I inch between each on the baking sheet. Chill the cookies for at least 30 minutes before baking them, as this helps to retain their shape.

7 Bake for 10 minutes until the cookies are a pale golden brown, making sure you rotate the baking sheets halfway through the cooking time. Remove the cookies from the oven and leave on the baking sheets for 2–3 minutes. This allows them to firm up so that they are less fragile when you handle them. Transfer the cookies to a wire rack using a metal spatula.

Cook's Tip
Cooling cookies on a wire rack allows air to circulate around them, preventing them from gathering moisture and becoming soggy as they cool.

ALL SHAPES AND SIZES

One of the greatest assets of rolled cookies is that they may be cut into any shape or size. There is a huge range of cutters available, but other ways of cutting and shaping cookies include using a pastry wheel or a knife, or even making your own template out of paper or card.

USING A KNIFE OR A PASTRY WHEEL TO SHAPE COOKIES

If you want to make squares, rectangles, triangles or bars, a sharp knife and a ruler are the perfect tools for the job. Instead of a knife, you could use a fluted pastry wheel to give an attractive edging.

I Roll out the cookie dough to a square or rectangular shape, turning it frequently by 90 degrees. During the early stages of rolling out, push in the edges of the dough with your cupped palms to keep the shape.

2 To make square or rectangular cookies such as shortbread fingers or bourbons, use a ruler to measure the dough so that it is rolled to the appropriate shape and size, then cut with a sharp knife or pastry cutter. (For example, for custard creams, cut the dough into 1½-inch strips, then cut each strip at intervals of 2 inches to make rectangles.)

3 To make triangular cookies, cut the dough into strips then into squares, then cut each square in half diagonally to make triangles.

4 To make neat diamond-shaped cookies, cut the dough into strips and then cut diagonally across the strips to make diamonds.

MAKING A TEMPLATE

For special occasions you may want to create a more complex cookie shape for which you do not have a cutter. In this case you will need to make a template. It's probably best to avoid very intricate designs, especially those with small protrusions, as these may distort or burn during baking, and will break off easily once cooked.

I Select the design, then either draw the design straight onto a piece of thin cardboard or trace it onto tracing or waxed paper first, then glue it onto cardboard. Wait for the glue to dry thoroughly before carefully cutting out the template.

2 Place the template on the rolled out cookie dough and hold it firmly in place. Using the point of a sharp knife, cut around the template to create the cookie shape.

MAKING RING COOKIES

It's hard to transfer ring cookies to baking sheets without pulling them out of shape. One solution is to place round pieces of cookie dough on the baking sheet, then cut out the centers with a smaller cutter. To make perfect rings, bake round cookies, then stamp out the centers while they are still warm.

I Roll out the dough then stamp into round pieces and transfer to a baking sheet. Bake the cookies according to the recipe instructions.

2 Remove the cookies from the oven and leave on the baking sheet. Using a small cookie cutter, stamp out the centers of the cookies before they have time to cool.

3 Leave the cookies on the baking sheet for 3–4 minutes, then transfer to a wire rack to cool completely.

Cook's Tips
• *To make pretty jammy sandwiches, only remove the centers from half the round-shaped dough, then sandwich the round pieces and rings together with a little jam.*
• *Young children love the mini cookies that are left over after punching out holes in larger cookies. Drizzle with a little icing made from sugar and water for an extra special treat.*

MAKING MULTI-COLORED ROLLED COOKIES

By using two or more different colored doughs you can make a range of attractive cookies. The colored doughs can be rolled, stamped out, then pieced together before baking, or the rolled doughs can be layered together then cut into cookie shapes.

TWO-TONE COOKIES

To make cookies with different colored middles, leave half the dough plain and knead in a little cooled melted chocolate into the other half, or use a few drops of food coloring.

1 Roll out each piece of dough to about ⅛ inch thick. Stamp out an equal number of cookies (round shapes or hearts) and place them on separate baking sheets. Chill for 30 minutes.

2 Using a smaller cutter, stamp out the centers from all of the cookies, then swap the plain centers for the flavored or colored centers and vice versa.

3 If you like, you can use a third, even smaller, cutter as well and swap the tiny centers once more to make triple-tone cookies.

PINWHEELS

These cookies are made by rolling together layers of colored dough.

1 Divide the cookie dough into two. Leave half plain and flavor the other half by kneading in 1 tablespoon sifted unsweetened cocoa powder and 1 teaspoon milk. Wrap and chill for about 30 minutes.

2 Roll out each piece of dough to a rectangle measuring 8 × 10 inches. Lightly brush the plain dough with lightly beaten egg white and place the colored dough on top. Roll up tightly from a long side, then cut into ¼ inch thick slices.

NEAPOLITAN SLICES

These cookies resemble mini slices of Neapolitan ice cream.

1 Divide the dough into three. Leave one third plain, flavor one third with cocoa (as for pinwheels) and color the remaining third pink. Wrap and chill for 30 minutes.

2 Roll out each piece of dough into a rectangle measuring 4 × 3 inches. Place the rectangles on top of each other, brushing between the layers with lightly beaten egg white. Cut the dough into ¼-inch thick slices, then cut each slice in half.

SEVEN STEPS TO SUCCESS

• Always chill the dough to firm it for at least 20 minutes and up to 1 hour before rolling. If you chill it for longer, leave it at room temperature for about 10 minutes before rolling out.

• Cookies should be rolled to a thickness of ⅛–¼ inch. Thicker cookies will have soggy centers when the outside has browned; thinner cookies will be very crisp and fragile.

• Use the minimum amount of flour when rolling out the dough. Lightly dust the work surface and the rolling pin using a flour dredger or fine sieve, sprinkling with a little more flour when needed. After cutting the cookies, brush off any excess flour with a dry pastry brush.

• If the dough is sticky, even after chilling, roll it out between two sheets of baking parchment or plastic wrap. After rolling, leave the parchment or plastic wrap in place, slide the dough onto a baking sheet and chill before stamping out the cookies with a cookie cutter.

• When stamping out the cookies, dip the cutter into flour, then press down firmly to cut right through the dough.

• Cut cookies closely together to minimize re-rolling scraps. The first rolling is always better.

• If you don't have a cutter, use a sharp knife or pastry wheel to cut the dough into squares or rectangles, or stamp out round pieces using a thin-rimmed glass.

Piped Cookies

For this type of cookie the mixture needs to be soft enough to pipe but firm enough to keep its shape during baking. Piped cookies are usually made by the creaming method, which gives them a crumbly, airy texture and makes blending in flavorings easy. Make sure that the butter is very soft before you start, as this will make mixing and piping quick and easy.

VIENNESE PIPED COOKIES

With a little practice, these cookies can be piped into any shape you like.

Makes 12

6 ounces/¾ cup sweet butter, softened
1½ ounces/3 tablespoons confectioners' sugar, sifted
½ teaspoon vanilla extract
6 ounces/1½ cups all-purpose flour
1½ ounces/3 tablespoons cornstarch

1 Preheat the oven to 350°F/Gas 4. Grease or line two baking sheets. Cream the butter and icing sugar together until very pale and fluffy. Add the vanilla extract and beat for a few more seconds.

2 Sift the flour and cornstarch together over the butter mixture and mix together until smooth.

3 Spoon the mixture into a pastry bag fitted with a large, star-shaped nozzle and pipe into the required shapes on the prepared baking sheets. Make sure the shapes are spaced well apart.

4 Bake the cookies for about 12 minutes, or until they are a pale golden color. Leave for a few minutes on the baking sheets to firm up slightly before carefully transferring them to a wire rack with a metal spatula to finish cooling.

Variations

Once you have mastered making and piping the basic recipe, try adding flavorings to vary the cookie mixture.
Chocolate *Substitute 2 tablespoons cocoa powder (unsweetened) for the same quantity of flour.*
Coffee *Omit the vanilla extract and blend 1 teaspoon instant coffee powder with 1 teaspoon just boiled water. Leave to cool, then add to the mixture with the flour and cornstarch.*
Strawberry *Use 1½ ounces/3 tablespoons strawberry-flavor blancmange powder instead of the cornstarch.*
Orange or lemon *Beat the finely grated rind of half an orange or half a lemon into the creamed mixture.*
Caramel *To give the cookies a mild caramel flavor, use unrefined confectioners' sugar.*

PERFECT PIPING

To perfect your piping technique, follow these three simple steps.

1 Drop the nozzle into the bag, pushing it down to fit firmly. Twist the nozzle end around so that there is a twist in the bag just above it, then push the twisted section of the bag inside the nozzle to close it off.

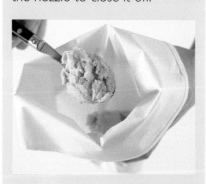

2 Fold the top of the bag over your hand to make a "collar". Spoon in the mixture. When the bag is about half full, gently twist the top to remove the air. Holding the top of the bag, push the mixture down.

3 To pipe, hold the twisted end firmly and use the other hand to guide the nozzle. Using firm, steady pressure, pipe the shape. Push down slightly then lift up.

PIPING SHAPES

Viennese cookie mixture can be piped it into all kinds of shapes.

VIENNESE COOKIES

Round swirls are the classic shape for Viennese cookies.

Spoon the mixture into a pastry bag fitted with a ½-inch star nozzle. Pipe rosettes 2 inches across onto greased baking sheets, spacing them far apart.

VIENNESE WHIRLS

Sandwich two Viennese cookies together with buttercream filling and a little sieved apricot jam.

SWISS FINGERS

Pretty piped fingers are very popular, and very simple to make.

Spoon the mixture into a pastry bag fitted with a ½-inch star nozzle. Pipe 2¼-inch lengths on greased baking sheets, spacing far apart.

OYSTER COOKIES

These pretty, sophisticated cookies resemble oyster shells.

Spoon the mixture into a pastry bag fitted with a ½-inch star nozzle and pipe about five lines to make shells. Make the shape wide at one end and tapered at the other.

CHOCOLATE VANILLA SWIRLS

These two-color cookies look lovely piped into paper cake cases.

1 Divide the Viennese cookie mixture into two equal parts and beat 1 tablespoon sifted cocoa powder (unsweetened) into half of it. Spoon the vanilla mixture down one side of a pastry bag fitted with a ½-inch star nozzle and then spoon the chocolate mixture down the other side.

2 Pipe the mixture into 12 paper cake cases in a muffin pan to make pretty striped swirls.

OTHER PIPED COOKIES

Many other cookie mixtures are piped to give them an even length, width and shape.

LANGUES DE CHATS

These classic French cookies are long, thin ovals with a slightly rough texture (like a cat's tongue).

Makes 18

*3 ounces/6 tablespoons sweet
    butter, softened*

*4 ounces/1 cup confectioners' sugar,
    sifted, plus extra for dusting*

2 extra large egg whites

2 tablespoons superfine sugar

*3 ounces/⅔ cup all-purpose
    flour, sifted*

1 Preheat the oven to 400°F/Gas 6. Grease two baking sheets or line them with baking parchment. Cream the butter and confectioners' sugar together until pale and fluffy.

2 In a separate bowl, whisk the egg whites to soft peaks, then add the superfine sugar 1 tablespoon at a time, whisking between each addition. Fold the whites into the butter mixture, then fold in the flour.

3 Spoon the mixture into a pastry bag fitted with a ½-inch plain nozzle and pipe 2½-inch lengths onto the prepared baking sheets. Allow 2 inches between each cookie for spreading.

4 Bake for 5–7 minutes, or until the edges are lightly browned. Leave to cool on the baking sheets for 5 minutes before transferring to a wire rack to cool completely.

FILIGREE CROWNS

These delicate, shaped cookies are made from finely piped lines of cookie mixture, which are first baked and then molded into crowns. They make stunning little containers for desserts such as ice cream, sorbet, mousse or fresh fruit.

Makes 6

1 egg white
2 ounces/¼ cup superfine sugar
1 ounce/¼ cup all-purpose flour

1 Preheat the oven to 400°F/ Gas 6. Draw six rectangles, each measuring about 8 x 3 inches, on six separate pieces of baking parchment.

2 Whisk the egg white and sugar together in a small mixing bowl until foamy. Sift the flour over the egg mixture and stir in thoroughly.

3 Spoon the cookie mixture into a waxed paper pastry bag and snip off the tip to create a small hole. On each rectangle of baking parchment, carefully pipe thin wiggly lines from side to side to fill the marked shape, then pipe a little extra mixture down one of the long edges.

4 Bake the cookies for about 3 minutes. Remove the tray from the oven and immediately roll the cookie around a straight-sided glass.

5 Peel away the paper and stand the crowns upright. Remove the glass. If the mixture hardens before you have molded the crowns, return to the oven for a few seconds. Cool and store in an airtight container.

SPANISH CHURROS

These little Spanish cake-cookies are made from sweetened choux pastry, which is piped into hot oil and then deep-fried. Serve sprinkled generously with cinnamon sugar.

Makes 25

3 ounces/6 tablespoons butter, diced
8 fluid ounces/1 cup water
4 ounces/1 cup all-purpose flour
2 ounces/4 tablespoons superfine sugar
3 eggs, lightly beaten
½ tsp ground cinnamon

1 Heat the butter and water in a small heavy pan until the butter has melted – do not allow the water to boil. Sift the flour and 1 tablespoon of the superfine sugar onto a piece of waxed paper.

2 Once the butter has melted, bring to a boil, then add the flour and sugar. Remove the pan from the heat and beat the mixture vigorously. Leave to cool for 5 minutes, then gradually beat in the eggs until the mixture is smooth and glossy.

3 Half-fill a large, heavy pan or deep-fryer with oil and heat to 375°F. Spoon the mixture into a pastry bag with a ½-inch star nozzle. Pipe five 4-inch lengths of the mixture into the hot oil, being careful not to cause the fat to splash or spit. Fry the churros for 2 minutes, or until golden and crisp.

4 Remove the churros from the oil with a slotted spoon and drain on kitchen paper. Repeat until all the mixture has been used. Mix the remaining superfine sugar with the ground cinnamon and sprinkle over the churros. Serve warm.

Pressed Cookies

Shaped cookies are amazingly simple to make using a commercial cookie press. The press comes with a range of patterned disks and may have several settings so that a variety of shapes and sizes can be made. Choose soft-textured cookie doughs that will easily push through the press.

VANILLA FLOWERS
These pretty cookies use vanilla extract for an irresistible flavor.

Makes 25

3½ ounces/scant ½ cup butter, softened
3½ ounces/½ cup superfine sugar
1 egg yolk
5½ ounces/scant 1½ cups all-purpose
  flour
1 teaspoon milk
1 teaspoon vanilla extract

1 Cream the butter and sugar together until pale and fluffy. Beat in the egg yolk. Sift the flour over the butter mixture and then fold in with the milk and vanilla extract to make a soft dough. Knead for a few seconds until smooth.

2 Fill the cookie press cylinder almost to the top with the dough and then screw on the plunger. Press out the dough onto greased baking sheets, spacing the cookies well apart.

3 Place the baking sheets in the refrigerator for at least 30 minutes, so that the cookies keep their shape while baking. Decorate with sugar or nuts, if using. Meanwhile, preheat the oven to 350°F/Gas 4.

4 Bake for 15 minutes, or until very lightly browned. Leave to cool on the baking sheets for 5 minutes, then transfer to a wire rack.

CHOCOLATE DAISIES
This dark chocolate mixture works perfectly in a cookie press.

Makes 12

6 ounces/¾ cup sweet butter,
  softened
1½ ounces/3 tablespoons confectioners'
  sugar, sifted
6 ounces/1½ cups all-purpose flour
1 ounce/2 tablespoons cocoa powder
  (unsweetened)
1½ ounces/3 tablespoons cornstarch

1 Preheat the oven to 350°F/Gas 4. Grease or line two baking sheets. Cream the butter and confectioners' sugar together until very pale and fluffy.

2 Sift the flour and cornstarch together over the butter mixture and mix together until smooth.

3 Put enough of the dough into the press to fill it almost to the top, then screw on the plunger.

4 Press out the dough onto the greased baking sheets. Make sure the shapes are spaced well apart.

5 Bake the cookies for about 12 minutes until just beginning to change color. Leave the cookies for a few minutes on the baking sheets to firm up slightly before carefully transferring them to a wire rack to cool completely.

PRESSED COOKIE TIPS AND TECHNIQUES
• To achieve a very short texture, thoroughly cream the butter and sugar until very light and fold in the flour gently.
• The dough must be very smooth to go through the fine holes in the cookie disks, so don't add chunky flavoring ingredients, such as chopped nuts, dried fruit, candied cherries or chocolate chips.
• The dough must be sufficiently soft to be easily squeezed through the press, but firm enough to hold its shape.
• If the mixture is too firm to press, add a few drops of milk
• If the dough is slightly soft and sticks to the cookie disk, put it in the refrigerator for about 30 minutes until it has firmed.
• Pressed cookies can be decorated with ingredients such as chocolate chips, sugar crystals or nuts before baking.

Molded Cookies

Shaping cookie dough in a mold gives a professional finish. The dough can be either shaped in a mold, then turned out for baking or baked in the shaped pan itself. It is not essential to buy special molds, as you can improvise with plain pans for both shaping and baking.

SHAPING SHORTBREAD

Shortbread molds usually have a carved design of a thistle and are available in different sizes. The mold should be brushed with a flavorless oil the first time it is used, then wiped with kitchen paper.

1 Make one quantity of shortbread mixture and roll out to a 6-inch round shape. Press it firmly into a 7-inch shortbread mold. Line a baking sheet with baking parchment.

2 Invert the mold onto the baking sheet, tapping the mold firmly to release the dough. Chill for about 30 minutes, until firm.

3 Preheat the oven to 325°F/ Gas 3. Bake the shortbread for 35–40 minutes, or until pale golden. Sprinkle the top with a little superfine sugar, then leave to cool.

SHAPING MADELEINES

These French lemon cookies are baked in shell-shaped pans.

Makes 15

1 egg
2½ ounces/generous ¼ cup
    superfine sugar
2½ ounces/9 tablespoons self-rising
    flour
¼ teaspoon baking powder
finely grated rind of ½ lemon
2½ ounces/5 tablespoons butter, melted
    and cooled

1 Preheat the oven to 425°F/ Gas 7. Brush the pans with melted sweet butter. Chill for 10 minutes, then brush lightly with butter again, dust with flour and shake off any excess.

2 Whisk the egg and sugar until thick and pale. (The mixture should leave a trail when the whisk is lifted.) Sift over half the flour with the baking powder and fold in the lemon rind. Pour half the melted butter around the edge of the bowl and fold in gently.

3 Sift over the remaining flour, then pour in the rest of the melted butter around the edge of the bowl. Fold in gently until combined.

4 Spoon the mixture into the molds, filling them just to the top. Bake for 10 minutes, until golden. Leave for a few moments, then ease out the madeleines with a metal spatula and transfer to a wire rack.

MAKING PETTICOAT TAILS

Shortbread is traditionally made into wedge-shaped petticoat tails.

1 Press one quantity of shortbread mixture into a 7-inch loose-based fluted quiche pan.

2 Prick the surface with a fork and mark the shortbread into eight wedges using a knife. If you do not have a fluted pan, use a straight-sided layer pan and press a pattern around the edge.

MAKING SQUARES AND BARS

Cookie dough can be baked in a loose-based square or rectangular pan, then cut into pieces.

1 Press one quantity of shortbread mixture into a 6-inch square pan, or press two quantities into a 7 x 11 inch rectangular pan.

2 To cut into squares, make two cuts lengthwise, then two cuts across for the square pan and four for the rectangular pan. To cut into bars, cut in half lengthwise first, then cut across widthwise into bars.

SMALL MOLDED COOKIES

These can be made in mini quiche pans or pretty metal chocolate molds.

Press shortbread dough into the pan or molds until level, then bake. Alternatively, turn out the molded round pieces onto greased or lined baking sheets. Chill before baking.

SHAPING COOKIES BY HAND

You can model cookie dough into all kinds of shapes. Classic hand-molded cookies include jumbles and pretzels. Choose a dough that will retain its shape when baked.

FORK COOKIES

These are the simplest molded cookies, made by rolling dough into balls, then flattening with a fork to make a pretty pattern on the top.

Makes 16

4 ounces/½ cup butter, softened
2 ounces/¼ cup superfine sugar
5 ounces/1¼ cups self-rising
   flour, sifted

1 Preheat the oven to 350°F/Gas 4. Lightly grease two baking sheets. Beat the butter in a bowl until creamy, then beat in the sugar. Stir in the flour and bring the dough together with your hands.

2 Shape into walnut-size balls and place on the baking sheets, spacing far apart. Dip a fork in cold water and use to flatten the cookies.

3 Bake for 10–12 minutes, until pale brown. Leave to cool on the baking sheets for a few minutes, then transfer to a wire rack to cool.

PRETZELS

These are complicated shapes, so require a more pliable dough.

Makes 40

4 ounces/½ cup butter, softened
4 ounces/1 cup confectioners'
   sugar, sifted
1 egg, lightly beaten
1 tablespoon light corn syrup
¼ teaspoon vanilla extract
9 ounces/2¼ cups all-purpose
   flour, sifted

1 Preheat the oven to 375°F/Gas 5. Beat the butter and sugar together until light and creamy. Beat in the egg, syrup and vanilla extract. Add the flour and stir to make a dough. Knead on a floured surface, then wrap and chill for 30 minutes.

2 Divide the dough into 40 pieces and cover the pieces that you aren't working on with plastic wrap. Roll one piece into a thin strand about 10 inches long.

3 Create a loop with the strand, bring the ends together and press them into the top of the circle. Make the rest of the pretzels in the same way. Chill for 30 minutes.

4 Bake for 10 minutes, until lightly browned, then cool on wire racks.

Bar Cookies

These are a cross between a cake and a cookie; some are thin and crunchy, others thick and chewy or light and spongy. Some bar cookies, such as brownies and flapjacks, are just a single layer, but many have two or more different layers that combine tastes and textures. Sometimes this base is partially or fully cooked first before the topping is added, then the oven temperature is lowered so that the topping doesn't overcook.

Always make bar cookies in the recommended pan size; even a small change in size will affect the cooking time and final result.

LAYERED FRUIT AND NUT BAR COOKIE

This indulgent treat combines several flavors and textures.

Makes 15
9 ounces/2¼ cups all-purpose flour
6 ounces/¾ cup chilled butter or
    hard margarine, diced
3 ounces/scant ½ cup superfine sugar
    or soft light brown sugar

For the filling
4 ounces/½ cup candied cherries,
    coarsely chopped
2 ounces/⅓ cup golden raisins
2 ounces/½ cup almonds, chopped

For the topping
4 ounces/½ cup butter or hard
    margarine, softened
4 ounces/generous ½ cup superfine
    sugar
2 eggs
2 ounces/½ cup all-purpose flour
2 ounces/½ cup ground almonds
confectioners' sugar, for dusting

1 Preheat the oven to 350°F/Gas 4. Line the base and grease a 7 x 11 x 1 inch cake pan. To make the base, sift the flour into a bowl. Additional dry flavorings such as ground spices or cocoa powder (unsweetened) (substitute for an equal quantity of flour) can be added at this stage.

2 Rub in the butter or margarine pieces until the mixture resembles breadcrumbs. Stir in the sugar. If you are adding chunky flavorings, such as coconut or chocolate chips, stir them in with the sugar. Mix with your hands until the dough comes together.

3 Press the mixture into the base of the pan. Level with the back of a spoon or a potato masher. Prick the base with a fork to let out the steam and to make sure it remains level as it cooks, then bake for 10 minutes. Remove from the oven.

4 Reduce the temperature to 325°F/Gas 3. Mix together the filling ingredients, then sprinkle evenly over the base. To make the topping, cream the butter and sugar together until pale and fluffy, then beat in the eggs. Sift over the flour and fold in with the ground almonds. Spread the topping carefully over the fruit and nuts.

5 Bake for 30 minutes, or until a light golden brown color and firm to the touch. Check the topping is cooked by inserting a wooden toothpick into it and leaving for a few seconds; it should come out clean. Leave to cool in the pan for 15 minutes. Lightly dust with confectioners' sugar and cut into bars.

Variations
• *Use chopped dried fruit or spread a thick layer of jam for the filling.*
• *Try flavoring the sponge cake topping with a little finely grated citrus rind.*

TOPPING IDEAS

There are dozens of different toppings for bar cookies. The base must be fairly firm but the topping can be softer, ranging from sponge cake to caramel, and from sticky meringue to chocolate. The following ideas are sufficient for a 7 x 11 inch pan.

CRUMBLE OR STREUSEL

This works best on top of a slightly soft or sticky base or filling such as jam, fruit puree or soft caramel.

Beat 4 ounces/½ cup butter until creamy, then mix in 2 ounces/ ¼ cup soft light brown sugar. Stir in 4 ounces/⅔ cup semolina and 4 ounces/1 cup plain whole-wheat flour until the mixture resembles breadcrumbs. Add ½ teaspoon ground ginger. Sprinkle over the base and press down. Bake at 325°F/Gas 3 for 40 minutes.

COCONUT

This light topping has a delicate flavor and lovely texture. Beat two eggs, then stir in 4 ounces/ generous ½ cup raw sugar, 1 ounce/ 3 tablespoons ground rice, and 5 ounces/1⅔ cups dried unsweetened shredded coconut. Spread over the base and bake at 350°F/Gas 4 for 25 minutes.

MERINGUE

This produces a wonderfully light, topping that melts in the mouth,

Whisk two egg whites with a pinch of salt in a clean bowl until they form soft peaks. Gradually whisk in 4 ounces/generous ½ cup superfine sugar, a spoonful at a time, until the mixture is stiff and glossy. Fold in ½ teaspoon cornstarch and 1 teaspoon lemon juice. Spread over the base and swirl with a metal spatula to form soft peaks. Bake at 275°F/Gas 1 for 40 minutes, until the meringue is set and tinged brown.

GRATED SHORTBREAD

To make this rich, buttery filling, cream together 4 ounces/½ cup softened butter and 1½ ounces/ 3 tablespoons soft light brown sugar. Combine 1 teaspoon sunflower oil, 1 teaspoon vanilla extract and 1 egg yolk and beat into the butter mixture. Sift over 7 ounces/1¾ cups all-purpose flour, 1 ounce/¼ cup cornstarch and ½ teaspoon baking powder. Mix well and knead on a lightly floured surface for 30 seconds. Put in plastic wrap and chill for about 30 minutes. Grate over the base or filling and press down. Bake at 300°F/Gas 2 for 45 minutes.

CITRUS CHEESECAKE

To make this zesty topping, put the finely grated rind of two lemons and two limes in a bowl with 8 ounces/ 1 cup melted butter, 2 tablespoons superfine sugar and three eggs. Whisk until thick and mousse-like. Sift over 1½ ounces/⅓ cup all-purpose flour and ½ teaspoon baking powder and fold in with 2 tablespoons lemon or lime juice. Pour over the base and bake at 350°F/Gas 4 for 25 minutes.

NUT CARAMEL

Put 6 ounces/⅔ cup soft light brown sugar, 2 tablespoons light corn syrup and 6 ounces/¾ cup butter in a pan. Heat gently until the sugar has dissolved, then bring to the boil and simmer for 5 minutes, until a rich golden color. Stir in 6 ounces/1 cup chopped roasted unsalted peanuts. Immediately spread over base and leave to cool.

CHOCOLATE

This topping is incredibly simple and always produces great results.

Chop 12 ounces semisweet, milk or white chocolate. Sprinkle over the hot cookie base, then return to the oven for 1 minute, until melted. Mark into bars when the chocolate is almost set.

BAKING THE PERFECT BROWNIE

Brownies, named after their dark rich color, should be moist and chewy; with a sugary crust on the outside, but soft on the inside. There are many different recipes for brownies, varying in richness. Plainer ones rely on cocoa powder (unsweetened) alone, others on vast quantities of melted chocolate. Often, a small amount of coffee is added that is barely perceptible to the taste, but cuts through the sweetness a little. True brownies have a very high proportion of sugar and fat and most contain nuts, usually walnuts or pecan nuts.

Light versions and those made from white chocolate are often referred to as "blondies." It is important to remove brownies from the oven as soon as the cooking time is up, even though they will still seem quite soft. They will firm up on standing and, if overcooked, the characteristic gooey texture will be ruined.

BROWNIE VARIATIONS

Double chocolate Add chocolate chips in place of the chopped walnuts.

Chunky choc and nut Use coarsely chopped chunks of white chocolate in place of half the walnuts.

Macadamia nut Replace the chopped walnuts with whole macadamia nuts.

Almond brownies Use almond extract and almonds instead of vanilla and walnuts.

CLASSIC CHOCOLATE BROWNIES

Richly colored and flavored, these are deliciously gooey and moist.

Makes 24

8 ounces semisweet chocolate

8 ounces/1 cup butter, diced

3 eggs

8 ounces/generous 1 cup superfine sugar

2 tablespoons strong black coffee

3 ounces/⅔ cup self-rising flour

pinch of salt

5 ounces/1¼ cups chopped walnuts

1 teaspoon vanilla extract

1 Preheat the oven to 180°C/375°F/ Gas 5. Grease and line a 7 x 11 inch pan. Break the chocolate into squares and place in a heatproof bowl with the butter.

2 Set the bowl over a pan of barely simmering water and leave for 5–10 minutes, stirring occasionally until the mixture is melted and smooth. Remove the bowl from the pan and then leave the chocolate mixture to cool for 5 minutes.

3 In a large bowl, beat the eggs, sugar and coffee until smooth, then gradually beat in the cooled melted chocolate mixture.

4 Sift the flour and salt over the mixture, then fold in together with the walnuts and vanilla extract.

5 Spoon the mixture into the prepared pan and bake for about 35 minutes, or until just firm to the touch in the centre. (Do not bake it for any longer than this, as the mixture will still be soft under the crust but will firm up as it cools. Overcooking gives a dry result.)

6 Leave the brownies to cool in the pan then turn out onto a board, trim off the crusty edges and cut into squares. using a serrated knife, with a gentle sawing action.

GREASING, LINING AND REDUCING THE SIZE OF PANS

When making bar cookies, it is important to line the baking pan with waxed paper or baking parchment. This makes it much easier to lift the baked brownies or bars from the pan. If you use waxed paper, you will need to brush a little flavorless oil over the paper before pouring in the mixture. If you use baking parchment, the paper does not need to be greased.

Base-lining Some recipes only require the base of the pan to be lined. This technique can be used to line any shape of pan, whether rectangular, square or round. Place the pan on a sheet of waxed paper or baking parchment and, using a pencil, carefully draw around the pan. Using a pair of scissors, cut just inside the drawn line so that the lining will fit neatly inside the pan.

Using a sheet of buttered paper or a piece of kitchen paper drizzled with a flavorless oil, such as sunflower or vegetable oil, grease the inside of the pan and place the lining paper in the base, pressing it into the corners.

Square and rectangular pans
To line both the base and sides of a square or rectangular pan, place the pan on a piece of waxed paper or baking parchment that is considerably larger than the pan. Using a pencil, draw around the pan. Cut a straight line from the edge of the paper to each corner of the square or rectangle. Turn the piece of paper over so the side marked with pencil is facing downward. Fold in each side along its pencil line.

Grease the pan, then fit the paper inside the pan, folding the corners to fit neatly.

Round pans To line a round pan, place it on a piece of waxed paper or baking parchment and use a pencil to draw around it. Cut out the circle just inside the line. Next cut a long strip of paper about ¾ inch wider than the depth of the pan. (It must be long enough to wrap around the outside of the pan with 1¼ inch to spare.) Fold up the lower edge by ½ inch, then make cuts about 1 inch apart from the edge to the fold.

Grease the pan, then position the paper strip(s) around the side of it, so that the snipped edge sits flat on the base. Place the paper circle in the base of the pan, covering the snipped paper. Lightly grease all the paper, if necessary.

Reducing pan size If the pan you are using is larger than the size required, you can reduce its size by fitting a strip of foil across the pan to make it the correct size. Make a long strip of triple thickness foil and cut it to fit three sides of the required pan.

Fold the strip of foil along one of the long edges to make a lap, and fit it inside the pan to make it the required size. The weight of the mixture will hold the lap down and keep the divider in place.

Short-cut Cookies

There are occasions when you may want to make cookies in a hurry and you either don't want to turn on the oven just to bake a single batch of cookies or take the time and trouble measuring and mixing. Using ready-made cookie dough that you've either made in advance or bought, baking in a microwave oven or following a no-bake cookie recipe may provide you with the perfect solution.

REFRIGERATOR COOKIES

These are so called because the dough can be made in advance and kept in the refrigerator for up to 2 weeks before being cooked. It means that cookies can be freshly baked on demand. They are ideal for those who enjoy the pleasures of home-baked cookies, but don't always have time to make them from scratch.

The cookie dough is shaped into a log, put in plastic wrap and chilled in the refrigerator. Because the dough has a high fat content, it should be chilled for at least 1 hour, and preferably for longer. This will firm it to make slicing easier and will also ensure that the cookies hold their shape when cooked. The texture of the cookies is partly determined by the thickness of the slices: thinner slices will make fairly crisp cookies, thicker ones will be slightly less crisp. Some cookies, such as those with chunks of chocolate or nuts, are best cut in thicker slices. When baking thicker cookies, lower the temperature slightly and cook for a few minutes longer to make sure that they're cooked through.

QUICK VANILLA COOKIES

Just a few drops of vanilla extract is needed for these.

Makes 32
5 ounces/10 tbsp butter, softened
5 ounces/¾ cup superfine sugar
1 egg, lightly beaten
½ tsp vanilla extract
8 ounces/2 cups all-purpose
   flour, sifted

1 Put the ingredients in a bowl and mix to a smooth dough. Lightly knead on a floured surface, then roll the dough into a log shape about 2 inches in diameter and 8 inches long. Put the log in plastic wrap and chill for at least 1 hour, or until firm enough to slice. For mini cookies, divide the dough in half and make two thinner logs.

2 Preheat the oven to 375°F/Gas 5. Cut the dough into ¼-inch slices. You can dip the knife in water and wipe it dry for a clean cut.

3 When you have cut the required number of cookies, re-wrap the remaining dough and put it back in the refrigerator.

4 Place the cookies about 1 inch apart on ungreased baking sheets. Bake for 12 minutes, or until just golden around the edges. Leave on the baking sheets for 2–3 minutes, then transfer to a wire rack to cool completely. Use the remaining cookie dough within 1 week of making, or double-wrap and freeze for up to 3 months.

BOUGHT COOKIE DOUGH

If you do not have the time to make your own cookie dough, ready-made chilled or frozen dough can be bought instead. This usually comes in tubs and, although several different varieties are available, chocolate chip cookie dough is the most popular. The mixture is ready to be spooned onto greased baking sheets, then baked according to the manufacturer's instructions. Once opened, the dough can be kept in its tub in the refrigerator for several days, so that you can bake fresh batches when required.

NO-BAKE COOKIES

A range of cookies can be made by mixing melted ingredients with dry ingredients and leaving them to set. The setting agent may be chocolate, which sets firmly, or syrups and marshmallows, which set to create a chewier cookie. The mixture may be spooned into paper cake cases or into a greased and base-lined shallow pan, then cut into squares, bars or triangles when set.

SETTING COOKIES WITH CHOCOLATE

The simplest no-bake cookies are made with breakfast cereals, such as cornflakes, combined with melted semisweet chocolate, light corn or maple syrup and butter. Others may contain crushed or broken plain cookies, dried fruit and nuts rather than cereal. Always leave the melted chocolate to cool before adding the dry ingredients.

To make a basic mixture, melt 2½ ounces/5 tablespoons sweet butter and 6 ounces semisweet chocolate together, then cool. Stir in 3 ounces broken graham crackers, 2 ounces/½ cup sliced almonds, 2 ounces/½ cup chopped dried fruit and 2 ounces roughly chopped white chocolate.

SETTING COOKIES WITHOUT CHOCOLATE

No-bake cookies can be set with a mixture of cooked sugar or light corn syrup combined with melted butter, marshmallows and soft toffees. The most effective mixture uses equal quantities of toffees, butter and marshmallows mixed with puffed rice cereal.

To make a basic mixture, melt 4 ounces each of butter, toffees and marshmallows in a pan, then stir in 4 ounces/2 cups puffed rice cereal.

MAKING ROUND COOKIES

Spoon the no-bake cookie mixture onto a sheet of waxed paper or baking parchment and wrap the mixture, packing it into a fat log-shape roll about 8 inches long. Chill until firm, then cut into ½-inch slices.

MAKING COOKIE WEDGES

Some cookies are made in a round shape and sliced into wedges like cakes.

1 Spoon the cookie mixture into a lightly greased and lined shallow 7-inch round or 6-inch square pan. Chill for 1–2 hours, or until very firm, but not rock hard.

2 Remove the mixture from the pan, then cut into thin wedges using a sharp knife.

MAKING COOKIE TRIANGLES

Rather than making individual cookies, you can make a triangular block of cookie mixture, then slice it once it has set.

1 Line the base and three sides of a deep, greased 7-inch square pan with plastic wrap. Prop up one side of the pan on a box so that it is at an angle of about 45 degrees.

2 Spoon the mixture into the pan and level the surface with the back of the spoon. Leave to stand until firm, then chill until completely set. To serve, remove the block from the pan, peel off the plastic wrap and cut into ½-inch triangular slices.

LAYERED NO-BAKE COOKIES

Most no-bake cookies are single-layered affairs, but some are richer and have two or more layers. Bear in mind that you need to be able to slice through the cookies cleanly, so don't make one layer much more fragile than the others. Canadian nanaimo bars are a classic layered no-bake cookie. The base is made of a non-crumbly cookie and nut mixture, the filling is firm and smooth, and the chocolate topping has a little oil added to it so it doesn't crack when cut.

MICROWAVE COOKIES

Many traditional cookie recipes written with oven-baking in mind need to be adjusted for microwave cooking, and there are some that simply cannot be converted successfully. Others, however, will turn out every bit as good but in a fraction of the time.

The key to cooking round cookies in a microwave is to arrange them in circles so that they cook evenly. Don't be tempted to add a cookie to the middle as it will cook more slowly than the rest.

SOFT ALMOND COOKIES

These almond cookies remain soft for some time after cooking.

Makes 12

2 ounces/¼ cup butter, softened
2 ounces/¼ cup soft light brown sugar
1 egg yolk
3 ounces/⅔ cup all-purpose flour
1 ounce/¼ cup ground almonds

1 Cream the butter and sugar together in a large mixing bowl until light and fluffy. Beat in the egg yolk. Sift over the flour and gently fold into the mixture together with the ground almonds. If you like, fold in other ingredients such as chopped candied cherries, a mixture of dried fruit or chopped nuts.

2 Place six tablespoonfuls of the mixture in a circle on a microwave-proof dish or a piece of baking parchment cut to fit the base of the oven. Cook for 1¾–2½ minutes on high (100 percent power), or until the surface of the cookies is dry.

3 Remove the cookies carefully from the microwave, as the edges will still be soft, and leave to stand for 1 minute before lifting them onto a wire rack. They will finish cooking and become firmer as they cool.

BAR MICROWAVE COOKIES

To achieve the best results with bar cookies and traybakes in a microwave, bake them in a round quiche pan, or 1½ inch-deep pie plate, then cut the cookies into wedges. The center may be difficult to cook properly in recipes such as shortbread, but this isn't a problem with high-fat, syrupy mixtures such as flapjacks.

STICKY LEMON FLAPJACKS

Made with rolled oats, flapjacks are deliciously thick and chewy.

Makes 8

3 ounces/6 tablespoons butter, diced
4 tablespoons light corn syrup
4 ounces/generous ½ cup raw sugar
6 ounces/1½ cups rolled oats
juice and finely grated rind of ½ lemon

1 Put the butter, syrup and sugar in a heatproof bowl. Microwave on medium (50 percent) power for 3–4 minutes, stirring halfway through.

2 Stir in the oats, lemon rind and juice. Spoon the mixture into an 8-inch microwave quiche pan and spread out.

3 Cook on full (100 percent) power for 3–3½ minutes, or until bubbling all over. Remove from the oven and mark into wedges when warm. Leave to cool in the dish.

DIFFERENT-SHAPED COOKIES

Microwave cookies don't have to be round, but whatever the shape, they should still be arranged in a ring. Irregular-shaped cookies should be positioned with the widest part toward the outer edge of the dish. When microwaving finger or stick-shaped cookies, avoid arranging them like the spokes of a wheel; instead, place them around the edge of the dish in one or two rows.

SESAME CHEESE TWISTS

These savory snacks are perfect to serve with soups or salads.

Makes 36

4 ounces/1 cup all-purpose flour

1/4 teaspoon salt

pinch of mustard powder

2 ounces/1/4 cup butter, diced and chilled

2 ounces/1/2 cup finely grated strong-flavored cheese, such as Cheddar

1 egg yolk

2 teaspoons cold water

2 tablespoons sesame seeds

1 Sift the flour, salt and mustard powder into a bowl. Rub in the butter until the mixture resembles fine breadcrumbs, then stir in the cheese. Mix the egg yolk and water together, sprinkle over the dry ingredients and mix to a firm dough. Lightly knead on a floured surface.

2 Roll out the dough to 1/4-inch thickness and cut into sticks about 3 inches long and 1/4 inch wide.

3 Hold the ends of the sticks and twist them in opposite directions. Sprinkle the sesame seeds on a plate and roll the twists in them until coated. Line a microwave tray with baking parchment and arrange 12 twists in a circle on it.

4 Cook on full (100 percent) power for 2–2½ minutes, until firm to the touch. Leave to stand for 2 minutes, then transfer to a wire rack to cool. Cook the remaining cheese twists in the same way.

Cook's Tip

There isn't a standard output or name or number for settings used by all microwave manufacturers, so cooking times are only a guide. The recipes given here are for 750-watt microwave ovens.

GETTING GOOD RESULTS

• Always use microwave-proof cookware. Glass and china are suitable, but avoid melamine, plastic and any dishes that contain metal.

• Microwaved cookies don't brown in the same way as conventionally baked ones, so colored mixtures, such as ginger and chocolate, work best.

• Improve the look of microwave cookies by icing them after cooking, or adding a dusting of sugar.

• Added ingredients such as chocolate, nuts and dried fruit should be cut into small, even-sized pieces.

• Don't cover the cookies during cooking, to allow the steam to escape.

• Microwaved cookies continue cooking for a short time after the machine is switched off, so stop microwaving just before they are ready. Open the door during cooking to check progress. The best way to discover whether they are done is to sacrifice one and break it open; if the center is beginning to change color, the cookies are ready. Use the same cooking time for subsequent batches.

• Foods with a high fat or sugar content cook very quickly in a microwave and can burn easily. Always cook for the minimum time, and watch carefully. Remember, if you reduce the number of cookies, the cooking time must also be reduced.

Baking Cookies

To make perfect cookies, you must take as much care with cooking them as you did with mixing and shaping the dough.

USING THE OVEN

Always allow time to preheat the oven; it will take about 15 minutes to reach the required temperature (although fan-assisted ovens may heat more quickly).

Unless the recipe instructs otherwise, bake cookies in the middle, or just above the middle, of the oven. If you are baking large quantities of cookies, do not put more than two baking sheets in the oven at once, because this can cause the oven temperature to drop. This particularly applies to cookies that have been chilled beforehand.

USING BAKING SHEETS

If you are using a new baking sheet, check that it fits into the oven before you arrange the cookies on it; ideally, there should be a small gap at either side and at the back of the baking sheet to allow hot air to circulate. If you need to divide the cookies between two or more baking sheets, put the same number of cookies on each sheet, so the batches cook at the same rate. If you put two baking sheets of cookies in the oven at the same time, switch them around halfway through the cooking time. If you need to cook a second batch of cookies right away, let the baking sheet cool before placing the next batch of raw cookies on it; a hot baking sheet might make the raw cookies spread, which will result in thin, irregular-size cookies.

TIME AND TEMPERATURE

Baking times may vary slightly with different ovens, and can depend on how chilled the cookies were when cooking commenced. Get to know your oven. If you feel that it is either too cool or too hot, use an oven thermometer to check the temperature. If it needs adjusting, change your oven temperature dial accordingly to correct this.

Always check cookies a few minutes before the end of the suggested cooking time. Unlike cakes, they will not loose volume or sink if the oven door is opened, although you should avoid doing this too frequently or the temperature will drop and the cookies will be less crisp. Second and subsequent batches of cookies may take slightly less time to cook.

COOKING GUIDELINES

Not all cookies are the same. Different types of cookie need to be cooked in different ways and at different temperatures.

DROP COOKIES

These are baked in a moderate oven, around 350°F/Gas 4. This gives them a chance to spread out a little before they set. To make cookies that are crisp on the outside, but with a slightly soft and chewy center, remove from the oven as soon as the edges are dark golden but the middle is still a little pale. For crisp cookies, wait until the whole cookie is lightly browned before removing from the oven. To achieve an even crisper result, spread out the mixture slightly to make a thinner layer before baking.

ROLLED, PIPED AND PRESSED COOKIES

These are usually chilled before baking to prevent them spreading too much during cooking. They are cooked in a moderate to hot oven, between 350°F/Gas 4 and 400°F/Gas 6.

1 Place the cookies on a baking sheet, then chill for 30 minutes.

2 Bake until pale golden; do not allow to color too much.

3 Leave to cool slightly on the baking sheets, then carefully transfer to wire racks to cool completely.

REFRIGERATOR COOKIES

These cookies have a relatively high fat content and so are baked at a moderately high temperature, around 375°F/Gas 5.

1 Slice the chilled cookie mixture and arrange on ungreased baking sheets. Do not use non-stick sheets or line the sheets with baking parchment, because this will make the cookies spread.

2 The cookies must be well chilled before baking, so either cook them as soon as they have been sliced or place the baking sheets in the refrigerator until ready to bake.

BAR COOKIES

This type of cookie is usually baked in a moderate to moderately low oven, between 325°F/Gas 3 and 350°F/Gas 4.

1 Bar cookies with a shortbread, pastry or crumb base are often partially baked before the topping is added. This allows the base to be cooked until crisp and firm without the topping becoming overcooked.

2 To test whether sponge or brownie mixtures are cooked, insert a toothpick into the mixture. It should come out clean.

COOLING COOKIES

Always follow the instructions in the recipe when cooling cookies. Most cookies are quite delicate so benefit from being left on the baking sheets for a minute or two to firm up, before removing to a wire rack to cool completely.

Use a thin metal spatula to transfer cookies to wire racks. Placing them on a wire rack allows air to circulate around the them, and prevents moisture being trapped, which can make them lose their crisp texture. Don't cram too many cookies on the rack at any one time and avoid placing hot cookies on top of each other; they are likely to lose their crispness.

Cookies such as tuiles that are to be molded into shape should be removed from the baking sheets after 30 seconds, while they are still warm and pliable. Others such as bar cookies may benefit from being allowed to cool in the baking pans. Placing the whole pan a wire rack can speed the cooling.

BAKING COOKIES AT HIGH ALTITUDE

At 9,800 feet above sea level, atmospheric pressure becomes lower, which makes liquid boil faster and causes greater evaporation. This affects cookie-baking in several ways: flavors, especially sweet ones, are more concentrated; slightly more liquid is necessary; and smaller quantities of raising agents are needed. It also helps if you marginally reduce the amount of fat in recipes and increase the quantity of flour.

	ALTITUDE		
	9,800 feet	**16,350 feet**	**22,900 feet**
Sugar For each 4 ounces/ generous ½ cup, reduce by:	2 teaspoons	1 tablespoon	2 tablespoons
Baking powder For each 1 teaspoon, reduce by:	⅛ teaspoon	¼ teaspoon	¼ teaspoon
Liquid For each 5 tablespoons, reduce by:	1 teaspoon	2 teaspoons	1 tablespoon
Oven temperature Increase by:	10°F/Gas ¼	25°F/Gas ½	35°F/Gas 1½

Cookie Decoration

Decorating cookies can add the final flourish to home-made cookies and can be one of the most enjoyable aspects of cookie-making. Cookies can be decorated before baking, while the cookies are still warm from the oven, or when they are completely cool.

DECORATING COOKIES BEFORE BAKING

Techniques for decorating unbaked cookies can range from the most simple sprinkling of sugar or nuts to brushing with a glossy glaze or painting intricate designs with edible food coloring.

SUGAR

A crunchy sugar topping is one of the easiest and most effective ways to decorate unbaked cookies. (It is also one of the most popular decorations for baked cookies.) Many different sugars can be used.

Superfine sugar can be sprinkled straight over raw cookies to give a subtle, crunchy texture. Coarse sugars such as raw sugar and irregular-shaped coffee crystals give a crunchier result. Pretty colored sugars and crushed white and brown sugar lumps also produce a lovely effect when sprinkled over raw cookies.

Moist cookie doughs can simply be sprinkled with sugar; drier cookies, such as refrigerator or rolled cookies, may benefit from being lightly brushed with a little water or milk before they are sprinkled with sugar. Alternatively, after rolling the dough, sprinkle it with sugar, then roll very lightly before cutting out the cookies.

Cookie dough that is shaped into a log before slicing can be rolled in sugar before the log is chilled and sliced. This will produce cookies with a crisp, sugary edge.

Cookies such as macaroons that produce a cracked surface during baking look particularly attractive dusted with sugar before baking. The sugar helps to accentuate the cracked effect. Flatten the balls of dough slightly, brush each with a little water and sift over a fine and even layer of confectioners' sugar before baking.

NUTS

Chopped and sliced nuts can be sprinkled over cookies in the same way as sugar. Nuts brown during baking, so avoid using on cookies that are baked at a high temperature or on cookies that are baked for a long time, as the nuts may overcook.

A whole nut can be pressed into the top of each individual cookie. (This technique is best suited to soft cookie doughs.) The nuts may be decorative, or they can be used to indicate the type of cookie. For example, you might want to press a whole hazelnut into a hazelnut cookie, or an almond into an almond flavored cookie.

Sliced almonds look stunning sprinkled over cookies but should be baked for no longer than 10 minutes in a moderately hot oven, or they will burn. This is the classic topping for tuiles.

GLAZES

Brushing a glaze over cookies can serve two purposes, either to provide a sticky surface that nuts or sugar can stick to, or simply to give an attractive finish.

To give cookies a rich, glossy finish, use a whole beaten egg or yolk. Brush the glaze lightly and evenly on the top, without it dripping over the edges – this is especially important where raising agents have been used, because it will prevent the cookies rising evenly. You can dilute the glaze by adding 1 tablespoon cold water or milk and adding a pinch of superfine sugar for sweet cookies; salt for savory ones.

Lightly beaten egg white produces a clear, shiny finish. Brush over the cookies halfway through the baking time, so that it soaks into the cookies slightly and does not set to a crackled glaze. It looks effective sprinkled with a little sugar.

PAINTED COOKIES

Edible food coloring can be painted directly onto unbaked cookies to make pretty patterns. This technique is best suited to drier, firmer cookie doughs, such as rolled and refrigerator cookies.

To decorate cookies, cut the dough into shapes, place them on baking sheets and chill for 30 minutes. Beat an egg yolk and mix in a few drops of food coloring. Using a fine paintbrush, paint patterns onto the cookies, and then bake. (Remember that the yellow egg yolk may affect the color of the food coloring.)

CANDY CENTERS

This technique is very simple to do yet is extremely effective.

Cut out the center of each cookie and fill it with crushed hard candy. The sweets will melt during baking, then harden when cooled to make a colorful center.

SIMPLE BAKED COOKIE DECORATIONS

As with unbaked cookies, you can transform simple baked cookies into something really special with just a few simple decorating techniques. A sprinkling of sugar takes just a few seconds, while dusting a design using a stencil or writing a simple message with a food coloring pen takes only a little longer. Food coloring pens work best on refrigerator or rolled cookies that have been only lightly baked, or on firm icing.

DECORATING COOKIES WITH SUGAR

Different types of sugar can be used to give a range of effects on various baked cookies.

Confectioners' sugar A light dusting of confectioners' sugar gives plain cookies a wonderfully professional finish and is a useful way of disguising any imperfections.

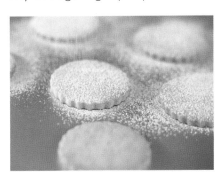

Use a fine sieve or sugar dredger to give an even coating. If you want a very light layer, hold the sieve or dredger high and shake gently; for a thicker finish, keep the sieve or dredger closer to the cookies. If you are dusting pairs of cookies sandwiched together, fill them first, then sprinkle with sugar.

Superfine sugar Simply sprinkling freshly baked cookies with a little superfine sugar is perhaps one of the quickest and easiest decorations to use.

Sprinkle sugar over the cookies while they are still warm so that the sugar sticks to them. (Soft light and dark brown sugars can also be used but, because they are so moist, even sprinkling is very difficult. Push through a medium sieve rather than sprinkling by hand.)

FLAVORED SUGARS

These are a good alternative to plain superfine sugar and give cookies a subtle hint more flavor. It is possible to buy flavored sugars, but it is just as easy to make your own.

Vanilla Put a vanilla bean in a jar of superfine sugar and leave for at least 2 weeks. Refill the jar with sugar as you use it.
Sweet spice Steep the sugar for two weeks with whole spices such as cloves. To make instant spiced sugar, use about ½ teaspoon ground cinnamon or apple pie spice for every 2 tablespoons sugar.

Coarse-grained sugars

Granulated and raw sugar look pretty sprinkled over cookies, but, because the grains are so large, they will not stick to the cookie on their own. The easiest way to overcome this problem is to use a glaze, such as beaten egg white, to stick the sugar to the cookie, then return the cookies to the oven for 2–3 minutes.

Cookies such as sweet pretzels are usually coated with sugar, then broiled until they start to caramelize. Brush the cooled cookies lightly with egg white and sprinkle generously with raw sugar. (Sprinkle on plenty of sugar to protect the cookie from the heat.) Place under a hot broiler for about 1 minute until the sugar is just starting to bubble. Return to wire racks to cool.

Citrus Add a strip of orange or lemon rind to the sugar and leave for 3 days. Shake the sugar before use as it may have become slightly damp from the rind.
Rosemary Add a sprig of fresh rosemary to the sugar and leave for 3–4 days.
Lavender Add lavender (about five heads) to the sugar and leave for 3–4 days.

DECORATING COOKIES WITH SUGAR GLAZES

Cookies such as lebkuchen are sometimes given a slightly shiny finish with a sugar glaze. These glazes may be clear or opaque and are usually brushed over the cookies while they are still hot or warm.

LEBKUCHEN GLAZE

This semi-opaque glaze gently softens the surface of the cookie, giving it a chewy texture.

Sift 6 ounces/1½ cups confectioners' sugar into a bowl. Add ½ teaspoon almond extract, 1 teaspoon lemon juice and 2 tablespoons hot water. Mix together until smooth, then brush over the hot lebkuchen and leave to cool.

CLEAR GLAZE

This simple sugar glaze gives cookies a lovely, glossy finish.

1 Heat 1 ounce/2 tablespoons sugar in 4 tablespoons water until the sugar dissolves. Boil rapidly for 5 minutes, or until reduced by half. (The glaze can be flavored with a strip of lemon or orange rind, if you like.)

2 Remove from the heat and leave to cool. Gradually beat in 4 ounces/ 1 cup sifted icing sugar, then brush over warm cookies and leave to set.

STENCILING DESIGNS

This is an easy way to decorate cookies. You can buy stencils that are specially made for cake and cookie decorating, or make your own by drawing a small design on thin cardboard and cutting it out. Make sure there is a contrast between the color of the cookie and the dusting ingredient; confectioners' sugar works well on chocolate cookies, while cocoa powder (unsweetened) is better on pale cookies. You can also color confectioners' sugar by blending cake decorators' petal dust with the sugar.

Place the stencil over the cookie. Dust with confectioners' sugar or cocoa powder through a fine sieve, then carefully remove the cardboard.

Paper doilies can be used to make an attractive lacy pattern. Place a large doily over several cookies at once and dust liberally with confectioners' sugar or cocoa powder.

To create a dramatic light and dark effect on cookies, lightly dust a whole cookie with confectioners' sugar, then cover half of it with a piece of cardboard or a sheet of paper and carefully dust the other half with cocoa powder.

FOOD-COLORING PENS

These pens look like felt-tip pens, but they are filled with edible food coloring. They come in a range of colors, from primary to pastels, and some are flavored.

They can be used directly onto the cookies or onto icing. They are most effective used on rolled and cut cookies that have been baked only until light golden rather than well browned; icing must be dry and firm.

Use the decorating pens in the same way as an ordinary pen. Draw designs, write messages, or use to color in shapes.

DECORATING COOKIES WITH ICING

Cookies can look lovely decorated with pretty colored icing. It is important to get the consistency of icing exactly right; too thick and it will be difficult to spread; too thin and it will run off the edges and soak into the cookie.

There are many different types of icing that can be used to decorate cookies, and they can range in color from the palest pastels to vibrant primary colors. Candied or fondant icings give a smooth, glossy finish and can be used to create simple finishing touches to the cookies, while royal icing can be swirled to give a textured pattern or piped into delicate and intricate designs. Whatever type of icing you use, iced cookies should usually be eaten within 3 or 4 days.

CANDIED ICING

This is the simplest type of icing to make and use. It is perfect for the tops of cookies, or for drizzling and piping simple designs.

To cover 24 cookies
4 ounces/1 cup confectioners' sugar
a few drops of vanilla extract
  (optional)
1 tablespoon hot water
a few drops of food coloring (optional)

Sift the confectioners' sugar into a bowl, then add the vanilla extract, if using. Gradually stir in the hot water until the mixture is the consistency of thick cream. Add the food coloring, and continue stirring until smooth.

Top coating This is the simplest technique for coating the top of cookies with candied icing.

Spoon a little icing onto the center of the cookie, then carefully spread it out almost to the edges using the back of the spoon. (To make a perfect shape, pipe the outline of the shape first. Leave to dry for 1–2 minutes, then spoon in the icing and spread out to fill the shape.)

Feathered candied icing Spoon a little icing over a cookie to cover it completely, then pipe several thin, straight parallel lines of icing in a contrasting color across the top of the cookie.

Starting at the middle of the cookie, draw a wooden toothpick or fine skewer through the lines in the opposite direction, gently dragging the color through the icing and creating a feathered effect on the cookie.

Cobweb icing Cover a cookie in icing, then pipe on fine, concentric circles of icing in a contrasting color, starting from the center and working outward.

Draw a toothpick from the center of the cookie to the outside edge, dividing the cookie into quarters, then repeat to divide it into eighths.

Drizzled icing Candied icing can be drizzled or piped over cookies to give a pretty finish.

Place the cookies on a wire rack. Using a paper pastry bag or teaspoon, drizzle fine lines of icing over the cookies. You can then drizzle more icing at right angles to these first lines, if you like.

Variation
To make white candied icing, add a few drops of lemon juice instead of vanilla extract; this enhances the whiteness.

ICING GLAZE

This is similar to candied icing, but is flavored with lemon juice and thinned with egg white, giving it a shinier, slightly harder set.

To cover 12 cookies

1 tablespoon lightly beaten egg white
1 tablespoon lemon juice
4 ounces/1 cup confectioners' sugar, sifted

Mix together the egg white and lemon juice in a bowl. Gradually beat in the confectioners' sugar until the mixture is completely smooth, then place the cookies on a wire rack. Spoon the icing evenly over the cookies and leave to set.

ROYAL ICING

This icing sets hard to give a good finish so is perfect for piping designs and messages on cookies such as gingerbread. It can be colored with a few drops of food coloring but is better left unflavored.

To cover 30 cookies

1 egg white, at room temperature or
1½ teaspoons albumen powder
8 ounces/2 cups confectioners' sugar,
sifted, plus extra if necessary

1 Beat the egg white for a few seconds with a fork. (If using albumen powder, mix according to the instructions.) Mix in the icing sugar a little at a time until the mixture stands in soft peaks and is thick enough to spread. If the icing is for piping, beat in a little more confectioners' sugar until the icing will stand in stiff peaks. Spread or pipe the icing over the cookies. Leave to set.

MAKING AND USING A PAPER ICING BAG

A paper bag for piping is easy to make once you know how.

1 Cut a piece of waxed paper or baking parchment into a 10-inch square, then cut it in half diagonally so that you have two triangles. Hold one triangle with the longest side away from you. Curl the left-hand point over into a cone to meet the point nearest you. Curl the right-hand point over the cone.

2 Bring the points of the folded triangles together to make a neat, narrow cone. Tuck the point of paper inside the cone, fold it over and secure with sticky tape.

3 If using a nozzle, cut off the pointed end of the bag. Position the nozzle so that it fits snugly.

4 Using a metal spatula, fill the bag with icing. Take care not to overfill the bag; half to two-thirds full is ideal.

5 Fold the top corners of the bag in toward the center, then fold over the top, firmly pushing the icing down toward the tip. Fold over the top corner again, making a pad to push with your thumb.

6 If you have not inserted a nozzle into the bag, snip a small, straight piece off the end of the bag for the icing to pass through. (It is better to snip off the small tip first. If the line of icing is too narrow, snip off a little bit more.)

7 Hold the pastry bag between your middle and forefingers and push down with your thumb. Place the tip in position over the cookie, then gently push the icing through the bag using your thumb. To stop the flow of icing, release the pressure from your thumb. The icing will continue to flow for a few seconds after the pressure has stopped so you should release your thumb before you reach the end of the line.

DECORATING COOKIES WITH CHOCOLATE

The taste, texture and versatility of chocolate makes it one of the most popular ingredients for decorating cookies. It can be used to coat cookies, pipe or drizzle patterns, or even write short messages.

MELTING CHOCOLATE

For most decorating techniques, chocolate needs to be melted. Take care doing this, as overheating will spoil both the texture and flavor. When melting chocolate, choose a variety with a high proportion of cocoa butter, as this will melt much more easily and smoothly.

Using a double boiler Break the chocolate into pieces and put it in the top of a double boiler or in a heatproof bowl set over a pan of hot water; the water should not touch the top container. Bring the water to simmering point, then turn down the heat to keep the water at a very gentle simmer.

Check the chocolate every few minutes, turning off the heat if necessary. Stir once or twice during melting, until the chocolate is completely smooth. Do not cover the bowl once the chocolate has melted, or condensation will form.

Using a microwave This is a quick and simple way of melting chocolate. Bear in mind that microwaved chocolate will retain its shape, so you will need to stir the chocolate to see if it has melted.

Break the chocolate into pieces and place in a microwave-safe bowl. Melt in bursts of 30–60 seconds, checking often and reducing the time as the chocolate begins to soften. Stop microwaving before all the chocolate has melted; the residual heat in the chocolate should complete the process.

As a guide, 4 ounces of chocolate will take about 1½ minutes on full (100 percent) power, and 8 ounces will take 2–2½ minutes. White chocolate should be melted on medium (50 percent) power.

Using direct heat This method is only suitable for recipes where the chocolate is melted with another liquid, such as milk or cream, or with other ingredients, such as butter and light corn syrup.

Put the liquid ingredients in the pan, then add the chopped or broken chocolate and melt slowly over the lowest heat. When the chocolate has started to melt, turn off the heat and stir constantly until the mixture is completely smooth.

Tempering chocolate This technique is used for couverture chocolate, making it easier to work with and giving it a glossy appearance when set.

Melt the chocolate in the usual way, then pour about two-thirds of it onto a marble slab or cold surface. Using a metal spatula, move the chocolate back and forth until it is thick and beginning to reach setting point. Return the chocolate to the bowl and melt again, stirring constantly.

USING MELTED CHOCOLATE

When you are decorating cookies with melted chocolate, handle the chocolate as little as possible and use a metal spatula to lift and move the decorated cookies around; the warmth of your fingers will leave prints on the chocolate and make the surface dull.

Always leave chocolate-coated cookies to set at room temperature, and do not store in the refrigerator unless it is exceptionally warm; chilling will cause the chocolate to lose its glossy appearance. Also make sure that the cookies are at room temperature rather than still warm from the oven or cold (if they have been stored in the refrigerator or freezer).

Coating cookies with chocolate

Before coating cookies in melted chocolate, make sure that the chocolate is just starting to cool; chocolate that is hot or even very warm will soak into the cookies and spoil the texture.

1 Place the cookies on a wire rack with a sheet of baking parchment underneath. Spoon cooled melted chocolate over each cookie, then tap the rack to help it run down the sides and to level the top. Leave to set on the rack, then cover with a second coat, if you like. Scrape the chocolate off the baking parchment, return to the bowl and re-melt to coat more cookies.

2 To decorate coated cookies, drizzle or pipe with a contrasting color of chocolate. For a smooth surface, do this before the first layer of chocolate has set; for a raised surface, wait until the first layer of chocolate has hardened.

Dipping cookies in chocolate

Round or shaped cookies are often half-coated in chocolate, and finger cookies sometimes have one or both ends dipped in chocolate. This method is simpler than completely covering cookies in chocolate. If you're planning to sandwich cookies together, they are best dipped in chocolate before filling, as the warmth of the chocolate may melt the filling if dipped afterward.

1 Melt the chocolate in a narrow deep bowl. Holding the cookie by the part that you don't want to coat, dip it briefly in the melted chocolate, then allow any excess to drip back into the bowl.

2 Place the cookie on a sheet of baking parchment and leave to set. When the chocolate is firm, carefully peel off the paper. If you want to sprinkle chopped nuts or other decorations on the top, do this before the chocolate sets.

Coating florentines with chocolate

The flat underside of florentines is traditionally coated with chocolate.

Holding the florentine between finger and thumb, spread the flat base with chocolate. With the prongs of a fork, create wavy lines in the chocolate. Place the florentine on a wire rack, and leave to set.

Piping chocolate

Use a small paper pastry bag with the end snipped off to pipe thin lines of chocolate.

Place cookies on a sheet of baking parchment and pipe over thin lines, first in one direction, then the other.

Coloring white chocolate

You can color melted white chocolate with cake decorator's petal dust. Do not use liquid or paste food colorings, as these will spoil the texture of the chocolate.

Cookie Fillings

From smooth custard creams to sticky jammie sweethearts, two cookies sandwiched together are better than one. The key to a good cookie filling is to make the mixture soft enough to spread or pipe but not too moist, because this can make the cookies soft and crumbly.

BUTTERCREAM

This simple cookie filling is very easy to make. Once filled, the cookies should be eaten within 3 days.

1 To make enough filling for about 12 pairs of average-size cookies, put 2 ounces/¼ cup softened sweet butter in a bowl and beat with a wooden spoon until very soft, smooth and creamy.

2 Gradually stir in 3½ ounces/ scant 1 cup confectioners' sugar and 1 teaspoon vanilla extract. Beat the ingredients well with an electric mixer until they are very light and smooth.

Variations
Orange, lemon or lime buttercream
Add 1 tablespoon finely grated citrus rind and replace the vanilla with juice, beating well to avoid curdling. The buttercream cannot be piped through a small nozzle because of the citrus rind.
Chocolate buttercream *Blend 2 teaspoons cocoa powder (unsweetened) with 4 teaspoons boiling water until smooth. Cool, then beat into the buttercream.*
Coffee buttercream *Replace the vanilla extract with 2 teaspoons instant coffee powder dissolved in 1 tablespoon near-boiling water. Cool before adding to the mixture.*

CRÈME AU BEURRE

This delicious buttercream has a rich taste and very smooth texture.

1 To make enough filling for about 12 pairs of average-size cookies, put 1½ ounces/3 tablespoons superfine sugar and 2 tablespoons water in a small, heavy pan and heat gently until the sugar has completely dissolved. Bring to the boil and boil steadily for 2–3 minutes, until the syrup reaches 225°F on a sugar thermometer or when a little syrup pulled apart between two dry teaspoons makes a fine thread.

2 Beat 1 egg yolk in a heatproof bowl for a few seconds. Gradually pour over the syrup in a steady, narrow stream, whisking constantly. Continue whisking until the mixture is thick and cold. Beat 3 ounces/ 6 tablespoons sweet butter until creamy. Gradually add the egg yolk mixture to the butter, whisking well after each addition.

CHOCOLATE GANACHE

This filling is a fairly soft, so chill for a few minutes before using to fill cookies. It is rich, so spread thinly.

1 To make enough filling for about 20 pairs of average-size cookies. Pour 4 fluid ounces/½ cup heavy cream into a small pan and bring to the boil. Remove the pan from the heat and add 4 ounces semisweet chocolate. Stir until melted and smooth.

2 Return the mixture to the heat and bring back to the boil. Transfer to a bowl and leave to cool. Chill for 10 minutes before using.

FILLING COOKIES WITH JAM

To make a smooth, slightly set jam filling, the jam needs to be boiled briefly to thicken it.

1 To make enough for 16 pairs of cookies, put 8 tablespoons jam in a small, heavy pan. Add 1 teaspoon lemon juice. Heat gently until runny, then boil for 3–4 minutes.

2 Remove the pan from the heat and leave to cool slightly, then push the jam through a fine sieve to remove any lumps. Leave the jam until barely warm, then use to sandwich the cookies together.

FILLING BRANDY SNAPS

Whipped cream, sometimes sweetened with a little sugar and flavored with brandy or a few drops of vanilla extract, makes a simple filling for these crisp rolled cookies. Using a well-chilled bowl for whipping the cream will give a lighter result.

1 To make enough cream to fill about 20 brandy snaps, pour 8 fluid ounces/1 cup whipping cream into a large chilled bowl. Sift 2 teaspoons confectioners' sugar over the cream and add about 2 tablespoons brandy. Whip the mixture, using an electric mixer or balloon whisk, until the cream just forms soft peaks.

2 Spoon the cream into a pastry bag fitted with a large star nozzle. Push the end of the nozzle into the end of the brandy snap and squeeze gently until the brandy snap is filled to the middle. Repeat with the other end of the brandy snap.

CHOCOLATE-FILLED COOKIES

Chunks of chocolate can be baked inside the cookie to make a delicious surprise filling.

Makes about 16

5 ounces/10 tablespoons butter, softened

5 ounces/¾ cup superfine sugar

1 egg yolk

1 tablespoon ground almonds

8 ounces/2 cups self-rising flour

1 ounce/¼ cup cocoa powder (unsweetened)

5 ounces semisweet chocolate

confectioners' sugar, for dusting

1 Preheat the oven to 375°F/ Gas 5 and grease or line two baking sheets. Cream the butter and sugar until pale and fluffy. Beat in the egg yolk and ground almonds. Sift over the flour and cocoa powder and fold into the mixture to make a firm dough. Knead for a few seconds, then put in plastic wrap and chill for 30 minutes.

2 Roll out just over a third of the dough to a thickness of ⅛ inch and stamp out 16 rounds using a 1½-inch cookie cutter. Break the chocolate into squares and put one in the center of each cookie round.

3 Roll out the remaining dough and cut into 16 larger round pieces using a 2-inch cutter. Place these over the chocolate-covered cookie rounds and press the edges together. Bake for 10 minutes, until firm. Dust the cookies with confectioners' sugar and transfer to a wire rack. Serve warm while the filling is still soft and melted.

CLASSIC COOKIE FILLINGS

These recipes will make enough to fill 12–15 pairs of cookies.

Custard cream Melt 1 ounce/ 2 tablespoons butter in a small pan, then beat in 8 ounces/ 2 cups sifted confectioners' sugar, 2 tablespoons milk and a few drops of vanilla extract until smooth.

Chocolate bourbon Beat together 2 ounces/¼ cup of softened butter, 3 ounces/¾ cup sifted confectioners' sugar, 1 tablespoon sifted cocoa powder (unsweetened) and 1 teaspoon light corn syrup until smooth.

Chocolate and orange Bring 4 fluid ounces/½ cup whipping cream to the boil. Remove from the heat and stir in 7 ounces chopped white chocolate until smooth. Stir in 1 teaspoon orange extract or liqueur.

Fudgy mocha Dissolve 2 teaspoons instant coffee powder in 1 teaspoon water in a heatproof bowl set over a pan of boiling water. Add four chopped chocolate-coated fudge fingers. Stir until melted, remove from the heat and whisk in 2 tablespoons heavy cream. Chill until firm enough to spread.

Honey and ginger Beat together 3 ounces/ 6 tablespoons softened butter, 3 ounces/¾ cup set honey and 3 ounces/¾ cup confectioners' sugar until light and creamy. Beat in 1½ ounces finely chopped, preserved stem ginger.

Storing Cookies

With few exceptions, cookies are best eaten on the day that they are made. Some, such as American-style soft cookies, are delicious when still slightly warm from the oven, but most cookies need to be cooled first to allow them to crisp. If you're not planning to eat them right away, store them as soon as they have cooled. This will prevent crisp cookies from becoming soft and soft ones from drying out and hardening. Store crisp and soft cookies separately; if kept together, not only will their texture suffer, but the flavors may mingle as well.

SOFT COOKIES

It is essential to keep these cookies in an airtight container, and, if possible, they should also be stored in the refrigerator to retain the freshly baked flavor.

Carefully pack cookies into an airtight container, and seal. If the lid of the container isn't tight-fitting, put the cookies inside a plastic bag first, or cover the whole container with plastic wrap before closing the lid. To restore the texture of soft cookies that have hardened – this may happen very quickly in dry climates – add a slice of brown bread to the container. Replace the bread daily.

CRISP COOKIES

The container for this type of cookie does not need to be absolutely airtight; unless the atmosphere is very humid, a slight flow of air will help them stay crisp.

Glass jars and ceramic containers with cork stoppers are ideal for storing crisp cookies. Place a little crumpled tissue paper in the base of the jar to help absorb any moisture. If cookies become soft, place them on a baking sheet and put in a preheated oven at 300°F/ Gas 2 for about 3 minutes to re-crisp. Remove and cool on a wire rack before storing.

COOKIES IN THE FREEZER

Undecorated baked cookies can be frozen successfully. Freeze the cookies on trays, then pack into an airtight container, interleaving with waxed paper or baking parchment. (Avoid freezing cream-filled cookies, such as brandy snaps, as these will quickly become soggy.) To thaw, leave at room temperature for about 20 minutes.

Iced cookies can also be frozen in the same way, but they should be removed from the airtight container and thawed on a wire rack – the icing may be spoiled if they are left to thaw while still packed in layers.

CHILLING AND FREEZING COOKIE DOUGH

As long as cookie dough doesn't contain leavening ingredients, it can be stored in the refrigerator overnight or, in some cases, for up to a week. Cookie dough can also be frozen for up to 3 months, but the flavors tend to lose their intensity after a month, so, for optimum results, the dough is best frozen for just a few weeks.

To store cookie dough in the refrigerator, put it in plastic wrap, or place it in a bowl and cover it tightly with plastic wrap. To freeze, doubly wrap the dough in plastic wrap, then store in an airtight container.

To freeze unbaked cookies, open-freeze them on trays, then pack into airtight containers, interleaving them with layers of waxed paper or baking parchment. Thaw unbaked cookies on baking sheets.

WHAT WENT WRONG AND WHY

Occasionally cookies don't turn out quite as you had hoped. If you have a problem when baking, try to work out why so that you can either remedy it at the time, or at least avoid it next time you bake cookies.

Problem	Cause	Remedy
The dough is very soft and won't hold its shape.	Too much liquid or fat, or too little flour, or the dough has become too warm.	Always measure ingredients carefully. Chill the dough for 30 minutes before baking. If it is still too soft, work in a little extra flour.
The dough is dry and crumbly and won't hold together.	Not enough liquid or fat, or too much flour, or the dough may not have been kneaded sufficiently.	Try gently kneading the dough; the warmth of your hands may bring it together. If the dough includes egg, check the right size was used. Knead in a little beaten egg, milk or soft butter.
The cookies are not evenly cooked.	The cookies are either of uneven sizes on the baking sheet; or some cookies were placed too near the edge of the sheet.	Make sure that all the cookies on a baking sheet are an even size. Leave at least a 1-inch gap around the edge of the baking sheet, and turn the sheets around halfway through baking.
The cookies stick to the baking sheet.	The baking sheet was not greased or greased unevenly. Alternatively, it may have been greased with salted butter.	Use melted sweet butter, or oil for greasing or, line the sheet with baking parchment.
The cookies crumble when removed from baking sheet.	Cookies that have a very high butter content are often more fragile than less rich ones.	Leave fragile cookies to cool on the baking sheet for at least 3 minutes before transferring to a wire rack.
The cookies are dry and too crisp on top.	The oven was too hot or the cookies were baked for too long.	If you have concerns about the temperature of your oven, use an oven thermometer. Check cookies a few minutes before end of cooking time.
The cookies spread out too much on the baking sheet.	The cookies were not chilled before baking, or the baking sheet was over-greased when the cookies were added.	Most cookies benefit from chilling before baking. Grease baking sheets only lightly. Some cookies, such as refrigerator cookies, should be baked on ungreased baking sheets. Always use cold baking sheets.
The cookies are burnt on the base but not on the top.	There are a number of possible causes: baking too low down in the oven, or at too low a temperature; the baking sheets may be of poor quality, or you may have used salted butter for greasing.	Check the oven temperature and bake cookies on the middle shelf. Avoid thin or very dark baking sheets. Butter burns at a lower temperature, so use oil for cookies baked at high temperatures or for a long time.

Presentation and Packaging

Whether you're making cookies to serve to guests, give as a gift or sell at a fund-raising event, it is worth spending a little time on pretty presentation and attractive and elegant packaging.

All cookies should be properly stored as soon as they have cooled or, if iced or decorated, as soon as they have set and hardened. Leave gift wrapping and packaging until the last minute so that the cookies are as fresh as possible. It is often useful to include information about the cookies as well, including a list of ingredients and advice on storing.

GIFT BOXES

You can buy a huge range of pretty storage containers that make perfect packaging for cookies. Stationers and department stores sell a range of beautiful gift boxes and containers in all shapes and sizes, patterns and colors. These are the simplest way to package cookies and look stunning tied with curled ribbon or raffia.

Line the box with either crumpled tissue paper or several layers of waxed paper. If the cookies are iced or fragile, then shallow boxes that will hold the cookies in one or just a few layers are better than very deep ones.

Certain types of cookie can be individually wrapped in tissue paper or cellophane before packing into the box. Amaretti, for example, are usually wrapped in pairs in twists of fine tissue paper.

JARS, TIN BOXES AND OTHER CONTAINERS

Reusable containers such as glass or ceramic storage jars, or tin boxes, are more practical than simple cardboard boxes, as they have the advantage of being airtight. They also have the advantage of becoming part of the gift as well.

As well as packaging cookies in more conventional jars and tin boxes, you could also consider packing cookies into a container such as a cup. Wrap the cookies in cellophane and tie with a ribbon, then place in the container. (This form of packaging is not airtight, so the cookies should be wrapped at the last minute.)

MAKING BOXES

It can be great fun making your own boxes or cartons to pack cookies in. It is also much cheaper than buying ready-made gift boxes, which can be surprisingly expensive. All you need is some fine cardboard, a metal ruler and a sharp knife.

MAKING A CUBE BOX

Following the template on the opposite page, draw the outline of the cube box on the back of a piece of colored, patterned or plain cardboard. Cut out the shape and carefully score along the dotted lines with a sharp craft knife.

1 Fold along the dotted lines, sticking tab A to edge A (keeping the tab inside the box), then tab B to edge B. Repeat with tab C to edge C and tab D to edge D.

2 To create the lid, simply fold in tabs E and tuck the flap inside the box to hold the lid in place.

MAKING A CARTON

Following the template shown below, draw the outline of the carton on the back of a piece of fine cardboard and carefully cut out.

1 Score along the dotted lines using a sharp craft knife and cut out the four slots. You can use a hole puncher to make the four holes as marked on the diagram.

2 Fold the carton along the scored lines, tucking tongue A into flaps B and tongue C into flaps D, so that the end of the tongue is on the inside of the carton. Fill the carton with cookies, then you can thread fine ribbon through the punched holes and tie together.

DECORATING BOXES

If you don't have time to make a box, you can cover a used box with colored paper. Stick on gift wrap or colored paper, then trim the paper back to the edges of the box.

CUBE BOX TEMPLATE

A   C
4 inches

A   C

4 inches   Base

C   D

C   D

E   E

E

CARTON TEMPLATE

6 inches

B   D

A   3 inches   Base   C

B   D

6 inches

BAGS

You can buy pretty ready-made bags made out of paper, cardboard and cellophane, which look very attractive filled with cookies. Fabric bags can also look very pretty. Both are ideal for cookies that are to be given and eaten on the same day.

SIMPLE BAGS

These are best made from clear or colored cellophane and make a perfect quick and easy wrapping for square or round cookies.

1 Cut a 10-inch square of cellophane. Put a pile of about six cookies in the center.

2 Gather up the edges around the cookies, then tie a ribbon tightly where you've gathered the cellophane together. If you use curling ribbon, pull the ribbon between your thumb and the blade of a pair of scissors to create very pretty corkscrew curls.

POINTED BAGS

These are perfect for wrapping small cookies and long, thin fingers.

1 Cut a 16-inch square of cellophane. Fold it in quarters, hold the corner where the folds join and cut a quarter circle.

2 Open out and cut in half. Pull the two points of one half to meet. Slide one of the points behind the other to make a cone. Secure with sticky tape. Half-fill with cookies, then gather and tie with ribbon.

TUBE BAGS

These little packages, tied at both ends, are perfect for wrapping long, thin finger-shaped cookies such as brandy snaps. Simply cut out a sheet of cellophane that is about twice the length of the cookies, then roll a few cookies together to make a little tube-shaped package. Tie each end of the tube with ribbon to keep the cookies in place.

GIFT TAGS

Adding a label or gift tag to gift-wrapped cookies is the final touch. They can either carry a message or information about the ingredients and advice on storing. You can buy ready-made gift tags, make your own from thin cardboard or even bake your own individual cookie gift tags and ice on a message.

EDIBLE GIFT TAGS

These are pretty and fun, and make a really unusual, themed label.

1 Sift 3 ounces/⅔ cup all-purpose flour, a pinch of baking soda and a pinch of salt into a mixing bowl. Rub in 1¼ ounces chilled, diced butter until the mixture resembles fine breadcrumbs. Stir in 1½ ounces/scant ¼ cup superfine sugar.

2 Blend together 1 tablespoon light corn syrup and ½ egg yolk in a separate bowl. Add these to the dry ingredients and mix to a firm dough. Knead the dough lightly, then wrap in plastic wrap and chill for 30 minutes.

3 Roll the dough out on a lightly floured surface to a thickness of ¼ inch, then stamp out gift-tag-size shapes using a cookie cutter.

4 Using a skewer, pierce a hole for the ribbon to thread through about ½ inch from the top. Place the cookies on lightly greased baking sheets and bake in a preheated oven at 350°F/Gas 4 for 12–15 minutes, or until lightly browned. Leave on the baking sheets for 3 minutes, then, using a metal spatula, transfer to a wire rack to cool.

5 Put a little royal icing – either white or colored – in a paper pastry bag fitted with a writing nozzle. Pipe on your message, then leave the icing to dry. Thread ribbon through the holes made with the skewer and tie onto the cookies' container.

Cook's Tip

If the gift tag hole closes up during baking, gently pierce it again while the cookies are still hot. They will be too brittle once they have cooled.

SENDING COOKIES BY POST

If you choose cookies that are robust, there is no reason why you can't post your gift of cookies, as long as you package them carefully and send by next-day delivery. Delicate iced cookies are not ideal for sending via post, because they are too likely to be damaged.

1 Line the base and sides of a strong box or tin box with bubble wrap or crumpled tissue paper to stop the cookies moving around.

2 Pack the cookies tightly into a box or tin box, interleaving the layers with baking parchment.

3 Cut a piece of corrugated paper or bubblewrap and place between the cookies and the lid, then place the box in a plastic bag. (This will protect the cookies against dampness or rain if the package is left on a doorstep or in a leaking mail box.)

4 Put the wrapped box in a slightly larger box, surrounded by more bubble wrap, foam pieces or crumpled paper to stop the two boxes knocking against each other.

5 Clearly address the package and label it "fragile," then take the box to the post office immediately and send it next-day delivery.

Cook's Tip

It is not really practical to send home-made cookies abroad, as the mail is often unreliable, and the arrival of stale cookies would be very disappointing for the recipient. In addition, some countries will have very strict rules about the importation and transportation of foodstuffs, even home-baked gifts, to protect their indigenous agriculture and to abide by local health and safety rules.

LISTING INGREDIENTS

When offering cookies as a gift, particularly when you do not present them in person, it is best to include information about the ingredients. Many people suffer from allergies and intolerance to certain foods, and many of the main food culprits are included in cookies. The most common are gluten in flour, dairy products in the form of butter and eggs, and nuts.

Even if you know that the person to whom you are giving the cookies has no allergy, it is best to let them know what they contain in case they share them with someone who does have an allergy or intolerance.

Tea-time Treats

Whether you are taking a well-earned five-minute break, entertaining friends for afternoon tea – a sadly forgotten custom these days – or attempting to stem the hunger pangs of ravenous children returning from school, this is the chapter to turn to. Tasty cookie treats range from Peanut-butter Cookies – perfect for the kids – to Cappuccino Swirls – ideal for those with more sophisticated tastes.

Butter Cookies

These crunchy, buttery cookies make a delicious afternoon treat served with a cup of tea or a glass of milk. The dough can be made in advance and chilled until you are ready to bake the cookies.

Makes 25–30

6 ounces/¾ cup sweet butter,
   at room temperature, diced
3½ ounces/½ cup golden
   superfine sugar
9 ounces/2¼ cups
   all-purpose flour
raw sugar, for coating

1 Put the butter and sugar in a bowl and beat until light and fluffy. Add the flour and, using your hands, gradually work it in until the mixture forms a smooth dough. Roll into a sausage shape about 12 inches long, then pat the sides flat to form either a square or triangular log.

2 Sprinkle a thick layer of raw sugar on a piece of waxed paper. Press each side of the dough into the sugar to coat. Wrap and chill for about 30 minutes, until firm. Meanwhile, preheat the oven to 325°F/Gas 3.

3 When ready to bake, remove the dough from the refrigerator and unwrap. Cut into thick slices and place slightly apart on non-stick baking sheets. Bake for 20 minutes, until just beginning to turn brown. Transfer to a wire rack to cool.

Variations

• *To flavor the cookies, add ground cinnamon, grated lemon or orange rind, or vanilla or almond extract to the butter mixture, or add whole candied cherries, chocolate chips, chopped nuts or dried fruit, such as chopped apricots, to the dough.*

• *As an alternative, coat the outside in granulated sugar or chopped toasted nuts.*

Sugar-crusted Shortbread Rounds

There should always be a supply of shortbread in the cookie jar – it is so delicious. It should melt in the mouth and taste buttery but never greasy.

Makes about 24

1 pound/2 cups butter

8 ounces/generous 1 cup
  superfine sugar

1 pound/4 cups all-purpose flour

8 ounces/scant 1½ cups ground rice
  or rice flour

1 teaspoon salt

raw sugar, to decorate

golden superfine sugar,
  for dusting

1 Place the butter and sugar in a bowl and cream together until light, pale and fluffy. Alternatively, process them in a food processor, then scrape the mixture into a bowl.

2 Sift together the flour, ground rice or rice flour and salt, and stir into the butter and sugar with a wooden spoon, until the mixture resembles fine breadcrumbs.

3 Working quickly, gather the dough together with your hand, then put it on a clean work surface. Knead lightly together until it forms a ball, but take care not to over-knead or the shortbread will be tough and greasy. Lightly roll into a sausage shape, about 3 inches thick. Put in plastic wrap and chill in the refrigerator until firm.

4 Preheat the oven to 375°F/ Gas 5. Line two baking sheets with baking parchment.

5 Pour the raw sugar onto a sheet of baking parchment. Unwrap the dough and roll it in the sugar until evenly coated. Using a large, sharp knife, slice the roll into disks about ½ inch thick.

6 Place the disks onto the baking sheets, spacing them far apart. Bake for 20–25 minutes, until very pale gold in color.

7 Remove from the oven and sprinkle with golden superfine sugar. Leave to cool on the baking sheet for 10 minutes before transferring to a wire rack to cool completely.

Cook's Tip
The rice flour adds a toothsome grittiness and shortness to the dough, which is what distinguishes home-made shortbread from the store-bought variety.

Peanut-butter Cookies

These must come close to the top of the list of America's favorites. For extra crunch, add 2 ounces/½ cup chopped peanuts with the peanut butter.

Makes 24

*4 ounces/½ cup butter at room
   temperature, diced*
*4½ ounces/¾ cup firmly packed soft light
   brown sugar*
1 egg
1 teaspoon vanilla extract
*8 ounces/1 cup crunchy
   peanut butter*
4 ounces/1 cup all-purpose flour
½ teaspoon baking soda
pinch of salt

1 With an electric mixer, cream together the butter and sugar until light and fluffy.

2 In another bowl, mix the egg and vanilla extract, then gradually beat into the butter mixture.

3 Stir in the peanut butter and blend thoroughly. Sift together the flour, baking soda and salt, and stir into the mixture to form a soft dough. Chill the dough for at least 30 minutes, until firm.

4 Preheat the oven to 350°F/ Gas 4. Lightly grease two baking sheets.

5 Spoon out rounded teaspoonfuls of the dough and roll into balls.

6 Place the balls on the prepared baking sheets and press flat with a fork into round shapes about 2½ inches in diameter, making a criss-cross pattern. Bake the cookies for about 12 minutes, or until lightly colored. Transfer to a wire rack to cool.

Toll House Cookies

Crunchy and delicious, these vanilla-flavored cookies are packed with chopped walnuts and chocolate chips and are certainly worth an afternoon break.

Makes 24

*4 ounces/½ cup butter or margarine
   ot room temperature, diced*
2 ounces/¼ cup granulated sugar
*3 ounces/½ cup soft dark
   brown sugar*
1 egg
½ tsp vanilla extract
*4½ ounces/generous 1 cup
   all-purpose flour*
½ teaspoon baking soda
pinch of salt
6 ounces/1 cup chocolate chips
2 ounces/½ cup walnuts, chopped

1 Preheat the oven to 350°F/ Gas 4. Grease two baking sheets.

2 With an electric mixer, cream together the butter or margarine and the two sugars until the mixture is light and fluffy.

3 In another bowl, combine the egg and the vanilla extract, then gradually beat into the butter mixture. Sift over the flour, baking soda and salt. Stir to blend.

4 Add the chocolate chips and chopped walnuts, and mix well to combine thoroughly.

5 Place rounded teaspoonfuls of the dough, spaced about 2 inches apart, on the prepared baking sheets. Bake for 10–15 minutes, until lightly colored. With a metal spatula, transfer to a wire rack to cool completely.

Buttermilk Cookies

It was once thought that buttermilk was especially good for children, but don't let them know, as that will give them the perfect excuse for not leaving any cookies for the adults in the family. These cookies are particularly good if served warm.

Makes 15

6 ounces/1½ cups all-purpose
   flour
pinch of salt
1 teaspoon baking powder
½ teaspoon baking soda
*2 ounces/4 tablespoons cold butter
   or margarine*
6 fluid ounces/¾ cup buttermilk

1 Preheat the oven to 425°F/Gas 7. Grease a baking sheet.

Cook's Tip
Buttermilk is slightly acidic and helps activate the raising agents.

2 Sift the dry ingredients into a large bowl. Rub in the butter or margarine until the mixture resembles coarse breadcrumbs.

3 Gradually pour in the buttermilk, stirring constantly with a fork until the mixture comes together and forms a soft dough.

4 Roll out the dough to about ½ inch thick, then stamp out 15 round pieces with a 2-inch cutter.

5 Place on the prepared baking sheet and bake for 12–15 minutes, until golden. Serve warm, or cool to room temperature.

Baking Powder Cookies

These all-purpose cookies are delicious served warm, spread with butter and jam or honey as an accompaniment to tea or coffee. Kids will enjoy them as an after-shool snack, perhaps served with hot drinking chocolate, on a chilly winter afternoon.

Makes 15

5½ ounces/1⅓ cups all-purpose
   flour
2 tablespoons granulated sugar
1 tablespoon baking powder
pinch of salt
*1½ ounces/5 tablespoons cold
   butter, diced*
4 fluid ounces/½ cup milk

1 Preheat the oven to 425°F/ Gas 7. Grease one or two baking sheets.

2 Sift together the flour, sugar, baking powder and salt into a bowl. Rub in the butter until the mixture resembles coarse crumbs.

3 Pour in the milk and stir with a fork to form a soft dough.

4 Roll out the dough to about ¼ inch thick. Stamp out round pieces with a 2½-inch cutter.

5 Place far apart on the prepared baking sheets and bake for about 12 minutes, until golden. Serve these soft cookies hot or warm, spread with butter for children's teas. To accompany tea or coffee, serve with butter and jam or honey.

Scottish Shortbread

Light, crisp shortbread looks very professional when shaped in a decorative mold. This recipe is sufficient to make two large shortbreads or eight individual ones.

Makes 2

6 ounces/¾ cup all-purpose
    flour
2 ounces/¼ cup cornstarch
2 ounces/¼ cup superfine sugar,
    plus extra for sprinkling
4 ounces/½ cup sweet butter,
    diced

1 Preheat the oven to 325°F/Gas 3. Lightly flour the shortbread mold and line two baking sheets with baking parchment. Sift together the flour, cornstarch and sugar into a large mixing bowl. Rub in the butter until you can knead the mixture into a soft dough.

2 Place half the dough into the mold and press gently but firmly to fit neatly. Carefully invert the mold onto one of the baking sheets and tap firmly to release the dough shape. Mold the remaining dough in the same way.

3 Bake the shortbreads for about 35–40 minutes, until just pale golden in color. Sprinkle a little superfine sugar evenly over the tops of the shortbreads and then leave them to cool on the baking sheets before serving.

Brittany Butter Cookies

These lightly glazed little cookies are similar to shortbread, but are even richer and more like cakes in texture. Traditionally, they are made with lightly salted butter.

Makes 18–20

6 egg yolks, lightly beaten

1 tablespoon milk

9 ounces/2¼ cups all-purpose flour

6 ounces/¾ cup superfine sugar

7 ounces/scant 1 cup butter at room temperature, diced

1 Preheat the oven to 350°F/Gas 4. Grease two heavy baking sheets. Mix 1 tablespoon of the egg yolks with the milk to make a glaze. Set aside.

2 Sift the flour into a bowl. Add the egg yolks, sugar and butter, and work them together until creamy.

3 Using your fingertips, bring in the flour, a little at a time, until it is all incorporated and the mixture forms a slightly sticky dough. Gather it together.

4 Using floured hands, pat out the dough to about ¼ inch thick and stamp out round pieces using a 3-inch cutter. Transfer the pieces to the prepared baking sheet, brush each with a little of the reserved egg and milk glaze, then, using the back of a knife, score gently with lines to create a lattice pattern.

5 Bake for about 12 minutes, or until golden. Cool on the baking sheet placed on a wire rack for 15 minutes, then carefully remove the cookies with a spatula and leave to cool completely on the rack.

Variation

To make a large Brittany butter cake, pat the dough with well-floured hands into a 9-inch loose-based cake pan or springform pan. Brush with the glaze and score the lattice pattern on top. Bake for 45–60 minutes, until firm to the touch and golden brown.

Ladies' Kisses

These old-fashioned cookies from the Piedmont region of Italy are sweet, light and a rare treat, just like their name. They certainly merit the best silver teapot and bone-china cups.

Makes 20

5 ounces/10 tablespoons butter,
    softened
4 ounces/generous ½ cup superfine
    sugar
1 egg yolk
½ teaspoon almond extract
4 ounces/1 cup ground almonds
6 ounces/1½ cups all-purpose flour
2 ounces semisweet chocolate

1 Cream the butter and sugar with an electric mixer until light and fluffy, then beat in the egg yolk, almond extract, ground almonds and flour until evenly mixed. Chill for about 2 hours until firm.

2 Preheat the oven to 325°F/Gas 3. Line several baking sheets with baking parchment.

3 Break off small pieces of dough and roll into balls with your hands, making 40 altogether.

4 Place the balls on the baking sheets, spacing them out as they will spread in the oven.

Cook's Tip
These cookies look extra dainty served in frilly petit fours cases.

5 Bake for 20 minutes, or until golden. Remove the baking sheets from the oven, lift off the parchment with the cookies still on it, then place on wire racks. Leave to cool. Repeat with the remaining mixture.

6 Lift the cooled cookies off the paper. Melt the chocolate in a bowl over a pan of hot water. Use to sandwich the cookies in pairs, then leave to cool and set before serving.

Tea Cookies

These cookies are very quick and easy to make. If you don't want to pipe the mixture, simply spoon it onto the baking parchment and press it down with a fork.

Makes 20

5 ounces/10 tablespoons butter,
    softened
3 ounces/¾ cup superfine sugar, sifted
1 egg, beaten
a few drops almond extract
8 ounces/2 cups all-purpose flour
2–3 large pieces candied peel, cut into
    small diamond shapes

Variation
Use 10 halved candied cherries instead of the candied peel.

1 Preheat the oven to 450°F/Gas 8. Line two baking sheets with baking parchment.

2 Cream the butter and sugar with an electric mixer until light and fluffy, then beat in the egg yolk, almond extract and flour.

3 Spoon the mixture into a pastry bag fitted with a star nozzle, and pipe 10 rosette shapes on each of the baking sheets.

4 Press a candied peel diamond into the center of each. Bake for 5 minutes, until golden. Cool.

Shortbread

You have to use butter to get exactly the right texture and flavor for these rich, melt-in-the-mouth, traditional Scottish cookies. Margarine simply won't do.

Makes 8

6 ounces/⅔ cup sweet butter at room
    temperature, diced
4 ounces/generous ½ cup superfine
    sugar
5 ounces/1¼ cups all-purpose
    flour
2 ounces/½ cup rice flour
¼ tsp baking powder
pinch of salt

1 Preheat the oven to 325°F/Gas 3. Grease a shallow, loose-based 8-inch cake pan.

2 With an electric mixer, cream the butter and sugar together until light and fluffy. Sift over the flours, baking powder and salt, and mix well to form a smooth dough.

3 Press the dough into the pan, smoothing the surface with the back of a spoon. Prick all over with a fork, then score into eight wedges using the back of a knife.

4 Bake the shortbread for 40–45 minutes. Leave it in the pan until it is cool enough to handle, then unmold carefully and re-cut the wedges while still hot.

Rolled Oat Wedges

Similar to the ever-popular flapjacks, these scrumptious, chewy wedges have a deeper, richer flavor and darker color that is derived from using molasses.

Makes 8

2 ounces/¼ cup butter, plus extra
    for greasing
1½ tablespoons molasses
2 ounces/¼ cup dark brown
    soft sugar
6 ounces/1¾ cups rolled oats
pinch of salt

1 Preheat the oven to 350°F/ Gas 4. Line an 8-inch shallow cake pan with waxed paper and then grease the paper with a little butter.

2 Place the butter, molasses and sugar in a pan set over a low heat. Cook, stirring constantly, until melted and thoroughly combined.

3 Remove the pan from the heat and stir in the rolled oats and salt.

4 Spoon into the prepared cake pan and smooth the surface. Bake for 20–25 minutes, until golden brown. Leave in the pan until cool enough to handle, then unmold and cut into eight equal wedges while still hot.

Ginger Cookies

These are a supreme treat for ginger lovers – richly spiced cookies packed with chunks of succulent preserved stem ginger. They are sure to give a boost when your energy starts to flag.

Makes 30 small or 20 large cookies

12 ounces/3 cups self-rising flour

pinch of salt

7 ounces/1 cup golden superfine sugar

1 tablespoon ground ginger

1 teaspoon baking soda

4 ounces/½ cup sweet butter

3½ ounces/generous ¼ cup light
   corn syrup

1 extra large egg, beaten

5 ounces preserved stem ginger in syrup,
   drained and coarsely chopped

1 Preheat the oven to 325°F/Gas 3. Line three baking sheets with baking parchment or lightly greased waxed paper.

2 Sift the flour into a large mixing bowl, add the salt, superfine sugar, ground ginger and baking soda, and stir to combine.

3 Dice the butter and put it in a small, heavy pan with the syrup. Heat gently, stirring, until the butter has melted. Remove from the heat and set aside to cool until just warm.

4 Pour the butter mixture over the dry ingredients, then add the egg and two-thirds of the ginger. Mix thoroughly, then use your hands to bring the dough together.

5 Shape the dough into 20 large or 30 small balls, depending on the size you require. Place them, spaced far apart, on the baking sheets and gently flatten the balls.

6 Press a few pieces of the remaining preserved stem ginger into the top of each of the cookies.

7 Bake for about 12–15 minutes, depending on the size of your cookies, until light golden in color. Remove from the oven and leave to cool for 1 minute on the baking sheets to firm up. Using a metal spatula, transfer the cookies to a wire rack to cool completely.

Spiced-nut Palmiers

First created at the beginning of the last century, these dainty French cookies are designed to be served with afternoon tea. They are said to look like the foliage of palm trees.

Makes 40

3 ounces/¾ cup chopped almonds,
  walnuts or hazelnuts

2 tablespoons superfine sugar,
  plus extra for sprinkling

½ teaspoon ground cinnamon

8 ounces puff pastry, thawed
  if frozen

1 egg, lightly beaten

1 Lightly butter two large baking sheets, preferably non-stick. In a food processor fitted with a metal blade, process the nuts, sugar and cinnamon until finely ground.

2 Sprinkle the work surface with superfine sugar and roll out the rough-puff or puff pastry to a rectangle measuring 20 x 8 inches and about ⅛ inch thick. Lightly brush the pastry all over with beaten egg and sprinkle evenly with about half of the nut mixture.

3 Fold in the long edges of the pastry to meet in the center and flatten with the rolling pin. Brush with egg and sprinkle with most of the remaining nut mixture. Fold in the edges to meet in the center, brush with egg and sprinkle with the remaining nut mixture. Fold one side of the pastry over the other.

4 Cut the pastry diagonally into ⅜-inch slices and place 1 inch apart on the baking sheets.

5 Spread the pastry edges apart to form a wedge shape. Chill the palmiers in the refrigerator for at least 15 minutes. Preheat the oven to 425°F/Gas 7.

6 Bake for about 8–10 minutes, until golden. Carefully turn them over halfway through the cooking time, using a metal spatula. Keep a careful eye on them as the sugar can easily scorch. Transfer to a wire rack to cool.

Spicy Pepper Cookies

Don't be put off by their peppery name – try these warmly spiced cookies, and you are sure to be pleasantly surprised by their fabulous flavor. They are also very quick and easy to make.

Makes 48

7 ounces/1¾ cups all-purpose flour

2 ounces/½ cup cornstarch

2 teaspoons baking powder

½ teaspoon ground cardamom

½ teaspoon ground cinnamon

½ teaspoon grated nutmeg

½ teaspoon ground ginger

½ teaspoon ground allspice

pinch of salt

½ teaspoon ground black pepper

8 ounces/1 cup butter or margarine
   at room temperature, diced

3½ ounces/scant ½ cup soft light
   brown sugar

½ teaspoon vanilla extract

1 teaspoon finely grated
   lemon rind

2 fluid ounces/¼ cup whipping cream

3 ounces/¾ cup finely ground almonds

1 Preheat the oven to 350°F/Gas 4. Sift together the flour, cornstarch, baking powder, ground cardamom, cinnamon, nutmeg, ginger, allspice, salt and pepper into a medium bowl. Set aside.

2 With an electric mixer, cream the butter or margarine and brown sugar together until light and fluffy. Beat in the vanilla extract and grated lemon rind.

3 With the mixer on low speed, add the flour mixture alternately with the whipping cream, beginning and ending with flour. Stir in the ground almonds.

4 Shape the dough into ¾-inch balls. Place them on ungreased baking sheets, about 1 inch apart. Bake for 15–20 minutes, until golden brown underneath.

5 Leave the cookies on the baking sheets for about 1 minute to firm up slightly before transferring them with a metal spatula to a wire rack to cool completely.

Cinnamon and Molasses Cookies

These molasses-flavored cookies are slightly moist, spicy and nutty. The white confectioners' sugar zigzag decoration contrasts appealingly with the dark color of the cookies.

Makes about 24

2 tablespoons black molasses

2 ounces/¼ cup butter or margarine

4 ounces/1 cup all-purpose flour

¼ tsp baking soda

½ tsp ground ginger

1 teaspoon ground cinnamon

1½ ounces/3 tablespoons soft light
   brown sugar

1 tablespoon ground almonds
   or hazelnuts

1 egg yolk

4 ounces/1 cup confectioners'
   sugar, sifted

1 Grease two baking sheets. Heat the molasses and butter or margarine gently until just beginning to melt.

2 Sift the flour into a bowl with the baking soda and spices, then stir in the sugar and ground nuts.

3 Beat the molasses mixture and egg yolk briskly into the flour mixture, drawing the ingredients together to form a firm but soft dough.

4 Roll out the dough on a lightly floured surface to ¼ inch thick and stamp out shapes, such as stars, hearts or rounds. Re-roll the trimmings and cut more shapes. Place on the prepared baking sheets and chill for 15 minutes.

5 Preheat the oven to 375°F/Gas 5. Prick the cookies lightly with a fork and bake for 12–15 minutes, until just firm. Using a metal spatula, transfer to wire racks and leave until crisp.

6 Mix the confectioners' sugar with a little lukewarm water to make it slightly runny, then drizzle over the cookies.

Cinnamon Refrigerator Cookies

Cookies don't come much easier to make than these. Keep a roll of dough in the refrigerator or freezer so that you can cut slices and bake fresh cookies any afternoon that you fancy them.

Makes 50

8 ounces/2 cups all-purpose flour

pinch of salt

2 teaspoons ground cinnamon

8 ounces/1 cup sweet butter at room temperature, diced

8 ounces/1 cup superfine sugar

2 eggs

1 teaspoon vanilla extract

1 Sift together the flour, salt and cinnamon into a bowl. Set aside.

2 With an electric mixer, cream the butter until soft. Add the sugar and continue beating until the mixture is light and fluffy. Beat together the eggs and vanilla extract, then gradually stir into the butter mixture.

3 Add the dry ingredients to the butter mixture and stir together to form a soft dough.

4 Divide the dough into four parts, then roll each part into a 2-inch diameter log. Wrap tightly in foil and chill or freeze until firm.

5 Preheat the oven to 375°F/Gas 5. Grease two baking sheets.

6 With a sharp knife, cut the dough into ¼-inch slices. Place the slices on the prepared baking sheets and bake for about 10 minutes, or until lightly colored. With a metal spatula, transfer to a wire rack to cool completely.

Lady Fingers

These long, delicate cookies are named after the pale, slim fingers of highborn gentlewomen. They are also known, much more mundanely, as sponge fingers.

Makes 18

3½ ounces/generous ¾ cup
   all-purpose flour
pinch of salt
4 eggs, separated
4 ounces/½ cup superfine sugar
½ teaspoon vanilla extract
confectioners' sugar,
   for sprinkling

1 Preheat the oven to 300°F/Gas 2. Grease two large baking sheets, then dust lightly with flour, and shake off the excess. Sift the flour and salt together twice and set aside.

2 With an electric mixer, beat the egg yolks with half of the sugar until thick enough to leave a ribbon trail when the beaters are lifted.

3 In another grease-free bowl, beat the egg whites to stiff peaks. Beat in the remaining sugar until very glossy.

4 Sift the flour mixture over the yolks and spoon about a quarter of the egg whites over the flour. Carefully fold in with a large metal spoon to slacken, adding the vanilla extract. Then gently fold in the remaining egg whites.

5 Spoon the mixture into a pastry bag fitted with a large plain nozzle. Pipe 4-inch long lines on the prepared baking sheets. Sift over a layer of confectioners' sugar. Tip off any excess sugar.

6 Bake for 20 minutes, until crusty on the outside with soft centers. Cool slightly on the baking sheets before transferring to a wire rack.

Walnut Cookies

Crisp and crunchy, these cookies are great for a mid-afternoon energy boost during a busy day. The recipe makes 60 little cookies, so cook them in batches – two trays at a time.

Makes 60

4 ounces/½ cup butter or margarine
   at room temperature, diced
6 ounces/scant 1 cup superfine
   sugar
4 ounces/1 cup all-purpose
   flour
2 teaspoons vanilla extract
4 ounces/1 cup walnuts,
   finely chopped

1 Preheat the oven to 300°F/Gas 2. Grease two baking sheets.

2 With an electric mixer, cream the butter or margarine until soft. Add 2 ounces/¼ cup of the sugar and continue to beat until light and fluffy. Stir in the flour, vanilla extract and chopped walnuts.

3 Drop teaspoonfuls of the batter onto the prepared baking sheets, spaced about 1 inch apart, and flatten slightly with the back of the spoon. Bake the cookies for about 25 minutes, until golden.

4 Transfer to a wire rack set over a baking sheet and sprinkle with the remaining sugar. Leave to cool.

Pecan Nut Puffs

As they don't keep very well, you have the perfect excuse to enjoy these melt-in-the-mouth, light-as-air cookies as freely as you like.

Makes 24

4 ounces/½ cup sweet butter at room
   temperature, diced
2 tablespoons granulated sugar
pinch of salt
1 teaspoon vanilla extract
4 ounces/1 cup pecan nuts
4 ounces/1 cup all-purpose
   flour, sifted
confectioners' sugar,
   for dusting

1 Preheat the oven to 300°F/Gas 2. Grease two baking sheets.

2 Using an electric mixer, cream the butter and sugar in a bowl until light and fluffy. Stir in the salt and vanilla extract.

3 Grind the pecan nuts in a food processor, blender or nut grinder. Stir several times to prevent the nuts from becoming oily.

4 Push the ground nuts through a sieve set over a bowl to aerate them. Any pieces that are too large to go through the sieve can be ground again.

5 Stir the nuts and flour into the butter mixture to make a dough. Roll the dough into marble-size balls between the palms of your hands. Place on the prepared baking sheets, spaced far apart, and bake for 45 minutes.

6 Leave the puffs to cool slightly, then, while they are still hot, roll them in confectioners' sugar. Leave to cool completely on a wire rack, then roll once more in the sugar.

Pecan Tassies

These are a kind of cross between a rich cookie and a sweet tart, although however you describe them, they will accompany a cup of tea to perfection.

Makes 24

4 ounces/½ cup cream cheese

4 ounces/½ cup butter, softened

4 ounces/1 cup all-purpose flour

For the filling

2 eggs

4 ounces/½ cup soft dark brown sugar

1 teaspoon vanilla extract

pinch of salt

1 ounce/2 tablespoons butter, melted

4 ounces/1 cup pecan nuts

1 Place one or two baking sheets in the oven and preheat to 350°F/Gas 4. Grease 24 mini muffin pans.

2 Chop the cream cheese and butter. Put in a mixing bowl. Sift over the flour, and mix to a dough.

3 Roll out the dough thinly. Stamp out 24 round pieces, using a floured, fluted 2½-inch cutter. Line the muffin pans with the pastry pieces and chill until required.

4 To make the filling, lightly whisk the eggs in a bowl. Whisk in the brown sugar, a few tablespoons at a time, and add the vanilla extract, salt and butter. Set aside.

5 Reserve 24 undamaged pecan nut halves and chop the remainder coarsely with a sharp knife.

6 Place a spoonful of chopped nuts in each pie shell and cover with a little of the filling. Set a pecan half on the top of each.

7 Bake on the hot baking sheets for about 20 minutes, until puffed and set. Transfer to a wire rack to cool. Serve at room temperature.

Tuiles d'Amandes

These cookies are named after the French roof tiles they resemble. Making them is a little tricky, so bake only four at a time. With a little practice, you will find them really quite easy.

Makes 24

2½ ounces/generous ½ cup whole
    blanched almonds, lightly toasted
2½ ounces/⅓ cup superfine
    sugar
1½ ounces/3 tablespoons sweet butter
    at room temperature, diced
2 egg whites
½ teaspoon almond extract
1¼ ounces/scant ⅓ cup all-purpose
    flour, sifted
2 ounces/½ cup sliced almonds

1 Preheat the oven to 400°F/Gas 6. Generously butter two heavy baking sheets.

2 Place the almonds and about 2 tablespoons of the superfine sugar in a food processor fitted with a metal blade, and process until the almonds are finely ground and well combined with the sugar.

3 Using an electric mixer, beat the butter until creamy, then add the remaining sugar and beat until light and fluffy. Gradually beat in the egg whites, then add the almond extract. Sift the flour over the butter mixture, gently fold in with a metal spoon, then fold in the ground almond mixture.

4 Drop tablespoonfuls of the mixture onto the prepared baking sheets about 6 inches apart. With the back of a wet spoon, spread each mound into a paper-thin 3-inch round. (Don't worry if holes appear, they will fill in.) Sprinkle a few sliced almonds evenly over the top.

5 Bake the cookies, one sheet at a time, for 5–6 minutes, until the edges are golden. Working quickly, use a spatula to loosen the edges of one cookie. Lift it on the spatula and place over a rolling pin, then press down the sides to curve it. Transfer the cookies to a wire rack as they become firm.

● **Cook's Tip**
If the cookies become too crisp to shape, return the baking sheet to the hot oven for 15–30 seconds, then continue as before. If they flatten or lose their crispness, reheat them on a baking sheet in a moderate oven, until they are completely flat, then reshape.

Sliced Almond Cookies

These attractive, golden cookies have the most wonderful texture and flavor – crisp and nutty in one bite. They're good with afternoon tea, especially a fragrant Chinese variety.

Makes 30

6 ounces/¾ cup butter or
   margarine, diced

8 ounces/2 cups self-rising flour

5 ounces/⅔ cup superfine sugar

½ teaspoon ground cinnamon

1 egg, separated

2 tablespoons cold water

2 ounces/½ cup sliced almonds

1 Preheat the oven to 350°F/Gas 4. Rub the butter or margarine into the flour. Reserve 1 tablespoon of the sugar and mix the rest with the cinnamon. Stir into the flour and then add the egg yolk and water and mix to a firm dough.

2 Roll out the dough on a lightly floured surface to about ½ inch thick. Sprinkle over the almonds. Continue rolling until the dough is about ¼ inch thick.

3 Using a floured fluted cutter, stamp out round pieces. Lift on a metal spatula onto an ungreased baking sheet. Re-form the trimmings and cut more pieces, using all the dough. Whisk the egg white lightly, brush it over the cookies and sprinkle with the reserved sugar.

4 Bake the cookies for about 10 minutes, or until golden. To remove from the baking sheet, slide a metal spatula under the cookies, which will still seem a bit soft, but will harden as they cool. Carefully transfer to a wire rack and leave until quite cold.

Melting Moments

These cookies are very crisp and light – and they quite simply melt in your mouth. The secret of their wonderful texture lies in using two different kinds of fat to make them.

Makes 16–20

1½ ounces/3 tablespoons butter or
    margarine at room temperature,
    diced
2½ ounces/5 tablespoons shortening
    at room temperature, diced
3 ounces/½ cup superfine sugar
½ egg, beaten
a few drops of vanilla or
    almond extract
5 ounces/1¼ cups self-rising flour
rolled oats, for coating
4–5 candied cherries, cut into quarters

1 Preheat the oven to 350°F/ Gas 4. Grease two baking sheets. Cream together the butter or margarine, shortening and sugar until light and fluffy, then gradually beat in the egg and vanilla or almond extract.

2 Stir the flour into the beaten mixture to form a soft dough.

Cook's Tip
To halve an egg, beat a whole egg in a measuring cup, then pour off half.

3 Roll the dough into 16–20 small balls in your hands.

4 Spread the rolled oats on a sheet of waxed paper and roll the balls in them to coat evenly.

5 Place the balls, spaced far apart, on the baking sheets, place a piece of cherry on top of each ball and bake for 15–20 minutes, until lightly browned. Leave to cool for a few minutes before transferring to a wire rack using a spatula.

Sugar-topped Vanilla Cookies

Buttery, crumbly vanilla cookies with an irresistible crunchy sugar topping, these are great with a cup of tea for adults or a glass of milk, or even a milkshake, for children.

Makes about 24

4 ounces/½ cup sweet butter, at room
  temperature, diced
2 ounces/¼ cup vanilla superfine
  sugar
I egg, beaten
¼ teaspoon vanilla extract
7 ounces/1¾ cups self-rising
  flour
3 tablespoons cornstarch

For the topping

I egg white
I tablespoon vanilla superfine
  sugar
3 ounces sugar cubes, crushed

I Preheat the oven to 350°F/Gas 4.
Put the butter and sugar in a bowl
and beat until the mixture is light
and fluffy. Beat in the egg and
vanilla extract. Sift together the
flour and cornstarch over the
mixture and mix to a soft but not
sticky dough.

2 Roll the mixture out on a lightly
floured surface. Using a flower
cookie cutter or ring cutter, stamp
out cookies and place on a non-stick
baking sheet. Re-roll any trimmings
and stamp out more cookies until
you have used up all the dough.

3 To make the topping, put the egg
white in a small bowl and whisk
until foamy. Whisk in the vanilla
sugar. Using a pastry brush, spread
generously on each cookie. Sprinkle
with the crushed sugar cubes.

4 Bake for about 15 minutes, or
until the topping is just beginning
to turn golden brown. Remove
from the oven and transfer to a
wire rack to cool.

Cook's Tip
*To make your own vanilla sugar,
take a vanilla bean and split it open
down one side. Place in a jar of
sugar and use as necessary. If you
don't have any vanilla sugar, increase
the quantity of vanilla extract to
½ teaspoon.*

Traditional Sugar Cookies

Always a popular choice, these cookies are often baked in more interesting shapes than the round kind shown here. Stamp out hearts, moons and stars if you have the right shaped cutters.

Makes about 36

12 ounces/3 cups all-purpose
  flour

1 teaspoon baking soda

2 teaspoons baking powder

½ teaspoon grated nutmeg

4 ounces/½ cup butter or
  margarine at room
  temperature, diced

8 ounces/1 cup superfine sugar

½ teaspoon vanilla extract

1 egg

4 ounces/½ cup milk

colored or raw sugar,
  for sprinkling

1 Sift the flour, baking soda, baking powder and nutmeg into a small bowl. Set aside.

2 With an electric mixer, cream together the butter or margarine, superfine sugar and vanilla extract until the mixture is light and fluffy. Add the egg and beat to mix well.

3 Add the flour mixture alternately with the milk to make a soft dough. Wrap in plastic wrap and chill for at least 30 minutes.

4 Preheat the oven to 350°F/Gas 4. Roll out the dough on a lightly floured surface to ⅛ inch thick. Stamp out round pieces or other shapes of your choice with lightly floured cutters.

5 Transfer to ungreased baking sheets. Sprinkle with colored or raw sugar. Bake for about 10 minutes, or until golden brown. Using a spatula, transfer the cookies to a wire rack to cool.

Cappuccino Swirls

A melt-in-the-mouth, mocha-flavored cookie drizzled with white and bittersweet chocolate is just the thing to have with that mid-morning café latte, as well as with afternoon tea with friends.

Makes 18

2 teaspoons instant coffee powder

2 teaspoons boiling water

5 ounces/1¼ cups all-purpose
   flour

4 ounces/½ cup cornstarch

15ml/1 tbsp cocoa powder
   (unsweetened)

8 ounces/1 cup sweet butter,
   at room temperature, diced

2 ounces/¼ cup golden superfine
   sugar

For the decoration

2 ounces white chocolate

1 ounce bittersweet chocolate

1 Preheat the oven to 375°F/Gas 5. Line two baking sheets with baking parchment. Put the coffee powder in a cup, add the boiling water and stir until dissolved. Set aside to cool. Sift together the flour, cornstarch and cocoa powder.

2 Put the butter and sugar in a bowl and beat until creamy. Add the coffee and the sifted flour and mix well. Spoon into a pastry bag fitted with a plain nozzle.

3 Pipe 18 spirals, slightly apart, onto the prepared baking sheets.

4 Bake for 10–15 minutes, or until firm but not browned. Remove from the oven and leave on the baking sheets for 1 minute, then transfer to a wire rack to cool.

5 Melt the white and bittersweet chocolate separately in heatproof bowls set over a pan of hot water.

6 Place the cooled cookies close together on kitchen paper. Using a teaspoon, take some white chocolate and flick over the cookies, moving your hand speedily from left to right to create small lines of chocolate drizzle over them.

7 When all the white chocolate has been used, repeat the process with the bittersweet chocolate, flicking it over the cookies so the bittersweet chocolate is at an angle to the white chocolate. Leave until the chocolate has set, and then remove the cookies from the paper.

Golden Ginger Macaroons

Macaroons are classic no-fuss cookies – easy to whisk up in minutes from the minimum ingredients, and always appreciated. A hint of ginger makes this recipe excitingly different.

Makes 18–20

1 egg white

3 ounces/scant ½ cup soft light brown sugar

4 ounces/1 cup ground almonds

1 teaspoon ground ginger

Variation

Other ground nuts, such as hazelnuts or walnuts, are good alternatives to the almonds. Ground cinnamon, or apple pie spice can be used instead of the ginger, if you like.

1 Preheat the oven to 350°F/ Gas 4. Line two baking sheets with baking parchment.

2 Whisk the egg white in a large, clean, grease-free bowl until stiff and standing in peaks, but not dry and crumbly, then gradually whisk in the brown sugar.

3 Sprinkle the ground almonds and ginger over the whisked egg white and gently fold them together.

4 Using two teaspoons, place spoonfuls of the mixture on the baking sheets, spaced apart. Bake for about 20 minutes, until golden.

5 Leave to cool slightly on the baking sheets before transferring to a wire rack to cool completely.

Nutty Nuggets

Nougat is an almost magical sweetmeat that emerges from honey-flavored meringue made with boiled syrup. However, any other nuts or candied fruits can be used instead of almonds.

Makes about 1¼ pounds

8 ounces/generous 1 cup sugar

8 ounces/⅔ cup clear honey or light corn syrup

1 extra large egg white

4 ounces/1 cup sliced almonds or chopped pistachio nuts, roasted

1 Line a 7-inch square cake pan with rice paper. Place the sugar, honey or syrup together with 4 tablespoons water in a large, heavy pan and heat gently, stirring frequently, until the sugar has completely dissolved.

2 Bring the syrup to the boil and boil gently, without stirring, to the soft crack stage (when the syrup is dropped into cold water, it separates into hard but not brittle threads) or until it registers 304°F on a sugar thermometer. Remove the syrup from the heat and leave to cool slightly.

3 Meanwhile, using an electric mixer, whisk the egg white in a large, clean, grease-free bowl until very stiff, but not dry and crumbly, then gradually drizzle in the syrup while whisking constantly.

4 Quickly stir in the almonds or pistachio nuts. Pour the mixture into the pan. Leave to cool completely but, before the nougat becomes too hard, cut it into squares. Store in an airtight container.

Chocolate Macaroons

The Italians claim to have invented these little cookies during the Renaissance, and this classic combination of almonds and chocolate certainly suggests that this is true.

Makes 20

2 ounces semisweet chocolate,
  chopped into small pieces
4 ounces/1 cup ground almonds
2 egg whites
7 ounces/1 cup superfine sugar
½ teaspoon vanilla extract
¼ teaspoon almond extract
confectioners' sugar,
  for dusting

1 Preheat the oven to 300°F/
Gas 2. Line two baking sheets with
baking parchment.

2 Melt the chocolate in the top of
a double boiler or in a heatproof
bowl placed over a pan of barely
simmering water.

3 In a clean, grease-free mixing
bowl, whisk the egg whites until
they form soft peaks. Gently fold
in the sugar, vanilla and almond
extract, and ground almonds along
with the cooled melted chocolate.
The mixture should just hold its
shape. If it is too soft, chill in the
refrigerator for 15 minutes.

4 Place mounded teaspoonfuls of
the mixture, spaced far apart,
on the prepared baking sheets and
flatten slightly. Brush each ball with a
little water and sift over a thin layer
of confectioners' sugar.

5 Bake the macaroons for
20–25 minutes, until just firm.
Transfer to a wire rack to cool.

Cook's Tip
*To make Chocolate Pine Nut Macaroons,
spread 3 ounces/¾ cup pine nuts in a
shallow dish. Press the balls of chocolate
macaroon dough into the nuts to cover
one side of each ball and place them,
nut side up, on lined baking sheets, then
bake as above.*

Coconut Macaroons

The French also claim to have invented macaroons, and recipes – almost all from monasteries and convents – date back many centuries. This is a little surprising considering their richness.

Makes 24

1½ ounces/⅓ cup all-purpose
  flour
pinch of salt
7½ ounces/2½ cups dried unsweetened
  shredded coconut
¼ pint/⅔ cup sweetened
  condensed milk
1 teaspoon vanilla extract

1 Preheat the oven to 350°F/
Gas 4. Line two baking sheets
with waxed paper and grease
the paper, or line with non-stick
baking parchment.

2 Sift the flour and salt into a large
bowl. Stir in the dried coconut.

3 Pour in the milk. Add the vanilla
and stir together from the center to
form a very thick batter.

4 Drop mounded tablespoonfuls
of batter 1 inch apart on the
prepared baking sheets. Bake the
macaroons for about 20 minutes,
or until golden brown. Transfer to
a wire rack to cool.

Cook's Tip
*For a very rich, sweet and tempting petit
four, make the macaroons smaller and,
when cooked, coat them in melted
semisweet chocolate. Place them on
waxed paper and leave to set. Serve with
small cups of strong, black coffee after a
dinner party.*

Macaroons

Freshly ground almonds, lightly toasted beforehand to intensify the flavor, give these cookies their rich taste and texture so, for best results, avoid using ready-ground almonds as a shortcut.

Makes 12

4 ounces/1 cup blanched
* almonds, toasted*
5½ ounces/¾ cup superfine
* sugar*
2 egg whites, lightly beaten
½ teaspoon almond or
* vanilla extract*
confectioners' sugar,
* for dusting*

1 Preheat the oven to 350°F/ Gas 4. Lightly grease a large baking sheet.

2 Reserve 12 of the toasted almonds for decorating the macaroons. In a food processor, grind the rest of the almonds with the sugar.

3 With the machine running, slowly pour in enough of the lightly beaten egg whites to form a soft dough. Add the almond or vanilla extract, and pulse to mix.

4 Remove the mixture from the machine and, with moistened hands, shape into walnut-size balls and arrange on the baking sheet.

5 Press one of the reserved almonds onto each ball, flattening the balls slightly, and dust lightly with confectioners' sugar.

6 Bake the macaroons for about 12 minutes, or until the tops are golden and feel slightly firm. Transfer to a wire rack and leave to cool completely.

Cook's Tip
To toast the almonds, spread them out on a baking sheet and bake in the preheated oven, at 350°F/Gas 4, for 10–15 minutes, or until golden. Leave to cool before grinding.

Madeleines

These little tea cakes were made famous by Marcel Proust, who referred to them in his novel, *Remembrance of Things Past*. They are best eaten on the day they are made.

Makes 12

5½ ounces/generous 1¼ cups
* all-purpose flour*
1 teaspoon baking powder
2 eggs
3 ounces/¾ cup confectioners' sugar,
* plus extra for dusting*
grated rind of 1 lemon or orange
1 tablespoon lemon or orange juice
3 ounces/6 tablespoons sweet butter,
* melted and slightly cooled*

1 Preheat the oven to 375°F/Gas 5. Generously butter a 12-cup madeleine pan. If you don't have one, use a muffin pan. Sift together the flour and baking powder.

2 Using an electric mixer, beat together the eggs and confectioners' sugar in a bowl for 5–7 minutes, until thick and creamy, when the mixture leaves a ribbon trail as the beaters are lifted. Gently fold in the lemon or orange rind and juice using a rubber spatula or metal spoon.

3 Beginning with the flour mixture, alternately fold in the flour and melted butter in four batches with a rubber spatula. Leave the mixture to stand for 10 minutes, then carefully spoon into the pan. Tap gently to release any air bubbles.

4 Bake for 12–15 minutes, rotating the pan halfway through cooking, until a skewer or cake tester inserted in the center comes out clean. Tip the madeleines onto a wire rack to cool completely, and dust with confectioners' sugar before serving.

Snickerdoodles

An irresistible name for irresistible cookies – two very good reasons why you will find everyone asking for more. Not only do they have a deliciously nutty flavor, but with their dusting of cinnamon sugar, they look attractive, too.

Makes 20

4 ounces/½ cup butter at room temperature, diced

4 ounces/generous ½ cup superfine sugar

1 teaspoon vanilla extract

2 eggs

2 fluid ounces/¼ cup milk

14 ounces/3½ cups all-purpose flour

1 teaspoon baking soda

2 ounces/½ cup walnuts, finely chopped

For the coating

5 tablespoons superfine sugar

2 tablespoons ground cinnamon

1 With an electric mixer, beat the butter until light and creamy. Add the sugar and vanilla extract, and continue to beat until fluffy. Beat in the eggs, then the milk.

2 Sift the flour and baking soda over the butter mixture and stir to blend. Stir in the nuts. Chill for 15 minutes. Preheat the oven to 375°F/Gas 5. Lightly grease two baking sheets.

3 To make the coating, mix the sugar and ground cinnamon in a shallow plate or bowl. Roll tablespoonfuls of the dough into walnut-size balls between the palms of your hands, then roll the balls in the sugar mixture. You may need to work in batches.

4 Place the balls, spaced about 2 inches apart, on the prepared baking sheets and flatten slightly with the back of a spoon or your fingers. Bake for about 10 minutes, or until golden. Using a spatula, transfer to a wire rack to cool.

Chewy Chocolate Cookies

The texture of these dark and delicious cookies is sublime – soft on the inside with a crisper, crunchier exterior – matched only by their subtle mocha flavor.

Makes 18

4 egg whites

11 ounces/2½ cups confectioners' sugar

4 ounces/1 cup cocoa powder (unsweetened)

2 tablespoons all-purpose flour

1 teaspoon instant coffee powder

1 tablespoon water

4 ounces/1 cup walnuts, finely chopped

1 Preheat the oven to 350°F/Gas 4. Line two or three baking sheets with waxed paper and grease the paper well. Whisk the egg whites until frothy.

2 Sift the sugar, cocoa powder, flour and coffee into the egg whites. Add the water and continue beating on low speed to blend, then on high for a few minutes, until the mixture thickens. Fold in the walnuts.

3 Place spoonfuls of the mixture 1 inch apart on the baking sheets. Bake in batches for 12–15 minutes, until firm and cracked on top but soft inside. Transfer to a wire rack to cool.

Coffee Biscotti

These crisp cookies are made twice as delicious with both freshly roasted ground coffee beans and strong aromatic brewed coffee in the mixture. They are great for perking you up when you need a morale boost in the middle of the afternoon.

Makes about 30

1 ounce/⅓ cup espresso-roasted coffee beans

4 ounces/1 cup blanched almonds

7 ounces/scant 2 cups all-purpose flour

1½ teaspoons baking powder

¼ teaspoon salt

3 ounces/6 tablespoons sweet butter, cubed

5 ounces/¾ cup superfine sugar

2 eggs, beaten

1½–2 tablespoons strong brewed coffee

1 teaspoon ground cinnamon, for dusting

1 Preheat the oven to 350°F/Gas 4. Put the espresso coffee beans in a single layer on one side of a large baking sheet and the almonds on the other. Roast for 10 minutes, then remove from the oven and leave to cool.

2 Process the coffee beans in a food processor or blender until fairly finely ground. Tip out into a bowl and set aside. Add the almonds to the food processor or blender and process until finely ground, but not oily.

3 Sift the flour, baking powder and salt into a bowl. Rub in the butter, then stir in the superfine sugar, ground coffee and almonds. Add the beaten eggs and just enough brewed coffee to make a fairly firm dough.

4 Lightly knead for a few seconds until smooth and then shape into two rolls about 3 inches in diameter. Place on a greased baking sheet and dust with cinnamon. Bake for 20 minutes.

5 Using a sharp knife, cut the rolls into 1½-inch slices on the diagonal. Arrange the slices on the baking sheet, return to the oven and bake for a further 10 minutes, or until lightly browned. Transfer to a wire rack to cool.

Toffee Cookies

Sheer – if slightly sticky – joy. The deliciously chewy base of these irresistible squares is topped with a luscious layer of chocolate and chopped nuts. Children might prefer milk or white chocolate instead of semisweet, or use a mixture and swirl the two colors together.

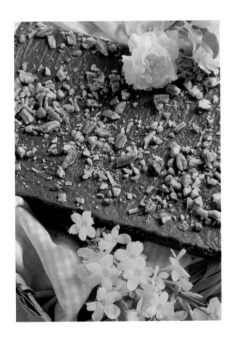

Makes 36
6 ounces/¾ cup sweet butter, melted

7 ounces/1¾ cups rolled oats

4 ounces/packed ½ cup soft light
   brown sugar

4 fluid ounces/½ cup light corn syrup

2 tablespoons vanilla extract

large pinch of salt

6 ounces/¾ cup semisweet
   chocolate, grated

1½ ounces/⅓ cup chopped walnuts

1 Preheat the oven to 400°F/Gas 6. Grease a shallow 15 x 10 inch baking pan.

2 Mix together the butter, oats, sugar, syrup, vanilla extract and salt, and press into the prepared pan. Bake for about 15–18 minutes, until the mixture is brown and bubbly.

3 Remove from the oven and immediately sprinkle on the chocolate. Set aside for 10 minutes, then spread the chocolate over the base. Sprinkle on the nuts. Transfer to a wire rack to cool. Cut into squares.

Rose Water Thins

These light, crunchy cookies are easy to make and bake in minutes. For an unusual tea party, serve them with North African mint tea – the two flavors are made for each other. The mixture makes about 60 cookies, so bake them in batches, two trays at a time.

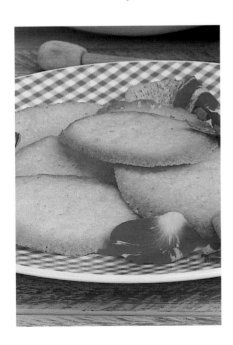

Makes 60
8 ounces/1 cup slightly salted butter

8 ounces/1 cup superfine sugar

1 egg

1 tablespoon light cream

11 ounces/2⅔ cups all-purpose
   flour

pinch of salt

1 teaspoon baking powder

1 tablespoon rose water

superfine sugar, for sprinkling

1 Preheat the oven to 375°F/ Gas 5. Line two baking sheets with baking parchment.

2 Soften the butter and mix with all the other ingredients to make a firm dough. Mold the mixture into an even roll and wrap in waxed paper.

3 Chill until it is firm enough to slice very thinly. This will take 1–1½ hours.

4 Arrange the cookies on the prepared baking sheets, allowing enough space for them to spread during cooking. Sprinkle with a little superfine sugar and bake for about 10 minutes, until they are just turning brown at the edges.

Fruity Corn Meal Cookies

These little yellow cookies come from the Veneto region in the north of Italy, where they would probably be served with a glass of wine. However, they make excellent tea-time treats.

Makes 48

3 ounces/½ cup golden raisins

4 ounces/1 cup finely ground yellow corn meal

6 ounces/1½ cups all-purpose flour

1½ teaspoons baking powder

pinch of salt

8 ounces/1 cup butter, softened

8 ounces/1 cup granulated sugar

2 eggs

1 tablespoon Marsala or 1 teaspoon vanilla extract

1 Soak the raisins in warm water for 15 minutes. Drain well. Preheat the oven to 350°F/Gas 4. Lightly grease two baking sheets.

2 Sift the corn meal, flour, baking powder and salt together into a mixing bowl. Set aside.

3 Cream the butter and sugar until light and fluffy. Beat in the eggs, one at a time. Beat in the Marsala or vanilla extract.

4 Add the dry ingredients to the butter mixture, beating until well blended. Stir in the raisins.

5 Drop mounded teaspoonfuls of the mixture onto the prepared baking sheets in rows about 2 inches apart. Bake for 7–8 minutes, or until the cookies are golden brown at the edges. With a metal spatula transfer to a wire rack to cool.

Cook's Tip

If you can find them, buy sun-dried golden raisins for the best flavor. They may not even need soaking to plump them up.

Amaretti

These ever-popular Italian almond cookies are very delicious and great with afternoon tea, although they are equally enjoyable served with a sweet white dessert wine later in the day.

Makes 36

7 ounces/1¾ cups almonds

all-purpose flour, for dusting

8 ounces/generous 1 cup superfine sugar

2 egg whites

½ teaspoon almond extract or 1 teaspoon vanilla extract

confectioners' sugar, for dusting

1 Preheat the oven to 325°F/Gas 3. Peel the almonds by dropping them into a pan of boiling water for 1–2 minutes. Drain well, then rub the almonds in a clean dishtowel to remove the skins.

2 Spread out the sweet and bitter almonds on a baking sheet and let them dry out in the oven for 10–15 minutes, but do not allow them to turn brown. Remove them from the oven and leave to cool. Turn the oven off. Dust the almonds with a little flour.

3 Grind the almonds with half of the sugar in a food processor.

4 Use an electric beater or wire whisk to whisk the egg whites in a grease-free bowl until they form soft peaks.

5 Gradually add half the remaining sugar and whisk until stiff peaks form. With a metal spoon gently fold in the remaining sugar, the almond or vanilla extract and the almonds.

6 Spoon the almond mixture into a pastry bag and, using a plain nozzle, pipe the mixture in walnut-size round pieces onto a baking sheet. Sprinkle lightly with the confectioners' sugar and leave to stand for 2 hours.

7 Preheat the oven to 350°F/Gas 4. Bake for 15 minutes, until pale gold. Remove from the oven and cool on a wire rack.

Citrus Drops

These soft, cake-like treats are deliciously tangy, with a zesty, crumbly base, and are traditionally filled with sweet, sticky lemon or orange curd, available in specialty shops.

Makes about 20

6 ounces/¾ cup sweet butter,
   at room temperature, diced
5 ounces/¾ cup superfine sugar
finely grated rind of 1 large lemon
finely grated rind of 1 orange
2 egg yolks
2 ounces/½ cup ground almonds
8 ounces/2 cups self-rising flour
lemon and/or orange curd
milk, for brushing
sliced almonds, for sprinkling

1 Preheat the oven to 325°F/Gas 3. Line two baking sheets with baking parchment. Beat the butter and sugar together until light and fluffy, then stir in the citrus rinds.

2 Stir the egg yolks into the butter mixture, then add the ground almonds and flour and mix well.

3 Divide the mixture into 20 pieces and shape into balls. Place on the baking sheets. Using the handle of a wooden spoon, make a hole in the center of each cookie. Put ½ teaspoon lemon or orange curd into each hole, and pinch the opening to semi-enclose the curd.

4 Brush the top of each cookie with milk and sprinkle with sliced almonds. Bake for about 20 minutes, until pale golden brown. Leave to cool slightly on the baking sheets to firm up, then transfer to a wire rack to cool completely.

Fig and Date Ravioli

These melt-in-the-mouth cushions of sweet pastry are filled with a delicious mixture of figs, dates and walnuts and dusted with confectioners' sugar. They are ideal for serving with tea.

Makes about 20

13-ounce packet sweet
  shortcrust pastry
milk, for brushing
confectioners' sugar, sifted,
  for dusting

For the filling

4 ounces/⅔ cup ready-to-eat dried figs
2 ounces/⅓ cup pitted dates
½ ounce/1 tablespoon chopped walnuts
2 teaspoons lemon juice
1 tablespoon clear honey

1 Preheat the oven to 350°F/Gas 4. To make the filling, put all the ingredients into a food processor and blend to a paste.

2 Roll out just under half of the shortcrust pastry, on a lightly floured surface, to a square. Place spoonfuls of the fig paste on the pastry in neat rows at equally spaced intervals, as when making ravioli.

3 Roll out the remaining pastry to a slightly larger square. Dampen all around each spoonful of filling, using a pastry brush dipped in cold water. Place the second sheet of pastry on top and press together around each mound of filling.

4 Using a zigzag pastry wheel or a pizza cutter, cut squares between the mounds of filling. Place the cookies on non-stick baking sheets and lightly brush the top of each with a little milk. Bake for 15–20 minutes, until golden.

5 Using a metal spatula, transfer the cookies to a wire rack to cool. When cool, dust with confectioners' sugar.

Baked Sweet Ravioli

These delicious sweet ravioli are made with a rich pastry flavored with lemon and filled with the traditional ingredients used in Sicilian cassata.

Serves 4

8 ounces/2 cups all-purpose flour

2½ ounces/⅓ cup superfine sugar

3½ ounces/scant ½ cup butter

1 egg

1 teaspoon finely grated lemon rind

confectioners' sugar and grated chocolate,
    for sprinkling

For the filling

6 ounces/¾ cup ricotta cheese

2 ounces/¼ cup superfine sugar

¾ teaspoon vanilla extract

1 egg yolk

1 tablespoon mixed candied fruits or
    candied peel

1 ounce bittersweet chocolate, finely
    chopped or grated

1 medium egg, beaten

1 Put the flour and sugar into a food processor and, working on full speed, add the butter in pieces until fully worked into the mixture. With the food processor running, add the egg and lemon rind. The mixture should form a dough that just holds together. Scrape the dough onto a sheet of plastic wrap, cover with another sheet, flatten and chill until needed.

2 To make the filling, push the ricotta through a sieve into a bowl. Stir in the sugar, vanilla extract, egg yolk, candied fruits or peel, and chocolate until combined.

3 Remove the dough from the refrigerator and leave to come to room temperature. Divide the dough in half and roll out each half between sheets of plastic wrap to make strips, measuring 6 x 22 inches. Preheat the oven to 350°F/Gas 4.

4 Arrange heaped tablespoons of the filling in two rows along one of the dough strips, making sure that there is a 1-inch clear space around each spoonful. Brush the dough between the heaps of filling with beaten egg. Place the second strip of dough on top and press down between each mound to seal.

5 Using a 2½-inch plain cutter, cut around each mound to make circular ravioli. Lift each one and, with your fingertips, seal the edges. Place on a greased baking sheet and bake for 15 minutes, until golden brown. Serve warm sprinkled with icing sugar and grated chocolate.

Spicy Fruit Cake from Siena

This is a delicious flat cake with a wonderful spicy flavor. This cake is very rich, so it should be cut into small wedges. Serve with tea or a glass of sparkling wine on special occasions.

Serves 12–14

butter for greasing
6 ounces/1 cup hazelnuts,
   coarsely chopped
3 ounces/½ cup whole almonds,
   coarsely chopped
8 ounces/1⅓ cups mixed candied
   fruits, diced
¼ teaspoon ground coriander
1 teaspoon ground cinnamon
¼ teaspoon ground cloves
¼ teaspoon grated nutmeg
2 ounces/½ cup all-purpose flour
4 ounces/⅓ cup honey
4 ounces/½ cup granulated sugar
confectioners' sugar, for dusting

1 Preheat the oven to 350°F/ Gas 4. Grease an 8-inch round cake pan with the butter. Line the base of the pan with non-stick baking parchment.

2 Spread the nuts on a baking tray and place in the oven for about 10 minutes, until lightly toasted. Set aside. Lower the oven temperature to 300°F/Gas 2.

3 Combine the candied fruits, all the spices and the flour in a bowl and stir together. Add the nuts and stir in thoroughly.

4 In a small heavy pan, stir together the honey and sugar, and bring to the boil. Cook the mixture until it reaches 280°F on a sugar thermometer, or when a small piece forms a hard ball when pressed between fingertips in iced water. Take care when doing this and use a teaspoon to remove a little mixture out of the pan for testing.

5 At this stage immediately pour the sugar syrup into the dry ingredients and stir in well until evenly coated. Pour into the prepared pan. Dip a spoon into water and use the back of the spoon to press the mixture evenly into the pan. Bake in the preheated oven for 1 hour.

6 When the cake is ready, it will still feel quite soft, but it will firm up as it cools. Leave to cool completely in the pan and then turn out onto a serving plate. Dust with confectioners' sugar before serving.

Cook's Tip
This will store in an airtight container for up to 2 weeks.

Orange Shortbread Fingers

These delicately scented cookies are a real tea-time treat, and they would be the perfect choice for a leisurely summer afternoon sitting in the shade in the garden.

Makes 18

4 ounces/½ cup sweet butter at room temperature, diced
2 ounces/4 tablespoons superfine sugar, plus extra for sprinkling
finely grated rind of 2 oranges
6 ounces/1½ cups all-purpose flour

1 Preheat the oven to 375°F/Gas 5. Grease a large baking sheet. Beat together the butter and sugar until soft and creamy. Beat in the orange rind.

2 Gradually add the flour and gently pull the dough together to form a soft ball. Roll out the dough on a lightly floured surface to about ½ inch thick.

3 Cut into narrow bars, sprinkle over a little extra superfine sugar and place on the baking sheet. Prick the surface with a fork and bake for about 20 minutes, until the cookies are a light golden color. Transfer the cookies to a wire rack and leave to cool.

Cook's Tip
Store the cookies in plastic bags or an airtight container for up to 2 weeks.

Variation
Use the rind of 1 or 2 lemons in place of the orange rind. Remember to use unwaxed fruit and wash thoroughly before use.

Coconut and Lime Macaroons

These pretty pistachio nut topped cookies are crunchy on the outside and soft and gooey in the center. The zesty lime topping contrasts wonderfully with the sweet coconut.

Makes 12–14

4 extra large egg whites

9 ounces/3 cups dried sweetened shredded coconut

5 ounces/¾ cup granulated sugar

2 teaspoons vanilla extract

1 ounce/¼ cup all-purpose flour

4 ounces/1 cup confectioners' sugar, sifted

grated rind of 1 lime

3–4 teaspoons lime juice

about ½ ounce/1 tablespoon pistachio nuts, chopped

1 Preheat the oven to 350°F/Gas 4. Line two baking sheets with baking parchment. Put the egg whites, dried coconut, sugar, vanilla extract and flour in a large, heavy pan. Mix well.

2 Place over a low heat and cook for 6–8 minutes, stirring constantly to make sure it does not stick. When the mixture becomes the consistency of thick oatmeal, remove from the heat.

3 Place spoonfuls of the mixture in rocky piles on the lined baking sheets. Bake for 12–13 minutes, until golden brown. Remove from the oven and leave to cool completely on the baking sheets.

4 To make the topping, put the confectioners' sugar and lime rind into a bowl and add enough lime juice to give a thick pouring consistency. Place a spoonful of icing on each macaroon and allow it to drip down the sides. Sprinkle over the pistachio nuts.

Variation

If you prefer, make Coconut and Lemon Macaroons by substituting grated lemon rind and juice.

Shape and Bake Cookies

The mixture for these simple Maryland-style cookies can be made and stored in the refrigerator. It's so easy to cook some each day – and there's nothing like a warm, freshly baked cookie.

Makes about 12 giant or 20 standard-size cookies

4 ounces/½ cup sweet butter, at room temperature, diced

4 ounces/generous ½ cup granulated sugar

4 ounces/generous ½ cup light brown sugar

1 extra large egg

1 teaspoon vanilla extract

7 ounces/1¾ cups self-rising flour

5 ounces/scant 1 cup chocolate chips

2 ounces/½ cup chopped toasted hazelnuts or walnuts

2 ounces/scant ½ cup raisins

1 Preheat the oven to 350°F/Gas 4. Line two baking sheets with baking parchment. Put the butter, granulated sugar and brown sugar in a large mixing bowl and beat together well until light and fluffy. Add the egg and vanilla extract and beat again until the mixture is well combined.

2 Add the flour, chocolate chips, chopped toasted hazelnuts or walnuts, and raisins, and mix together, until the ingredients have just blended. The dough will now have a slightly crumbly consistency.

3 Depending on whether you want giant or standard-size cookies, place tablespoonfuls or teaspoonfuls of the mixture, spaced far apart, on the prepared baking sheets. Bake for 15 minutes, until golden brown.

4 Leave the cookies on the baking sheets for 5 minutes, then use a metal spatula to transfer to a wire rack to cool.

Cook's Tip
If you don't want to bake the mixture all at once, simply spoon it into a plastic container, cover the surface with plastic wrap to prevent it from drying out and replace the lid. Keep in the refrigerator for up to 1 week. When required, remove the dough from the refrigerator 15 minutes before you want to bake the cookies to soften slightly, and shape and bake as before.

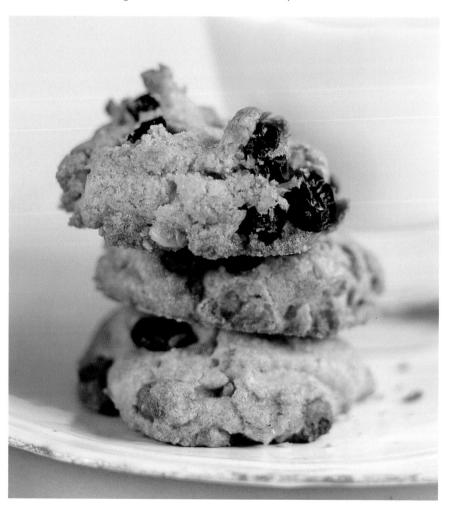

Apple and Elderflower Stars

These delicious, crumbly apple cookies are topped with a sweet yet very sharp icing. Packaged in a pretty box, they would make a delightfully festive gift for someone special.

Makes about 18

4 ounces/½ cup sweet butter, at room
   temperature, diced
3 ounces/scant ½ cup superfine
   sugar
½ teaspoon apple pie spice
1 extra large egg yolk
1 ounce dried apple rings,
   finely chopped
7 ounces/1¾ cups self-rising flour
1–2 teaspoons milk, if necessary

For the topping

7 ounces/1¾ cups confectioners'
   sugar, sifted
4–6 tablespoons elderflower cordial
granulated sugar, for sprinkling

1 Preheat the oven to 375°F/Gas 5. Cream together the butter and sugar until light and fluffy. Beat in the apple pie spice and egg yolk. Add the chopped apple and flour and stir together well. The mixture should form a stiff dough, but if it is too dry, add some milk.

2 Roll the dough out on a floured surface to ¼ inch thick. Draw a five-pointed star on cardboard. Cut out and use as a template for the cookies. Alternatively, use a star cookie cutter.

3 Place the cookies on non-stick baking sheets and bake for about 10–15 minutes, or until just beginning to brown around the edges. Using a metal spatula, carefully transfer the cookies to a wire rack to cool.

4 To make the topping, sift the confectioners' sugar into a bowl and add just enough elderflower cordial to mix to a fairly thick but still pourable consistency.

5 When the cookies are completely cool, trickle the icing randomly over the stars. Immediately sprinkle with granulated sugar and leave to set.

Greek Honey Crunch Creams

**With its scent of liquorice and aniseed, Greek honey lends a wonderful flavor to these cookies.
If you like your honey less strong, try using orange blossom or lavender instead.**

Makes 20

*9 ounces/2¼ cups self-rising
  flour*

2 teaspoons baking soda

2 ounces/¼ cup superfine sugar

*4 ounces/½ cup sweet
  butter, diced*

*finely grated rind of
  1 large orange*

4 ounces/½ cup Greek honey

*1 ounce/¼ cup pine nuts or
  chopped walnuts*

For the filling

*2 ounces/¼ cup sweet butter,
  at room temperature, diced*

*4 ounces/1 cup confectioners'
  sugar, sifted*

1 tablespoon Greek honey

1 Preheat the oven to 400°F/Gas 6.
Line three or four baking sheets
with baking parchment. Sift the
flour, baking soda and superfine
sugar into a bowl. Add the butter
and rub in until the mixture
resembles breadcrumbs. Stir in the
orange rind.

2 Put the honey in a small pan and
heat until just runny but not hot.
Pour over the dry mixture and mix
to a firm dough.

3 Divide the dough in half and
shape one half into 20 small balls
about the size of a hazelnut in its
shell. Place the balls on the baking
sheets, spaced far apart, and gently
flatten. Bake for 6–8 minutes, until
golden brown. Leave to cool and
firm up on the baking sheets. Use a
metal spatula to transfer the cookies
to a wire rack and leave them to
cool completely.

4 Shape the remaining dough into
20 balls and dip one side of each
one into the pine nuts or walnuts.
Place the cookies, nut sides up, on
the baking sheets, gently flatten and
bake for 6–8 minutes, until golden
brown. Leave to cool and firm up
slightly on the baking sheets before
carefully transferring the cookies to
a wire rack, still nut sides up, to
cool completely.

5 To make the filling, put the butter,
sugar and honey in a bowl and beat
together until light and fluffy. Use
the mixture to sandwich the
cookies together in pairs using a
plain cookie for the base and a nut-
coated one for the top.

Cook's Tip
*Greek honey is also called Hymettus
honey, named after the mountain. It is
very dark and aromatic, with a unique
taste, and is one of the most expensive
honeys in the world.*

Cookies for Kids

There's nothing quite like coming home from school to a plate of freshly baked cookies and a glass of milk. This chapter is packed with fabulous, fun ideas that kids will love, from simple cookies with pretty sugar icing to utterly adorable puppy faces, and indulgent ice-cream sandwiches.

Orange Biscotti

These crisp, crunchy cookies are based on a traditional Italian recipe in which the cookies are packed with nuts and twice baked. This version is flavored with orange instead of the nuts, and shaped into long, thin sticks. They are a little softer than the classic biscotti, which are very hard.

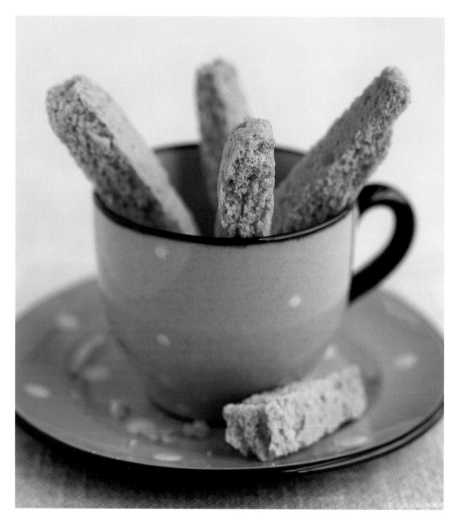

3 Bake the dough for 25 minutes, then remove from the oven and leave to stand for about 5 minutes until slightly cooled.

4 Using a sharp knife, carefully cut the mixture widthwise into thin sticks, about ½ inch wide.

5 Space the cookies out slightly on the baking sheet so there's a gap in between each one, allowing air to circulate, then return to the oven and bake for a further 20 minutes, until crisp. Transfer the biscotti to a wire rack and leave to cool. Serve dusted with a little confectioners' sugar.

Makes about 20

2 ounces/ ¼ cup sweet butter, at room temperature, diced
3½ ounces/ ½ cup light brown sugar
1 egg
finely grated rind of 1 small orange, plus 2 teaspoons juice
6 ounces/1½ cups self-rising flour
1½ teaspoons baking powder
good pinch of ground cinnamon
2 ounces/½ cup polenta
confectioners' sugar, for dusting

1 Preheat the oven to 325°F/Gas 3. Grease a large baking sheet. In a large bowl, beat together the butter and sugar until smooth and creamy. Beat in the egg, then the orange rind and juice, flour, baking powder, cinnamon and polenta.

2 Tip the mixture onto a lightly floured surface and knead. Place the dough on the baking sheet and flatten out with the palm of your hand to make a rectangle about 10 x 7 inches.

Five-spice Fingers

These light, crumbly cookies have an unusual Chinese five-spice flavoring. Pipe them into finger shapes, then arrange them on cut-out paper hand shapes and add a bracelet or watch stamped out from citrus rind.

Makes 28

4 ounces/½ cup butter or margarine
    at room temperature, diced
2 ounces/½ cup confectioners'
    sugar
4 ounces/1 cup all-purpose flour
2 teaspoons Chinese five-spice
    powder
grated rind and juice of ½ orange

1 Preheat the oven to 350°F/Gas 4. Lightly grease two baking sheets. Put the butter or margarine and half the confectioners' sugar in a bowl and beat well with a wooden spoon, until the mixture is smooth and creamy.

2 Add the flour and five-spice powder and beat again until thoroughly mixed. Spoon the mixture into a large pastry bag fitted with a large star nozzle.

3 Pipe short lines of mixture, about 3 inches long, on the prepared baking sheets. Leave enough room for them to spread.

4 Bake for 15 minutes, until lightly browned. Leave to cool slightly, before transferring to a wire rack, using a metal spatula.

5 Sift the remaining confectioners' sugar into a small bowl and stir in the orange rind. Add enough juice to make a thin icing. Brush over the cookies while they are still warm.

Cook's Tip
These cookies are delicious served with ice cream or creamy desserts.

Variation
Use apple pie spice instead of five-spice, if you prefer.

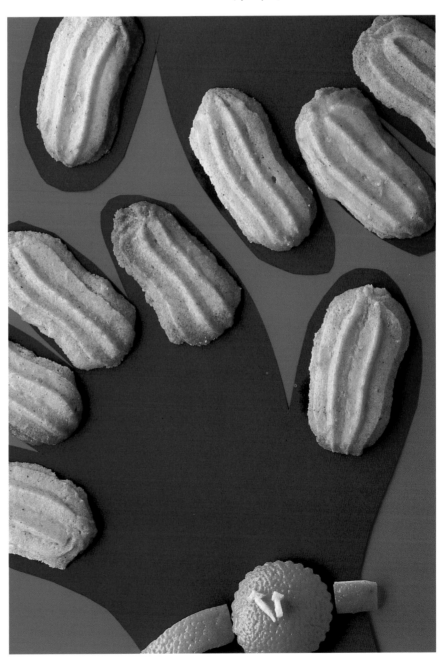

Pink Sugared Hearts

Pretty and pink, these delightful cookies are always a hit with Barbie-loving girls. Rolling the edges of the cookies in colored sugar to accentuate their shape really adds to the fun of decorating.

Makes 32

8 ounces/2 cups all-purpose flour

6 ounces/¾ cup sweet butter, chilled and diced

4¼ ounces/⅔ cup superfine sugar

1 egg yolk

For the decoration

2 ounces/¼ cup granulated sugar

pink food coloring

8 ounces/2 cups confectioners' sugar

2–3 tablespoons lemon juice

1 Preheat the oven to 350°F/Gas 4. Grease two baking sheets.

2 Put the flour and diced butter into a food processor, then process until the mixture resembles fine breadcrumbs. Add the sugar and egg yolk to the food processor and process until the mixture begins to form a ball.

3 Turn the dough out onto a lightly floured surface and knead until smooth. Shape the dough into a ball, put in plastic wrap and chill for at least 30 minutes.

4 Working in batches, roll out the dough thinly on a lightly floured surface and cut out heart shapes using a 2-inch cutter. Transfer to the baking sheets, spacing them slightly apart. Bake for 10 minutes, or until pale golden. Transfer to a wire rack to cool.

5 To decorate, put the granulated sugar in a bowl and add a small dot of pink food coloring. Using the back of a teaspoon, work the food coloring into the sugar until it is completely pink.

6 Put the confectioners' sugar in a separate bowl and add 2 tablespoons of the lemon juice, stirring until smooth but spreadable. If the paste is too thick, add a little more lemon juice and stir until well combined.

Cook's Tip

To make festive cookies, try cutting out tree shapes, and use green food coloring instead of pink. Alternatively, cut out star shapes and use silver or gold food coloring to tint the sugar. Children will love these festive shapes and will enjoy leaving a plate of cookies and a glass of milk out for Santa.

7 Using a metal spatula spread a little icing onto each cookie, to within ¼ inch of the edge.

8 Turn each iced cookie on its side and gently roll in the colored sugar so that the edges of the icing become coated in pink. Leave the cookies to set for about 1 hour.

Jammie Bodgers

These buttery cookies are an absolute classic. Sandwiched with buttercream and a generous spoonful of strawberry jam, they make a perfect snack served with a glass of milk at tea time, or are equally good wrapped tightly, and popped in a lunchbox as a post-sandwich treat.

Makes 20

8 ounces/2 cups all-purpose flour

6 ounces/¾ cup sweet butter, chilled and diced

4¼ ounces/⅔ cup superfine sugar

1 egg yolk

For the filling

2 ounces/¼ cup sweet butter, at room temperature, diced

3½ ounces/scant 1 cup confectioners' sugar

4–5 tablespoons strawberry jam

Cook's Tip

If you don't have a small cutter for the cookie centers, use a sharp knife to cut out triangles or squares instead.

1 Put the flour and butter in a food processor and process until the mixture resembles breadcrumbs. Add the sugar and egg yolk and process until the mixture starts to form a dough.

2 Turn out onto a floured surface and knead until smooth. Shape into a ball, put in plastic wrap and chill for at least 30 minutes. Preheat the oven to 350°F/Gas 4. Grease two baking sheets.

3 Roll out the dough thinly on a lightly floured surface and cut out round pieces using a 2½-inch cookie cutter. Re-roll the trimmings and cut out more pieces until you have 40.

4 Place half the round pieces on a prepared baking sheet. Using a small heart-shaped cutter, about ¾ inch in diameter, cut out the centers of the remaining pieces. Place these pieces on the second baking sheet.

5 Bake the cookies for about 12 minutes until pale golden, then transfer to a wire rack and leave to cool completely.

6 To make the buttercream, beat together the butter and sugar until smooth and creamy.

7 Using a metal spatula, spread a little buttercream onto each whole cookie. Spoon a little jam onto the buttercream, then gently press the cut-out cookies on top, so that the jam fills the heart-shaped hole.

Applesauce Cookies

These soft and chewy, fruit-flavored cookies are a favorite with children and ideal to make if you have a glut of apples in the autumn. They're best eaten within a day or two of baking, or they can be frozen and then thawed as you need them.

Makes 36

1 pound cooking apples, peeled, cored and chopped

3 tablespoons water

4 ounces/generous ½ cup superfine sugar

4 ounces/½ cup butter or margarine at room temperature, diced

4 ounces/1 cup all-purpose flour

½ teaspoon baking powder

¼ teaspoon baking soda

pinch of salt

½ teaspoon ground cinnamon

2 ounces/½ cup chopped walnuts

1 Cook the apples with the water in a covered pan over a low heat until tender. Puree in a blender, then measure out 6 fluid ounces/¾ cup.

2 Preheat the oven to 375°F/Gas 5. Grease two baking sheets. Cream together the sugar and butter or margarine until well mixed. Beat in the apple puree.

3 Sift the flour, baking powder, baking soda, salt and ground cinnamon into the mixture and stir to blend thoroughly. Fold in the chopped walnuts.

4 Drop teaspoonfuls of the dough onto the prepared baking sheets, spacing them about 2 inches apart.

5 Bake the cookies for about 10 minutes, or until they are golden brown. With a spatula, transfer to a wire rack and leave to cool. Store in an airtight container for up to 2 days, or freeze for up to 4 months.

Lemony Peanut Pairs

These simple-to-make cookies are filled with peanut butter, but you could use buttercream or chocolate-and-nut spread instead. Make a selection with different fillings and let the kids choose.

Makes 8–10

1½ ounces/3 tablespoons soft light
 brown sugar
2 ounces/¼ cup soft margarine
1 teaspoon grated lemon rind
3 ounces/¾ cup whole-wheat flour
2 ounces/¼ cup chopped
 candied pineapple
1 ounce/2 tablespoons smooth
 peanut butter
sifted confectioners' sugar, for dusting

1 Preheat the oven to 375°F/Gas 3. Grease a baking sheet.

2 Cream the sugar, margarine and lemon rind together. Work in the flour and knead until smooth, then roll out thinly.

3 Stamp out rounds. Place on the baking sheet. Press on the pineapple. Bake for 20 minutes. Cool. Sandwich with peanut butter. Dust with sugar.

Iced Ginger Cookies

If your children enjoy cooking with you, mixing and rolling the dough and cutting out all sorts of different shapes, this is the ideal recipe to let them practice on.

Makes 16

4 ounces/½ cup soft brown sugar
4 ounces/½ cup soft margarine
pinch of salt
a few drops of vanilla extract
6 ounces/1¼ cups whole-wheat
 flour
1 tablespoon cocoa powder
 (unsweetened), sifted
2 teaspoons ground ginger
*candied icing and candied cherries,
 to decorate*

1 Preheat the oven to 375°F/Gas 5. Lightly grease one or two large baking sheets.

2 Cream together the sugar, margarine, salt and vanilla extract until very soft and light.

3 Work in the flour, cocoa powder and ginger, adding a little water, if necessary, to bind the mixture. Knead lightly on a floured surface until smooth.

4 Roll out the dough to about ¼ inch thick. Stamp out shapes using floured cookie cutters and place on the baking sheet.

5 Bake the cookies for about 10–15 minutes, until just firm to a light touch. Leave to cool on the baking sheets until completely firm, then transfer to a wire rack to cool completely. Decorate the tops with candied icing and pieces of candied cherries.

Gingerbread Family

You can have great fun with these cookies by creating characters with different features. By using an assortment of different gingerbread cutters, you can make a gingerbread family of all shapes and sizes. If you want to make decorating the cookies simpler, use just one color of chocolate rather than three. Colored writer icing and candy are also good for decorating.

Makes about 12

12 ounces/3 cups all-purpose flour

1 teaspoon baking soda

1 teaspoon ground ginger

4 ounces/½ cup sweet butter, chilled and diced

6 ounces/scant 1 cup light brown sugar

1 egg

2 tablespoons black molasses or light corn syrup

2 ounces each semisweet, milk and white chocolate, to decorate

1 Preheat the oven to 350°F/ Gas 4. Grease two large baking sheets.

2 Put the flour, baking soda, ginger and diced butter into the food processor. Process until the mixture begins to resemble fine breadcrumbs.

3 If necessary, scrape down the sides of the food processor bowl with a wooden spoon or spatula to remove any crumbs that have become stuck.

4 Add the sugar, egg and black molasses or syrup to the food processor and process the mixture until it begins to form into a ball.

5 Turn the dough out onto a lightly floured surface, and knead until smooth and pliable.

6 Roll out the dough on a lightly floured surface. (You might find it easier to roll half of the dough out at a time.) Cut out figures, using people-shaped cutters, then transfer to the baking sheets. Re-roll any trimmings and cut out more figures.

7 Bake for 15 minutes until slightly risen and starting to color around the edges. Leave for 5 minutes, then transfer to a wire rack to cool.

8 To decorate the cookies, break each type of chocolate into a separate bowl. One at a time, set a bowl over a pan of simmering water and heat, stirring frequently, until melted. Spoon the melted chocolate into paper pastry bags, snip off the merest tip, then pipe faces and clothes onto the cookies. Leave to set.

Cook's Tip

You can use any color of sugar for these cookies: the darker the sugar, the darker the final cookies will be. Similarly, molasses will produce a darker cookie than light corn syrup will.

Peanut Crunch Cookies

These delicious sweet and nutty cookies are so easy to make. They puff up into lovely domed round shapes during baking, giving them a really professional look. If you prefer cookies with a slightly less "nutty" texture, use smooth peanut butter rather than the crunchy variety.

Makes 25

4 ounces/ ½ cup sweet butter,
   at room temperature, diced
4 ounces/generous ½ cup light
   brown sugar
I egg
5 ounces/I ¼ cups self-rising flour
½ teaspoon baking powder
5 ounces/generous ½ cup crunchy
   peanut butter
confectioners' sugar,
   for dusting

I Preheat the oven to 375°F/Gas 5. Grease two baking sheets.

2 Put the butter and sugar in a mixing bowl and beat until pale and creamy. Beat in the egg, then add the flour, baking powder and peanut butter. Beat until the ingredients are thoroughly mixed.

3 Place heaped teaspoonfuls of the mixture onto the greased baking sheets; space enough apart to allow the cookies to spread while baking. (If necessary, spoon the dough onto the baking sheets in batches.)

4 Bake the cookies for about 20 minutes until risen; they will still be quite soft to the touch.

5 Leave the cookies on the baking sheets for about 5 minutes, then transfer to a wire rack to cool. To serve, lightly dust with sugar.

Ice-cream Sandwiches

Home-made wafer cookies have a flavor unlike anything you can buy at the supermarket. These crisp, nutty cookies make perfect ice-cream sandwiches for a summertime treat. They're also fun to make and are a good accompaniment to almost any fruity or creamy dessert.

Makes 6 sandwiches

2 ounces/ ¼ cup sweet butter

2 egg whites

3 ounces/scant ½ cup superfine
  sugar

2 ounces/ ½ cup all-purpose flour

1½ ounces/scant ½ cup ground almonds

2 tablespoons sliced almonds
  (optional)

raspberry ripple or vanilla ice cream,
  to serve

confectioners' sugar, for dusting

1 Preheat the oven to 400°F/Gas 6. Line two large baking sheets with baking parchment. Put the butter in a small pan and melt over a very low heat.

2 Put the egg whites and sugar in a bowl and whisk lightly with a fork until the egg whites are broken up. Add the flour, melted butter and ground almonds and mix until evenly combined.

3 Drop 6 level tablespoonfuls of mixture onto each baking sheet, spacing them far apart. Spread the mixture to rounds about 2¾ inches in diameter. Sprinkle with almonds, if using, and bake for 10–12 minutes, until golden around the edges. Peel away the paper and transfer to a wire rack to cool.

4 Place a scoop of slightly softened ice cream onto one cookie and top with another, gently pressing them together. Dust with sugar and serve.

Cook's Tip
Don't be tempted to use waxed paper instead of baking parchment, as the cookies may stick to it.

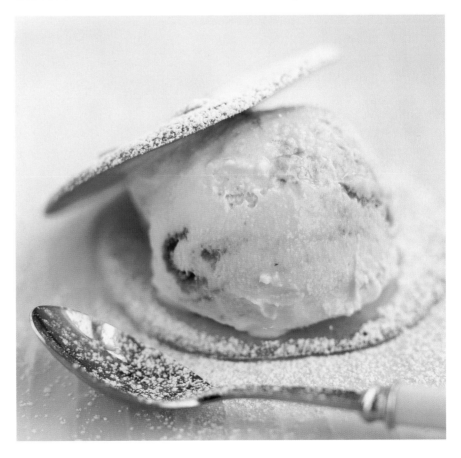

Flower Power Cookies

Look out for little piped sugar flower decorations in the supermarket. Some are in pretty pale colors, while others are much brighter and more vibrant. The latter are best for these colorful cookies, as they contrast better with the pretty pastel-colored icing.

Makes 28

8 ounces/2 cups all-purpose flour

6 ounces/¾ cup sweet butter, chilled and diced

finely grated rind of 1 orange

4¼ ounces/⅔ cup light brown sugar

1 egg yolk

For the decoration

2 tablespoons orange juice

7 ounces/1¾ cups confectioners' sugar

green, yellow and orange food colorings

*multi-colored sugared flowers,
   to decorate*

1 Put the flour, butter and orange rind into a food processor. Process until the mixture resembles fine breadcrumbs. Add the sugar and egg yolk to the food processor and process until the mixture starts to bind together.

2 Turn the mixture out onto a lightly floured surface and knead until it forms a dough. Shape the dough into a ball, wrap tightly in plastic wrap and chill in the refrigerator for at least 30 minutes.

3 Preheat the oven to 350°F/Gas 4. Grease two baking sheets. Roll out the dough thinly on a floured surface and cut out round pieces using a fluted cookie cutter about 2½ inches in diameter.

4 Transfer the cookies to the baking sheets, spacing them slightly apart. Bake for 12–15 minutes, until pale golden, then transfer to a wire rack to cool completely.

5 To decorate the cookies, put the orange juice in a bowl and gradually stir in the confectioners' sugar until the mixture has the consistency of thick pouring cream. Divide the mixture among three bowls and stir a few drops of a different food coloring into each bowl.

6 Spoon a little green icing onto one third of the cookies, spreading it to within ½ inch of the cookie edges. Top each one with a sugared flower (ideally of a contrasting color). Decorate the remaining cookies in the same way, using the yellow icing on half the cookies and the orange icing on the remaining half. Leave to set for about 1 hour.

Alphabetinis

These funny little letters are great for kids – and might even be a good way to encourage them to practice their spelling. They are great fun to make and even better to eat.

Makes about 30

2 egg whites
1 tablespoon cornstarch
2 ounces/ ½ cup all-purpose flour
5 ounces/ ¾ cup superfine sugar
2 teaspoons vanilla extract
3½ ounces milk chocolate

1 Preheat the oven to 350°F/Gas 4. Line two large baking sheets with baking parchment.

2 In a clean glass bowl, whisk the egg whites until peaking. Sift the cornstarch and all-purpose flour over the egg whites and add the sugar and vanilla extract. Fold in using a large metal spoon.

3 Spoon half the mixture into a plastic bag and gently squeeze it into a corner of the bag. Snip off the tip of the corner so that the cookie mixture can be squeezed out in a thin line, ½ inch wide.

4 Very carefully, pipe letters onto one of the lined baking sheets, making each letter about 2½ inches tall. Spoon the remaining cookie mixture into the bag and pipe more letters onto the second lined baking sheet.

5 Bake the cookies for 12 minutes, or until crisp and golden. Carefully transfer to a wire rack to cool.

6 Break the chocolate into pieces and put in a heatproof bowl set over a pan of simmering water. Heat, stirring frequently, until melted.

7 Spoon the melted chocolate into a small paper pastry bag (or use a smaller plastic bag) and snip off the merest tip.

8 Pipe the chocolate in lines over the cookies to highlight the shape of each letter. Leave to set for at least 1 hour.

Puppy Faces

Children of any age can have fun making these little pups – you could even use the family pet as a model. These cookies are decorated with the widely available, white "ready-to-roll" icing, but you can knead in a little black, brown or yellow food coloring to make different-colored dogs.

Makes 10

3½ ounces/scant 1 cup all-purpose flour

2 ounces/½ cup rolled oats

½ teaspoon apple pie spice

2 ounces/¼ cup sweet butter, chilled and diced

3½ ounces/½ cup superfine sugar

1 egg yolk

For the decoration

4 tablespoons apricot jam

9 ounces white ready-to-roll icing

10 round colored candies

black and red writer icing tubes

confectioners' sugar, for dusting

1 Put the flour, rolled oats, mixed spice and butter into the food processor. Process until the mixture resembles fine breadcrumbs.

2 Add the sugar, egg yolk and 1 teaspoon water to the food processor and blend until the mixture begins to form a ball.

3 Turn the dough out onto a lightly floured surface and knead until smooth. Put in plastic wrap and chill for 30 minutes.

4 Preheat the oven to 400°F/Gas 6. Grease a large baking sheet.

5 Roll out the dough on a floured surface and cut out round pieces using a 2½-inch cutter. Transfer to the baking sheet, spacing slightly apart. Bake for 12 minutes, until pale golden. Transfer to a wire rack to cool.

6 Press the jam through a sieve. Brush a little jam over each cookie to within ¼ inch of the edge.

7 Roll out half the icing as thinly as possible on a surface dusted with confectioners' sugar. Cut out 10 round pieces using the 2½-inch cutter, and lay one over each cookie. To make the eyes, halve the colored candied, brush the icing lightly with water and press the candies into the cookies.

8 Use the black writer tube to pipe the noses and mouths, finishing with little red tongues.

9 To make the ears, divide the remaining icing into 20 pieces. Roll each piece into a ball and flatten between the thumb and forefinger to make a flat pear shape. Lightly brush the icing with water and secure the ears. Arrange the cookies in a single layer on a tray.

Tree Cookies

These cookies look really effective with their chocolate "trunks" and brightly colored "fruits". Kids will love helping to decorate them. Arrange the cookies in a line on the tea table (preferably on a multi-colored cloth, if you have one).

Makes 10

2 ounces/ ¼ cup sweet butter,
  at room temperature, diced
4 ounces/ ½ cup light brown sugar
1 egg
5 ounces/1 ¼ cups self-rising flour
½ teaspoon baking soda
finely grated rind of 1 lemon

For the decoration

2 ounces/½ cup confectioners' sugar
2 teaspoons lemon juice
10 milk chocolate fingers
brightly colored candies,
  such as M&Ms

1 Preheat the oven to 350°F/Gas 4. Grease two baking sheets.

2 In a large bowl, beat together the butter and sugar until smooth and creamy. Beat in the egg. Add the flour, baking soda and lemon rind and mix until smooth.

3 Place 5 large spoonfuls of the mixture onto each baking sheet, spacing them far apart. Bake for 15 minutes until the cookies have risen. Leave on the baking sheet for 5 minutes to firm up, then transfer to a wire rack to cool.

Variation

To create pretty blossoming trees, attach pastel-colored sugar flowers to the cookies instead of colored sweets.

4 To decorate the cookies, mix together the confectioners' sugar and lemon juice to make a thick paste. Use a little paste to secure one end of a chocolate finger to each cookie.

5 Attach the colored candies in the same way, securing each one with a little paste. Leave the cookies to set for at least 1 hour. (Handle the decorated cookies with care.)

Butter Gems

These tiny shortbread-based cookies are topped with rosettes of soft buttercream and a pretty sprinkling of brightly colored sugar. They make a great treat for even the smallest of mouths.

Makes about 40

4 ounces/ ½ cup sweet butter, at room
    temperature, diced
2 ounces/ ¼ cup superfine sugar
6 ounces/1 ½ cups all-purpose flour

For the decoration

2 ounces/4 tablespoons sweet butter,
    at room temperature, diced
1 teaspoon vanilla extract
3½ ounces/scant 1 cup confectioners'
    sugar
1 ounce/2 tablespoons granulated sugar
green, lilac or pink food colorings

1 Put the diced butter and the sugar in a large bowl and beat together until smooth and creamy. Add the flour to the creamed butter and mix well to form a thick paste.

2 Turn the dough onto a lightly floured surface and knead until smooth. Wrap the dough in plastic wrap and chill for at least 30 minutes.

3 Preheat the oven to 350°F/Gas 4. Grease two baking sheets.

4 Roll out the dough on a lightly floured surface and cut out round pieces using a 1¼-inch cookie cutter. Space slightly apart on the baking sheets and bake for 10 minutes, or until pale golden. Transfer to a wire rack to cool completely.

5 To decorate the cookies, beat the butter with the vanilla extract and confectioners' sugar until smooth and creamy. Spoon the buttercream into a pastry bag fitted with a star-shaped nozzle, then pipe a rosette onto each cookie.

6 Put the granulated sugar into a small bowl and add several drops of the food coloring. Using the back of a teaspoon, work the coloring into the sugar until it is deeply colored. Sprinkle a little of the sugar over the cookies.

Dolly Cookies

These pretty cookies look like they belong at a doll's tea party and are great fun for kids to make and decorate. The cookies are made by simply chilling a roll of dough, then slicing off pieces onto a baking sheet so you don't even need cookie cutters. Baking doesn't get much easier than this.

Makes 14

4 ounces/½ cup sweet butter,
  at room temperature, diced
2 ounces/¼ cup superfine
  sugar
pink food coloring
1 teaspoon vanilla extract
6 ounces/1½ cups all-purpose
  flour
3½ ounces white chocolate
3 ounces multi-colored
  candies

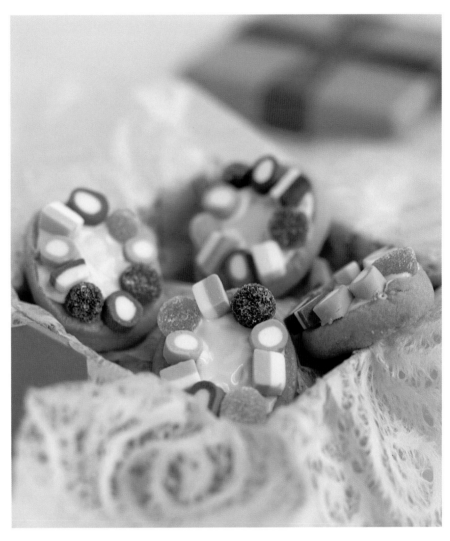

1 Put the butter and sugar in a bowl with a dash of pink food coloring and the vanilla extract. Beat together until smooth and creamy.

2 Add the flour to the butter and sugar mixture and stir well until thoroughly combined. Turn the dough out onto a lightly floured surface and knead until smooth.

3 Using your hands, roll the dough into a thick sausage shape, about 4½ inches long and 2 inches in diameter. Put the dough in plastic wrap and chill for at least 30 minutes.

4 Preheat the oven to 350°F/Gas 4. Grease two large baking sheets.

5 Cut the dough into ¼-inch slices and space them slightly apart on the baking sheets. Bake for 15–18 minutes, or until the cookies begin to color. Transfer to a wire rack to cool completely.

6 Break the chocolate into pieces and put in a heatproof bowl set over a pan of simmering water. Heat, stirring frequently, until the chocolate has melted. Using a sharp knife, cut the sweets in half.

7 Using a metal spatula swirl a little chocolate onto each cookie and decorate with a ring of candies. Leave to set.

Marshmallow Toasties

These soft cookie squares topped with a layer of strawberry jam and melted marshmallow make a sweet, sticky treat for kids of all ages. When you're toasting the marshmallows, watch them very closely, because once they start to color, they brown extremely quickly.

Makes 12

4½ ounces/generous ½ cup sweet
  butter, at room temperature,
  diced
3 ounces/scant ½ cup superfine
  sugar
finely grated rind of 1 lemon
2 teaspoons vanilla extract
3 ounces/¾ cup ground almonds
1 egg
4 ounces/1 cup self-rising flour
5 ounces/½ cup strawberry jam
7 ounces pink and white
  marshmallows
confectioners' sugar, for dusting

1 Preheat the oven to 350°F/Gas 4. Grease the base and sides of a 9-inch square baking pan and line with baking parchment.

2 Put the butter, sugar and lemon rind in a bowl and beat until creamy. Beat in the vanilla extract, ground almonds and egg, then add the flour and stir well.

3 Turn the mixture into the pan and spread in an even layer. Bake for 20 minutes, until pale golden and just firm. Leave to cool in the pan for 10 minutes.

4 Spread the cookie base with jam. Using scissors, cut the marshmallows in half, then arrange them, cut sides down, in an even layer over the jam. Preheat the broiler to medium.

5 Put the pan under the grill for about 2 minutes, until the marshmallows are melted and pale golden. Remove from the heat and gently press down each marshmallow with the back of a spoon to create an even layer of melted marshmallow. Return to the grill for a further minute, until the surface is very toasted. Leave to cool.

6 To serve, dust lightly with sugar, cut into 12 squares or bars and remove from the pan.

Chocolate Cookies on Sticks

Let your imagination run riot when decorating these fun chocolate cookies. Use plenty of brightly colored candies, or create a real chocolate feast by using only chocolate decorations. Whichever you choose, these cookies are very sweet, so should be kept as a real treat for special occasions.

3 Spoon the milk chocolate into the outlines on the paper, reserving one or two spoonfuls of chocolate. Using the back of a spoon, carefully spread the chocolate to the edges to make neat shapes.

4 Press the end of a wooden popsicle stick into each of the shapes, and spoon over a little more melted milk chocolate to cover the stick. Sprinkle the chocolate shapes with the crumbled cookies.

Makes 12

4¼ ounces milk chocolate

3 ounces white chocolate

2 ounces chocolate-coated sweetmeal cookies, crumbled into chunks

a selection of small colored candies, chocolate chips or chocolate-coated raisins

12 wooden popsicle sticks

1 Break the milk and white chocolate into pieces and put in separate heatproof bowls. Place each bowl in turn over a pan of gently simmering water and heat, stirring frequently, until melted.

2 Meanwhile, draw six 2¾-inch round shapes on baking parchment and six 3½ x 2¾ inch rectangles. Invert the paper onto a large tray.

5 Pipe or drizzle the cookies with the melted white chocolate, then sprinkle the cookies with the colored candies, chocolate chips or chocolate-coated raisins, pressing them gently to make sure they stick.

6 Chill for about 1 hour, until set, then carefully peel away the paper.

Marshmallow Crispie Cakes

This is a delicious variation of a perennially popular childhood cookie, which even very young children will love to help make. The marshmallows make them wonderfully sticky.

Makes 45

9-ounce bag of toffees
2 ounces/¼ cup butter
3 tablespoons milk
4 ounces/1 cup marshmallows
6 ounces/6 cups crisped rice cereal

1 Lightly brush an 8 x 13 inch roasting pan with a little oil. Put the toffees, butter and milk in a pan and heat gently, stirring until the toffees have melted.

2 Add the marshmallows and crisped rice cereal and stir until well mixed and the marshmallows have melted.

Variation

Instead of using toffees, try using semisweet chocolate instead. Melt the chocolate by putting it into a heatproof bowl set over a pan of hot water on a low heat. Do not allow the water to touch the base of the bowl, or the chocolate may become too hot.

3 Spoon the mixture into the prepared roasting pan, level the surface and leave to set.

4 When cool and hard, cut into squares, remove from the pan, and put into paper cases to serve.

Sweet Peanut Wafers

Delicate wafers filled with a sweet, peanut-flavored buttercream make a fun, no-bake recipe that kids of any age can help with. Just remember to chill the wafer sandwiches after they have been assembled, otherwise they will be almost impossible to cut.

Makes 12

2½ ounces/4 tablespoons sweet butter,
    at room temperature, diced
2½ ounces/generous ½ cup
    confectioners' sugar
4 ounces/ ½ cup crunchy peanut butter
12 fan-shaped wafers
2 ounces semisweet chocolate

1 Put the butter and sugar in a bowl and beat with a hand-held electric whisk until very light and creamy. Beat in the peanut butter.

2 Using a small metal spatula, spread a thick layer of the mixture onto a wafer and spread to the edges.

3 Place another wafer on top of the peanut buttercream and press it down very gently. Spread the top wafer with more buttercream, then place another wafer on top and press down gently.

4 Use the remaining buttercream and wafers to assemble three more fans in the same way. Spread any remaining buttercream around the sides of the fans. Chill for at least 30 minutes until firm.

5 Using a serrated knife, carefully slice each fan into three equal wedges and arrange in a single layer on a small tray.

6 Break the chocolate into pieces and put in a heatproof bowl placed over a pan of gently simmering water. Stir frequently until melted.

7 Remove the bowl from the heat and leave to stand for a few minutes to cool slightly.

8 Drizzle lines of chocolate over the wafers, then leave to set in a cool place for at least 1 hour.

Peanut-butter and Jelly Cookies

These cookies are a twist on the original American peanut-butter cookie and are a real hit with kids and adults alike. Give them a try – you'll love the crunchy nuts and sweet raspberry centers.

Makes 20–22

8-ounce jar crunchy peanut butter
(with no added sugar)

3 ounces/6 tablespoons sweet butter,
at room temperature, diced

3½ ounces/½ cup golden superfine
sugar

2 ounces/¼ cup light
brown sugar

1 extra large egg, beaten

5 ounces/1¼ cups self-rising
flour

9 ounces/scant 1 cup seedless
raspberry jam

1 Preheat the oven to 350°F/Gas 4. Line three or four baking sheets with baking parchment. Put the peanut butter and unsalted butter in a large bowl and beat together until well combined and creamy.

2 Add the superfine and brown sugars and mix. Add the beaten egg and blend well. Sift in the flour and mix to a stiff dough.

3 Roll the dough into walnut-size balls between the palms of your hands. Place the balls on the prepared baking sheets and gently flatten each one with a fork to make a rough-textured cookie with a ridged surface. (Don't worry if the dough cracks slightly.)

4 Bake for 10–12 minutes, or until cooked but not browned. Using a metal spatula, transfer to a wire rack to cool.

5 Spoon jam onto one cookie and top with a second. Continue to sandwich the cookies in this way.

Old-fashioned Ginger Cookies

As these spicy cookies bake, the kitchen will be filled with a wonderfully tempting aroma. Children love them as a mid-morning snack with a glass of ice cold milk.

Makes 60

11 ounces/2½ cups all-purpose flour

1 teaspoon baking soda

1½ teaspoons ground ginger

¼ teaspoon ground cinnamon

¼ teaspoon ground cloves

4 ounces/½ cup butter or margarine at room temperature, diced

12 ounces/1¾ cups superfine sugar

1 egg

4 tablespoons black molasses

1 teaspoon fresh lemon juice

1 Preheat the oven to 325°F/Gas 3. Grease three baking sheets.

2 Sift the flour, baking soda and spices into a small bowl. Set aside.

3 Place the butter or margarine and two-thirds of the sugar in a bowl and cream together with an electric mixer until light and fluffy. Lightly beat the egg and stir it in.

4 Stir in the molasses and lemon juice. Add the flour mixture and mix in thoroughly with a wooden spoon to make a soft dough.

5 Shape the dough into ¾-inch balls. Roll the balls in the remaining sugar to coat and place them on the prepared baking sheets, spaced about 2 inches apart to allow for the dough spreading.

6 Bake for about 12 minutes, or until the cookies are just firm to the touch. With a spatula, transfer the cookies to a wire rack and leave to cool.

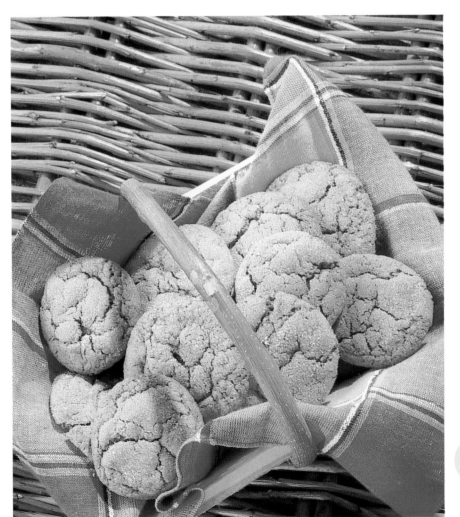

Cook's Tip

You'll need to cook trays of these cookies in batches. It is best not to put more than two trays in the oven at one time.

Raspberry Sandwich Cookies

Children will love these sweet, sticky treats, so chances are there will be none left to store. If you need to keep them, layer with waxed paper in an airtight container.

Makes 32

4 ounces/1 cup blanched almonds

6 ounces/1½ cups all-purpose flour

6 ounces/¾ cup butter

4 ounces/generous ½ cup superfine sugar

grated rind of 1 lemon

1 teaspoon vanilla extract

1 egg white

pinch of salt

1½ ounces/⅓ cup sliced almonds, chopped

12 ounces/1¼ cups raspberry jam

1 tablespoon lemon juice

1 Finely grind the almonds with 3 tablespoons of the flour.

2 Cream together the butter and sugar until light and fluffy. Stir in the lemon rind and vanilla. Add the ground almonds and remaining flour and mix to form a dough. Gather it into a ball, wrap in waxed paper and chill for 1 hour.

3 Preheat the oven to 325°F/ Gas 3. Line two baking sheets with waxed paper.

4 Divide the dough into four. Roll out on a lightly floured surface to ⅛ inch thick. With a floured 2½-inch cutter, stamp out round pieces, then stamp out the centers from half of them with a piping nozzle. Place equal numbers of rings and rounds ½ inch apart on the baking sheets.

5 Whisk the egg white with the salt until just frothy. Brush only the rings with the egg white, then sprinkle over the chopped almonds. Bake for 12–15 minutes, until lightly browned. Cool for 2–3 minutes on the sheets before transferring to a wire rack.

6 In a small, heavy pan, heat the jam with the lemon juice until it melts and comes to a simmer. Brush the jam over the round pieces and sandwich together with the rings.

Toffee Apple and Oat Crunchies

An unashamedly addictive mixture of chewy oats, soft apple and wonderfully crunchy toffee, this cookie won't win big prizes in the looks department but is top of the class for flavor.

Makes about 16

5 ounces/10 tablespoons sweet butter

6 ounces/scant 1 cup light brown sugar

3½ ounces/½ cup granulated sugar

1 extra large egg, beaten

3 ounces/⅔ cup all-purpose flour

½ teaspoon baking soda

pinch of salt

9 ounces/2½ cups rolled oats

2 ounces/scant ½ cup golden raisins

2 ounces dried apple rings, coarsely chopped

2 ounces chewy toffees, coarsely chopped

1 Preheat the oven to 350°F/Gas 4. Line two or three baking sheets with baking parchment. In a large bowl, beat together the butter and both sugars until creamy. Add the beaten egg and stir well until thoroughly combined.

2 Sift together the flour, baking soda and salt. Add to the butter, sugar and egg mixture, and mix in well. Finally, add the oats, raisins, chopped apple rings and toffee pieces, and stir gently until just combined.

3 Using a small ice-cream scoop or large tablespoon, place heaps of the mixture far apart on the prepared baking sheets. Bake for about 10–12 minutes, or until lightly set in the center and just beginning to brown at the edges.

4 Remove from the oven and leave to cool on the baking sheets for a few minutes. Using a metal spatula, transfer the cookies to a wire rack to cool completely.

Celebration Cookies

Food and festivals go together – from China to America and from January to December, you cannot have a celebration without cooking something special to eat. Of course, you don't have to wait for Diwali to enjoy Neuris, Hanukkah to feast on Rugelach or Easter to bake a batch of Simnel Cookies. Making any of the cookies in this chapter will turn an ordinary day into a special occasion and an international celebration.

Almond Orange Cookies

The combination of shortening and almonds gives these traditional cookies a lovely flaky texture, so that they melt in the mouth. Serve them whenever you have guests – they are perfect with coffee or hot chocolate.

Makes 36

9 ounces/generous 1 cup shortening

4½ ounces/generous ½ cup
   superfine sugar

2 eggs, beaten

grated rind and juice of 1 small orange

11 ounces/2¾ cups all-purpose
   flour, sifted with 1 teaspoon
   baking powder

7 ounces/1¾ cups ground almonds

For dusting

2 ounces/½ cup confectioners'
   sugar mixed with 1 teaspoon
   ground cinnamon

1 Preheat the oven to 400°F/Gas 6. Place the softened shortening in a large bowl and beat with an electric whisk until light and aerated. Gradually beat in the superfine sugar.

2 Whisk in the eggs, orange rind and juice. Whisk for 3–4 minutes more, then stir in the flour mixture and almonds to form a dough.

3 Roll out on a lightly floured surface to ½ inch thick. Stamp out 36 round pieces with a plain cutter. Lift the pieces onto baking sheets and bake for about 10 minutes, until golden. Leave on the baking sheets for 10 minutes to cool and firm slightly. Sift the confectioners' sugar mixture evenly over the cookies and leave to cool completely.

Mexican Wedding Cookies

Almost hidden beneath their veil of confectioners' sugar, these little shortbread cookies are traditionally served at weddings and are absolutely delicious. Serve them after dinner with coffee or, perhaps, a glass of the Mexican coffee liqueur – Kahlúa.

Makes 30

9 ounces/1 cup butter, softened

6 ounces/1½ cups confectioners'
   sugar

1 teaspoon natural vanilla extract

11 ounces/2¾ cups all-purpose
   flour

pinch of salt

5 ounces/1¼ cups pecan nuts,
   finely chopped

1 Preheat the oven to 375°C/ Gas 5. Beat the butter in a large bowl until it is light and fluffy, then beat in 4 ounces/1 cup of the confectioners' sugar, with the vanilla extract.

2 Gradually add the flour and salt to the creamed mixture, beating well after each addition, until it starts to form a dough. Add the finely chopped pecans with the remaining flour. Knead the dough lightly until combined.

3 Divide the dough into 30 equal pieces and roll them into balls. Space about ¼ inch apart on baking sheets. Press each ball lightly with your thumb, to flatten it slightly.

4 Bake for 10–15 minutes, until the cookies are starting to brown. Cool on the baking sheets for 10 minutes, then, using a metal spatula, transfer to wire racks to cool completely.

5 Put the remaining confectioners' sugar in a bowl. Add a few cookies at a time, shaking them gently until they are heavily coated. Serve immediately or store in an airtight container.

Cinnamon and Orange Tuiles

The tempting aroma of cinnamon and orange evokes a feeling of Christmas and, served with coffee, these chocolate-dipped tuiles are perfect for festive occasions.

Serves 15

2 egg whites

3½ ounces/½ cup superfine sugar

1½ teaspoons ground cinnamon

finely grated rind of 1 orange

2 ounces/½ cup all-purpose flour

3 ounces/6 tablespoons butter, melted

For the dipping chocolate

3 ounces continental semisweet
   chocolate

3 tablespoons milk

5–6 tablespoons heavy or
   whipping cream

1 Preheat the oven to 400°F/ Gas 6. Line two or three large baking sheets with non-stick baking parchment.

2 Whisk the egg whites until softly peaking, then whisk in the sugar until smooth and glossy. Add the cinnamon and the orange rind, sift over the flour and fold in with the melted butter. When well blended, add 1 tablespoon of recently boiled water to thin the mixture.

3 Place 4–5 teaspoons of the mixture on each tray, far apart. Flatten out and bake, one sheet at a time, for 7 minutes, until just golden. Cool for a few seconds then remove from the sheet with a metal spatula and immediately roll around the handle of a wooden spoon. Place on a rack to cool.

4 Melt the chocolate in the milk, then stir in the cream. Dip one or both ends of the cookies in the chocolate and leave to cool.

Lavender Heart Cookies

In folklore, lavender has always been linked with love, as has food, so make some heart-shaped cookies and serve them on Valentine's Day or any other romantic anniversary.

Makes about 18

4 ounces/½ cup sweet butter at room
   temperature, diced

2 ounces/¼ cup superfine sugar

6 ounces/1½ cups all-purpose
   flour

2 tablespoons fresh lavender florets or
   1 tablespoon dried culinary lavender,
   coarsely chopped

2 tablespoons superfine sugar,
   for sprinkling

1 Using an electric mixer, cream together the butter and superfine sugar until fluffy. Stir in the flour and lavender and bring the mixture together in a soft ball. Cover with plastic wrap and chill for about 15 minutes.

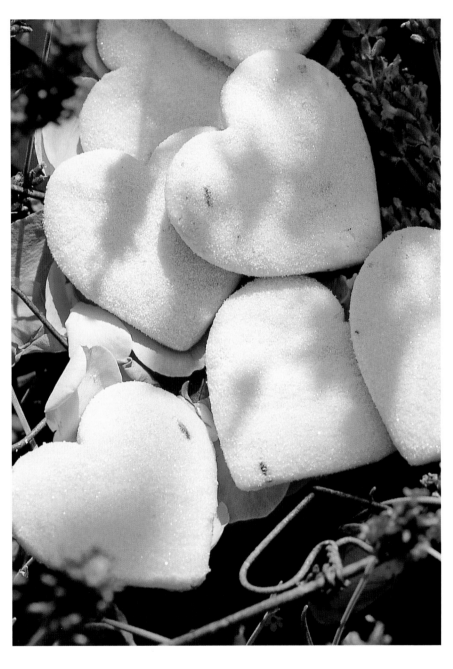

2 Preheat the oven to 400°F/Gas 6. Roll out the dough on a lightly floured surface and stamp out about 18 cookies, using a 2-inch heart-shaped cookie cutter. Place on a heavy baking sheet and bake for about 10 minutes, until golden.

3 Leave the cookies standing for 5 minutes to set. Using a metal spatula, transfer carefully from the baking sheet onto a wire rack to cool completely. The cookies can be stored in an airtight container for up to 1 week.

Cook's Tip
If you are using fresh lavender, make sure that it has not been sprayed with any chemicals or subjected to traffic pollution.

Double Gingerbread Cookies

Packed in little bags, these festive two-tone cookies would make a lovely Christmas gift. They are easy to make, but will have everyone wondering how you did it.

Makes 25

For the golden gingerbread

6 ounces/1½ cups all-purpose
    flour
¼ teaspoon baking soda
pinch of salt
1 teaspoon ground cinnamon
2½ ounces/5 tablespoons sweet butter,
    cut into pieces
3 ounces/scant ½ cup superfine
    sugar
2 tablespoons maple syrup
1 egg yolk, beaten

For the chocolate gingerbread

6 ounces/1½ cups all-purpose
    flour
pinch of salt
2 teaspoons apple pie spice
½ teaspoon baking soda
1 ounce/¼ cup cocoa powder
    (unsweetened)
3 ounces/⅓ cup sweet
    butter, chopped
3 ounces/⅓ cup light brown sugar
1 egg, beaten

1 To make the golden gingerbread mixture, sift together the flour, baking soda, salt and cinnamon into a large bowl. Rub the butter into the flour mixture with your fingertips until the mixture resembles fine breadcrumbs. Add the sugar, syrup and egg yolk and mix to a firm dough. Knead lightly. Put in plastic wrap and chill in the refrigerator for 30 minutes before shaping.

2 To make the chocolate gingerbread mixture, sift together the flour, salt, spice, baking soda and cocoa powder. Knead the butter into the flour in a large bowl. Add the sugar and egg and mix to a firm dough. Knead lightly. Put in plastic wrap and chill for 30 minutes.

3 Roll out half of the chocolate dough on a floured surface to an 11 x 1½ inch rectangle, ½ inch thick. Repeat with half of the golden gingerbread dough. Using a knife, cut both lengths into seven long, thin strips. Lay the strips together, side by side, alternating the chocolate and golden dough.

4 Roll out the remaining golden gingerbread dough with your hands to a long sausage, ¾ of an inch wide and the length of the strips. Lay the sausage of dough down the center of the striped dough.

Cook's Tip
As the shaping and combining of the two gingerbread doughs is crucial to the success of these cookies, and because you will have to handle them frequently, it is important to chill the doughs thoroughly before you start shaping.

5 Carefully bring the striped dough up around the sausage and press it gently in position, to enclose the sausage completely.

6 Roll the remaining chocolate dough to an 11 x 5 inch rectangle. Bring the chocolate dough up around the striped dough, to enclose it. Press gently into place. Wrap and chill for 30 minutes.

7 Preheat the oven to 350°F/Gas 4. Grease a large baking sheet. Cut the gingerbread roll into thin slices and place them, slightly apart, on the prepared baking sheet.

8 Bake for about 12–15 minutes, until just beginning to color around the edges. Leave on the baking sheet for 3 minutes, then transfer to a wire rack to cool completely.

Simnel Cookies

Enjoy these mini variations on the sweet, marzipan-covered simnel cake that is traditionally eaten at Easter and, originally, on Mothering Sunday in Britain. Children will enjoy decorating them.

Makes about 18

6 ounces/¾ cup sweet butter, at room
   temperature, diced
4 ounces/generous ½ cup superfine
   sugar
finely grated rind of 1 lemon
2 egg yolks
8 ounces/2 cups all-purpose flour
2 ounces/¼ cup currants

For the topping

4 ounces/¾ cup marzipan
7 ounces/1¾ cups confectioners'
   sugar, sifted
2–3 shades of food coloring
mini sugar-coated chocolate Easter eggs

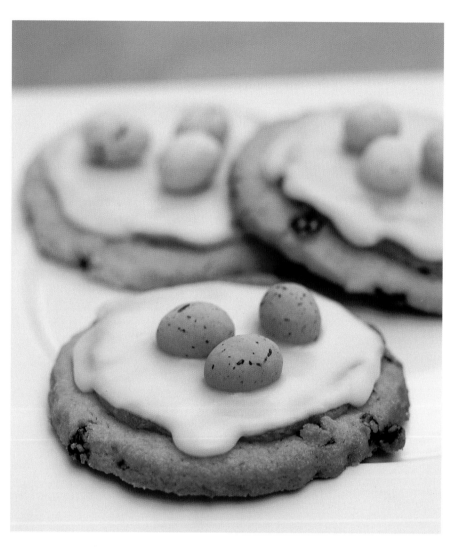

1 Preheat the oven to 350°F/Gas 4. Put the butter, sugar and lemon rind in a bowl and cream with a wooden spoon or electric mixer until light and fluffy. Beat in the egg yolks, then stir in the flour and currants and mix to a firm dough. If it is a little soft, chill in the refrigerator until firm.

2 Roll the dough out on a sheet of baking parchment to just under a ¼-inch thickness. Using a 3½-inch fluted cutter, stamp out round pieces and place, spaced slightly apart, on two non-stick baking sheets.

3 To make the topping, roll out the marzipan to just under a ¼-inch thickness and use a 2½-inch plain or fluted cutter to stamp out the same number of round pieces as there are cookies. Place a marzipan round on top of each cookie and press down very gently to fix the marzipan to the cookie dough.

4 Bake the cookies for about 12 minutes, or until just golden. Remove from the oven and leave to cool on the baking sheets.

5 Put the confectioners' sugar in a bowl and add just enough water to mix to a smooth, soft, spreadable consistency. Divide the icing among two or three bowls and add a few drops of different food coloring to each one. Stir until evenly mixed.

6 Divide the cooled cookies into three batches and spread each batch with icing of a different color. While the icing is still wet, gently press a few sugar-coated eggs on top of each cookie and leave to set.

Sweet Hearts

These cookies are for Valentine's Day or an anniversary, but you could use different-shaped cutters in the same way to make cookies for other occasions – stars and bells for Christmas, perhaps, or fluted "flowers" for a special birthday or Mother's Day present.

Makes 12–14

2 ounces/¼ cup sweet butter, softened

3 ounces/scant ½ cup superfine sugar

1 egg yolk

5 ounces/1¼ cups all-purpose flour

1 ounce bittersweet chocolate, melted and cooled

1–2 ounces bittersweet chocolate, to decorate

1 Preheat the oven to 350°F/Gas 4. Line two baking sheets with baking parchment. Put the butter, sugar and egg yolk in a mixing bowl and beat well. Stir in the flour and then knead until smooth.

2 Divide the dough in half, then knead the melted chocolate into one half until it is evenly colored.

3 Roll out the chocolate dough between two sheets of baking parchment, to a thickness of about ⅛ inch. Then roll out the plain dough in the same way.

4 Cut out hearts from both doughs using a 3-inch cookie cutter. Place the hearts on the prepared baking sheets.

5 Using a smaller heart-shaped cutter, stamp out the centers from all the hearts. Place a light-colored heart in the center of a larger chocolate heart and vice versa.

6 Bake the cookies for about 10 minutes, or until just beginning to turn brown. Remove from the oven and leave to cool.

7 To decorate, melt the chocolate in a microwave or in a heatproof bowl set over a pan of hot water. Put into a disposable pastry bag. Leave the chocolate to cool slightly.

8 Snip the end off the pastry bag and carefully pipe dots directly onto the outer part of the large chocolate hearts (with the plain centers). Then pipe zigzags on the pale part of the large plain hearts (with the chocolate centers). Put the cookies aside in a cool place and leave until they are set.

Variation

For a tasty variation, make chocolate and orange hearts by kneading 2 teaspoons very finely grated orange rind into the plain dough.

Rugelach

Jewish cookies, traditionally served during the eight-day festival of Hanukkah, these little crescents have a spicy fruit-and-nut filling. They can, of course, be enjoyed at any time of the year.

3 Divide the dough into four. Take one piece and leave the rest in the refrigerator, as it is important to keep the dough as cold as possible, because it is very sticky and therefore difficult to roll out. Sprinkle a sheet of baking parchment with flour and quickly roll out the dough to a round shape as thin as possible. Cut into six wedges; sprinkle with a quarter of the filling.

4 Starting at the wide end, roll each triangle up toward the point. Curve each roll into a crescent and place, the pointed side down, on the prepared baking sheets. Repeat with the remaining dough and filling.

5 Brush with beaten egg and bake for about 15–20 minutes, or until golden brown. Transfer to a wire rack and leave to cool.

Makes about 24
4 ounces/½ cup sweet butter, chilled
   and diced
4 ounces/½ cup cream cheese
4 fluid ounces/½ cup sour cream
9 ounces/2¼ cups all-purpose flour
beaten egg, to glaze

For the filling
2 ounces/¼ cup superfine sugar
2 teaspoons ground cinnamon
4 tablespoons raisins, chopped
4 tablespoons ready-to-eat dried
   apricots, chopped
3 ounces/¾ cup walnuts,
   finely chopped

1 To make the dough, put the butter, cream cheese and sour cream into a food processor and process until just creamy and combined. Add the flour and process briefly, using the pulse button, until the mixture just comes together, taking care not to overmix. Remove, put in plastic wrap and chill for at least 6 hours.

2 Preheat the oven to 350°F/ Gas 4. Line two large baking sheets with baking parchment. To make the filling, put all the filling ingredients in a bowl and mix until thoroughly combined.

Oznei Haman

These little cookies, shaped like tricorns – three-cornered hats – are eaten at the Jewish feast called Purim, which celebrates the Jews' deliverance from the scheming Haman.

Makes about 20

4 ounces/½ cup sweet butter, at room
   temperature, diced
4 ounces/generous ½ cup superfine
   sugar
½ teaspoon vanilla extract
3 egg yolks
9 ounces/2¼ cups all-purpose flour
beaten egg to seal and glaze

For the filling

1½ ounces/3 tablespoons poppy seeds
1 tablespoon clear honey
1 ounce/2 tablespoons superfine sugar
finely grated rind of 1 lemon
1 tablespoon lemon juice
1½ ounces/⅓ cup ground almonds
1 medium egg, beaten
1 ounce/scant ¼ cup raisins

1 Beat the butter with the sugar until light and creamy. Beat in the vanilla and egg yolks. Sift over the flour, stir in, then work into a dough with your hands. Knead until smooth. Put in plastic wrap and chill.

2 For the filling, put the poppy seeds, honey, sugar, lemon rind and juice into a pan with 4 tablespoons water and bring to the boil, stirring. Remove from the heat and beat in the almonds, egg and raisins. Cool.

3 Preheat the oven to 350°F/Gas 4. Line two large baking sheets with baking parchment. Roll out the dough on a lightly floured surface to a ⅛-inch thickness. Using a plain round 3-inch cutter, stamp out rounds. Place a heaped teaspoon of filling on each round. Brush the edges with beaten egg, then bring the sides to the center to form a tricorne shape. Seal the edges well together and place on the prepared baking sheets, spaced slightly apart.

4 Brush with beaten egg and bake for 20–30 minutes, or until golden brown. Transfer to a wire rack and leave to cool.

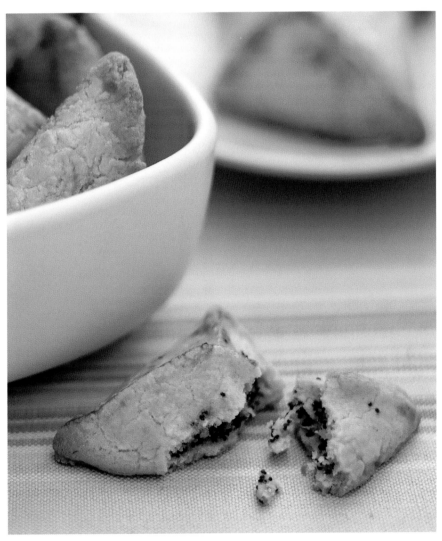

Hamantashen

These triangular-shaped pastries are eaten at Purim, the Jewish festival celebrating the story of Esther, Mordecai and Haman. Their shape represents the hat of Haman, whose plot to exterminate all the Jews of Persia was foiled. They can be made with a cookie or yeast dough.

Makes about 24

4 ounces/½ cup sweet butter,
    at room temperature

9 ounces/generous 1 cup sugar

2 tablespoons milk

1 egg, beaten

1 teaspoon vanilla or almond extract

pinch of salt

7–9 ounces/1½–2¼ cups all-purpose flour

confectioners' sugar, for dusting
    (optional)

For the apricot filling

9 ounces/generous 1 cup dried apricots

1 cinnamon stick

3 tablespoons sugar

For the poppy seed filling

4½ ounces/1 cup poppy seeds,
    coarsely ground

4 fluid ounces/½ cup milk

3 ounces/½ cup golden raisins,
    coarsely chopped

3–4 tablespoons sugar

2 tablespoons light corn syrup

1–2 teaspoons grated lemon rind

1 teaspoon vanilla extract

For the prune filling

9 ounces/generous 1 cup pitted
    ready-to-eat prunes

hot, freshly brewed tea or water, to cover

4 tablespoons plum jam

Cook's Tip

Every Jewish family has its own favorite filling for this hefty little pastry-cake. Their size can also vary, from small and dainty to the size of a hand.

1 Cream the butter and sugar in a large bowl until pale and fluffy. Mix together the milk, egg, vanilla or almond extract and salt in another bowl. Sift the flour into a third bowl.

2 Beat the butter mixture with one-third of the flour. Gradually add the remaining flour, alternating with the milk mixture. If the dough is too stiff, add a little extra milk. Cover and chill for 1 hour.

3 To make the apricot filling, put the apricots, cinnamon and sugar in a pan and add enough water to cover. Simmer for 15 minutes or until the apricots are tender and most of the liquid has evaporated. Remove the cinnamon stick, then puree the fruit in a food processor or blender with a little of the cooking liquid to the consistency of thick jam.

4 To make the poppy seed filling, put all the ingredients, except the vanilla, in a pan and simmer for 5–10 minutes, until the mixture has thickened and most of the milk has been absorbed. Stir in the vanilla.

5 To make the prune filling, put the prunes in a bowl and add enough hot tea or water to cover. Cover and set aside for 30 minutes, or until the prunes have absorbed the liquid. Drain, then puree in a food processor or blender with the jam.

6 Preheat the oven to 350°F/Gas 4. Roll out the dough on a lightly floured surface to ⅛–¼ inch thick. Stamp out 3-inch round pieces with a plain cutter.

7 Place 1–2 tablespoons of filling in the center of each round piece, then pinch the pastry together to form three corners, leaving a little of the filling showing in the middle.

8 Place the pastries on a baking sheet and bake for 15 minutes, or until pale golden. Serve the pastries warm or cold, dusted with confectioners' sugar, if you like.

Coconut Pyramids

These delightful, moist and chewy coconut cookies are sold in Israeli street markets during Passover, but are also popular in many other countries, too.

Makes 15

8 ounces/1 cup dried unsweetened
   shredded coconut
4 ounces/generous ½ cup superfine sugar
2 egg whites

I Preheat the oven to 375°F/Gas 5. Grease a large baking sheet with a little oil.

2 Mix together the dried coconut and sugar. Lightly whisk the egg whites. Fold enough egg white into the coconut to make a fairly firm mixture. You may not need quite all the egg whites.

3 Form the mixture into pyramids by taking a teaspoonful and rolling it first into a ball. Flatten the base and press the top into a point. Arrange the pyramids on the baking sheet.

4 Bake for 12–15 minutes on a low shelf. The tips should begin to turn golden, and the pyramids should be just firm, but still soft inside.

5 Slide a metal spatula underneath to loosen them. Leave to cool, then transfer to a wire rack.

Easter Cookies

These are enjoyed as a traditional part of the Christian festival of Easter. Traditionally, butter could not be eaten during the Lenten fast, so these cookies were a welcome treat.

Makes 16–18

4 ounces/½ cup butter at room
   temperature, diced
3 ounces/scant ½ cup superfine
   sugar, plus extra for sprinkling
1 egg, separated
7 ounces/1¾ cups all-purpose
   flour
½ teaspoon apple pie spice
½ teaspoon ground cinnamon
2 ounces/¼ cup currants
1 tablespoon chopped
   candied peel
1–2 tablespoons milk

1 Preheat the oven to 400°F/Gas 6. Lightly grease two baking sheets. Beat together the butter and sugar in a bowl until light and fluffy, then beat in the egg yolk.

2 Sift together the flour, mixed spice and cinnamon over the creamed mixture, then, using a metal spoon, gently fold in with the currants and peel, adding sufficient milk to mix to a fairly soft dough.

3 Turn out the dough onto a floured surface, knead lightly until just smooth, then roll out using a floured rolling pin, to about ¼ inch thick. Stamp the dough into round pieces using a 2-inch fluted cutter. Carefully transfer the round pieces to the prepared baking sheets and bake for 10 minutes.

Cook's Tip
Cinnamon is one of the exceptions to the rule that you should, if possible, buy spices whole and grind them freshly when you need them. Although cinnamon sticks are widely available, they are difficult – almost impossible – to grind yourself.

4 Beat the egg white, then brush over the cookies. Sprinkle with superfine sugar and return to the oven for a further 10 minutes, or until golden. Using a metal spatula, transfer to a wire rack to cool.

Kourabiedes

Lightly spiced and delicately flavored with orange-flower water and almonds, these crisp little crescents are perfect for parties and festive occasions such as christenings and weddings.

Makes about 20

4 ounces/½ cup sweet butter,
  softened
pinch of ground nutmeg
2 teaspoons orange flower water
2 ounces/½ cup confectioners' sugar,
  plus extra for dusting
3½ ounces/¾ cup all-purpose flour
4 ounces/1 cup ground almonds
1 ounce/¼ cup whole almonds, toasted
  and chopped

1 Preheat the oven to 325°F/ Gas 3. Line two large baking sheets with baking parchment. Beat the butter in a large bowl until soft and creamy.

2 Beat in the nutmeg and orange flower water. Add the confectioners' sugar and beat until fluffy.

3 Add the flour, ground and chopped almonds and mix well, then use your hands to bring the mixture together to form a dough, being careful not to overwork it.

4 Shape pieces of dough into sausages about 3 inches long. Curve each one into a crescent shape and place, spaced far apart, on the prepared baking sheets. Bake for about 15 minutes, or until firm but still pale in color. Cool for about 5 minutes, then dust with a little confectioners' sugar.

Spicy Hearts and Stars

These soft, sweet cookies have a wonderfully chewy texture and a deliciously warm, fragrant flavor. Serve with coffee at the end of a festive meal, or make them as a gift on a special occasion.

Makes about 25

4 ounces/½ cup sweet butter, softened

4 ounces/generous ½ cup light
   brown sugar

1 egg

2 ounces/1½ tablespoons light corn syrup

2 ounces/1½ tablespoons black molasses

14 ounces/3½ cups self-rising flour

2 teaspoons ground ginger

For the toppings

7 ounces semisweet or milk chocolate

5 ounces/1¼ cups confectioners'
   sugar, sifted

1 Beat together the butter and sugar until creamy. Beat the egg, syrup and molasses together. Sift in the flour and ginger and mix to form a firm dough. Chill for 20 minutes. Meanwhile, preheat the oven to 350°F/Gas 4 and line two large baking sheets with a layer of baking parchment.

2 Roll out the dough on a lightly floured surface to just under ½ inch thick and use cookie cutters to stamp out heart and star shapes. Place, spaced slightly apart, on the prepared baking sheets and bake for about 10 minutes, or until risen. Cool on a wire rack.

3 To make the toppings, melt the chocolate in a microwave or in a heatproof bowl set over a pan of barely simmering water. Use the melted chocolate to coat the heart-shaped cookies. Put the confectioners' sugar into a bowl and mix with enough warm water to make a coating consistency, then use this to glaze the star-shaped cookies.

Italian Pastry Twists

Deep-fried pastry twists, hearts or knots, traditionally flavored with vin santo, a sherry-like Italian wine, are served hot, dusted with confectioners' sugar, at Italian carnival time.

Makes 40

9 ounces/2¼ cups all-purpose flour

1 egg

pinch of salt

1 ounce/2 tablespoons granulated sugar

½ teaspoon vanilla extract

1 ounce/2 tablespoons butter, melted

3–4 tablespoons sherry

oil, for deep-frying

confectioners' sugar, for dusting

1 Sift the flour into a large mixing bowl and make a well in the center. Add the egg, salt, sugar, vanilla extract and melted butter.

2 Mix with your hands until the mixture starts to come together. When the dough becomes stiff, add enough sherry to make the dough soft and pliable. Knead until smooth and then put in plastic wrap and chill for about 1 hour.

3 Roll out the pastry thinly on a lightly floured surface and cut into 40 strips, each about 7 x ½ inches. Tie each strip loosely into a knot.

4 Heat the oil in a pan to 375°F and deep-fry the knots, in batches, for 2–3 minutes, until puffed up and golden.

5 Drain the pastry twists on kitchen paper, dust generously with confectioners' sugar and serve either hot or cold.

Variation

If you prefer the flavor, you could use Marsala instead of sherry.

Cook's Tip

Fry the cookies in flavorless oil, such as vegetable or sunflower.

Apricot Meringue Bars

Whenever you serve them, these unusual meringue-topped cookies make any occasion special. They would be lovely served, Mediterranean style, with a glass of chilled white wine.

Makes 16

2 ounces/½ cup all-purpose flour

2 ounces/¼ cup butter, softened

½ teaspoon vanilla extract

large pinch of salt

1 extra large egg, separated

4 ounces/generous ½ cup superfine sugar

2 ounces/½ cup chopped walnuts

2 ounces/½ cup chopped pecan nuts

4 ounces/⅓ cup apricot jam

1 Preheat the oven to 350°F/Gas 4. Grease a 9-inch square baking pan. Beat together the flour, butter, vanilla extract, salt, egg yolk and 2 ounces/¼ cup of the sugar. Spread the mixture in the base of the baking pan, prick it all over with a fork and bake for 10 minutes.

2 Beat the egg white until stiff. Gradually beat in the remaining sugar until the mixture is smooth and glossy. Gently fold in the chopped walnuts and pecan nuts, but do not over-mix.

3 Remove the pan from the oven, spread the apricot jam over the base and spread the meringue mixture to cover it evenly.

4 Return to the oven and bake for 20 minutes, until the meringue is crisp and light brown. Cool on a wire rack, then cut into bars.

Cook's Tip
Apricot Meringue Bars may be stored in an airtight container for up to 3 days.

Moravian Tarts

These birthday cookies are irresistible when freshly baked, so don't be surprised if there aren't any left over. They need to be thoroughly chilled, so make the dough the day before you need them.

Makes 35

4 ounces/½ cup sweet butter

½ teaspoon vanilla extract

large pinch of salt

5 ounces/¾ cup superfine sugar

1 egg, beaten

4 ounces/1 cup all-purpose flour

¼ teaspoon baking soda

1½ teaspoons ground cinnamon

1 egg white, lightly beaten

35 pecan nut halves

1 Cream the butter, vanilla extract, salt and 4 ounces/½ cup of the sugar until light and fluffy. Gradually add the egg, beating constantly.

2 Sift the flour, baking soda and ½ teaspoon of the cinnamon into another bowl, and stir a little at a time into the creamed mixture. Form the mixture into a dough, put in plastic wrap and chill overnight. Remove from the refrigerator 30 minutes before using.

3 Preheat the oven to 350°F/Gas 4. Lightly grease a baking sheet. Roll out the dough until it is about ⅛ inch thick. Stamp out round pieces with a 2-inch cutter.

4 Place the round pieces on the prepared baking sheet and brush the tops with the egg white. Mix the remaining ground cinnamon with the remaining superfine sugar. Sprinkle over the rounds and press a pecan nut half into each center. Bake for 8–10 minutes until golden brown.

Mexican Aniseed Biscochitos

It is time to revive the tradition of baking cookies flavored with aniseed, as they are absolutely delicious. There are versions of this recipe served at fiestas in many other countries as well.

Makes 24

6 ounces/1½ cups all-purpose
   flour
1 teaspoon baking powder
pinch of salt
4 ounces/½ cup sweet butter at room
   temperature, diced
4 ounces/½ cup superfine sugar
1 egg
1 teaspoon whole aniseed
1 tablespoon brandy
2 ounces/¼ cup superfine sugar mixed
   with ½ teaspoon ground cinnamon,
   for sprinkling

1 Sift together the flour, baking powder and salt. Set aside.

2 Beat the butter with the sugar until soft and fluffy. Add the egg, aniseed and brandy and beat until incorporated. Fold in the dry ingredients until just blended to a dough. Chill for 30 minutes.

3 Preheat the oven to 350°F/ Gas 4. Lightly grease two baking sheets.

4 On a lightly floured surface, roll out the chilled dough to about ⅛ inch thick.

5 With a lightly floured cutter, pastry wheel or knife, stamp out or cut out the dough into squares, diamonds, stars or other shapes. The traditional shape for biscochitos is a fleur-de-lis, but you might find this a little too ambitious.

6 Place the cookies on the prepared baking sheets, spaced apart, and sprinkle lightly with the cinnamon sugar.

7 Bake for about 10 minutes, or until just barely golden. Cool on the baking sheet for 5 minutes, before transferring to a wire rack, with a metal spatula, and leave to cool completely. The cookies can be stored in an airtight container for up to 1 week.

Fourth of July Blueberry Softbakes

These are simply wonderful when eaten still warm from the oven. However, they are also good if left to cool and then packed for a traditional Independence Day picnic.

Makes 10

5 ounces/1¼ cups all-purpose flour

1½ teaspoons baking powder

1 teaspoon ground cinnamon

2 ounces/¼ cup sweet butter,
    at room temperature, diced

2 ounces/¼ cup raw sugar, plus extra
    for sprinkling

4 fluid ounces/½ cup sour cream

3½ ounces/1 cup fresh blueberries

2 ounces/½ cup semi-dried cranberries

Variation

For Halloween or Thanksgiving, substitute fresh cranberries for the blueberries and chopped preserved stem ginger for the semi-dried cranberries.

1 Preheat the oven to 375°F/ Gas 5. Line two baking sheets with baking parchment. Sift together the flour, baking powder and cinnamon into a large mixing bowl. Add the diced butter and rub in with your fingers until the mixture resembles fine breadcrumbs. Stir in the raw sugar.

2 Add the sour cream, blueberries and cranberries and stir until just combined. Spoon ten mounds of the mixture, spaced far apart, onto the prepared baking sheets. Sprinkle with the extra raw sugar and bake for about 20 minutes, or until golden and firm in the center. Serve warm.

Cinnamon Balls

These almond balls should be soft inside, with a strong cinnamon flavor. Great for parties, they also harden with keeping, so it is a good idea to freeze some and use them when required.

Makes 16

oil, for greasing

6 ounces/1½ cups ground almonds

3 ounces/scant ½ cup superfine sugar

1 tablespoon ground cinnamon

2 egg whites

confectioners' sugar, for dredging

1 Preheat the oven to 350°F/Gas 4. Oil a large baking sheet. Mix together the ground almonds, sugar and cinnamon. Whisk the egg whites in a grease-free bowl until they begin to stiffen, and fold enough into the almonds and sugar to make a fairly firm mixture.

2 Dampen your hands and roll small spoonfuls of the mixture into balls. Place on the baking sheet and bake for about 15 minutes.

3 Slide a metal spatula under the balls to release them from the baking sheet and leave to cool.

4 Sift a few tablespoonfuls of confectioners' sugar onto a plate. When the cinnamon balls are completely cold, slide them onto the plate. Roll the cinnamon balls gently over the plate to cover completely in sugar. Store in an airtight container or in the freezer.

Baklava

This, the queen of all pastries, is enjoyed all year but is specially associated with the **Persian New Year on March 21st**, celebrating the first day of spring. Leave the baklava to cool in the pan.

Makes about 30

12 ounces/3 cups ground pistachio nuts

5 ounces/1¼ cups confectioners' sugar

1 tablespoon ground cardamom

5 ounces/⅔ cup sweet butter, melted

1 pound phyllo pastry

For the syrup

1 pound/2 cups granulated sugar

½ pint/1¼ cups water

2 tablespoons rose water

Variation

Baklava may also be made with sliced almonds, and drizzled with honey instead of syrup.

1 To make the syrup, place the sugar and water in a pan, bring them to the boil and simmer for 10 minutes, until syrupy. Stir in the rose water. Mix together the nuts, confectioners' sugar and cardamom. Preheat the oven to 325°F/Gas 3. Brush a baking pan with butter.

2 Taking one sheet of phyllo pastry at a time, and keeping the remainder covered with a damp cloth, brush with melted butter and lay in the base of the pan. Continue until you have six buttered layers in the pan. Spread half of the nut mixture over, pressing down with a spoon.

3 Take another six sheets of phyllo pastry, brush with butter and lay over the nut mixture. Sprinkle over the remaining nuts and top with a final layer of six phyllo sheets.

4 Cut the pastry into small lozenge shapes. Pour the remaining butter over the top. Bake for 20 minutes, increase the heat to 400°F/Gas 6 and bake for 15 minutes. Drizzle most of the syrup over the pastry, reserving the rest for serving.

Persian Rice Flour Cookies

These prettily decorated cookies are traditionally served on special occasions with black tea. However, they taste as good with coffee or even a glass of chilled dry white wine.

Makes about 22

*3 ounces/⅔ cup confectioners'
  sugar, sifted*

8 ounces/1 cup sweet butter, softened

10 ounces/2½ cups rice flour

3 ounces/⅔ cup self-rising flour

1 egg yolk

1 tablespoon rose water

For the topping

*5 ounces/1¼ cups confectioners'
  sugar, sifted*

rose water

pink food coloring

*crystallized rose petals or violets
  or pink sugar balls or
  sugar vermicelli*

1 Mix together the sugar, butter, flours, egg yolk and rose water and gather into a ball. Wrap and chill. Meanwhile, preheat the oven to 325°F/Gas 3. Line two baking sheets with baking parchment.

2 Shape the mixture into balls. Place far apart on the prepared baking sheets and flatten each one slightly.

3 Bake for 15–20 minutes, until firm but still quite pale in color. Leave to cool completely on the baking sheets.

4 To make the topping, put the confectioners' sugar into a bowl and add just enough rose water to mix to a thick, flowing consistency. Add just a light touch of pink food coloring to make a very pale shade.

5 Drizzle the icing in random squiggles and circles over all the cookies. Place a few crystallized rose petals or violets or pink sugar balls on top, or sprinkle with a little sugar vermicelli. Leave to set completely before serving the cookies.

Neuris

These melt-in-the-mouth sweet and spicy samosas are traditionally eaten during the Hindu festival of Diwali and are also given as little gifts to friends and family at this time.

Makes 12

3 ounces/1 cup dried unsweetened
   shredded coconut
2 ounces/¼ cup light brown sugar
1 ounce/¼ cup cashew nuts,
   chopped
2 ounces/⅓ cup seedless raisins
8 fluid ounces/1 cup unsweetened
   condensed milk
large pinch grated nutmeg
½ teaspoon ground cinnamon
12 sheets phyllo pastry, about
   11 x 7 inches each
sunflower oil, for brushing

For the topping

1 tablespoon unsweetened
   condensed milk
1 tablespoon superfine sugar
desiccated coconut

1 To make the filling, put the coconut, brown sugar, cashews, raisins and condensed milk into a small pan. Bring to the boil, stirring occasionally. Reduce the heat to very low and cook for about 10 minutes, stirring, until the milk has been absorbed. Stir in the nutmeg and cinnamon, then set aside to cool.

2 Preheat the oven to 350°F/ Gas 4. Line two baking sheets with baking parchment.

3 Brush one sheet of phyllo pastry with a little sunflower oil. Fold the sheet in half lengthwise, then brush with more oil and fold widthwise. Brush the edges of the folded pastry with water.

4 Place a spoonful of the cooled filling on one half of the folded pastry sheet. Fold the other half of the sheet over the filling, then press together the edges to seal. Trim off the rough edges and place on the baking sheet. Continue making neuris in this way until all the pastry and filling has been used up.

5 To make the topping, put the condensed milk and sugar into a small pan and heat gently, stirring constantly until the sugar has completely dissolved.

6 Brush the topping over the neuris and sprinkle them with the coconut. Bake for about 20 minutes, until crisp and golden brown. Transfer to a wire rack and leave to cool before serving.

Jeweled Elephants

These delightful, stunningly robed elephants make a lovely gift for young animal-lovers, or make a perfect edible decoration for a special occasion. If you make holes in them before baking, you could use them as original Christmas tree decorations.

Makes 10

1 quantity lebkuchen mixture (see
  Chocolate Fruit and Nut Cookies)
1 quantity icing glaze
red food coloring
8 ounces ready-to-roll sugar paste
a little royal icing
small candy-covered chocolates or chews
gold dragées

1 Preheat the oven to 350°F/Gas 4. Grease two large baking sheets.

2 Make a paper template for the elephant. Roll out the lebkuchen mixture. Use the template and a sharp knife to cut out elephant shapes. Space them, slightly apart, on the baking sheet, and bake for 3 minutes. Then transfer the elephants to a wire rack to cool.

3 Put a little icing glaze in a waxed paper pastry bag fitted with a fine nozzle. Alternatively, cut off the tip of the bag.

4 Knead some red food coloring into half of the sugar paste. Roll a little red sugar paste on a work surface, with your fingertips, to make ropes. Secure them around the feet and tips of the trunks, using icing from the bag. Shape more red sugar paste into flat oval shapes, about ¾ inch long, and stick them to the elephants' heads. Shape smaller ovals and secure them at the top of the trunks with icing glaze.

5 Roll out the white sugar paste. Stamp out round shapes, using a 2½-inch cookie cutter. Secure to the elephants' backs with royal icing so that the edge of the sugar paste is about 1 inch above the top of the legs. Trim off the excess paste around the top of the white sugar paste shapes.

6 Pipe ½-inch tassels around the edges of the flat ovals. Pipe dots of white icing at the tops of the elephants' trunks, around their necks and at the tops of their tails and also use it to draw small eyes. Halve the small candies and press them into the sugar paste, above the tassels. Decorate the headdress, sweets and white sugar paste with gold dragées, securing them with dots of icing. Leave for several hours to harden.

Variation

If you have the time and you want to make these charming cookies even more special, you could color the sugar paste for their decorations in a variety of brilliant, jewel-like colors, so that each one is different.

Cook's Tip

If you are artistic, you can draw the elephant template freehand. Otherwise, you could trace around a picture. If you cannot find a picture the right size, enlarge or reduce one on a photocopier and then trace around it.

Almond Cigars

These simple, Moroccan-inspired pastries can be prepared in minutes. They are perfect served with strong black coffee or as an after-dinner treat and are great with sweet Moroccan mint tea.

Makes 8–12
9 ounces/1⅔ cups marzipan
1 egg, lightly beaten
8–12 sheets phyllo pastry
melted butter, for brushing

1 Knead the marzipan until soft and pliable, then put it in a mixing bowl and mix in the lightly beaten egg. Cover and chill in the refrigerator for 1–2 hours.

2 Preheat the oven to 375°F/Gas 5. Lightly grease a baking sheet. Place a sheet of phyllo pastry on a piece of waxed paper, keeping the remaining pastry covered with a damp cloth. Brush the first sheet of phyllo with some of the melted butter.

3 Shape 2–3 tablespoons of the almond paste into a cylinder and place at one end of the pastry. Fold the pastry over to enclose the ends of the paste, then roll up to form a cigar shape. Place on the baking sheet and make 7–11 more cigars in the same way.

4 Bake the pastries for about 15 minutes, or until golden brown in color. Transfer to a wire rack to cool before serving.

Variation
Similar pastries are made throughout North Africa. In Tunisia, they are coated in syrup and sesame seeds after baking. To make the syrup, heat 5 ounces/⅔ cup sugar with ½ pint/1¼ cups water, stirring until dissolved. Add 1 tablespoon lemon juice, bring to the boil, and boil until syrupy. Remove from the heat and stir in 1 tablespoon orange-flower water. Soak the cigars in the hot syrup for 2–3 minutes, then sprinkle with sesame seeds. Cool before serving.

Honey and Nut Clusters

These are popular at all family celebrations in Italy. To serve, cut in squares or small bars and keep in the refrigerator. They are delightfully sticky and taste fabulous.

Makes 48

4 ounces/1 cup almonds

4 ounces/1 cup shelled hazelnuts

2 egg whites

4 ounces/½ cup clear honey

4 ounces/generous ½ cup superfine
 sugar

1 Preheat the oven to the lowest temperature. Line an 8-inch square pan with non-stick baking parchment.

2 Spread out the almonds and hazelnuts on separate baking sheets and toast in the oven for about 30 minutes. Tip onto a clean dishtowel and rub off the skins. Coarsely chop both types of nut.

3 Whisk the egg whites in a clean bowl until stiff, then gently stir in the chopped nuts.

4 Put the honey and sugar into a small, heavy pan and bring to the boil. Stir in the nut mixture and cook over a medium heat for 10 minutes.

5 Turn the mixture into the pan and level the top. Cover with another piece of baking parchment, put weights (such as food cans) on top and chill for at least 2 days.

Cook's Tip

If you like, you can use blanched almonds, so you don't have to rub off their skins. They will still taste more intense if toasted in the oven first.

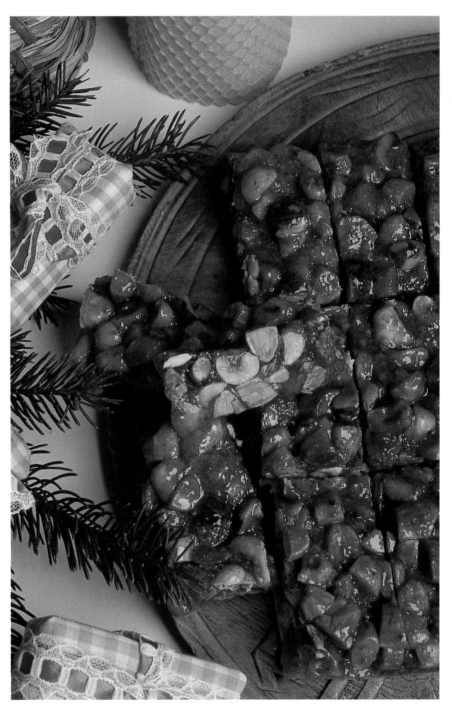

Christmas Tree Angels

Why not make these charming edible decorations to brighten your Yuletide? However, don't hang them on the tree until Christmas Eve, or they'll all be gone by Christmas Day.

Makes 20–30

3½ ounces/scant ½ cup raw
    sugar
7 ounces/scant1 cup light
    corn syrup
1 teaspoon ground ginger
1 teaspoon ground cinnamon
¼ teaspoon ground cloves
4 ounces/½ cup sweet butter,
    cut into pieces
2 teaspoons baking soda
1 egg, beaten
1¼ pounds/4½ cups all-purpose
    flour, sifted

For the decoration

1 egg white
6–8 ounces/1½–2 cups confectioners'
    sugar, sifted
silver and gold balls
fine ribbon

1 Preheat the oven to 325°F/Gas 3. Line two large baking sheets with baking parchment. Put the sugar, syrup, ginger, cinnamon and cloves into a heavy pan and bring to the boil over a low heat, stirring constantly. Once the mixture has boiled, remove the pan from the heat.

2 Put the pieces of butter in a large heatproof bowl and pour over the hot sugar and syrup mixture. Add the baking soda and stir well until the butter has completely melted. Beat the egg into the mixture, then stir in the flour. Mix thoroughly and then knead to form a smooth dough.

3 Divide the dough into four pieces and roll out, one at a time, between sheets of baking parchment, to a thickness of about ⅛ inch. Keep the unrolled dough in a plastic bag until needed, to prevent it from drying out. Stamp out festive shapes, such as Christmas trees, using cookie cutters, or make angels, as follows.

4 To make simple angels, stamp out round pieces of dough of any size you like, using a plain cutter. Don't make them too big, or they might be too heavy to hang on the Christmas tree. As shown in the photograph, cut off two segments from either side of the round pieces to give a body and two wings. Place the wings, rounded side facing down, behind the body, and press lightly together with your fingers.

5 Roll a small piece of dough for the head, place at the top of the body, and flatten with your fingers. Using a skewer, make a wide hole in the cookies through which ribbon can be threaded when they are cooked. Place on the baking sheets. Bake the cookies for 10–15 minutes, until golden brown. Transfer to a wire rack to cool.

6 To make the decoration, beat the egg white with a fork. Whisk in confectioners' sugar until you have an icing of soft-peak consistency.

7 Put the icing in a pastry bag fitted with a plain writing nozzle, and decorate the cookies with simple designs. Add silver and gold balls before the icing has set. Finally, thread fine ribbon through the holes in the cookies.

Brandy Snaps

Eat these on high days and holidays as an indulgent treat. They look incredibly tempting and are very easy to make, as long as you work quickly and in small batches.

Makes 18

2 ounces/¼ cup butter

5 ounces/⅔ cup superfine sugar

1½ tablespoons corn syrup

1½ ounces/⅓ cup all-purpose flour

½ teaspoon ground ginger

For the filling

8 fluid ounces/1 cup whipping cream

2 tablespoons brandy

1 With an electric mixer, cream together the butter and sugar until light and fluffy, then beat in the corn syrup. Sift over the flour and ginger and mix to a coarse dough.

2 Transfer the dough to a lightly floured work surface and knead until smooth. Cover with plastic wrap and chill in the refrigerator for 30 minutes. Preheat the oven to 375°F/Gas 5. Grease a baking sheet.

3 Working in batches of four, form walnut-size balls of dough. Place far apart on the prepared baking sheet and flatten slightly. Bake for about 10 minutes, until golden.

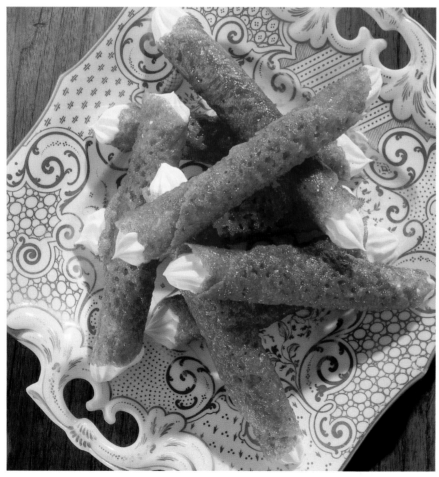

4 Remove from the oven and leave to cool for a few moments. Working quickly, slide a metal spatula under each cookie, turn over, and wrap around the handle of a wooden spoon. When firm, slide off the snaps and place on a wire rack to cool completely.

5 To make the filling, whip the cream and brandy together with a hand-held electric mixer until soft peaks form. Spoon the flavored cream into a pastry bag fitted with a star nozzle, and pipe into each end of the brandy snaps just before serving.

Glazed Ginger Cookies

These also make good hanging cookies for decorating trees and garlands. For this, make a hole in each one with a skewer and thread with fine ribbon.

Makes about 20

1 quantity golden gingerbread mixture
  (see *Double Gingerbread Cookies*)
2 quantities icing glaze
red and green food colorings
6 ounces white almond paste

1 Preheat the oven to 350°F/Gas 4. Grease a large baking sheet. Roll out the gingerbread dough on a floured surface and, using a selection of floured cutters, cut out a variety of shapes, such as trees, stars, crescents and bells. Transfer to the baking sheet and bake for 8–10 minutes, until just beginning to color around the edges. Leave the cookies on the baking sheet for 3 minutes.

2 Transfer the cookies to a wire rack and leave to cool completely. Place the wire rack over a large tray or plate. Using a teaspoon, spoon the icing glaze over the cookies until they are completely covered. Leave in a cool place to dry for several hours.

3 Knead red food coloring into half of the almond paste and green into the other half. Roll a thin length of each colored paste and then twist the two together into a rope.

4 Secure a rope of almond paste around a cookie, dampening the icing with a little water, if necessary, to hold it in place. Repeat on about half of the cookies. Dilute a little of each food coloring with water. Using a fine paintbrush, paint festive decorations over the plain cookies. Leave to dry completely and then wrap in tissue paper to give as a gift or store in an airtight container until required.

Decorated Chocolate Lebkuchen

Wrapped in paper or cellophane, or beautifully boxed, these decorated cookies make a lovely Christmas present. Don't make them too far in advance, as the chocolate will gradually discolor.

Makes 40

1 quantity lebkuchen mixture
  (see *Chocolate Fruit and Nut Cookies*)
4 ounces semisweet chocolate, chopped
4 ounces milk chocolate, chopped
4 ounces white chocolate, chopped
chocolate vermicelli, for sprinkling
cocoa powder (unsweetened) or
  confectioners' sugar, for dusting

Variation

Traditionally, lebkuchen contains other spices as well as ginger and cloves – star anise, cinnamon, nutmeg and black pepper, so you can add a pinch of each of these, to the basic mixture if you like. The molasses can also be replaced by clear honey.

1 Grease two baking sheets. Roll out just over half the lebkuchen mixture to ¼ inch thick. Stamp out 20 heart shapes with a 1¾-inch heart-shaped cutter. Transfer to one of the prepared baking sheets. Gather the trimmings together with the remaining dough and cut into 20 pieces. Roll into balls and place on the second baking sheet. Flatten each ball slightly with your fingers.

2 Chill both sheets for 30 minutes. Preheat the oven to 350°F/Gas 4. Bake for 8–10 minutes. Cool on a wire rack.

3 Melt the semisweet chocolate in a heatproof bowl set over a small pan of hot water. Melt the milk and white chocolate, in turn, in separate bowls over hot water.

4 Make three small paper pastry bags out of waxed paper. Spoon a little of each chocolate into the three paper piping bags.

5 Spoon a little semisweet chocolate over one-third of the cookies, spreading it to cover completely.

Cook's Tip

If the chocolate in the bowls starts to set before you have finished decorating, put the bowls back over the heat for about 1–2 minutes. If the chocolate in the pastry bags starts to harden, microwave briefly or put in a clean bowl over a pan of simmering water until soft.

6 Snip the merest tip from the bag of white chocolate and drizzle it over some of the coated cookies, to give a decorative zigzag finish.

7 Sprinkle the chocolate vermicelli over the semisweet chocolate-coated cookies that have not been decorated. Coat the remaining cookies with the melted milk and white chocolate and decorate some of these with more chocolate from the pastry bags, contrasting the colors. Sprinkle more undecorated cookies with vermicelli. Leave the cookies to set.

8 Transfer the undecorated cookies to a plate or tray and dust lightly with sifted cocoa powder or confectioners' sugar.

Christmas Cookies

You don't have to be a talented artist to produce these little edible masterpieces. They are amazingly easy to make and decorate. Use whatever shape of cutter you have at hand.

Makes 30

6 ounces/¾ cup sweet butter at room
*   temperature, diced*
11 ounces/generous 1½ cups
*   superfine sugar*
1 egg
1 egg yolk
1 teaspoon vanilla extract
grated rind of 1 lemon
pinch of salt
11 ounces/2⅔ cups all-purpose flour

For the decoration (optional)
colored candied icing and small candies
*   such as silver balls and colored*
*   sugar crystals*

1 Preheat the oven to 375°F/Gas 5. With an electric mixer, cream the butter until soft. Add the sugar gradually and continue beating until light and fluffy.

2 Gradually stir in the egg and egg yolk. Add the vanilla extract, lemon rind and salt. Stir to mix well.

3 Sift the flour over the mixture and stir to blend. Gather the dough into a ball, put in plastic wrap and chill for 30 minutes.

4 On a lightly-floured surface, roll out the dough until about ⅛ inch thick.

5 Stamp out shapes or round pieces with floured cutters and place on a non-stick baking sheet.

6 Bake for about 8 minutes, until lightly colored. Transfer to a wire rack and leave to cool completely before decorating, if you like, with icing and candies.

Jeweled Christmas Trees

These attractive and unusual cookies make an appealing gift. They look wonderful hung on a
Christmas tree or in front of a window where they will catch the light.

Makes 12

6 ounces/1½ cups all-purpose
  flour
3 ounces/6 tablespoons butter, diced
1½ ounces/3 tablespoons superfine
  sugar
1 egg white
2 tablespoons orange juice
8 ounces colored fruit candies
colored ribbons, to decorate

1 Preheat the oven to 350°F/Gas 4.
Line two baking sheets with non-
stick baking parchment. Sift the flour
into a mixing bowl.

2 Add the butter and rub it into
the flour with your fingertips
until the mixture resembles fine
breadcrumbs. Stir in the sugar, egg
white and enough orange juice to
form a soft dough. Knead on a
lightly floured surface until smooth.

3 Roll out thinly and stamp out as
many shapes as possible, using a
floured Christmas tree cutter.
Transfer the shapes to the baking
sheets, spacing them far apart.
Knead the trimmings together,
cover and set aside, or if there is
still room on the baking sheets,
stamp out more trees.

4 Using a ½-inch round cookie
cutter or the end of a large plain
pastry nozzle, stamp out and
remove six round pieces from each
tree shape. Cut each candy into
three and place a piece in each hole.
Make a small hole at the top of each
tree to thread through the ribbon.

5 Bake for 15–20 minutes, until the
cookies are golden and the candies
have melted and filled the holes.
Cool on the baking sheets. Repeat
until you have used up the rest of
the dough and candies. Thread short
lengths of ribbon through the holes
so that the cookies can be hung up.

Speculaas

These Dutch cookies are made from a spicy dough wrapped around a wonderfully rich marzipan filling. They are eaten in Holland around the Feast of St Nicholas, on December 6th.

Makes about 35

6 ounces/1½ cups ground hazelnuts

6 ounces/1½ cups ground almonds

6 ounces/scant 1 cup superfine sugar

6 ounces/1½ cups confectioners' sugar

1 egg, beaten

2–3 teaspoons lemon juice

9 ounces/2¼ cups self-rising flour

1 teaspoon apple pie spice

3 ounces/⅓ cup light brown sugar

4 ounces/½ cup sweet butter, at room
  temperature, diced

2 eggs

1 tablespoon milk

1 tablespoon superfine sugar

about 35 blanched almond halves

1 For the filling, put the ground hazelnuts, almonds, superfine sugar, confectioners' sugar, beaten egg and 2 teaspoons lemon juice in a bowl and mix to a firm paste, adding more lemon juice if needed. Divide the mixture in half and roll each piece into a sausage shape about 10 inches long. Put in plastic wrap and chill in the refrigerator.

2 To make the dough, sift the flour and apple pie spice into a large mixing bowl then stir in the brown sugar. Add the butter and rub in well with your fingertips.

3 Beat one of the eggs, add to the mixture and mix together to form a dough. Knead lightly, then put in plastic wrap and chill in the refrigerator for 15 minutes. Meanwhile, preheat the oven to 350°F/Gas 4 and line a large baking sheet with baking parchment.

4 Roll out the pastry on a lightly floured surface to a 12-inch square and cut in half to make two equal rectangles. Beat the remaining egg and brush some all over the pastry rectangles.

5 Place a roll of filling on each piece of pastry and roll the pastry to enclose the filling. Place, join side down, on the baking sheet.

6 Beat the remains of the egg with the milk and superfine sugar and brush over the rolls. Press almond halves along the top. Bake for 35 minutes, until golden brown. Leave to cool before cutting diagonally into slices.

Chinese Fortune Cookies

Whether you're a rabbit or a dragon, a snake or a tiger, these charming cookies are sure to delight and are a wonderful way to celebrate the Chinese New Year with family and friends.

Makes about 35

2 egg whites

2 ounces/½ cup confectioners' sugar, sifted, plus extra for dusting

1 teaspoon almond or vanilla extract

1 ounce/2 tablespoons sweet butter, melted

2 ounces/½ cup all-purpose flour

1 ounce/⅓ cup dried unsweetened shredded coconut, lightly toasted

tiny strips of paper with "good luck", "health, wealth and happiness" and other appropriate messages typed or written on them, to decorate

1 Preheat the oven to 375°F/Gas 5. Prepare two or three sheets of baking parchment (they can be used more than once) by cutting them to the size of a baking sheet. Draw two or three circles of about a 3-inch diameter, with a little distance between them, on each sheet of parchment. Place one of these sheets of parchment on the baking sheet and set aside.

2 Put the egg whites into a clean, grease-free bowl and whisk until foamy and white. Whisk in the confectioners' sugar, a little at a time. Beat in the almond or vanilla extract and the butter. Stir in the flour and mix lightly until smooth.

Cook's Tip

You need to work quickly to shape the cookies. Placing the hot cookies on the rim of wine glasses sets them with a curve in the center.

3 Place a teaspoonful of mixture into the center of each marked circle on the prepared parchment and spread out evenly to fit the circle. Sprinkle with a little coconut. Bake one sheet at a time (as you will only have enough time to shape one sheetful of cookies before they set) for about 5 minutes, or until very lightly brown on the edges.

4 Remove the cookies from the oven, immediately loosely fold in half and place on the rim of a glass. Leave until firm, then transfer to a wire rack. Continue baking one sheet of cookies at a time.

5 Tuck the messages into the side of each cookie. Dust very lightly with confectioners' sugar before serving.

Kids' Party Pieces

There's nothing quite like an extra-special cookie to make a kids' party go with a swing. This chapter is packed with fun ideas that kids will love, including cookie bracelets to slip around the wrist, novelty cookies that look like mini pizzas and a giant birthday cookie studded with candles to take the place of the more traditional birthday cake.

Gingerbread Jungle

These snappy biscuits in animal shapes are always popular at birthday parties and on picnics. Children will love helping to make and ice them.

Makes 14

6 ounces/1½ cups self-rising
   flour
½ teaspoon baking soda
½ teaspoon ground cinnamon
2 teaspoons superfine sugar
2 ounces/¼ cup butter
3 tablespoons light corn syrup
2 ounces/½ cup confectioners'
   sugar
1–2 teaspoons water

1 Preheat the oven to 375°F/ Gas 5. Lightly oil two large baking sheets.

2 Put the flour, baking soda, cinnamon and superfine sugar in a bowl and mix together.

3 Place the butter and syrup in a pan and melt over a low heat, stirring occasionally. Pour over the dry ingredients.

4 Mix together well with a wooden spoon and then use your hands to pull the mixture together to make a smooth dough.

5 Turn the mixture out onto a lightly floured surface and roll out to about ¼ inch thick.

6 Use lightly-floured animal cutters to stamp out shapes from the cookie dough. Arrange them on the prepared baking sheets, leaving enough room between the cookies to allow space for them to rise.

7 Press the trimmings back into a ball, roll it out again and stamp out more animal shapes. Continue until all the dough has been used. Bake the cookies for 8–12 minutes, until lightly browned.

8 Leave on the baking sheets to cool slightly, before carefully transferring with a metal spatula to a wire rack to cool completely.

9 Sift the confectioners' sugar into a small bowl and add enough water to make a fairly soft icing, stirring well to mix smoothly.

10 Spoon the icing into a pastry bag fitted with a small, plain nozzle and pipe decorations on the cookies. Leave to set before serving.

Cook's Tip
You don't have to be especially artistic to decorate the cookies. It is simple to pipe a letter of the alphabet, for example, which could be either the initial of each child's name or that of the type of animal – L for lion, E for elephant and so on. If you like, mix a little liquid edible food coloring with the icing.

Variation
Any cutters can be used with the same mixture. Obviously, the smaller the cutters, the more cookies you will make.

Gingerbread Teddies

These endearing teddies, dressed in striped pyjamas, would make a perfect gift for friends of any age. If you can't get a large cutter, make smaller teddies or use a traditional gingerbread-man cutter. Children love to help make them, but might need a hand with the decorating.

Makes 6

3 ounces white chocolate, chopped

6 ounces ready-to-roll white
    sugar paste

blue food coloring

1 ounce semisweet or
    milk chocolate

For the gingerbread

6 ounces/1½ cups all-purpose
    flour

¼ teaspoon baking soda

pinch of salt

1 teaspoon ground ginger

1 teaspoon ground cinnamon

2½ ounces/⅓ cup sweet butter,
    diced

3 ounces/scant ½ cup superfine
    sugar

2 tablespoons maple or light
    corn syrup

1 egg yolk, beaten

1 To make the gingerbread, sift together the flour, baking soda, salt, ginger and cinnamon into a large bowl. Add the butter and rub it into the flour with your fingertips until the mixture resembles fine breadcrumbs.

2 Stir in the sugar, syrup and egg yolk and mix to a firm dough with a wooden spoon. Knead lightly on a floured surface. Put in plastic wrap and chill in the refrigerator for 30 minutes.

3 Preheat the oven to 350°F/ Gas 4. Grease two large baking sheets.

4 Unwrap the gingerbread dough and roll out on a floured surface, then stamp out teddies, using a floured 5-inch shaped cutter.

5 Carefully transfer the teddies to the prepared baking sheets and bake for 10–15 minutes, until just beginning to color around the edges. Leave on the baking sheets for 3 minutes, then transfer to a wire rack to cool.

6 Melt half the white chocolate in a heatproof bowl set over a pan of hot water. Spoon the melted chocolate into a paper pastry bag and snip off the tip. Make a neat template for the teddies' clothes: draw an outline of the cutter onto paper, finishing at the neck, halfway down the arms and around the legs.

7 Thinly roll the sugar paste on a surface dusted with confectioners' sugar. Use the template to cut out the clothes, and secure them to the cookies with the melted chocolate.

8 Use the sugar paste trimmings to add ears, eyes and snouts.

9 Dilute the blue coloring with a little water and use to paint the striped pyjamas using a fine-tipped paint brush.

10 Melt the remaining white chocolate and the semisweet or milk chocolate in separate heatproof bowls set over pans of hot water. Put in separate paper pastry bags and snip off the tips. Use the white chocolate to pipe a decorative outline around the pyjamas and use the semisweet or milk chocolate to pipe the teddies' faces.

Gingerbread House Cookies

For a party of young children, these gingerbread house cookies provide plenty of entertainment. You could incorporate a house-decorating session as one of the party games, allowing the children to design their own houses and take them home after the party.

Makes 10

4 ounces/ ½ cup sweet butter,
  at room temperature, diced
4 ounces/generous ½ cup light
  brown sugar
1 egg
4 ounces/scant ⅓ cup black molasses
  or light corn syrup
14 ounces/3½ cups self-rising flour
1 teaspoon ground ginger
  (optional)

For the decoration

1 tube white decorating icing
1 tube pastel-colored decorating icing
selection of small multi-colored candies,
  sugar flowers and silver balls

1 Put the butter and sugar in a large bowl and beat together until pale and creamy. Beat in the egg and molasses or syrup, then add the flour and ginger, if using. Mix together to make a thick paste.

2 Turn the mixture onto a lightly floured surface and knead until smooth. Put in plastic wrap and chill for 30 minutes.

3 Preheat the oven to 350°F/Gas 4. Grease three baking sheets. On a piece of cardboard, draw a 4¼ x 3¼ inch rectangle. Add a pitched roof. Cut out the shape to use as a template.

4 Roll out the dough on a lightly floured surface. (It might be easier to roll out half the quantity of dough at a time.)

5 Using the template, cut out house shapes. Transfer to the baking sheets and re-roll the trimmings to make more. Bake for 12–15 minutes, until risen and golden. Transfer the cookies to a wire rack to cool.

6 Use the icing in the tubes to pipe roof tiles, window and door frames and other decorative touches. Secure candies and decorations to finish, cutting them into smaller pieces if preferred.

Secret Message Cookies

These fortune cookies are light and wafery, and what they lack in substance, they certainly make up for in their fun factor. These are great for older kids who can prepare birthday messages, jokes or predictions to tuck into the cookies as soon as they're baked.

Makes 18

3 egg whites
2 ounces/ ½ cup confectioners'
  sugar
1½ ounces/3 tablespoons sweet
  butter, melted
2 ounces/ ½ cup all-purpose flour

1 Preheat the oven to 400°F/Gas 6. Line two baking sheets with baking parchment and grease. Cut a piece of paper into 18 small strips, measuring 2½ × ¾ inches. Write a message on each one.

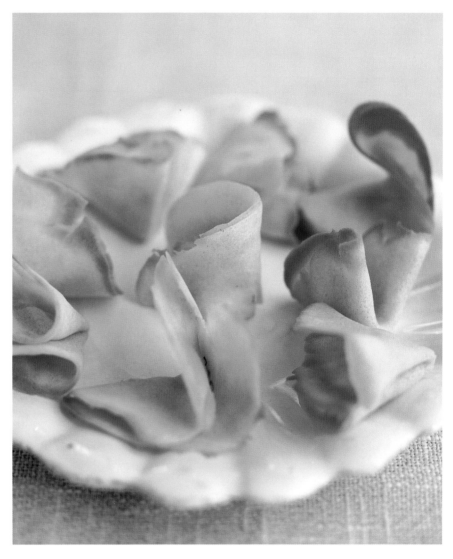

2 Lightly whisk the egg whites and confectioners' sugar until the whites are broken up. Add the melted butter and flour and beat until smooth.

3 Using a 2-teaspoon measure, spoon a little of the paste onto one baking sheet and spread to a 3-inch round shape with the back of a spoon. Add two more spoonfuls of mixture to the baking sheet and shape in the same way.

4 Bake for 6 minutes, until the cookies are golden. Meanwhile, prepare three more cookies on the second baking sheet.

5 Remove the first batch of cookies from the oven and replace with the second batch.

6 Working quickly, peel a hot cookie from the paper and fold it in half, tucking a message inside the fold. Rest the cookie over the rim of a glass or bowl and, very gently, fold again. (It probably won't fold over completely.) Fold the remaining two cookies in the same way.

7 Continue to bake and shape the remaining cookies in the same way until all the batter and messages have been used.

Cook's Tips
• *The secret to success is to spread the batter as thinly as possible on the paper. This will give a really crisp, light result.*
• *Don't be tempted to bake more than three cookies at once, or they'll harden before you can shape them.*

Giant Birthday Cookie

This enormous cookie is one for cookie-lovers of any age. Complete with candles, it makes the perfect party centerpiece. To personalize the cookie, write the recipient's name on top in icing.

Makes one 11-inch cookie

6 ounces/¾ cup sweet butter,
   at room temperature, diced
4¼ ounces/⅔ cup light
   brown sugar
1 egg yolk
6 ounces/1½ cups all-purpose
   flour
1 teaspoon baking soda
finely grated rind of 1 orange
   or lemon
3 ounces/scant 1 cup
   rolled oats

For the decoration

4¼ ounces/generous ½ cup
   cream cheese
8 ounces/2 cups confectioners'
   sugar
1–2 teaspoons lemon juice
birthday candles
white and milk chocolate-coated
   raisins or peanuts
cocoa powder, for dusting
gold or silver balls,
   for sprinkling

1 Preheat the oven to 375°F/ Gas 5. Grease an 11-inch metal tart pan and place on a large baking sheet.

2 Put the diced butter and the sugar in a large bowl and beat together until pale and creamy.

3 Add the egg yolk to the butter and sugar mixture and stir well to mix. Add the flour, baking soda, grated orange or lemon rind and rolled oats and stir thoroughly until evenly combined.

4 Turn the mixture into the pan and flatten with a wet wooden spoon.

5 Bake for 15–20 minutes, until risen and golden. Leave to cool in the pan. (If any of the mixture has seeped under the ring during baking, trim it off with a knife while still warm.)

6 Carefully slide the cookie from the pan onto a large, flat serving plate or board.

7 To decorate, beat the cream cheese in a bowl, then add the confectioners' sugar and 1 teaspoon of the lemon juice. Beat until smooth and peaking, adding more juice if required.

8 Spoon the mixture into a pastry bag and pipe swirls around the edge of the cookie. Press the candles into the frosting. Sprinkle with chocolate raisins or peanuts and dust with cocoa powder. Finish by sprinkling with gold or silver balls.

Mini Party Pizzas

These cute little cookie confections look amazingly realistic, and older children will love them. They're fun to make and are simply a basic cookie topped with icing, marzipan and dark cherries.

Makes 16

3½ ounces /7 tablespoons sweet butter,
  at room temperature, diced
3½ ounces/ ½ cup golden
  superfine sugar
1 tablespoon light corn syrup
6 ounces/1½ cups self-rising flour

For the topping

5 ounces/1¼ cups confectioners'
  sugar
4–5 teaspoons lemon juice
red food coloring
3½ ounces yellow marzipan,
  shredded
8 dark candied cherries, halved
a small piece of angelica,
  finely chopped

1 Preheat the oven to 350°F/Gas 4. Grease two baking sheets.

2 In a bowl, beat together the butter and sugar until creamy. Beat in the syrup, then add the flour and mix to a smooth paste.

3 Turn the mixture onto a lightly floured surface and cut into 16 even-size pieces. Roll each piece into a ball, then space far apart on the baking sheets, slightly flattening each one.

4 Bake for about 12 minutes, or until pale golden. Leave on the baking sheets for 3 minutes, then transfer to a wire rack to cool.

5 To make the topping, put the confectioners' sugar in a bowl and stir in enough lemon juice to make a fairly thick, spreadable paste. Beat in enough food coloring to make the paste a deep red color.

Cook's Tip

Make sure you use a red food coloring rather than cochineal, which will color the icing pink. Red food coloring is more readily available in paste form.

6 Spread the icing to within ¼ inch of the edges of the cookies. Sprinkle with the shredded marzipan and place a halved cherry in the center. Arrange a few pieces of chopped angelica on top so that the cookies resemble little cheese and tomato pizzas.

Jelly-bean Cones

Chocolate-dipped cookie cones filled with jelly beans make great treats for kids of all ages. The filled cones look very pretty arranged in glasses or other small containers to keep them upright. This way they can double as a tasty treat and a delightful table decoration.

Makes 10

3 egg whites

3½ ounces/½ cup superfine sugar

1 ounce/2 tablespoons sweet butter, melted

1½ ounces/⅓ cup all-purpose flour

2 tablespoons light cream

3½ ounces semisweet chocolate

jelly beans or other small candies

1 Preheat the oven to 375°F/Gas 5. Line two baking sheets with baking parchment and lightly grease.

2 Put the egg whites and sugar in a bowl and whisk lightly with a fork until the egg whites are broken up. Add the melted butter, flour and cream and stir well to make a smooth batter.

3 Using a 1-tablespoon measure, place a rounded tablespoon of the mixture on one side of a baking sheet. Spread to a 3½ inch round shape with the back of the spoon. Spoon more mixture onto the other side of the baking sheet and spread out to make another round shape.

4 Bake for about 8–10 minutes, until the edges are deep golden. Meanwhile, spoon two more round shapes of cookie mixture onto the second baking sheet.

5 Remove the first batch of cookies from the oven and replace with the second batch. Peel away the paper from the baked cookies and roll them into cone shapes. Leave to set. Continue in this way until you have made 10 cones.

6 Break the chocolate into a heatproof bowl set over a pan of simmering water and stir until melted. Dip the wide ends of the cookies in the chocolate and prop them inside narrow glasses to set, then fill with jelly beans or sweets.

Chocolate Party Cookies

You don't need a special cutter to make these party cookies. They're shaped using an ordinary round cutter to which you add a V-shaped cone when cutting them out – quite simple once you've made one or two. Children will find these fun cookies irresistible.

Makes 15

5 ounces/1¼ cups self-rising
   flour
3½ ounces/7 tablespoons sweet
   butter, diced
2 ounces/¼ cup light brown
   sugar
1 egg yolk
1 teaspoon vanilla extract

For the decoration

3 ounces/6 tablespoons sweet
   butter, softened
1 teaspoon vanilla extract
4 ounces/1 cup confectioners'
   sugar
2 chocolate fingers

1 Put the flour and butter in a food processor and process until the mixture resembles fine breadcrumbs. Add the sugar, egg yolk and vanilla and blend to a smooth dough. Put in plastic wrap and chill for 30 minutes.

2 Preheat the oven to 400°F/ Gas 6. Grease a large baking sheet. Roll the dough out thinly on a floured surface. Lay a 2-inch round cookie cutter on the dough. Using a ruler, mark a point 2 inches away from the edge of the cutter, then cut two lines from either side of the cutter to the point, to make cornet shapes. Cut around the rest of the cutter and transfer the cornet shape to the baking sheet. Make 14 more in the same way, re-rolling the trimmings to make the full quantity.

3 Using a sharp knife, make shallow cuts ¼ inch apart across the cone area of each cookie, then make more cuts diagonally across the first to create a "wafer" effect. Be careful not to cut all the way through the biscuit.

4 Bake for 8–10 minutes, until pale golden. Leave for 2 minutes then transfer to a wire rack to cool.

5 For the buttercream, beat together the butter, vanilla and confectioners' sugar until smooth. Add 1 teaspoon hot water and beat again until the mixture is very light and airy. Place in a pastry bag fitted with a large plain nozzle. Pipe swirls onto the tops of the biscuits so that they look like swirls of ice cream.

6 Cut the fingers across into 2-inch lengths. Carefully cut each piece lengthwise into four small lengths. Push a finger into each biscuit.

Cook's Tip

The biscuits and buttercream can be made ahead, but assemble them on the day they're served, as the cream will gradually soften the biscuits.

Stained-glass Windows

Baking colored sweets inside a cookie frame creates a stunning stained-glass effect, particularly if you hang the cookies in front of a window or near a lamp or wall light, where the light can shine through. The translucent cookie center will stay brittle for a day or so before softening and finally melting, so don't be tempted to hang them up for too long.

Makes 12–14

6 ounces/1½ cups all-purpose flour

½ teaspoon baking soda

½ teaspoon ground cinnamon

3 ounces/6 tablespoons sweet butter, chilled and diced

3 ounces/scant ½ cup superfine sugar

2 tablespoons light corn syrup

1 egg yolk

5 ounces brightly colored, clear hard candies

1 Put the flour, baking soda, cinnamon and butter into a food processor. Process until the mixture resembles breadcrumbs.

2 Add the sugar, syrup and egg yolk to the food processor, then process again until the mixture starts to cling together in a dough.

3 Turn the dough out onto a lightly floured surface and knead until smooth. Put in plastic wrap and chill in the refrigerator for at least 30 minutes.

4 Preheat the oven to 350°F/Gas 4. Line two large baking sheets with baking parchment.

5 Roll out the dough thinly on a lightly floured surface. Cut into 2½-inch wide strips, then cut diagonally across the strips to create about 12 diamond shapes.

6 Carefully transfer the diamond shapes to the lined baking sheets, spacing them slightly apart.

7 Using a sharp knife, cut out a smaller diamond shape from the center of each cookie and remove to leave a ½-inch frame.

8 Using a skewer, make a hole at one end of each cookie (large enough to thread fine ribbon).

9 Bake the cookie diamonds for about 5 minutes. Meanwhile, lightly crush the candies (still in their wrappers) by tapping them gently with the end of a rolling pin.

10 Remove the cookies from the oven and quickly fill the center of each one with about two crushed candies of the same color.

11 Return the cookies to the oven for a further 5 minutes, until the candies have melted. Remove from the oven and use a skewer to re-mark the skewer holes if they have shrunk during baking.

12 If the candies haven't spread to fill the cookie center during baking, while still hot, carefully spread the melted candies with the tip of a skewer.

13 Leave the cookies on the baking parchment until the melted candies have hardened. Once the centers are hard, gently peel away the paper from the cookies.

14 Thread fine ribbon of different lengths through the holes in the cookies, then hang as decorations around the home.

Cook's Tip

Make sure you re-mark the skewer holes while the cookies are still hot, as they'll probably break if you try to make the holes once they've cooled.

Silly Faces

These funny little characters can be made using almost any type of cookie mix, as long as the baked cookies are quite big and not too craggy. Silly faces are great fun for kids to decorate.

5 Bake the cookies for 10–12 minutes, until just turning golden around the edges. Transfer to a wire rack to cool.

6 To decorate, beat together the butter and confectioners' sugar in a bowl until smooth and creamy.

7 Using a small metal spatula spread a little buttercream along the top edge of each cookie, then secure the strawberry, apple or licorice strands. Either snip the strands to make straight hair, or twist the strands to make curly hair.

8 Use a dot of buttercream to secure a candied cherry to the middle of each cookie for a nose. Pipe eyes and mouths using the writer icing, then add halved sweets, attached with buttercream, for the centers of the eyes.

Makes 14

4 ounces/½ cup sweet butter, at room
   temperature, diced
4 ounces/generous ½ cup golden
   superfine sugar
1 egg
4 ounces/scant ⅓ cup light
   corn syrup
14 ounces/3½ cups self-rising flour

For the decoration

3 ounces/6 tablespoons sweet butter,
   at room temperature, diced
5 ounces/1¼ cups confectioners' sugar
strawberry, apple or licorice strands
candied cherries, halved
red and black writer icing
small multi-colored candies

1 Put the butter and sugar in a large bowl and beat together until pale and creamy. Beat in the egg and light corn syrup, add the flour and mix together to make a thick paste.

2 Turn the mixture onto a lightly floured surface and knead until smooth. Put in plastic wrap and chill for 30 minutes.

3 Preheat the oven to 350°F/Gas 4. Grease two baking sheets.

4 Roll out the chilled dough on a lightly floured surface and cut out round pieces using a 3½-inch cookie cutter. Transfer the pieces to the baking sheets, re-rolling the trimmings to make more cookies.

Train Cookies

These simple party cookies are so easy, yet incredibly effective, particularly if you let them trail across the party table. The quantity makes enough for two trains, but double it if required.

Makes 10

5 ounces/1¼ cups all-purpose
    flour
3½ ounces/7 tablespoons sweet butter,
    chilled, diced
2 ounces/½ cup golden confectioners'
    sugar
1 egg yolk
1 teaspoon vanilla extract

For the decoration

1½ ounces/3 tablespoons butter, softened
3 ounces/¾ cup golden confectioners'
    sugar
blue food coloring
large bag of colored licorice

1 Put the flour and butter in a food processor. Process until the mixture resembles fine breadcrumbs. Add the sugar, egg yolk and vanilla; blend to a smooth dough. Put in plastic wrap and chill for 30 minutes.

2 Preheat the oven to 400°F/Gas 6. Grease a large baking sheet. Roll out the dough and cut 3 x 1½ inch rectangles, re-rolling the scraps to make more cookies. Cut two 1¼ x ¾ inch rectangles and secure to the top of the larger rectangles for the engines.

3 Place on the baking sheet and bake for about 10 minutes, until pale golden around the edges. Leave for 2 minutes on the baking sheet, then transfer to a wire rack to cool completely.

4 To decorate the biscuits, put the butter and confectioners' sugar in a bowl with a dash of blue food coloring and beat until smooth and creamy. Chop plenty of the liquorice pieces into small dice.

Cook's Tip

If you don't want to use licorice, try other colorful candies or even chocolate. Round chocolates make good wheels, and chopped chocolate, or polka dots make good "cargo".

5 Spread a little buttercream along one long side of all the biscuits, except the engines, and press the chopped licorice into the buttercream. Halve some square pieces and secure to the engines for windows and another piece on the front of the engine for the funnel. Secure two wheels on all the biscuits. Arrange the biscuits in a trail across the table.

Gold Medals

These cookies are great for kids' parties. You can present each child with a huge cookie medal when they sit down at the table, or hand them out to winners of party games.

Makes 10

2 ounces/¼ cup sweet butter, at room
   temperature, diced
4 ounces/generous ½ cup superfine sugar
1 egg
5 ounces/1¼ cups self-rising flour
¼ tsp baking soda

For the decoration

1 egg white
7 ounces/1¾ cups confectioners' sugar
small brightly colored candies

1 Preheat the oven to 350°F/Gas 4. Grease two baking sheets with a little butter.

2 In a bowl, beat together the butter and sugar until smooth and creamy, then beat in the egg. Add the flour and baking soda and mix well to combine.

3 Place large spoonfuls of the mixture on the baking sheets, spacing them far apart to allow room for spreading. Bake for about 15 minutes, or until pale golden and slightly risen.

4 Using a skewer, make quite a large hole in the cookie, ½ inch from the edge. Transfer to a wire rack and leave to cool.

5 To make the icing, beat the egg white in a bowl using a wooden spoon. Gradually beat in the confectioners' sugar to make a thick paste that just holds its shape. Spoon the icing into a small plastic bag and snip off the merest tip.

6 Write icing numbers in the center of the cookies. Secure a circle of candies around the edge of each cookie with a little more of the icing, then leave to set.

7 Once the icing has hardened, carefully thread each cookie with a piece of ribbon.

Chocolate Dominoes

A recipe for children to eat rather than make, these fun bars are ideal for birthday parties, when you can match the spots on the dominoes to the children's ages.

Makes 16

6 ounces/¾ cup soft margarine

6 ounces/generous ¾ cup superfine
sugar

5 ounces/1¼ cups self-rising
flour

1 ounce/¼ cup cocoa powder
(unsweetened), sifted

3 eggs

For the topping

6 ounces/¾ cup butter

1 ounce/¼ cup cocoa powder
(unsweetened)

11 ounces/2¾ cups confectioners'
sugar

a few licorice strips and 4-ounce packet
candy-coated chocolate drops,
to decorate

1 Preheat the oven to 350°F/ Gas 4. Lightly brush a 7 x 11 inch rectangular baking pan with a little oil and line the base with waxed paper.

2 Put all the cake ingredients into a large bowl and beat until smooth.

3 Spoon the cake mixture evenly into the prepared cake pan and level the surface with a metal spatula.

4 Bake for 30 minutes, or until the cake springs back when pressed with the fingertips.

5 Cool in the pan for 5 minutes, then loosen the edges with a knife and transfer to a wire rack. Peel off the lining paper and leave the cake to cool completely. When cold, turn it out onto a chopping board.

6 To make the topping, place the butter in a bowl. Sift together the cocoa and confectioners' sugar into the bowl and beat until smooth. Spread the topping evenly over the cake with a metal spatula.

7 Cut the cake into 16 bars. Place a strip of licorice, across the middle of each bar, then decorate with candy-coated chocolate drops to make the domino spots.

Variation
To make Traffic Light Cakes, omit the cocoa and add an extra 3 tablespoons all-purpose flour. Omit cocoa from the icing and add an extra 4 tablespoons confectioners' sugar and ½ teaspoon vanilla extract. Spread over the cakes and decorate with a row of red, yellow and green candied cherries.

Name Cookies

You could decorate these cookies for children coming to a party, either in vibrant, bright colors or in more delicate pastels. It can be a fun idea to prop a name cookie up against the glass at each place setting around the tea table and let the children find their own seats.

Makes 20

7 ounces/scant 1 cup sweet butter,
  chilled and diced
10 ounces/2½ cups all-purpose
  flour
finely grated rind of 1 orange
3½ ounces/scant 1 cup confectioners'
  sugar
2 egg yolks

For the decoration

1 egg white
7 ounces/1¾ cups confectioners' sugar
2 different food colorings
jelly beans or silver balls

1 Put the butter, flour and orange rind in a food processor and process until the mixture resembles fine breadcrumbs. Add the confectioners' sugar and egg yolks and blend until smooth. Put in plastic wrap and chill for 30 minutes.

2 Preheat the oven to 400°F/Gas 6. Grease two baking sheets.

3 Roll out the dough on a floured surface and cut out cookies in a variety of shapes, such as squares, hearts and round forms. Make sure each cookie is at least 3 inches across.

4 Transfer the cookies to the baking sheets, spacing them slightly apart, and bake for 10–12 minutes, until pale golden around the edges.

5 Leave the cookies on the baking sheet for about 2 minutes to firm up, then transfer to a wire rack to cool completely.

6 To make the icing, put the egg white and confectioners' sugar in a bowl and beat together until smooth, and the icing only just holds its shape.

7 Divide the icing between two bowls, then beat a few drops of food coloring into each bowl to make two different colors.

8 Spoon the two different icings into separate small plastic bags and gently squeeze into one corner.

Variation

If you prefer, add food coloring to only one of the bowls of icing, leaving the second bowl of icing white. This can look very pretty, particularly if you choose a pastel color for the second bowl of icing and decorate with silver balls.

9 Cut off the merest tip from each bag so the icing can be piped in a very thin line, then write the names or initials of party guests on the cookies. Pipe decorative borders around the edges of the cookies using both colors of icing. Use either straight lines, flutes, dots of icing or squiggled lines of piping to decorate.

10 Chop the jelly beans, if using, into small pieces. Secure the jelly beans or the silver balls onto the icing on the cookies to finish. Leave the cookies to set for at least 1 hour.

Peanut Cookies

Packing up a party picnic? Got another kind of birthday party coming up? Make sure that some of these fabulous nutty cookies are on the menu. Remember to make sure that none of the children have a nut allergy.

Makes 25

8 ounces/1 cup butter

2 tablespoons smooth peanut butter

4 ounces/1 cup confectioners' sugar

2 ounces/¼ cup cornstarch

8 ounces/2 cups all-purpose flour

4 ounces/1 cup unsalted peanuts

1 Put the butter and peanut butter in a bowl and beat together. Add the confectioners' sugar, cornstarch and all-purpose flour and mix together to make a soft dough.

2 Preheat the oven to 350°F/ Gas 4. Lightly oil two baking sheets. Roll the mixture into 25 small balls, using the palms of your hands, and place on the baking sheets. Leave plenty of room for the cookies to spread.

3 Press the tops of the balls of dough flat, using either the back of a fork or your fingertips.

4 Press a few of the peanuts into each of the cookies. Bake for about 15–20 minutes, until lightly browned. Leave to cool for a few minutes before lifting them carefully onto a wire rack with a metal spatula.

Cook's Tip
For a party, make monster cookies by rolling bigger balls of dough. Remember to leave plenty of room on the baking sheets for them to spread during cooking.

Party Bracelets

These tiny cookies are threaded onto fine ribbon along with an assortment of brightly colored candies that have a ready-made hole in the middle. Make the cookies a day or two in advance, and simply thread together with the candies on the day of the party.

Makes 10

2 ounces/ ¼ cup sweet butter, at room
   temperature, diced
4 ounces/generous ½ cup superfine
   sugar
1 teaspoon vanilla extract
pink or green food coloring
1 egg
7 ounces/1¾ cups self-rising
   flour

For the decoration

2 large bags of hard candies with
   holes in the center
narrow pastel-colored ribbon,
   for threading

1 Preheat the oven to 350°F/Gas 4. Grease two baking sheets.

2 In a bowl, beat together the butter, sugar and vanilla extract until pale and creamy. Add a dash of pink or green food coloring, then beat in the egg. Add the flour and mix well to form a dough.

3 Turn the dough onto a lightly floured surface and roll out under the palms of your hands into two long, thin sausage shapes, each about 16 inches long.

4 Cut each roll across into ¼-inch lengths and space them slightly apart on the baking sheets. Place the baking sheets in the refrigerator for about 30 minutes.

5 Bake the cookies for about 8 minutes, until slightly risen and beginning to color. Remove from the oven and, using a skewer, immediately make holes for the ribbon to be threaded through. (You may find it easier to bake one sheet of cookies at a time.) Transfer the cookies to a wire rack to cool.

6 Thread the cookies onto 22-inch lengths of narrow ribbon, alternating with the sweets. (You should end up with about seven cookies on each ribbon.) Tie the ends of the ribbons together in bows to finish.

Cook's Tip

When you make the holes in the cookies, you will need to work quickly. If the cookies start to harden before you have time to make holes in all of them, pop the remaining cookies back in the oven very briefly to re-soften.

Sweet Necklaces

These are too awkward for very young children to make but ideal as novelty Christmas or birthday party presents. Arrange in a pretty, tissue-lined box or another container for presentation.

Makes 12

1 quantity lebkuchen mixture
(see *Chocolate Fruit and Nut Cookies*)
7 ounces royal icing
pink food coloring
selection of small candies
6 yards fine pink, blue or
white ribbon

1 Preheat the oven to 350°F/Gas 4. Grease two large baking sheets. Roll out slightly more than half of the lebkuchen mixture on a lightly-floured surface to a thickness of ¼ inch.

2 Stamp out stars using a lightly floured 1-inch star cutter. Carefully transfer to a prepared baking sheet, spacing them evenly and allowing room for them to rise. Taking care not to distort the shape of the stars, make a large hole in the center of each, using a metal or wooden skewer.

Variation
You can adapt this technique to use with other kinds of cookie dough for children who don't like ginger. However, lebkuchen is ideal because it is quite substantial and firm, so holds its shape. It is traditionally used for threaded shapes.

3 Gather the trimmings together with the remaining dough. Roll the dough under the palms of your hands, to make a thick, even sausage about 1 inch in diameter. Cut into ½-inch thick slices. Using the skewer, carefully make a hole in the center of each round piece. Place on the second baking sheet.

4 Bake for about 8 minutes, or until slightly risen and just beginning to color. Remove from the oven and, while still warm, re-make the skewer holes, as the gingerbread will have spread slightly during baking. Leave to cool on a wire rack.

5 Put half the royal icing in a paper pastry bag and snip off the tip. Use to pipe neat outlines all around the edges of each of the gingerbread stars.

6 Color the remaining icing with the pink coloring. Spoon into another paper pastry bag fitted with a star nozzle.

7 Cut the candies into smaller pieces and use to decorate the cookies, attaching them with icing. Leave to harden.

8 Cut the ribbon into 20-inch lengths. Thread a selection of the cookies onto each ribbon.

Variation
To make edible tinsel to drape on your Christmas tree, string stars together decorated with green, red and white icing.

Chocolate Heaven

This has to be a favorite chapter for almost everyone – chocolate cookies are universally popular, loved by young and old alike. This is hardly surprising, with such mouth-watering recipes as Chunky Chocolate Drops and Giant Triple Chocolate Cookies. Some, such as Rich Chocolate Cookie Slice, are astonishingly simple to make, while others, such as Mini Chocolate Marylands, take a little more time and effort, but they're certainly worth it.

Chocolate Thumbprint Cookies

Chunky, chocolatey and gooey all at the same time, these gorgeous cookies are filled with a spoonful of chocolate spread after baking to really add to their indulgent feel.

Makes 16

4 ounces/ ½ cup sweet butter,
  at room temperature, diced

4 ounces/generous ½ cup light
  brown sugar

1 egg

3 ounces/ ⅔ cup all-purpose flour

1 ounce/ ¼ cup cocoa powder
  (unsweetened)

½ teaspoon baking soda

4 ounces/generous 1 cup
  rolled oats

5–6 tablespoons chocolate spread

1 Preheat the oven to 350°F/Gas 4. Grease a large baking sheet. In a bowl, beat together the butter and sugar until creamy.

2 Add the egg, flour, cocoa powder, baking soda and rolled oats to the bowl and mix well.

3 Using your hands, roll spoonfuls of the mixture into balls. Place the balls on the baking sheet, spacing them far apart to allow room for spreading. Flatten slightly.

4 Dip a thumb in flour and press into the center of each cookie to make an indent. Bake the cookies for 10 minutes. Leave for 2 minutes, then transfer to a wire rack to cool.

5 Spoon a little chocolate spread into the center of each cookie.

Chocolate Molasses Snaps

These elegantly thin, molasses-flavored snap cookies have a delicate hint of spice and a decorative lick of chocolate on top. They are particularly good with a steaming cup of hot coffee.

Makes about 35

3½ ounces/7 tablespoons sweet
   butter, diced
6 fluid ounces/¾ cup light
   corn syrup
2 fluid ounces/¼ cup black
   molasses
9 ounces/2¼ cups all-purpose
   flour
5 ounces/¾ cup golden superfine
   sugar
1 teaspoon baking soda
¼ teaspoon apple pie
   spice
3½ ounces milk chocolate
3½ ounces white chocolate

1 Preheat the oven to 350°F/Gas 4. Line two or three baking sheets with baking parchment. Put the butter, syrup and molasses in a small pan. Heat gently, stirring constantly, until the butter has melted. Remove from the heat and set aside until required.

2 Sift the flour into a large mixing bowl. Add the sugar, baking soda and apple pie spice, and mix well using a wooden spoon. Slowly pour in the butter and molasses mixture and stir to combine well.

3 Place large teaspoonfuls of the mixture far apart on the prepared baking sheets. Bake the cookies for 10–12 minutes, until just beginning to brown around the edges. Leave them to cool for a few minutes on the baking sheets. When firm enough to handle, transfer the cookies to a wire rack to cool completely.

4 Melt the milk chocolate and white chocolate separately in the microwave or in heatproof bowls set over pans of hot water. Swirl a little of each into the center of each cookie and leave to set.

Mini Chocolate Marylands

These tasty little cookies are perfect for any age group. They're easy to make and even young children can get involved with helping to press the chocolate chips into the unbaked dough.

Makes 40–45

4¼ ounces/generous ½ cup sweet butter, at room temperature, diced

3½ ounces/½ cup superfine sugar

1 egg

1 egg yolk

1 teaspoon vanilla extract

6 ounces/1½ cups self-rising flour

3½ ounces/generous ½ cup milk

3½ ounces/generous ½ cup chocolate chips

1 Preheat the oven to 350°F/Gas 4. Grease two baking sheets.

2 In a large bowl, beat together the butter and sugar until pale and creamy. Add the egg, egg yolk, vanilla extract, flour, milk and half the chocolate chips and stir well until thoroughly combined.

3 Using two teaspoons, place small mounds of the mixture on the baking sheets, spacing them slightly apart to allow room for spreading.

4 Press the remaining chocolate chips onto the mounds of cookie dough and press down gently.

5 Bake for 10–15 minutes, until pale golden. Leave the cookies on the baking sheet for 2 minutes to firm up, then transfer to a wire rack to cool completely.

Cook's Tip

This recipe makes quite a large quantity. If you like, you can freeze half of the cookies for another time. Simply thaw, then return to the oven for a few minutes to re-crisp before serving.

Chocolate Pretzels

These scrumptious snacks look so charming twisted into little knots that it is tempting to take "just one more". Sweet pretzels are a specialty of Germany and Austria.

Makes 28

4 ounces/1 cup all-purpose flour
pinch of salt
3 tablespoons cocoa powder
   (unsweetened)
4 ounces/½ cup butter
5 ounces/⅔ cup superfine
   sugar
1 egg
1 egg white, lightly beaten,
   for glazing
sugar crystals, for sprinkling

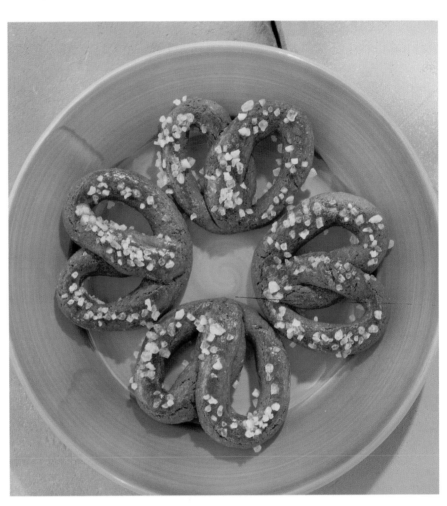

1 Sift together the flour, salt and cocoa powder. Set aside. Grease two baking sheets.

2 With an electric mixer, cream the butter until light. Add the sugar and continue beating until light and fluffy. Beat in the egg. Add the dry ingredients and stir to blend. Gather the dough into a ball, wrap in waxed paper and chill for 1 hour, or freeze for 30 minutes.

5 Brush the pretzels with the egg white. Sprinkle sugar crystals over the tops to decorate and bake for 10–12 minutes, until firm. Transfer to a wire rack to cool.

3 Roll the dough into 28 small balls. If the dough is sticky, lightly flour your hands first. Chill the dough balls until needed. Preheat the oven to 375°F/Gas 5.

4 Roll each ball into a rope about 10 inches long. With each rope, form a loop with the two ends facing you. Twist the ends and fold back onto the circle, pressing in, to make a pretzel shape. Place on the prepared baking sheets.

Cook's Tip
To make mocha-flavored pretzels, replace 2 teaspoons of the cocoa with instant coffee powder.

Chocolate Box Cookies

These prettily decorated, bite-size cookies look as though they've come straight out of a box of chocolates. They're great for a special tea or for wrapping as gifts, and older children will love getting thoroughly absorbed in making and decorating them.

Makes about 50

6 ounces/1½ cups self-rising
   flour
1 ounce/¼ cup cocoa powder
   (unsweetened)
1 teaspoon apple pie spice
2 ounces/¼ cup sweet butter, at room
   temperature, diced
4 ounces/generous ½ cup
   superfine sugar
1 egg
1 egg yolk

For the decoration

5 ounces milk chocolate
5 ounces white chocolate
3¾ ounces semisweet chocolate
whole almonds or walnuts
cocoa powder, for dusting

1 Preheat the oven to 350°F/Gas 4. Grease two baking sheets.

2 Put the flour, cocoa powder, spice and butter into a food processor. Process until the ingredients are thoroughly blended. Add the sugar, egg and egg yolk and mix to a smooth dough.

3 Turn the dough out onto a lightly floured surface and knead gently. Cut the dough in half and roll out each piece under the palms of your hands to form two long logs, each 13 inches long.

4 Cut each log into ½-inch slices. Place the slices on the prepared baking sheet, spacing slightly apart, and chill for at least 30 minutes.

5 Bake for 10 minutes, until slightly risen. Transfer to a wire rack to cool.

6 To decorate, break the chocolate into three separate heatproof bowls. Place each bowl, in turn, over a pan of gently simmering water and stir frequently until melted.

7 Divide the cookies into six batches. Using a fork, dip one batch, a cookie at a time, into the milk chocolate to coat completely. Place on a sheet of baking parchment.

8 Taking the next batch of cookies, half-dip in milk chocolate and place on the baking parchment.

9 Continue with the next two batches of cookies and the white chocolate. Completely coat one batch, then half-coat the second.

10 Continue with the remaining cookies, completely coating one batch in the semisweet chocolate and half-dipping the other. Press a whole nut onto the tops of the semisweet-coated cookies.

11 Put the leftover white chocolate in a small plastic bag and squeeze it into one corner. Snip off the tip, then drizzle lines of chocolate over the milk-chocolate-coated cookies.

12 Dust the white chocolate-coated cookies with a little cocoa powder. Store all the cookies in a cool place until ready to serve.

Cook's Tip

Once you have mastered the art of decorating the cookies, vary the combinations. Try drizzling bittersweet or milk chocolate over the different cookies.

Chocolate Florentines

These big, flat, crunchy cookies are just like traditional florentines but use tiny seeds instead of nuts. Rolling the edges in milk chocolate or white chocolate makes them feel like a real treat.

Makes 12

2 ounces/¼ cup sweet butter

2 ounces/¼ cup superfine sugar

1 tablespoon milk

1 ounce/scant ¼ cup pumpkin seeds

1½ ounces/generous ¼ cup sunflower seeds

2 ounces/scant ½ cup raisins

1 ounce/2 tablespoons multi-colored candied cherries, chopped

2 tablespoons all-purpose flour

4¼ ounces milk or white chocolate

1 Preheat the oven to 350°F/Gas 4. Line two baking sheets with baking parchment and grease the paper well.

2 In a pan, melt the butter with the sugar, stirring, until the sugar has dissolved, then cook until bubbling. Remove the pan from the heat and stir in the milk, pumpkin and sunflower seeds, raisins, candied cherries and flour. Mix well.

3 Spoon 6 teaspoonfuls of the mixture onto each baking sheet, spacing them far apart. Bake for 8–10 minutes, until the cookies are turning dark golden. Using a metal spatula, push back the edges of the cookies to neaten. Leave on the baking sheets for about 5 minutes to firm up, then transfer to a wire rack to cool.

4 Break up the chocolate and put in a heatproof bowl set over a pan of gently simmering water. Heat, stirring frequently, until melted. Roll the edges of the cookies in the chocolate and leave to set on a clean sheet of baking parchment for about 1 hour.

Variation
If you prefer, use semisweet chocolate to decorate the cookies.

Chocolate Refrigerator Cookies

The dough must be chilled thoroughly before it can be sliced and baked. Keep a "log" of dough, wrapped in foil, in the freezer ready for baking whenever you need a chocolate boost.

Makes about 50

8 ounces/2 cups all-purpose flour

pinch of salt

2 ounces semisweet chocolate, chopped

8 ounces/1 cup sweet butter at room temperature, diced

8 ounces/1 cup superfine sugar

2 eggs

1 teaspoon vanilla extract

4 ounces/1 cup walnuts, finely chopped

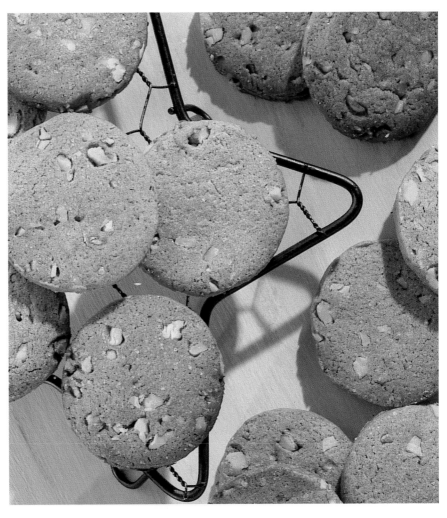

1 Sift together the flour and salt into a small bowl. Set aside. Melt the chocolate in the top of a double boiler, or in a heatproof bowl set over a pan of hot water. Set aside.

2 With an electric mixer, cream the butter until soft. Add the sugar and continue beating until the mixture is light and fluffy.

3 Mix the eggs with the vanilla extract, then gradually stir into the butter mixture.

4 Stir in the melted chocolate, then the flour mixture followed by the nuts and mix to form a firm dough.

5 Divide the dough into four pieces and roll each into 2-inch diameter logs. Wrap tightly in foil or plastic wrap and chill in the refrigerator or place in the freezer until firm.

6 Preheat the oven to 375°F/Gas 5. Grease two or three baking sheets. Cut the dough into ¼-inch slices. Place on the baking sheets and bake for 10 minutes. Transfer to a wire rack to cool.

Variation

To make two-tone cookies, make half chocolate and half plain dough. Roll out the plain dough. Roll out the chocolate dough, place on top of the plain dough and roll up. Wrap and chill, then cut and bake as above.

Chocolate Marzipan Cookies

These crisp little cookies are deliciously sweet and have a delightful almond surprise inside. Piped with zigzag lines of white chocolate, they make a perfect party treat.

Makes 36

7 ounces/scant 1 cup sweet butter
 at room temperature, diced
7 ounces/scant 1 cup light
 brown sugar
1 egg
11 ounces/2⅔ cups all-purpose
 flour
4 tablespoons cocoa powder
 (unsweetened)
7 ounces white almond paste
4 ounces white chocolate, chopped

1 Preheat the oven to 375°F/Gas 5. Lightly grease two large baking sheets. Cream the butter with the sugar in a bowl until pale and fluffy.

2 Add the egg and beat well. Sift the flour and cocoa powder over the mixture. Stir in, first with a wooden spoon, then with clean hands, pressing the mixture together to make a fairly soft dough. If the dough seems rather sticky and might be difficult to roll, put it in plastic wrap and chill for about 30 minutes.

3 Roll out about half the dough on a lightly floured surface to a thickness of about ¼ inch. Using a 2-inch cutter, stamp out round pieces, re-rolling the dough as required until you have about 36 rounds.

4 Cut the almond paste into about 36 equal pieces. Roll into balls, flatten slightly and place one on each dough round. Roll out the remaining dough, stamp out more rounds, then place on top of the almond paste. Press the dough edges to seal. Bake the cookies for 10–12 minutes until well risen.

5 Transfer the cookies to a wire rack, using a spatula, and leave to cool completely. Melt the white chocolate, spoon into a paper pastry bag and pipe zigzag lines onto the cookies. Leave to set before serving.

Chunky Chocolate Drops

Do not allow these cookies to cool completely on the baking sheet, or they will become too crisp and will break when you try to lift them.

Makes 18

6 ounces semisweet chocolate,
  chopped

4 ounces/½ cup sweet butter,
  diced

2 eggs

3½ ounces/½ cup granulated sugar

2 ounces/¼ cup soft light brown sugar

1½ ounces/⅓ cup all-purpose flour

1 ounce/¼ cup cocoa powder
  (unsweetened)

1 teaspoon baking powder

2 teaspoons vanilla extract

pinch of salt

4 ounces/1 cup pecan nuts, toasted and
  coarsely chopped

6 ounces/1 cup semisweet
  chocolate chips

4 ounces good quality white chocolate,
  chopped into ¼-inch pieces

4 ounces good quality milk chocolate,
  chopped into ¼-inch pieces

1 Preheat the oven to 325°F/Gas 3. Grease two large baking sheets. Melt the semisweet chocolate and butter in a pan over a low heat, stirring constantly until smooth. Remove from the heat and set aside to cool slightly.

2 In a large mixing bowl, using an electric mixer, beat the eggs and sugars for 2–3 minutes until pale and creamy. Gradually pour in the melted chocolate mixture, beating until well blended.

3 Beat in the flour, cocoa powder, baking powder, vanilla extract and salt until just blended. Stir in the nuts, chocolate chips and chocolate pieces.

4 Drop mounded tablespoonfuls of the mixture onto the prepared baking sheets, 4 inches apart. Gently flatten each to 3-inch round shapes with the back of the spoon. Bake for 8–10 minutes, until the tops are shiny and cracked and the edges look crisp; do not over-bake, or the cookies will become fragile.

5 Remove the baking sheets to a wire rack to cool for 2 minutes, then transfer the cookies to the rack to cool completely.

Chocolate Wands

Shaping these long, wafery chocolate cookies is fun, but you need to work quickly so it might take a few attempts to get the technique just right. Bake only two cookies at a time; any more and they will become brittle before you have time to shape them into wands.

Makes 10–12

3 egg whites

3½ ounces/ ½ cup superfine sugar

1 ounce/2 tablespoons sweet
butter, melted

2 tablespoons all-purpose flour

1 tablespoon cocoa powder
(unsweetened)

2 tablespoons light cream

3½ ounces milk chocolate and
multi-colored sprinkles, to decorate

1 Preheat the oven to 350°F/Gas 4. Line two large baking sheets with baking parchment and grease the paper well.

2 In a bowl, briefly beat together the egg whites and sugar until the whites are broken up.

3 Add the melted butter, flour, cocoa powder and cream to the egg whites and beat with a wooden spoon until smooth.

Cook's Tip
These cookies look best when the wands are really slender. Use a wooden spoon with a thin handle for shaping the cookies around. Alternatively, use a chunky pencil wrapped in kitchen foil.

4 Place 2 teaspoonfuls of the mixture to one side of a baking sheet and spread the mixture into an oval shape, about 6 inches long. Spoon more mixture onto the other side of the baking sheet and shape in the same way.

5 Bake for 7–8 minutes until the edges begin to darken. Meanwhile, prepare two more cookies on the second baking sheet so you can put them in the oven while shaping the first batch into wands.

6 Leave the baked cookies on the paper for 30 seconds, then carefully lift one off and wrap it around the handle of a wooden spoon. As soon as it starts to hold its shape, ease it off the spoon and shape the second cookie in the same way.

7 Continue baking and shaping the cookies in this way until all the mixture has been used up.

8 Break the chocolate into pieces and place in a heatproof bowl set over a pan of gently simmering water. Heat, stirring occasionally, until the chocolate has melted.

9 Dip the ends of the cookies in the chocolate, turning them until the ends are thickly coated.

10 Sprinkle the chocolate-coated ends of the cookies with colored sprinkles and place on a sheet of baking parchment. Leave for about 1 hour until the chocolate has set.

Chocolate Kisses

These rich little cookies look attractive mixed together on a plate and dusted with confectioners' sugar. Serve them with ice cream or simply with a cup of coffee.

Makes 24

3 ounces semisweet chocolate, chopped

3 ounces white chocolate, chopped

4 ounces/½ cup butter at room temperature, diced

4 ounces/generous ½ cup superfine sugar

2 eggs, beaten

8 ounces/2 cups all-purpose flour

confectioners' sugar, to decorate

1 Put the semisweet and white chocolate into separate small, heatproof bowls and melt the chocolates, in turn, over a pan of hot, but not boiling water, stirring until smooth. Remove the bowls from the heat and set them aside to cool slightly.

2 Beat together the butter and superfine sugar until pale and fluffy. Beat in the eggs a little at a time, beating well after each addition.

3 Sift the flour over the butter, sugar and egg mixture and mix in lightly and thoroughly.

4 Halve the mixture and divide it between the two bowls of chocolate. Mix each chocolate in well. Knead the doughs until smooth, put in plastic wrap and chill for 1 hour. Preheat the oven to 375°F/Gas 5. Grease two baking sheets.

5 Take rounded teaspoonfuls of the doughs and shape them roughly into balls. Roll the balls between the palms of your hands to make neater ball shapes. Arrange the balls on the prepared baking sheets and bake for about 12 minutes. Dust with sifted confectioners' sugar and then transfer to a wire rack to cool.

Chocolate Cinnamon Tuiles

These crisp French cookies acquired their name because their shape is said to resemble that of a curved tile. Classically plain, this special version is flavored with cocoa and cinnamon.

Makes 12

1 egg white
2 ounces/¼ cup superfine sugar
2 tablespoons all-purpose flour
1½ ounces/3 tablespoons butter, melted
1 tablespoon cocoa powder (unsweetened)
½ teaspoon ground cinnamon

1 Preheat the oven to 400°F/Gas 6. Lightly grease two large baking sheets. Whisk the egg white in a clean, grease-free bowl until it forms soft peaks. Gradually whisk in the sugar to make a smooth, glossy mixture.

2 Sift the flour over the mixture and fold in evenly. Stir in the butter. Transfer about 3 tablespoons of the mixture to a small bowl and set aside.

3 In a separate small bowl, mix together the cocoa and ground cinnamon. Stir them into the larger quantity of mixture.

Cook's Tip
Work as quickly as possible when removing the tuiles from the baking sheets – if they firm up too quickly, pop the baking sheet back in the switched-off oven for a minute and try again.

4 Leaving room for spreading, drop spoonfuls of the chocolate-flavored mixture onto the prepared baking sheets, then spread each gently with a metal spatula to make a neat round shape.

5 Using a small spoon, carefully drizzle the reserved unflavored mixture over the round shapes to create a marbled effect.

6 Bake for 4–6 minutes until just set. Using a spatula, lift each cookie carefully and quickly drape it over a rolling pin, to give a curved shape as it hardens.

7 Leave the tuiles to cool until set, then remove them gently and place on a wire rack to cool completely. Serve on the same day.

Triple Chocolate Sandwiches

Chocolate shortbread is a brilliant base for sandwiching or coating in lashings of melted chocolate. Kids of any age can enjoy making them, as they don't need to be perfectly uniform.

Makes 15

4¼ ounces/generous ½ cup sweet butter, chilled and diced

5 ounces/1¼ cups all-purpose flour

2 tablespoons cocoa powder (unsweetened)

2 ounces/¼ cup superfine sugar

3 ounces white chocolate

1 ounce/2 tablespoons sweet butter

4 ounces milk chocolate

1 Put the butter, flour and cocoa in a food processor. Process until the mixture resembles breadcrumbs. Add the sugar and process again until the mixture forms a dough.

2 Transfer the dough to a clean surface and knead lightly. Put in plastic wrap and chill for 30 minutes.

3 Preheat the oven to 400°F/Gas 6. Grease a large baking sheet.

4 Roll out the chilled dough on a floured surface to a 13 x 6¼ inch rectangle. Lift onto the baking sheet and trim the edges.

5 Cut the dough in half lengthwise, then cut across at ¾-inch intervals to make 30 small bars.

6 Prick each bar with a fork and bake for 12–15 minutes, until just beginning to darken around the edges. Remove from the oven and cut between the bars again while the cookies are still warm. Leave for 2 minutes, then transfer to a wire rack to cool.

7 To make the filling, break the white chocolate into a heatproof bowl. Add half the butter and set the bowl over a pan of gently simmering water and stir frequently until melted.

8 Spread a little of the filling evenly onto one of the bars. Place another bar on top and push together to sandwich the cookies. Continue in the same way with the remaining cookies and filling.

9 To make the topping, break the milk chocolate into a heatproof bowl. Add the remaining butter and set over a pan of simmering water, stirring frequently until melted. Using a teaspoon, drizzle the chocolate over the top of the cookies, then leave to set.

Chocolate Crackle-tops

Older children will enjoy making these distinctive-looking cookies and everyone will love eating them. The dough needs to be chilled for an hour but then is easy to handle and roll.

Makes 38

7 ounces semisweet chocolate, chopped

3½ ounces/scant ½ cup sweet butter

4 ounces/generous ½ cup superfine sugar

3 eggs

1 teaspoon vanilla extract

7½ ounces/scant 2 cups all-purpose flour

1 ounce/¼ cup cocoa powder (unsweetened)

½ teaspoon baking powder

pinch of salt

6 ounces/1½ cups confectioners' sugar, for coating

1 In a pan set over a low heat, melt the chocolate and butter together until smooth, stirring frequently.

2 Remove the pan from the heat. Stir in the sugar, and continue stirring for 2–3 minutes until the sugar dissolves. Add the eggs, one at a time, beating well after each addition. Stir in the vanilla extract.

3 Sift the flour, cocoa powder, baking powder and salt into a bowl. Gradually stir into the chocolate mixture in batches, until blended.

4 Cover the dough, cool and chill for at least 1 hour, until the dough is cold and is able to hold its shape.

5 Preheat the oven to 325°F/ Gas 3. Grease two or more large baking sheets.

6 Place the confectioners' sugar in a deep bowl. Using a small ice-cream scoop or teaspoon, scoop out the cold dough and, between the palms of your hands, roll into 1½-inch balls.

7 Drop each ball into the confectioners' sugar and roll until heavily coated. Remove with a slotted spoon and tap against the side of the bowl to remove excess sugar. Place on the prepared baking sheets about 1½ inches apart.

8 Bake for 10–15 minutes, until the tops feel slightly firm when touched. Remove the baking sheet to a wire rack for 2–3 minutes, then with a metal spatula, place the cookies on the wire rack to cool completely.

Marbled Caramel Chocolate Slice

The classic millionaire's slice is made even more special here with a decorative and tasty marbled chocolate topping – guaranteed to make you feel like a lottery winner.

Makes about 24

For the base

9 ounces/2¼ cups all-purpose
    flour

3 ounces/scant ½ cup superfine
    sugar

6 ounces/¾ cup sweet butter,
    softened

For the filling

3½ ounces/7 tablespoons sweet
    butter, diced

3½ ounces/scant ½ cup light
    brown sugar

2 x 14-ounce cans sweetened
    condensed milk

For the topping

3½ ounces semisweet chocolate

3½ ounces milk chocolate

2 ounces white chocolate

I Preheat the oven to 350°F/
Gas 4. Line and lightly grease a
13 x 9 inch jelly roll pan. Put the
flour and superfine sugar in a
bowl and rub in the butter until
the mixture resembles fine
breadcrumbs. Work with your
hands until the mixture forms
a dough.

2 Put the dough into the prepared
pan and press it out with your hand
to cover the base. Then use the
back of a tablespoon to smooth it
evenly into the pan. Prick all over
with a fork and bake for about
20 minutes, or until firm to the
touch and very light brown. Set
aside and leave in the pan to cool.

3 To make the filling, put the butter,
brown sugar and condensed milk
into a pan and heat gently, stirring,
until the sugar has dissolved. Stirring
constantly, bring to the boil. Reduce
the heat and simmer the mixture
very gently, stirring constantly, for
about 5–10 minutes, or until it has
thickened and has turned a caramel
color. Take care that the mixture
does not burn on the base of the
pan, as this will spoil the flavor.
Remove from the heat.

4 Pour the filling mixture over the
cookie base, spread evenly, then
leave until cold.

5 To make the topping, melt each
type of chocolate separately in a
microwave or in a heatproof bowl
set over a pan of hot water. Spoon
lines of semisweet and milk
chocolate over the set caramel filling.

6 Add small spoonfuls of white
chocolate. Use a skewer to form a
marbled effect on the topping.

Chocolate Fudge Triangles

These delightful white-chocolate fudge sandwiches are surprisingly easy to make and perfect for a children's party, although chocolate-loving adults will enjoy them, too.

Makes 48

1 pound 5 ounces good quality white chocolate, chopped

14 fluid ounces/1¾ cups sweetened condensed milk

1 tablespoon vanilla extract

1½ teaspoons lemon juice

pinch of salt

7½ ounces/scant 2 cups hazelnuts or pecan nuts, chopped (optional)

6 ounces semisweet chocolate, chopped

1½ ounces/3 tablespoons sweet butter, chopped

2 ounces semisweet chocolate, melted, to decorate

1 Line an 8 inch square cake pan with foil. Melt the white chocolate with the condensed milk in a pan over a low heat, stirring frequently. Remove from the heat and stir in the vanilla extract, lemon juice, salt, and nuts, if using. Spread half the mixture in the pan. Chill in the refrigerator for 15 minutes.

2 Melt the semisweet chocolate with the butter in a pan over a low heat, stirring until smooth. Remove from the heat, cool slightly, then pour over the chilled white layer and chill for 15 minutes.

3 Gently reheat the remaining white chocolate and condensed milk mixture until melted and pour it over the set semisweet chocolate layer. Smooth the top with a metal spatula, then chill in the refrigerator for 2–4 hours, until set.

4 Using the foil to lift it, remove the fudge from the pan and turn onto a chopping board. Remove the foil and, using a sharp knife, cut into 24 squares. Cut each square into two triangles. To decorate, drizzle with melted chocolate.

Chocolate, Maple and Walnut Swirls

Gloriously sticky and richly flavored, these swirls are like a cross between cookies and slices of cake. Serve them as a weekend coffee-time treat when you've had a busy morning.

Makes 12

1 pound/4 cups strong white
   bread flour

½ teaspoon ground cinnamon

2 ounces/¼ cup sweet
   butter, diced

2 ounces/¼ cup superfine
   sugar

1 sachet rapid-rise
   dried yeast

1 egg yolk

4 fluid ounces/½ cup water

4 tablespoons milk

1½ ounces/3 tablespoons sweet
   butter, melted

3 tablespoons maple syrup,
   to finish

For the filling

2 ounces/¼ cup light brown sugar

6 ounces/1 cup semisweet
   chocolate chips

3 ounces/¾ cup chopped walnuts

1 Grease a deep 9-inch springform cake pan. Sift the flour and cinnamon into a bowl, then rub in the butter until the mixture resembles breadcrumbs.

2 Stir in the sugar and yeast. In a separate bowl, beat the egg yolk, with the measured water and milk, then stir the mixture into the dry ingredients to make a soft dough.

3 Knead until smooth, then roll out to about 16 × 12 inches. Brush evenly with melted butter.

4 To make the filling, sprinkle the dough evenly with the brown sugar, then the semisweet chocolate chips and, finally, the chopped walnuts.

5 Roll up the dough from a long side like a jelly roll, then cut into 12 thick even-size slices.

6 Pack the slices closely together in the prepared cake pan. Cover and leave in a warm place for 1½ hours, until well risen and springy to the touch. Preheat the oven to 425°F/Gas 7.

7 Bake for 30–35 minutes, until well risen, golden brown and firm. Remove from the pan and transfer to a wire rack. To finish, spoon the maple syrup over the top. Pull the pieces apart to serve.

Cook's Tip
Make sure you use rapid-rise yeast, as other kinds need dissolving first.

Chocolate Salami

This after-dinner sweetmeat resembles a salami in shape, hence its curious name – although, of course, the flavor is somewhat different. It is very rich and will serve a lot of people. Slice it very thinly and serve with espresso coffee and amaretto liqueur.

Serves 8–12

24 Petit Beurre cookies, broken
    into pieces
12 ounces bittersweet chocolate, broken
    into squares
8 ounces/1 cup sweet butter, softened
4 tablespoons amaretto liqueur
2 egg yolks
2 ounces/½ cup sliced almonds,
    lightly toasted and thinly
    shredded lengthwise
1 ounce/¼ cup ground almonds

Variation

If you like, substitute pistachio nuts for the sliced almonds.

1 Place the cookies in a food processor and process until crushed into coarse crumbs.

2 Place the chocolate in a large heatproof bowl. Place the bowl over a pan of barely simmering water, add a small pat of the butter and all the liqueur and heat until the chocolate melts, stirring occasionally.

3 Remove the bowl from the heat, leave the chocolate to cool for a minute or two, then stir in the egg yolks, followed by the remaining butter, a little at a time. Tip in most of the crushed cookies, leaving behind a good handful, and stir well to mix. Stir in the shredded almonds. Leave the mixture in a cold place for about 1 hour, until it begins to soften.

4 Process the remaining crushed cookies in the food processor until they are very finely ground. Tip into a bowl and mix with the ground almonds. Cover and set aside until you are ready to serve.

5 Turn the chocolate and cookie mixture onto a sheet of lightly oiled waxed paper, then shape into a 14-inch-long sausage, using a metal spatula, tapering the ends slightly so that the roll looks like a salami. Wrap securely in the paper and freeze the roll for at least 4 hours, until solid.

6 To serve, unwrap the "salami". Spread the finely ground cookies and almonds out on a clean sheet of waxed paper and roll the salami in them until evenly coated. Transfer to a board and leave to stand for about 1 hour before serving in slices.

Cook's Tip

Take care when melting chocolate that it does not overheat. The base of the bowl must not touch the water, and the chocolate must be melted very gently. If you think the water is getting too hot, remove the pan from the heat.

Choc-tipped Cookies

Get those cold hands wrapped around a steaming hot drink and tuck into these tasty cookies. They're delightfully easy to make and quite delicious to eat.

Makes 22

4 ounces/½ cup butter or margarine
    at room temperature, diced
3 tablespoons confectioners' sugar,
    sifted
5 ounces/1¼ cups all-purpose flour
few drops vanilla extract
3 ounces semisweet chocolate,
    chopped

1 Preheat the oven to 350°F/Gas 4. Lightly grease two baking sheets. Put the butter or margarine and confectioners' sugar in a mixing bowl and cream together until very soft.

2 Add the flour and vanilla extract to the creamed mixture and mix until thoroughly combined.

3 Spoon the mixture into a large pastry bag fitted with a large star nozzle and pipe 4–5-inch lines onto the prepared baking sheets, leaving space for expansion.

4 Cook for 15–20 minutes, until pale golden brown. Leave on the baking sheets to cool slightly before lifting on to a wire rack. Leave the cookies to cool completely.

5 Put the chocolate in a small heatproof bowl and melt over a pan of hot, but not boiling water.

6 Dip both ends of each cookie into the melted chocolate, return the cookies to the wire rack as they are diped and leave them to set. Serve the cookies with mugs of hot chocolate topped with swirls of whipped cream and dusted with chocolate powder.

Variation

Make round cookies if you prefer, and dip each cookie into the melted chocolate to half coat.

Fruity Chocolate Cookie-cakes

The combination of spongy cookie, fruity preserve and semisweet chocolate makes irresistible eating for kids of all ages. As cookies go, these are a little time consuming, but that's all part of the fun.

Makes 18

3½ ounces/ ½ cup superfine
* sugar*
2 eggs
2 ounces/ ½ cup all-purpose flour
3 ounces/6 tablespoons apricot-orange
* marmalade or apricot jam*
4¼ ounces semisweet chocolate

1 Preheat the oven to 375°F/ Gas 5. Grease 18 muffin pans, preferably non-stick. (If you don't have that many muffin pans, you'll need to bake the cookies in batches.)

2 Stand a mixing bowl in very hot water for a couple of minutes to heat through, keeping the inside of the bowl dry. Put the sugar and eggs in the bowl and whisk with a hand-held electric mixer until light and frothy, when the beaters leave a ribbon trail when lifted. Sift the flour over the mixture and stir in gently using a large metal spoon.

3 Divide the mixture among the muffin pans. Bake for 10 minutes until just firm and pale golden around the edges. Using a metal spatula, lift from the pans and transfer to a wire rack to cool.

4 Press the marmalade or jam through a sieve to remove any rind or fruit pieces. Spoon a little of the smooth jam onto the center of each cookie.

5 Break the chocolate into pieces and place in a heatproof bowl set over a pan of gently simmering water. Heat, stirring frequently, until melted and smooth.

6 Spoon a little chocolate onto the top of each cookie and spread gently to the edges with a metal spatula. Once the chocolate has just started to set, very gently press it with the back of a fork to give a textured surface. Leave to set for at least 1 hour.

Chocolate Caramel Nuggets

Inside each of these buttery cookies lies a soft-centered chocolate-coated caramel. They're at their most delicious served an hour or so after baking, so you might want to shape them in advance, then put the baking sheet of uncooked nuggets in the refrigerator until you are ready to bake them.

Makes 14

5 ounces/1¼ cups self-rising flour

3½ ounces/7 tablespoons sweet butter,
*   chilled and diced*

2 ounces/¼ cup golden superfine
*   sugar*

1 egg yolk

1 teaspoon vanilla extract

14 soft-centered chocolate caramels

confectioners' sugar and cocoa
*   powder (unsweetened),*
*   for dusting*

1 Put the flour and diced butter in a food processor and process until the mixture resembles fairly fine breadcrumbs.

2 Add the sugar, egg yolk and vanilla extract to the food processor and process to a smooth dough. Put the dough in plastic wrap and chill for 30 minutes.

3 Preheat the oven to 400°F/Gas 6. Grease a large baking sheet.

4 Roll the dough thinly on a lightly floured surface and cut out 28 round pieces, using a 2-inch cutter.

5 Place one chocolate caramel on a round piece, then lay a second round piece on top. Pinch the edges of the dough together so that the chocolate caramel is completely enclosed, then place on the baking sheet. Make the remaining cookies in the same way. Bake for about 10 minutes, until pale golden.

6 Transfer to a wire rack and leave to cool. Serve lightly dusted with confectioners' sugar and cocoa powder.

Chocolate Whirls

These cookies are so easy that you don't even have to make any dough. They're made with ready-made puff pastry rolled up with a chocolate filling. They're not too sweet and are similar to Danish pastries, so you could even make them as a special treat for breakfast.

Makes about 20

3 ounces/⅓ cup golden superfine
  sugar
1½ ounces/6 tablespoons cocoa powder
  (unsweetened)
2 eggs
1 pound 2 ounces puff pastry
1 ounce/2 tablespoons butter, softened
3 ounces/generous ½ cup
  golden raisins
3½ ounces milk chocolate

1 Preheat the oven to 425°F/Gas 7. Grease two baking sheets.

2 Put the sugar, cocoa powder and eggs in a bowl and mix to a paste.

3 Roll out the pastry on a lightly floured surface to make a 12-inch square. Trim off any rough edges using a sharp knife.

4 Dot the pastry all over with the softened butter, then spread with the chocolate paste and sprinkle the raisins over the top.

Cook's Tip
Use a sharp knife to cut the cookie slices from the pastry roll, and wipe the blade clean with a cloth every few slices.

5 Roll the pastry into a sausage-shape, then cut the roll into ½-inch slices. Place the slices on the baking sheets, spacing them apart.

6 Bake the cookies for 10 minutes, until risen and pale golden. Transfer to a wire rack and leave to cool.

7 Break the milk chocolate into pieces and put in a heatproof bowl set over a pan of gently simmering water. Heat, stirring frequently until melted and smooth.

8 Spoon or pipe lines of melted chocolate over the cookies, taking care not to completely hide the swirls of chocolate filling.

Chocolate Truffle Cookies

Deeply decadent, these melt-in-the-mouth cookies are given a wicked twist by the addition of cherry brandy – the perfect way to end a dinner party.

Makes 18

2 ounces/½ cup all-purpose
   flour

1 ounce/¼ cup cocoa powder
   (unsweetened)

½ teaspoon baking powder

3½ ounces/½ cup superfine
   sugar

1 ounce/2 tablespoons butter, diced

1 egg, beaten

1 teaspoon cherry brandy or fresh
   orange juice

2 ounces/½ cup confectioners'
   sugar

1 Preheat the oven to 400°F/
Gas 6. Line two baking sheets with
baking parchment.

2 Sift the flour, cocoa and baking
powder into a bowl and stir in
the sugar. Rub in the butter until the
mixture resembles breadcrumbs. Mix
together the beaten egg and cherry
brandy or orange juice and stir into
the flour mixture. Cover with plastic
wrap and chill in the refrigerator for
30 minutes.

3 Put the confectioners' sugar into
a bowl. Shape walnut-size pieces of
dough roughly into a ball and drop
into the sugar. Toss until thickly coated
then place on the baking sheets.

4 Bake for about 10 minutes, or
until just set. Transfer to a wire rack
to cool completely.

White Chocolate Brownies

These scrumptious brownies are best served cut into very small portions – not only because they are incredibly rich, but also because kids find tiny, bite-size cookies utterly irresistible.

Makes 18

3 ounces/6 tablespoons sweet
    butter, diced
14 ounces white chocolate,
    chopped
3 eggs
3½ ounces/½ cup golden
    superfine sugar
2 teaspoons vanilla extract
3½ ounces/¾ cup golden raisins
coarsely grated rind of 1 lemon,
    plus 1 tablespoon juice
7 ounces/1¾ cups all-purpose
    flour

1 Preheat the oven to 375°F/ Gas 5. Grease and line an 11 x 8 inch shallow baking pan with baking parchment.

2 Put the butter and 11 ounces of the chocolate in a bowl and melt over a pan of gently simmering water, stirring frequently.

3 Remove the bowl from the heat and beat in the eggs and sugar, then add the vanilla extract, raisins, lemon rind and juice, flour and the remaining chocolate.

4 Tip the mixture into the pan and spread into the corners. Bake for about 20 minutes, until slightly risen, when the surface is only just turning golden. The center should still be slightly soft. Leave to cool in the pan.

5 Cut the brownies into small squares and then carefully remove them from the pan.

Rich Chocolate Cookie Slice

These rich, semisweet chocolate refrigerator cookies are perfect served with strong coffee, either as a mid-morning treat or even in place of dessert. They are always very popular.

Makes about 10
10 ounces fruit and nut semisweet chocolate

4½ ounces/½ cup sweet butter, diced

3½ ounces graham crackers

3½ ounces white chocolate

1 Grease and line the base and sides of a 1-pound loaf pan with baking parchment. Break the fruit and nut chocolate into even-size pieces and place in a heatproof bowl along with the diced sweet butter.

2 Set the bowl over a pan of simmering water and stir gently until melted. Cool for 20 minutes.

3 Break the graham crackers into small pieces with your fingers. Finely chop the white chocolate.

4 Stir the broken biscuits and white chocolate into the cooled, melted fruit and nut chocolate until combined. Turn the mixture into the prepared pan and pack down gently. Chill for 2 hours, or until set.

5 To serve, turn out the mixture and remove the lining paper. Cut into slices with a sharp knife.

Variation
You can use this simple, basic recipe for all kinds of variations. Try different kinds of chocolate, such as ginger, hazelnut, honey and almond, peanut or mocha.

Giant Triple Chocolate Cookies

Here is the ultimate cookie, packed full of chocolate and macadamia nuts. You will have to be patient when they come out of the oven, as they are too soft to move until completely cold.

Makes 12 large cookies

3½ ounces milk chocolate

3½ ounces white chocolate

11 ounces bittersweet chocolate
(minimum 70 percent
cocoa solids)

3½ ounces/7 tablespoons sweet
butter, at room temperature,
diced

1 teaspoon vanilla extract

5 ounces/¾ cup light brown sugar

5 ounces/1¼ cups self-rising flour

3½ ounces/scant 1 cup macadamia
nut halves

1 Preheat the oven to 350°F/Gas 4. Line two baking sheets with baking parchment. Coarsely chop the milk and white chocolate and put them in a bowl.

2 Chop 7 ounces of the bittersweet chocolate into very large chunks, at least ¾ inch in size. Set aside.

3 Break up the remaining bittersweet chocolate and place in a heatproof bowl set over a pan of barely simmering water. Stir until melted and smooth. Remove from the heat and stir in the butter, then the vanilla extract and brown sugar.

4 Add the flour and mix gently. Add half the bittersweet chocolate chunks, all the milk and white chocolate and the nuts and fold together.

5 Spoon 12 mounds onto the baking sheets. Press the remaining bittersweet chocolate chunks into the top of each cookie. Bake for about 12 minutes, until just beginning to color. Cool on the baking sheets.

Chocolate-chip Oat Cookies

Easy to make and delicious to eat. These vanilla-flavored cookies are exceedingly irresistible, so you'll need to keep the cookie jar or biscuit barrel well stocked up with this family favorite.

Makes 60

4 ounces/1 cup all-purpose flour

½ teaspoon baking soda

¼ teaspoon baking powder

pinch of salt

4 ounces/½ cup butter or margarine
  at room temperature, diced

4 ounces/generous ½ cup
  superfine sugar

3½ ounces/½ cup soft light
  brown sugar

1 egg

½ teaspoon vanilla extract

3 ounces/scant 1 cup rolled oats

6 ounces/1 cup semisweet
  chocolate chips

1 Preheat the oven to 350°F/
Gas 4. Lightly grease three or four
baking sheets.

2 Sift the flour, baking soda, baking
powder and salt into a mixing bowl.
Set aside.

3 With an electric mixer, cream
together the butter or margarine
and the sugars. Add the egg and
vanilla and beat until light and fluffy.

4 Add the flour mixture and beat
on low speed until thoroughly
blended. Stir in the rolled oats and
chocolate chips. The dough should
be crumbly. Drop heaped
teaspoonfuls onto the prepared
baking sheets, spacing the dough
about 1 inch apart.

5 Bake for about 15 minutes, until
just firm around the edge but still
soft to the touch in the center.
Transfer the cookies to a wire rack
and leave to cool.

Variation

*For an elegant look, melt semisweet
chocolate over a pan of hot, but not
boiling water, stirring until smooth. Dip
the baked cookies into the chocolate to
cover one half of the cookie.*

Double Chocolate Cookies

Keep these scrumptious treats under lock and key unless you're feeling especially generous. With two types of chocolate, they would certainly make a special gift for a good friend.

Makes 18–20

4 ounces/½ cup sweet butter
  at room temperature, diced

4 ounces/½ cup light brown
  sugar

1 egg

1 teaspoon vanilla extract

5 ounces/1¼ cups self-rising flour

3 ounces/scant 1 cup rolled oats

4 ounces semisweet chocolate,
  coarsely chopped

4 ounces white chocolate,
  coarsely chopped

3 Place small spoonfuls of the mixture in 18–20 rocky heaps on the prepared baking sheets, leaving space for spreading.

4 Bake for 15–20 minutes, until beginning to turn pale golden brown. Cool for 2–3 minutes on the baking sheets, then, using a spatula, transfer the cookies to wire racks to cool completely.

Variation

If you're short of time when making these cookies, substitute chocolate chips for the chopped chocolate. Chopped preserved stem ginger would make a delicious addition as well.

1 Preheat the oven to 375°F/Gas 5. Lightly grease two baking sheets. Cream the butter with the sugar in a bowl until pale and fluffy. Add the egg and vanilla extract and beat well.

2 Sift the flour over the mixture and fold in lightly with a metal spoon, then add the oats and chopped semisweet and white chocolate and stir well until evenly mixed.

Cook's Tip

Rolled oats are also known as "old-fashioned oats." Fine oatmeal is also excellent for making cookies.

Chocolate-chip Hazelnut Cookies

Hazelnuts impart a delicious nutty flavor to these little cookies. They would make a wonderful late night snack with a steaming mug of hot chocolate, topped with whipped cream.

Makes 36

4 ounces/1 cup all-purpose flour

1 teaspoon baking powder

pinch of salt

3 ounces/⅓ cup butter or margarine
   at room temperature, diced

4 ounces/generous ½ cup superfine
   sugar

2 ounces/¼ cup soft light brown sugar

1 egg

1 teaspoon vanilla extract

4½ ounces/⅔ cup chocolate chips

2 ounces/½ cup hazelnuts, chopped

1 Preheat the oven to 350°F/Gas 4. Grease two or three baking sheets. Sift the flour, baking powder and salt into a small bowl. Set aside.

2 With an electric mixer, cream together the butter or margarine and the sugars. Beat in the egg and vanilla extract. Add the flour mixture and beat well with the mixer on low speed.

3 Stir in the chocolate chips and half of the chopped hazelnuts.

4 Drop teaspoonfuls of the mixture onto the prepared baking sheets, to form ¾-inch mounds. Space the cookies 1–2 inches apart.

5 Flatten each cookie lightly with a wet fork. Sprinkle the remaining hazelnuts on top of the cookies and press lightly into the surface.

6 Bake for 10–12 minutes, until golden. With a metal spatula, transfer the cookies to a wire rack and leave to cool completely.

Cook's Tip

If you need to skin the hazelnuts yourself, spread them out on a baking sheet and toast lightly under the broiler or in a preheated oven, at 350°F/ Gas 4, then tip into a clean dishtowel. Rub with the dishtowel and the skins should slip off easily. Pick off any obstinate pieces.

Chocolate-coated Nut Brittle

Equal amounts of pecan nuts and almonds set in crisp caramel, then coated in semisweet chocolate, make a sensational gift – if you can bear to give them away.

Makes 20–24

4 ounces/1 cup mixed pecan nuts and
    whole almonds

4 ounces/generous ½ cup superfine
    sugar

4 tablespoons water

7 ounces semisweet chocolate,
    chopped

1 Lightly grease a baking sheet. Mix the nuts, sugar and water in a heavy pan. Cook over a low heat, stirring until the sugar has dissolved.

2 Bring to the boil, then lower the heat to medium and cook without stirring until the mixture turns a rich golden brown and registers 300°F on a sugar thermometer.

3 To test without a thermometer, drop a small amount of the mixture into ice water. It should become brittle enough to snap.

4 Quickly remove the pan from the heat and tip the mixture onto the prepared baking sheet, spreading it evenly. Leave until completely cold and set hard.

5 Break the nut brittle into pieces. Melt the chocolate and dip the nut brittle to half-coat them. Leave on a sheet of baking parchment to set, then store in an airtight container.

Cook's Tip

This brittle looks best in coarse chunks, so don't worry if the pieces break unevenly, or if there are few small gaps in the chocolate coating.

Indulgent Cookies

In case all the previous recipes haven't spoilt
you for choice, here is a superb collection of
mouth-watering treats that will prove totally
irresistible – from blissful Tiramisu Cookies to
light-as-air Praline Pavlova Cookies. There is
something special to indulge everyone,
whether your tastes are for the rich and
creamy, fresh and fruity or dark and chocolatey.
There are even breakfast cookies that cook
overnight while you sleep.

Florentine Cookies

These are not your traditional Florentines but an utterly yummy cookie version with a soft crumbly base and a wonderfully sticky chewy topping.

Makes 24

4 ounces/½ cup sweet butter, at room
    temperature, diced

4 ounces/generous ½ cup
    superfine sugar

1 egg

a few drops of almond extract (optional)

8 ounces/2 cups self-rising flour

For the topping

6 ounces/1½ cups ready-to-eat dried
    apricots, chopped

2 ounces/½ cup dried mango pieces,
    chopped

3½ ounces/scant 1 cup sliced
    almonds

4 tablespoons all-purpose flour

2 ounces/¼ cup sweet butter

2 ounces/¼ cup golden
    superfine sugar

4 tablespoons golden light
    corn syrup

1 Preheat the oven to 375°F/Gas 5. Lightly grease two baking sheets. Cream together the butter and sugar until the mixture is light and fluffy, then beat in the egg, making sure it is well combined. Stir in the almond extract, if using, and the flour and mix to a firm yet soft dough, working it together with your hands.

Variation

For an even more self-indulgent treat, make the topping using maple, rather than light corn syrup. Make sure you buy the pure syrup that has not been blended with other cheaper syrups, as it has an incomparable flavor.

2 Roll the dough out on a floured surface and, using a 3-inch plain round cookie cutter, stamp out 24 round pieces. Place them on the prepared baking sheets, spaced slightly apart to allow for spreading.

3 To make the topping, put the apricots, mango pieces, almonds and flour in a bowl and toss gently together to mix. Put the butter, sugar and syrup in a small pan and heat gently until the butter has melted and the mixture is smooth and combined. Pour the butter mixture over the fruit and nuts and mix thoroughly.

4 Spoon the mixture on top of the cookies, spreading it right to the edges. Bake for 12–14 minutes, until golden brown and crisp on top. Leave the cookies on the baking sheets for 5 minutes to firm up slightly, then transfer to a wire rack to cool completely.

Candied Peel Crumble Cookies

Crumbly, melt-in-the-mouth cookies, these incorporate candied peel, walnuts and white chocolate chips and are coated with a zingy lemon glaze.

Makes about 24

6 ounces/¾ cup sweet butter, at room
   temperature, diced

3½ ounces/½ cup superfine sugar

1 egg, beaten

finely grated rind of 1 lemon

7 ounces/1¾ cups self-rising flour

3½ ounces/generous ½ cup
   candied peel, chopped

3 ounces/¾ cup chopped walnuts

2 ounces/⅓ cup white chocolate chips

For the glaze

2 ounces/½ cup confectioners'
   sugar, sifted

1 tablespoon lemon juice

thin strips of candied peel, to
   decorate (optional)

1 Preheat the oven to 350°F/Gas 4. Grease two baking sheets or line them with baking parchment. Put the butter and sugar in a large bowl and cream together. Add the egg and beat thoroughly. Add the lemon rind and flour and stir together gently. Finally, fold the candied peel, walnuts and chocolate chips into the mixture.

2 Place tablespoonfuls of mixture, spaced slightly apart, on the baking sheets and bake for 12–15 minutes, until cooked but still pale in color. Transfer the cookies to a wire rack.

3 For the glaze, put the confectioners' sugar in a bowl and stir in the lemon juice. Spoon glaze over each cookie. Decorate with candied peel, if using.

Midnight Cookies

These cookies are so called because you can make them up before you go to bed and leave them to bake slowly in the switched-off oven. Hey presto – there they are in the morning, lightly crunchy on the outside and deliciously soft in the middle. A wonderfully indulgent way to start the day.

Makes 9

1 egg white

3½ ounces/½ cup superfine sugar

2 ounces/½ cup ground almonds

3½ ounces/generous ½ cup milk
chocolate chips

3½ ounces/scant ½ cup candied
cherries, chopped

2 ounces/⅔ cup dried sweetened,
shredded coconut

1 Preheat the oven to 425°F/
Gas 7. Line a baking sheet with
baking parchment. Put the egg
white in a large, clean, grease-
free bowl and whisk until stiff
peaks form.

2 Add the superfine sugar to the
whisked egg white, a spoonful at a
time, whisking well between each
addition until the sugar is fully
incorporated. The mixture should
be completely smooth and glossy in
appearance. Use an electric mixer
for speed.

3 Fold in the almonds, chocolate
chips, cherries and coconut. Place
9 spoonfuls on the baking sheet.
Place in the oven, close the door
then turn the oven off. Leave
overnight (or at least 6 hours during
the day) and don't open the door.
Serve the cookies for breakfast.

Banana Cream Cookies

These delicious cookies are inspired by the classic childhood dessert bananas and cream. The warm banana cookies are coated in crisp, sugar-frosted cornflakes and, for the ultimate indulgence, are delicious served warm drizzled with clear honey.

Makes about 24

2 eggs

9 ounces/1¼ cups soft light
   brown sugar

1 teaspoon vanilla extract

3½ fluid ounces/scant ½ cup
   sunflower oil

3½ ounces/scant ½ cup crème
   fraîche

7 ounces/1¾ cups all-purpose flour

7 ounces/1¾ cups self-rising flour

2 ounces/2½ cups frosted cornflakes

4¼ ounces dried small bananas,
   chopped, or 2 bananas, peeled
   and chopped

confectioners' sugar, sifted,
   for dredging

1 Preheat the oven to 350°F/Gas 4. Line two or three baking sheets with baking parchment. Put the eggs and brown sugar in a large bowl and whisk together until well blended. Stir in the vanilla extract. Add the oil and crème fraîche and stir in well. Add the flour and mix well. (The mixture will be quite runny at this stage.) Cover with plastic wrap and chill in the refrigerator for about 30 minutes.

2 Put the frosted cornflakes in a large bowl. Remove the cookie dough from the refrigerator and stir in the bananas. Using a tablespoon, drop heaps into the flakes. Lightly toss so each cookie is well coated, then remove and place on the prepared baking sheets. Flatten very slightly with your fingertips.

3 Bake for 15–20 minutes, or until risen and golden brown and crispy. Transfer the cookies to a wire rack and dredge with sifted confectioners' sugar. Serve while still warm.

Praline Pavlova Cookies

Crisp, melt-in-the-mouth meringue with a luxurious velvety chocolate filling is topped with nutty praline – just the thing for a special tea party or simply when you feel in need of a treat.

Makes 14

2 extra large egg whites

large pinch of ground cinnamon

3½ ounces/½ cup superfine
    sugar

2 ounces/½ cup pecan nuts,
    finely chopped

For the filling

2 ounces/¼ cup sweet butter,
    at room temperature, diced

3½ ounces/scant 1 cup confectioners'
    sugar, sifted

2 ounces semisweet chocolate

For the praline

4 tablespoons superfine sugar

½ ounce/1 tablespoon finely chopped
    toasted almonds

2 Place 14 spoonfuls of meringue on the prepared baking sheets, spaced far apart. Using the back of a wetted teaspoon, make a small hollow in the top of each meringue so it looks like a little nest. Bake in the oven for 45–60 minutes, until dry and just beginning to color. Remove from the oven and set aside to cool.

1 Preheat the oven to 275°F/ Gas 1. Line two baking sheets with baking parchment. Put the egg whites in a bowl and whisk until stiff. Stir the cinnamon into the sugar. Add a spoonful of sugar to the egg whites and whisk well. Continue adding the sugar, a spoonful at a time, whisking well until the mixture is thick and glossy. Stir in the chopped pecan nuts.

3 To make the filling, beat together the butter and confectioners' sugar until light and creamy. Break the chocolate into even-size pieces and place in a heatproof bowl. Set over a pan of barely simmering water and stir occasionally until melted. Remove from the heat and leave to cool slightly. Add the chocolate to the butter mixture and stir well. Divide the filling among the meringues, putting a little in each hollow.

4 To make the praline, put the sugar in a small non-stick frying pan. Heat gently until the sugar melts to form a clear liquid. When the mixture begins to turn brown, stir in the nuts. When the mixture is a golden brown, remove from the heat and pour immediately onto a lightly oiled or non-stick baking sheet. Leave to cool completely and then break into small pieces. Sprinkle over the meringues and serve.

Cook's Tip

These cookies should be eaten immediately, once they have been assembled. To make them ahead of time, store the unfilled meringues in an airtight container and place the filling in a covered container in a cool place. Make the praline on the day itself.

Variation

Use toasted hazelnuts, instead of almonds, to make the praline.

Tiramisu Cookies

These delicate cookies taste like the wonderful Italian dessert with its flavors of coffee, chocolate, rum and rich creamy custard. Serve with coffee or cups of frothy hot chocolate.

Makes 14

2 ounces/¼ cup butter, at room
   temperature, diced
3½ ounces/½ cup superfine sugar
1 egg, beaten
2 ounces/½ cup all-purpose flour

For the filling

5 ounces/⅔ cup mascarpone cheese
1 tablespoon dark rum
½ teaspoon instant coffee powder
1 tablespoon light brown sugar

For the topping

3 ounces white chocolate
1 tablespoon milk
2 tablespoons crushed chocolate flakes

1 To make the filling, put the mascarpone cheese in a bowl. Mix together the rum and coffee powder, stirring well until the coffee has dissolved. Add the rum and coffee mixture and the sugar to the cheese and mix together well. Cover with plastic wrap and chill until required.

2 Preheat the oven to 400°F/Gas 6. Line two or three baking sheets with baking parchment. To make the cookies, cream together the butter and sugar in a bowl until light and fluffy. Add the beaten egg and mix well. Stir in the flour and mix thoroughly again until well combined.

3 Put the mixture into a pastry bag fitted with a ½-inch plain nozzle, and pipe 28 small blobs onto the baking sheets, spaced slightly apart. Cook for about 6–8 minutes until firm in the center and just beginning to brown on the edges. Remove from the oven and set aside to cool.

4 When ready to assemble, spread a little of the filling onto half the cookies and place the other halves on top. Put the chocolate and milk in a heatproof bowl and melt over a pan of hot water. Take care not to overheat. When the chocolate has melted, stir vigorously to make a smooth spreadable consistency. Spread the chocolate topping evenly over the cookies, then sprinkle with crushed chocolate flakes to finish.

Chocolate and Prune Cookies

When freshly baked, these cookies have a deliciously gooey centre. As they cool down, the mixture hardens slightly to form a firmer, fudge-like consistency. Try these with a glass of brandy.

Makes 18

5 ounces/⅔ cup butter, at room
    temperature, diced
5 ounces/¾ cup superfine sugar
1 egg yolk
9 ounces/2¼ cups self-rising
    flour
1 ounce/¼ cup cocoa powder
    (unsweetened)
about 3½ ounces semisweet chocolate,
    coarsely chopped

For the topping

2 ounces semisweet chocolate
9 ready-to-eat prunes, halved

1 Preheat the oven to 375°F/Gas 5. Line two baking sheets with baking parchment. Cream the butter and sugar together until light and creamy. Beat in the egg yolk. Sift over the flour and cocoa powder and stir in to make a firm yet soft dough.

2 Roll out about a third of the dough on baking parchment. Using a 2-inch round cookie cutter, stamp out 18 round pieces and place them on the baking sheets.

3 Sprinkle the chopped chocolate in the center of each cookie.

4 Roll out the remaining dough in the same way as before and, using a 3-inch round cookie cutter, stamp out 18 "lids". Carefully lay the lids over the cookie bases and press the edges well together to seal. Don't worry if the lids crack slightly when you do this.

5 Bake for about 10 minutes, until the cookies have spread a little and are just firm to a light touch. Leave them on the baking sheets for about 5 minutes to firm up slightly, then, using a metal spatula, transfer to a wire rack to cool completely.

6 For the topping, melt the chocolate in a heatproof bowl set over a pan of hot water. Dip the cut side of the prunes in the chocolate then place one on top of each cookie. Spoon any remaining chocolate over the prunes.

Chocolate Fruit and Nut Cookies

These simple, chunky gingerbread cookies make a delicious gift, especially when presented in a decorative box. The combination of walnuts, almonds and cherries is very effective, but you can use any other mixture of candied fruits and nuts.

Makes 20

2 ounces/4 tablespoons superfine sugar

5 tablespoons water

8 ounces semisweet chocolate, chopped

1½ ounces/½ cup walnut halves

3 ounces/⅓ cup candied cherries, chopped into small wedges

4 ounces/1 cup whole blanched almonds

For the lebkuchen

4 ounces/½ cup sweet butter

4 ounces/½ cup light brown sugar

1 egg, beaten

4 ounces/⅓ cup black molasses

14 ounces/3½ cups self-rising flour

1 teaspoon ground ginger

½ teaspoon ground cloves

¼ teaspoon chilli powder

1 To make the lebkuchen, cream together the butter and sugar until pale and fluffy. Beat in the egg and black molasses.

2 Sift the flour, ginger, cloves and chilli powder into the bowl. Using a wooden spoon, gradually mix the ingredients together to make a stiff paste. Turn onto a lightly floured surface and knead lightly until smooth. Wrap and chill for 30 minutes.

3 Shape the dough into a roll, about 8 inches long. Chill for 30 minutes. Preheat the oven to 350°F/Gas 4. Grease two baking sheets.

4 Cut the dough roll into 20 slices and space them on the baking sheets. Bake for 10 minutes. Leave on the baking sheets for 5 minutes, then transfer to a wire rack and leave to cool.

5 Put the sugar and water in a small, heavy pan. Heat gently, stirring constantly until the sugar has completely dissolved. Bring to the boil and boil without stirring for 1 minute, until slightly syrupy.

6 Remove the pan from the heat and leave for 3 minutes, to cool slightly, and then stir in the chocolate until it has completely melted and made a smooth sauce.

7 Place the wire rack of cookies over a large tray or board. Spoon a little of the chocolate mixture over the cookies, spreading it to the edges with the back of the spoon.

8 Gently press a walnut half into the center of each cookie. Arrange pieces of candied cherry and almonds alternately around the nuts. Leave to set in a cool place.

Cook's Tip
Carefully stack the cookies in a pretty box or tin, lined with tissue paper, or tie in cellophane bundles.

Variation
If you prefer, make simpler chocolate-covered lebkuchen. Simply omit the walnuts, cherries and almonds and sprinkle the cookies with cocoa powder (unsweetened) before serving.

Cranberry and Chocolate Squares

There is no doubt that the contrasting flavors of tangy, sharp cranberries and sweet chocolate were made for each other – and make fabulous cream-topped squares.

Makes 12

4 ounces/½ cup sweet butter

4 tablespoons cocoa powder

7½ ounces/scant 1 cup light brown sugar

5 ounces/1¼ cups self-rising flour

2 eggs, beaten

4 ounces/1 cup fresh or thawed frozen cranberries

For the topping

¼ pint/⅔ cup sour cream

3 ounces/6 tablespoons superfine sugar

2 tablespoons self-rising flour

2 ounces/4 tablespoons soft margarine

1 egg, beaten

½ teaspoon vanilla extract

5 tablespoons coarsely grated semisweet chocolate, for sprinkling

1 Preheat the oven to 350°F/ Gas 4. Grease a 7 x 10 inch cake pan and dust lightly with flour. Combine the butter, cocoa powder and sugar in a pan and stir over a low heat until melted and smooth.

2 Remove from the heat and stir in the flour and eggs. Stir in the cranberries, then spread the mixture in the prepared cake pan.

3 To make the topping, mix all the ingredients, except the chocolate, in a bowl. Beat until smooth, then spread over the mixture in the pan.

4 Sprinkle evenly with the coarsely grated chocolate and bake for about 40 minutes, or until risen and firm. Leave to cool completely in the pan, then cut into 12 squares. Store in an airtight container.

Chocolate-dipped Crescents

A very simple idea, but these hazelnut-flavored cookies do look special. Walnuts or pecan nuts can be used instead of hazelnuts, but they must be finely ground.

Makes 35

11 ounces/2⅔ cups all-purpose flour
pinch of salt
8 ounces/1 cup sweet butter at room
   temperature, diced
2 ounces/¼ cup superfine sugar
1 tablespoon hazelnut liqueur
   or water
1 teaspoon vanilla extract
3 ounces semisweet chocolate,
   finely grated
2½ ounces/⅔ cup hazelnuts, toasted
   and finely chopped
confectioners' sugar, for dusting
12 ounces semisweet chocolate, melted,
   for dipping

1 Preheat the oven to 325°F/ Gas 3. Grease two large baking sheets. Sift the flour and salt into a small bowl.

2 In a large bowl, using an electric mixer, beat the butter until creamy. Add the sugar and beat until fluffy, then beat in the hazelnut liqueur or water and vanilla extract. Using a wooden spoon, gently stir in the flour mixture, until just blended, then fold in the grated chocolate and chopped hazelnuts.

3 With floured hands, shape the dough into 2 x ½ inch crescent shapes. Place on the prepared baking sheets, 2 inches apart. Bake for 20–25 minutes, until the edges are set and the cookies slightly golden. Remove the baking sheets to a wire rack to cool for 10 minutes. Transfer the cookies to wire racks to cool completely.

4 Line the baking sheets with baking parchment. Dust the cooled cookies with confectioners' sugar. Using a pair of kitchen tongs, or your fingers, dip half of each crescent into the melted chocolate. Place on the prepared baking sheets. Leave in a cool place until the chocolate has set firmly.

Viennese Whirls

These crisp, melt-in-the-mouth piped cookies are filled with a creamy coffee buttercream. Needless to say, they are delicious served with Viennese coffee or hot chocolate.

Makes 20

6 ounces/¾ cup butter

2 ounces/½ cup confectioners' sugar

½ teaspoon vanilla extract

4 ounces/1 cup all-purpose flour

2 ounces/½ cup cornstarch

confectioners' sugar and cocoa powder
(unsweetened), to dust

For the filling

1 tablespoon ground coffee

4 tablespoons light cream

6 tablespoons butter, softened

4 ounces/1 cup confectioners'
sugar, sifted

Cook's Tip

*For mocha Viennese whirls, substitute
1 ounce/¼ cup cocoa powder (unsweetened)
for 1 ounce/¼ cup of the flour.*

1 Preheat the oven to 350°F/Gas 4.
Grease two baking sheets. Cream
together the butter, confectioners'
sugar and vanilla extract until light.
Stir in the flour and cornstarch and
mix until smooth.

2 Using two tablespoons, spoon the
mixture into a pastry bag fitted with
a ½-inch fluted nozzle.

3 Pipe small rosettes, spaced far
apart, on the prepared baking
sheets. Bake for 12–15 minutes,
until golden. Using a metal spatula,
transfer to a wire rack to cool.

4 To make the filling, put the ground
coffee in a heatproof bowl. Heat the
cream in a small pan to just below
boiling point and then pour it over
the coffee. Leave to steep for
4 minutes, then strain through a fine
sieve into a clean bowl.

5 Beat together the butter,
confectioners' sugar and coffee-flavored
cream until light and thoroughly
combined. Use to sandwich the
cooled cookies together in pairs.
Dust the whirls lightly with a little
confectioners' sugar and cocoa powder.

Pecan Toffee Shortbread

Coffee shortbread is topped with pecan-studded toffee – what could be more scrumptious? Cornstarch gives it a crunchy light texture, but all-purpose flour can be used if you like.

Makes 20

1 tablespoon ground coffee

1 tablespoon near-boiling water

4 ounces/½ cup butter, softened

2 tablespoons smooth peanut butter

3 ounces/scant ½ cup superfine sugar

3 ounces/⅔ cup cornstarch

6½ ounces/1⅔ cups all-purpose flour

For the topping

6 ounces/¾ cup butter

6 ounces/¾ cup soft light brown sugar

2 tablespoons light corn syrup

6 ounces/1 cup shelled pecan nuts, halved

1 Preheat the oven to 350°F/Gas 4. Grease and line a 7 × 11 inch pan with waxed paper.

2 Put the ground coffee in a small. heatproof bowl and pour the hot water over it. Leave to steep for 4 minutes. Strain through a sieve into a bowl. Discard the grounds.

3 Cream the butter, peanut butter, sugar and coffee until light. Sift the cornstarch and flour together and mix in to make a smooth dough.

4 Press into the base of the pan and prick all over with a fork. Bake for 20 minutes. To make the topping, put the butter, sugar and syrup in a pan and heat until melted. Bring the mixture to the boil.

5 Simmer for 5 minutes, then stir in the pecan nuts. Spread the topping evenly over the base. Leave in the pan until cold, then cut into squares or bars. Remove from the pan and serve.

Mocha Viennese Swirls

Sophisticated cookies that look elegant and taste superb, these swirls can be served with morning coffee to impress your guests or just please your friends.

Makes 20

9 ounces semisweet chocolate, chopped

7 ounces/scant 1 cup sweet butter at room temperature, diced

2 ounces/½ cup confectioners' sugar

2 tablespoons strong black coffee

7 ounces/1¾ cups all-purpose flour

2 ounces/½ cup cornstarch

about 20 blanched almonds

1 Preheat the oven to 375°F/ Gas 5. Lightly grease two large baking sheets.

2 Melt 4 ounces of the chocolate in a heatproof bowl set over a pan of hot water, then remove from the heat and leave to cool slightly. Cream the butter with the confectioners' sugar in a bowl until smooth and pale. Beat in the melted chocolate, then the black coffee.

3 Sift the flour and cornstarch over the mixture. Fold in lightly and evenly to make a soft mixture.

4 Spoon the mixture into a pastry bag fitted with a large star nozzle and pipe 20 swirls on the prepared baking sheets, allowing room for spreading during baking.

5 Gently press an almond into the center of each swirl. Bake for about 15 minutes, until the cookies are firm and just beginning to brown. Leave to cool for about 10 minutes on the baking sheets, then, using a metal spatula, transfer carefully to a wire rack to cool completely.

6 Melt the remaining chocolate in a heatproof bowl over a pan of hot water. Dip the base of each swirl into the chocolate to coat. Place on a sheet of baking parchment and leave to set.

Cook's Tip
If the mixture is too stiff to pipe, soften it with a little more black coffee.

Chocolate Amaretti

Although it is always said that chocolate does not go with wine, make an exception with these scrumptious little cookies and serve them, Italian style, with a glass of chilled champagne.

Makes 24

5 ounces/1¼ cups blanched
   whole almonds
3½ ounces/½ cup superfine sugar
1 tablespoon cocoa powder
   (unsweetened)
2 tablespoons confectioners' sugar
2 egg whites
pinch of cream of tartar
1 teaspoon almond extract
24 sliced almonds, to decorate

1 Preheat the oven to 350°F/Gas 4. Spread out the almonds on a baking sheet and bake for 10–12 minutes, until golden brown. Leave to cool. Reduce the oven temperature to 325°F/Gas 3. Line a large baking sheet with baking parchment.

2 Process the almonds with half the sugar in a food processor until they are finely ground. Transfer to a bowl and sift in the cocoa and confectioners' sugar. Set aside.

3 Using an electric mixer, beat the egg whites and cream of tartar until stiff peaks form. Sprinkle in the remaining sugar, a tablespoon at a time, and continue beating until the whites are glossy and stiff. Beat in the almond extract.

4 Sprinkle over the almond-sugar mixture and gently fold into the beaten egg whites until just blended. Spoon the mixture into a large pastry bag fitted with a plain ½-inch nozzle. Pipe 1½-inch round pieces about 1 inch apart on the prepared baking sheet. Gently press a sliced almond into the center of each.

5 Bake the cookies for about 12–15 minutes, or until crisp and golden. Remove the baking sheets to a wire rack and leave to cool for about 10 minutes. With a metal spatula, transfer the amaretti to the wire rack to cool completely. Wrap individually in tissue paper before packing in a box if giving as a gift.

Chocolate Almond Torrone

The name of this log-shaped cookie is usually translated as "nougat," but this is a reference to its nutty flavor rather than its texture. Serve this Italian specialty in thin slices.

Makes 20

4 ounces semisweet chocolate, chopped

2 ounces/4 tablespoons sweet butter

1 egg white

4 ounces/generous ½ cup superfine sugar

2 ounces/½ cup ground almonds

3 ounces/¾ cup chopped toasted almonds

5 tablespoons chopped candied peel

For the coating

6 ounces white chocolate, chopped

1 ounce/2 tablespoons sweet butter

4 ounces/1 cup sliced almonds, toasted

1 Melt the chocolate with the butter in a heatproof bowl set over a pan of hot water, stirring until the mixture is smooth.

2 In a clean, grease-free bowl, whisk the egg white with the sugar until stiff. Gradually beat in the melted chocolate, then stir in the ground almonds, chopped toasted almonds and candied peel.

Cook's Tip
The mixture can be shaped into a simple round roll instead of the triangular shape, if you prefer.

3 Tip the mixture onto a large sheet of baking parchment and, using your hands, shape it into a thick roll.

4 As the mixture cools, use the baking parchment to press the roll firmly into a triangular shape. Twist the baking parchment over the triangular roll and chill in the refrigerator until completely set.

5 To make the coating, melt the white chocolate with the butter in a heatproof bowl set over a pan of hot water. Unwrap the chocolate roll and spread the white chocolate quickly over the surface. Press the almonds in a thin even coating over the chocolate, working quickly.

6 Chill again until firm, then cut the torrone into thin slices to serve.

Chocolate Hazelnut Galettes

There's stacks of sophistication in these triple-tiered chocolate galettes sandwiched with a light creamy filling. They are elegant enough to serve for dessert.

Makes 4

6 ounces semisweet chocolate,
   chopped

3 tablespoons light cream

2 tablespoons sliced hazelnuts

4 ounces white chocolate,
   chopped

6 ounces/¾ cup ricotta cheese

1 tablespoon dry sherry

4 tablespoons finely chopped
   hazelnuts, toasted

physalis, dipped in white chocolate,
   to decorate

1 Melt the semisweet chocolate in a heatproof bowl set over a pan of hot water, then remove from the heat and stir in the cream.

2 Draw 12 circles about 3 inches in diameter on sheets of baking parchment. Turn the parchment over and spread the semisweet chocolate over each marked circle, covering in a thin, even layer. Sprinkle sliced hazelnuts over four of the circles, then leave until set.

Cook's Tip

The chocolate could be spread over heart shapes instead, for a special Valentine's Day dessert.

3 Melt the white chocolate in a heatproof bowl set over a pan of hot water. Remove the bowl from the heat, then stir in the ricotta cheese and dry sherry. Fold in the chopped, toasted hazelnuts. Leave to cool until the mixture holds its shape.

4 Remove the round chocolate pieces from the baking parchment and sandwich them together in stacks of three, spooning the white chocolate cream between each layer and using the hazelnut-covered round pieces on top. Chill before serving with chocolate-dipped physalis.

Rocky Road Chocolate Bars

This is a dream to make with kids. They love smashing up the cookies and can do most of the rest, apart from melting the chocolate and lining the pan. However, when it comes to flavor, the contrast of melting chocolate, crunchy cookies and soft marshmallows is not just kid's stuff.

Makes 16 bars

8 ounces/1 cup butter

4 ounces bittersweet chocolate with more than 60 percent cocoa solids, coarsely broken up

2 tablespoons superfine sugar

2 tablespoons light corn syrup

2 tablespoons good quality cocoa powder (unsweetened)

12 ounces mixed graham crackers and gingersnaps

2 ounces mini marshmallows

3 ounces mixed white and milk chocolate chips

confectioners' sugar, for dusting (optional)

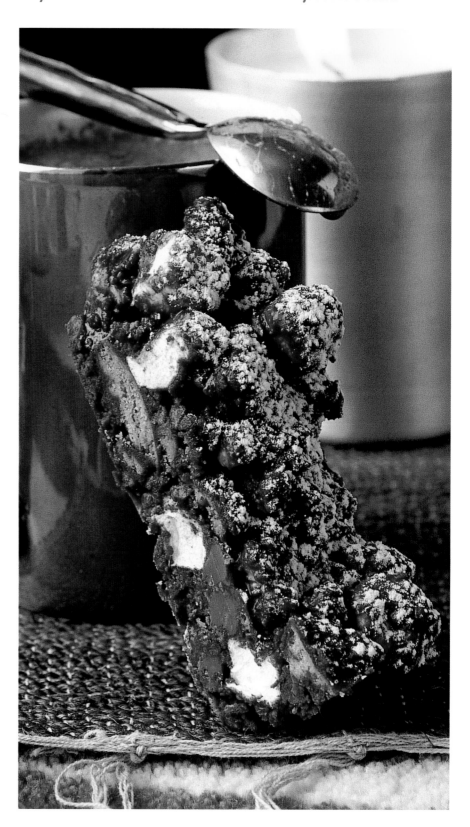

1 Line an 8-inch square cake pan, measuring about 1 inch deep, with baking parchment. Put the butter in a pan with the chocolate, sugar, syrup and cocoa powder. Place over a gentle heat until completely melted.

2 Put the graham crackers and gingersnaps in a large plastic bag and smash to coarse chunks with a rolling pin. Stir these into the chocolate mixture, followed by the marshmallows and chocolate chips. Mix well together.

3 Spoon the mixture into the pan, but don't press down too much – it should look like a rocky road. Chill for at least 1 hour, or until firm.

4 Remove from the pan and cut into 16 bars. If you like, dust the bars with confectioners' sugar before serving.

Late Night Cookies

Take a pile of these to bed with you, and all that will be left next morning will be the crumbs in the duvet. These are dangerous cookies. Crisp yet crumbly and packed with chocolate chips, they are a must with a tall glass of ice-cold milk or stacked with an obscene amount of ice cream.

**Makes about 12 large or
20 regular cookies**

3 ounces/6 tablespoons butter, softened

3 ounces/6 tablespoons golden
   superfine sugar

3 ounces/6 tablespoons soft light brown
   sugar, sifted

1 extra large egg, beaten

½ teaspoon vanilla extract

5 ounces/1¼ cups self-rising flour

1 ounce/¼ cup cocoa powder
   (unsweetened)

¼ teaspoon salt

4 ounces chopped semisweet chocolate
   or chocolate chips

ice cream or milk, to serve

1 Preheat the oven to 350°F/ Gas 4. Butter two heavy, non-stick baking sheets. Cream the butter and both sugars together until pale and fluffy. Beat in the egg and vanilla extract.

2 Sift the flour with the cocoa and salt. Gently fold into the egg mixture with the chopped chocolate or chocolate chips. Place four heaped tablespoonfuls of the mixture, spaced far apart, on each baking sheet. Press down and spread out with the back of a wet spoon.

3 Bake for 12 minutes. Cool on the baking sheet for 1 minute, then remove to a cooling rack. Repeat with the remaining mixture. Store in an airtight container when cold. Serve with ice cream sandwiched between, or eat on their own with a glass of ice-cold milk.

Ice-cream Sandwich Cookies

These are great when you get those midnight munchies – either keep the cookies in an airtight container and sandwich together each time with the softened ice cream of your choice or make the sandwiches complete with ice cream and coating and freeze until required.

Makes 12

4 ounces/½ cup sweet butter, at room temperature, diced

4 ounces/generous ½ cup superfine sugar

1 egg, beaten

7 ounces/1¾ cups all-purpose flour

1 ounce/¼ cup cocoa powder (unsweetened), sieved

ice cream, to fill

toasted nuts, cookie crumbs, chocolate flakes or raw sugar, to coat

1 Preheat the oven to 350°F/Gas 4. Cream the butter and sugar together until light and fluffy, then beat in the egg. Stir in the flour and cocoa powder to make a firm dough.

2 Roll the dough out to a thickness of ¼ inch on baking parchment. Using a 3-inch plain round cookie cutter, stamp out 24 round pieces and place on the prepared baking sheets. Alternatively cut into squares or rectangles of equal size. Bake the cookies for about 15 minutes. Set aside on the baking sheets to cool.

3 To make the ice cream cookies, spread 2 good spoonfuls of softened ice cream on a cookie and press a second on top. Squeeze so the filling reaches the edges.

4 Put your chosen coating on a plate and roll the cookies in it to coat the sides. Either eat right away or wrap individually in foil and freeze. The cookies may be kept for up to 2 weeks in the freezer.

Cook's Tip

For super-deluxe cookies, half-dip the ice cream cookies in melted chocolate. Shake off the excess, place on a sheet of baking parchment and freeze at once. When the chocolate has set, either eat or wrap in foil and freeze for later.

Nut Bar Cookies

If you love chocolate, condensed milk, nuts and crumb crust, then these are the cookies for you. It's fortunate that they are incredibly easy to make, because they are even easier to eat and are sure to become firm favorites with all the family. Children enjoy helping to make them.

Makes 16–18

9 ounces graham crackers

4 ounces/½ cup butter, melted

5 ounces/scant 1 cup milk
  chocolate chips

7 ounces mixed whole nuts, such as
  pecan nuts, hazelnuts, brazil nuts,
  walnuts and almonds

7 fluid ounce/scant 1 cup can sweetened
  condensed milk

Cook's Tip

*If you prefer, use a shallow 8-inch
cake pan instead, and cut the cookies
into squares.*

1 Preheat the oven to 350°F/Gas 4. Crush the graham crackers in a plastic bag with a rolling pin.

2 Put the graham cracker crumbs in a bowl and stir in the melted butter. Mix well. Press the mixture evenly into the base of a 4 x 14 inch cake pan.

3 Sprinkle the chocolate chips over the graham cracker base. Arrange the nuts on top and pour the condensed milk over the top evenly.

4 Bake for 25 minutes, or until bubbling and golden. Cool in the pan, loosen from the sides, then cool completely and slice into thin bars.

Apple Crumble and Custard Slice

These luscious apple slices are easy to make using ready-made sweet pastry and custard. Just think, all the ingredients of one of the world's most popular desserts – in a cookie.

Makes 16

12 ounces ready-made sweet pastry

1 large cooking apple, about 9 ounces

2 tablespoons superfine sugar

4 tablespoons ready-made thick custard

For the crumble topping

4 ounces/1 cup all-purpose flour

½ teaspoon ground cinnamon

4 tablespoons granulated sugar

3½ ounces/7 tablespoons sweet
butter, melted

1 Preheat the oven to 375°F/ Gas 5. Roll out the pastry and use to line the base of an 11 x 7 inch shallow cake pan. Prick the pastry with a fork, line with foil and baking beans and bake blind for about 10–15 minutes. Remove the foil and baking beans and return the pastry to the oven for a further 5 minutes, until cooked and golden brown.

2 Meanwhile, peel, core and chop the apple evenly. Place in a pan with the sugar. Heat gently until the sugar dissolves, then cover with a lid and cook gently for 5–7 minutes until a thick puree is formed. Beat with a wooden spoon and set aside to cool.

3 Mix the cold apple with the custard. Spread over the pastry.

4 To make the crumble topping, put the flour, cinnamon and sugar into a bowl and pour over the melted butter. Stir thoroughly until the mixture forms small clumps. Sprinkle the crumble over the filling.

5 Return to the oven and bake for about 10–15 minutes, until the crumble topping is cooked and a golden brown. Leave to cool in the pan, then slice into bars to serve.

Creamy Fig and Peach Squares

A sweet cream-cheese and dried-fruit filling with a hint of mint makes these cookies really special. They are ideal for quietening hunger pangs after school or work.

Makes 24

12 ounces/3 cups all-purpose flour

7 ounces/scant 1 cup sweet
   butter, diced

1 egg, beaten

superfine sugar, for sprinkling

For the filling

1¼ pounds/2½ cups ricotta cheese

4 ounces/generous ½ cup
   superfine sugar

1 teaspoon finely chopped
   fresh mint

2 ounces/⅓ cup ready-to-eat dried
   figs, chopped

2 ounces/⅓ cup ready-to-eat dried
   peaches, chopped

1 Preheat the oven to 375°F/ Gas 5. And then lightly grease a 13 x 9 inch jelly roll pan or shallow cake pan. Put the flour and butter into a bowl. Rub in the butter until the mixture resembles fine breadcrumbs. Add the egg and enough water to mix to a firm but not sticky dough.

2 Divide the pastry into two and roll out one piece to fit the base of the prepared pan. Place in the pan and trim.

3 To make the filling, put all the ingredients in a bowl and mix together. Spread over the pastry base. Roll out the remaining pastry and place on top of the filling. Prick lightly all over with a fork then sprinkle with superfine sugar.

4 Bake for about 30 minutes until light golden brown. Remove from the oven and sprinkle more superfine sugar thickly over the top. Cool and cut into slices to serve.

White Chocolate Macadamia Nut Slices

Keep these luxury slices for a celebratory afternoon tea. Not only do they have a superbly rich flavor, but their crunchy texture will also make them a firm favorite among your guests. For a special occasion serve with a spoonful of whipped cream.

Makes 16

5 ounces/1¼ cups macadamia
   nuts

14 ounces white chocolate

2 ounces/¼ cup ready-to-eat
   dried apricots

3 ounces/⅓ cup sweet butter

1 teaspoon vanilla extract

3 eggs

5 ounces/⅔ cup light brown
   sugar

4 ounces/1 cup self-rising
   flour

1 Preheat the oven to 375°F/Gas 5. Lightly grease two 8-inch layer cake pans and line the base of each with waxed paper or baking parchment.

2 Coarsely chop the nuts and half the white chocolate, making sure that the pieces are more or less the same size, then cut the apricots into similar-size pieces.

3 Place the remaining white chocolate and the butter in the top of a double boiler or a heatproof bowl set over a pan of hot water. Melt over a gentle heat, stirring occasionally until smooth. Remove the bowl from the heat and leave to cool slightly.

4 Stir in the vanilla extract. Whisk the eggs and sugar in a mixing bowl until thick and pale, then whisk in the melted chocolate mixture.

5 Sift the flour over the mixture and fold in gently and evenly. Stir in the nuts, chopped white chocolate and apricots.

6 Spoon the mixture into the prepared pans, smooth the top level with a spatula and bake for 30–35 minutes, until golden brown. Leave in the pans to cool slightly then turn out the cakes and leave to cool completely on a wire rack. Serve cut into slices or wedges, with a spoonful of fresh whipped cream, if you like.

Cook's Tip
You might find it easier to use sharp kitchen scissors rather than a knife to snip the apricots into small pieces.

Variation
Use blanched almonds or hazelnuts in place of the macadamia nuts, if you prefer.

Florentines with Grand Marnier

Orange liqueur adds a note of glorious luxury to these ever-popular nut and dried fruit cookies. These mini versions would be delicious with dessert or after-dinner coffee and liqueurs.

Makes about 24

2 ounces/¼ cup soft light brown sugar

1 tablespoon clear honey

1 tablespoon Grand Marnier

2 ounces/¼ cup butter

1½ ounces/3 tablespoons
   all-purpose flour

1 ounce/¼ cup hazelnuts,
   coarsely chopped

2 ounces/½ cup sliced
   almonds, chopped

2 ounces/¼ cup candied
   cherries, chopped

4 ounces bittersweet chocolate, melted,
   for coating

1 Preheat the oven to 350F/Gas 4. Line three or four baking sheets with baking parchment. Combine the sugar, honey, Grand Marnier and butter in a small pan and melt over a low heat.

2 Remove the pan from the heat and tip in the flour, hazelnuts, almonds and cherries. Stir well.

Variation

For an extra decoration, pour semisweet or white chocolate into a paper pastry bag, snip off the end and pipe zigzag lines over the plain side of each Florentine.

3 Spoon small heaps of the mixture onto the baking sheets. Bake for about 10 minutes, until golden brown. Leave the cookies on the baking sheets until the edges begin to harden a little, then remove and cool on a wire rack.

4 Spread the melted chocolate over the underside of each Florentine with a knife. When the chocolate is just beginning to set, drag a fork through to give wavy lines. Leave to set completely.

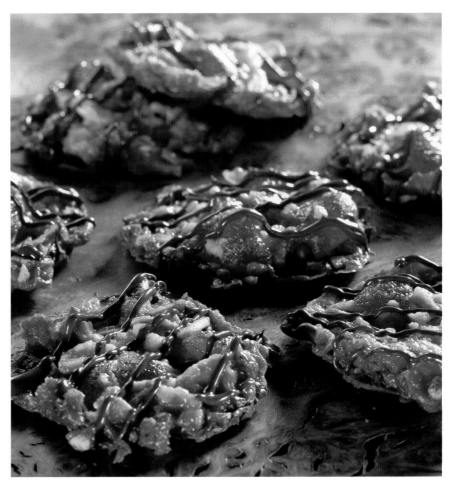

Cointreau Chocolate Colettes

Small chocolate cases, filled with swirled chocolate and Cointreau cream, make indulgent treats. Serve them with a glass of Cointreau liqueur at the end of a special meal.

Makes 14

4 ounces bittersweet chocolate, broken
   into squares
confectioners' sugar, for dusting

For filling

2½ ounces bittersweet chocolate
1 ounce/2 tablespoons sweet butter
2 tablespoons Cointreau
4 tablespoons heavy
   cream, whipped

1 Put the chocolate in a heatproof bowl. Stand the bowl over a pan of hot water and heat gently until the chocolate has melted.

2 Using a small, clean paintbrush, brush the insides of 14 petit-four cases with a thin coating of melted chocolate and leave to set completely. Repeat three or four times. When finally set, carefully peel off the paper cases.

3 Make the filling. Melt the chocolate and butter in a heatproof bowl set over a pan of simmering water, stirring until smooth.

4 Remove from the heat. When cool (but still liquid), stir in the Cointreau and fold in the whipped heavy cream.

5 Chill this mixture until firm, then pipe into the chocolate cases. Dust with confectioners' sugar.

Cook's Tip
When making the cases, it is best to make several thin layers of chocolate.

Two-tone Chocolate Florentines

Fruit and nut florentines make a deliciously sticky treat to serve with coffee. Store them in an airtight container in the refrigerator. They'll keep for up to 1 week – unless, of course, they're eaten sooner, which is highly likely.

Makes about 30

4 fluid ounces 1½ cup heavy
  cream
2 ounces/¼ cup sweet butter
3½ ounces/½ cup granulated sugar
2 tablespoons clear honey
5 ounces/1¼ cups sliced almonds
1½ ounces/⅓ cup all-purpose
  flour
½ teaspoon ground ginger
2 ounces/⅓ cup diced candied
  orange peel
2½ ounces/½ cup diced preserved
  stem ginger
7 ounces semisweet chocolate,
  chopped
5 ounces good quality white
  chocolate, chopped

1 Preheat the oven to 350°F/Gas 4. Lightly grease two large baking sheets. Heat the cream, butter, sugar and honey in a pan over a medium heat, stirring constantly until the sugar has dissolved. Bring the mixture to the boil, stirring constantly.

2 Remove from the heat and stir in the almonds, flour and ground ginger until thoroughly blended. Stir in the orange peel, preserved stem ginger and 2 ounces/⅓ cup chopped semisweet chocolate.

3 Drop teaspoonfuls of the mixture onto the prepared baking sheets at least 3 inches apart. Spread each round shape as thinly as possible with the back of the spoon.

4 Bake in batches for 8–10 minutes, until the edges are golden brown and the cookies are bubbling. Do not under-bake, or they will be sticky, but be careful not to over-bake as they burn easily.

5 If you wish, use a 3-inch cookie cutter to neaten the edges of the florentines while on the baking sheet.

6 Remove the baking sheet to a wire rack to cool for 10 minutes. Using a metal spatula, transfer the florentines to the wire rack to cool completely.

7 In a bowl set over a small pan of hot water, melt the remaining semisweet chocolate. Cool slightly.

8 In a separate bowl, melt the white chocolate in the same way. Remove the bowl from the pan and cool for about 5 minutes, stirring occasionally until the chocolate is slightly thickened.

9 Using a small metal spatula, spread the flat side of half the florentines with the semisweet chocolate, swirling it to create a decorative pattern. Place on a wire rack, chocolate side up.

10 Coat the remaining florentines with the melted white chocolate in the same way. Leave in a cool place for about 10 minutes to set.

Variation
Use candied cherries in place of half or all of the orange peel, if you prefer.

Cook's Tip
Dip the spoon in water to prevent it from sticking when you are spreading out the mixture on the baking sheets.

Coffee Sponge Drops with Cheese and Ginger Filling

These little cookies are delicious with a filling of low-fat farmer's cheese and chopped preserved stem ginger, but if you like, you can serve them on their own.

Makes 12

2 ounces/½ cup all-purpose flour

1 tablespoon instant coffee powder

2 eggs

3 ounces/scant ½ cup superfine sugar

For the filling

4 ounces/½ cup low-fat farmer's cheese

1½ ounces/¼ cup chopped preserved stem ginger

1 Preheat the oven to 375°F/Gas 5. Line two baking sheets with baking parchment. Sift the flour and coffee powder together. To make the filling, beat together the farmer's cheese and stem ginger. Chill.

2 Whisk the eggs and sugar in a bowl until thick.

3 Carefully add the sifted flour and coffee powder to the egg mixture and gently fold in with a metal spoon, being careful not to knock out any air.

4 Spoon into a pastry bag with a ½-inch plain nozzle. Pipe 1½-inch round shapes onto the baking sheets. Bake for 12 minutes. Cool. Sandwich together with the filling.

Sablés with Chèvre Cheese and Strawberries

Sablés are little French cookies, made from egg yolk and butter. Crisp and slightly sweet, they contrast perfectly with the tangy goat's cheese and juicy strawberries.

Makes 24

3 ounces/⅓ cup butter

5 ounces/1¼ cups all-purpose flour

3 ounces/¾ cup blanched hazelnuts, lightly toasted and ground

2 tablespoons superfine sugar

2 egg yolks, beaten with 2–3 tablespoons water

4 ounces chèvre cheese

4–6 large strawberries, cut into small pieces

hazelnuts and fresh mint, to decorate

I Put the butter, flour, ground hazelnuts, sugar and beaten egg yolks into a food processor and process to a smooth dough. Scrape out the dough. Shape into a log about 1½ inches thick. Put in plastic wrap and chill.

Variation

These sablés are ideal served with fruit. Beat 3 ounces/⅓ cup cream cheese with 1 tablespoon confectioners' sugar and a little lemon or orange rind. Spread a little on the sablés and top with a few pieces of sliced kiwi fruit, peach, nectarine and a few raspberries.

2 Preheat the oven to 400°F/Gas 6. Line a large baking sheet with baking parchment. With a sharp knife, slice the dough into ¼-inch thick round pieces and arrange on the prepared baking sheet. Bake for 7–10 minutes, until golden brown. Transfer to a wire rack to cool and crisp slightly.

3 Crumble the chèvre cheese with your fingers into small pieces on a plate. Mound a little chèvre cheese onto each sablé, top with a piece of strawberry and sprinkle with a few hazelnuts. Transfer to a platter or individual plates, decorate with mint leaves and serve the sablés while still warm.

Dessert Cookies

Mousses, sorbets, ice creams and fresh fruit salads are among the many desserts complemented by delicate, elegant or richly flavored cookies – and, of course, there is nothing so delicious as special little nibbles served with coffee and liqueurs. The recipes in this chapter will be an inspiration for those who love to entertain, as they provide that professional finishing touch that turns a good meal into a truly memorable occasion.

Biscotti

These lovely Italian cookies are part-baked, sliced to reveal a feast of mixed nuts and then baked again until crisp and golden. Traditionally they're served dipped in vin santo, a sweet, sherry-like dessert wine, but they would also go well with zabaglione or creamy chocolate mousse.

Makes 24

2 ounces/¼ cup sweet butter
   at room temperature, diced
4 ounces/generous ½ cup superfine
   sugar
6 ounces/1½ cups self-rising flour
pinch of salt
2 teaspoons baking powder
1 teaspoon ground coriander
finely grated rind of 1 lemon
2 ounces/scant ½ cup polenta
1 egg, lightly beaten
2 teaspoons brandy or orange-
   flavored liqueur
2 ounces/½ cup unblanched almonds
2 ounces/½ cup pistachio nuts

1 Preheat the oven to 325°F/Gas 3. Lightly grease a baking sheet. Cream together the butter and sugar in a bowl.

2 Sift the flour, salt, baking powder and coriander into the bowl. Add the lemon rind, polenta, egg and brandy or liqueur and mix together to make a soft dough.

3 Stir in the nuts until evenly combined. Halve the mixture. Shape each half into a flat "sausage" about 9 inches long and 2½ inches wide. Bake for about 30 minutes, or until risen and firm. Remove the "sausages" from the oven.

4 When cool, cut each "sausage" diagonally into 12 thin slices. Return to the baking sheet and cook for a further 10 minutes, or until crisp.

5 Transfer to a wire rack to cool completely. Store in an airtight container for up to 1 week.

Cook's Tip
Use a sharp, serrated knife to slice the cooled cookies, otherwise they will crumble and break.

All Butter Cookies

Crisp, buttery cookies are perfect with strawberries and cream or any creamy dessert or fruit compote. These are refrigerator cookies, as the mixture is chilled until it is firm enough to cut neatly into thin slices. The dough can be frozen and when thawed enough to slice, can be baked, but do allow a little extra cooking time.

Makes 28–30

10 ounces/2½ cups all-purpose
  flour
7 ounces/scant 1 cup sweet butter
3½ ounces/scant 1 cup
  confectioners' sugar, plus
  extra for dusting
2 teaspoons vanilla extract

1 Put the flour in a food processor. Add the butter and process until the mixture resembles coarse breadcrumbs. Add the confectioners' sugar and vanilla extract and process again until the mixture comes together to form a dough.

2 Turn out the dough onto a lightly floured surface. Knead lightly and then shape into a thick sausage, 12 inches long and 2 inches in diameter. Put in plastic wrap or in foil, and chill for at least 1 hour, until firm.

Cook's Tip
Do make sure that you use a sharp knife for cutting the dough roll into individual cookies. Not only is it safer, but also the results will be neater.

3 Preheat the oven to 400°F/Gas 6. Grease two baking sheets. Using a sharp knife, cut ¼-inch thick slices from the dough and space them slightly apart on the baking sheets.

4 Bake for 8–10 minutes, alternating the position of the baking sheets in the oven halfway through cooking, if necessary, until the cookies have turned pale golden around the edges. Leave for 5 minutes, then transfer to a wire rack to cool. Serve dusted with confectioners' sugar.

Cinnamon Pinwheels

These impressive sweet pastries make a superb and attractive accompaniment to ice cream, sorbets, mousses and other creamy desserts. Cinnamon has a deliciously fragrant aroma and gives these simple-to-make pinwheels a warm spicy flavor. If you find they turn slightly soft during storage, re-crisp them briefly in the oven.

Makes 20–24

2 ounces/¼ cup superfine sugar, plus a little extra for sprinkling

2 teaspoons ground cinnamon

9 ounces puff pastry

beaten egg, to glaze

1 Preheat the oven to 425°F/Gas 7. Thoroughly grease a large baking sheet. Put the superfine sugar and ground cinnamon in a small bowl and mix well. Set the bowl aside until required.

2 Roll out the pastry on a lightly floured surface to an 8-inch square and sprinkle with half the sugar mixture. Roll out the pastry to a 10-inch square so that the sugar is pressed into it.

3 Brush with the beaten egg and then sprinkle with the remaining sugar mixture. Loosely roll up the pastry into a log, brushing the end of the pastry with a little more egg to secure the edge in place.

4 Using a sharp knife, cut the log into fairly thin slices and transfer them to the prepared baking sheet. Bake for about 10 minutes, or until golden and crisp. Sprinkle with a little more sugar and transfer to a wire rack to cool.

Spanish Churros

These sugar-coated deep-fried bites are sold from roadside stalls all over Spain and are eaten from paper cones while piping hot. For a special treat serve with a lemon sorbet.

Makes 24

8 fluid ounces/1 cup water
1 tablespoon granulated sugar,
　plus extra for coating
pinch of salt
6 ounces/1½ cups all-purpose
　flour
1 egg
oil, for deep-frying
½ lime or lemon

1 Pour the measured water into a heavy pan, add the sugar and salt and bring to the boil over a low heat, stirring until the sugar has dissolved. Remove from the heat, tip in the flour and beat until smooth.

2 Beat in the egg until the mixture is smooth and satiny. Set aside.

3 Heat 2-inch depth of oil, with the lime or lemon, in a deep frying pan to 375°F, or until a cube of bread browns in 30–60 seconds.

4 Pour the batter into a large pastry bag with a fluted nozzle. Pipe 3-inch strips of batter and then add to the oil, a few at a time. Fry for 3–4 minutes, until golden. Remove, drain on kitchen paper and roll in granulated sugar.

Golden Pillows

These tasty little Mexican snacks are delicious served warm with syrup or honey, but they can also be sprinkled with sugar and cinnamon, if you prefer. They are lovely with ice cream.

Makes 30

8 ounces/2 cups all-purpose
　flour, sifted
1 tablespoon baking powder
pinch of salt
2 tablespoons margarine
6 fluid ounces/¾ cup water
corn oil, for frying
syrup or clear honey, to serve

1 Put the flour, baking powder and salt into a large bowl. Add the margarine, and then lightly rub in, using just your fingertips, until the mixture resembles coarse breadcrumbs.

2 Gradually stir in the water, using a fork, until the mixture clings together to form a soft dough.

3 Shape the dough into a ball, then turn onto a lightly floured surface and knead very gently until smooth. Roll out thinly to a rectangle measuring about 18 x 15 inches. Using a sharp knife, cut about 3-inch squares. For a decorative edge, use a fluted pastry wheel to cut out the squares.

4 Heat the oil to 375°F, or until a cube of day-old bread browns in 30–60 seconds.

5 Deep-fry the squares, a few at a time, in the oil. As they brown and puff up, turn them over to cook the other side. Remove with a slotted spoon and drain well on kitchen paper. Serve the pillows warm, with syrup or honey.

Tea Finger Cookies

The unusual ingredient in these cookies is Earl Grey tea, with bergamot, which imparts a distinctive aroma and flavor.

3 Using your hands, roll the dough on a lightly floured surface into a long cylinder, about 9 inches long.

4 Gently press down on the top of the dough cylinder with the palm of your hand to flatten slightly. Put the dough in plastic wrap and chill for about 1 hour, until the dough is firm enough to slice.

5 Using a sharp knife, cut the dough cylinder widthwise into ¼-inch slices and place, slightly apart, on the prepared baking sheets.

6 Sprinkle the cookies with a little raw sugar, then bake for 10–15 minutes, until lightly browned. Using a metal spatula, transfer the cookies to a wire rack and leave to cool.

Makes about 36

5 ounces/10 tablespoons sweet butter, at room temperature, diced

4 ounces/generous ½ cup light brown sugar

1–2 tablespoons Earl Grey tea leaves

1 egg, beaten

7 ounces/1¾ cups all-purpose flour

raw sugar, for sprinkling

1 Preheat the oven to 375°F/Gas 5. Line two or three baking sheets with baking parchment.

2 Beat the butter and sugar until light and creamy. Stir in the Earl Grey tea leaves until well combined. Beat in the egg, then carefully fold in the flour.

Variation

You could use other exotic types of tea for making these cookies. Try aromatic flower or fruit teas, such as jasmine, rose congou or pouchong, chrysanthemum, passion fruit or strawberry. All work well in creating an unusual flavor.

Rosemary-scented Citrus Tuiles

These delicious crisp cookies are flavored with tangy orange and lemon rind, and made beautifully fragrant with fresh rosemary – an unusual but winning combination.

Makes 18–20

2 ounces/¼ cup sweet butter, diced

2 egg whites

4 ounces/generous ½ cup superfine
   sugar

finely grated rind of ½ lemon

finely grated rind of ½ orange

2 teaspoons finely chopped
   fresh rosemary

2 ounces/½ cup all-purpose flour

1 Preheat the oven to 375°F/Gas 5. Line a baking sheet with baking parchment. Melt the butter in a pan over a low heat. Leave to cool. Whisk the egg whites until stiff, then gradually whisk in the sugar.

2 Fold in the lemon and orange rinds, rosemary and flour and then the melted butter. Place 2 large tablespoonfuls of mixture on the baking sheet. Spread each to a thin disk about 3½ inches in diameter. Bake for 5–6 minutes, until golden.

3 Remove from the oven and lift the tuiles using a metal spatula and drape over a rolling pin. Transfer to a wire rack when set in a curved shape. Continue baking the rest of the mixture in the same way.

Striped Cylinder Cookies

These cookies can be made in different flavors and colors and look wonderful tied in bundles or packed into decorative jars or boxes. Eat them with ice cream or light desserts.

Makes 25

1 ounce white chocolate, melted
red and green food coloring dusts
2 egg whites
3½ ounces/½ cup superfine sugar
2 ounces/½ cup all-purpose flour
2 ounces/¼ cup sweet butter,
* melted*

1 Preheat the oven to 375°F/Gas 5. Line two baking sheets with baking parchment. Divide the melted chocolate in half and add a little food coloring dust to each half. Using two waxed paper pastry bags, fill each with colored chocolate and fold down the tops. Snip off the tips.

2 Place the egg whites in a bowl and whisk until stiff. Add the sugar gradually, whisking well after each addition. Add the flour and melted butter and whisk until smooth.

3 Drop four separate teaspoonfuls of the mixture onto the prepared baking sheets and spread into thin rounds. Pipe lines or zigzags of green and red chocolate over each round.

4 Bake one sheet at a time for about 3 minutes, until pale golden in color. Loosen the rounds with a metal spatula and return to the oven for a few seconds to soften. Have two or three lightly oiled wooden spoon handles to hand.

5 Taking one round cookie out of the oven at a time, turn it over and roll it around a spoon handle. Leave for a few seconds to set. Repeat to shape the remaining cookies. Put the second sheet of cookies in the oven to bake. Repeat the process of loosening, softening and rolling the cookies into shape.

6 When the cookies are set, slip them off the spoon handles onto a wire rack. Repeat with the remaining mixture and the red and green colored chocolate until all the mixture has been used, baking only one sheet of cookies at a time. If the cookies are too hard to shape, simply return them to the oven for a few seconds to soften.

7 When the cookies are cold, tie them together with colored ribbon and pack into boxes, glass jars or tins as gifts.

Cook's Tip

Don't be tempted to speed things up by baking more than one sheet of cookies at a time, as you won't be able to shape them all before some of them harden and set flat or scorch.

Ginger Glass Cookies

As thin, delicate and elegant as fine glass, these ginger cookies are ideal served with creamy desserts, sorbets and luxury ice creams.

Makes about 18

2 ounces/¼ cup sweet butter,
   diced

1½ ounces/3 tablespoons clear
   corn syrup

3½ ounces/½ cup superfine sugar

1½ ounces/⅓ cup all-purpose
   flour

1 teaspoon ground ginger

1 Put the butter and liquid glucose in a heatproof bowl set over a pan of gently simmering water. Stir together until melted. Set aside.

Cook's Tip

Use unlipped baking sheets so you can roll the cookies thinly.

2 Put the sugar in a bowl and sift over the flour and ginger. Stir into the butter mixture, then beat well until combined. Cover with plastic wrap and chill for about 25 minutes, until firm. Meanwhile, preheat the oven to 350°F/Gas 4 and line two or three baking sheets with baking parchment.

3 Roll teaspoonfuls of the cookie mixture into balls between your hands and place them, spaced far apart to allow room for spreading, on the prepared baking sheets.

4 Place a second piece of baking parchment on top and roll the cookies as thinly as possible. Peel off the top sheet. Then stamp each cookie with a 3- or 3½-inch plain round cutter.

5 Bake for 5–6 minutes, or until golden. Leave for a few seconds on the baking sheets to firm up slightly, then either leave flat or curl over in half. Leave to cool completely.

Butterfly Cookies

Melt-in-the-mouth puff pastry interleaved with sugar, nuts and cinnamon produces a slightly outrageous-looking cookie that teams well with ice creams and fruit salads.

Makes about 12

*1¼-pound packet ready-made
   puff pastry*

1 egg, beaten

*4 ounces/generous ½ cup
   granulated sugar*

1 ounce/¼ cup chopped mixed nuts

1 teaspoon ground cinnamon

1 Preheat the oven to 400°F/Gas 6. Roll out the pastry on a lightly floured surface to a rectangle measuring 20 x 6½ inches. Cut widthwise into four pieces. Brush each piece with beaten egg.

Cook's Tip

If using frozen puff pastry, thaw it first, but keep it chilled. Handle the dough lightly so it doesn't toughen.

2 Mix together 3 ounces/ 6 tablespoons of the sugar, the nuts and cinnamon in a bowl. Sprinkle this mixture evenly over three of the pieces of pastry. Place the pieces one on top of the other, ending with the uncoated piece, placing this one egg side down on the top. Press lightly together with the rolling pin.

3 Cut the stack of pastry sheets widthwise into ¼-inch slices. Carefully place one strip on a non-stick baking sheet and place the next strip over it at an angle. Place a third strip on top at another angle so that it looks like a butterfly. Don't worry if the strips separate slightly when you are transferring them to the baking sheet.

4 Using your fingers, press the center very flat. Sprinkle with a little of the reserved sugar. Continue in this way to make more cookies until all the pastry is used up.

5 Bake the cookies for about 10–15 minutes, or until golden brown all over. Leave to cool completely on the baking sheet before serving with your dessert.

Sablés with Caramel Glaze

These are very buttery French cookies with a dark caramel glaze. The leftover glaze can be kept in the refrigerator and used to flavor fruit salads and especially oranges, both of which are good served with sablés. Use on the day of baking for the most delicious results.

Makes about 18

7 ounces/1¾ cups all-purpose flour
pinch of salt
3 ounces/⅔ cup confectioners'
 sugar
4½ ounces/generous ½ cup
 sweet butter, chilled
 and diced
3 egg yolks
½ teaspoon vanilla extract
1 egg yolk, for glazing

For the caramel syrup

2 ounces/¼ cup granulated sugar
4 teaspoons water
½ teaspoon lemon juice
2 fluid ounces/¼ cup water

1 First make the caramel syrup. Put the sugar, 4 teaspoons water, and lemon juice into a small pan. Place over a gentle heat and stir until no longer cloudy. Boil until bubbly and allow to become a rich golden brown. Once this color, remove the pan immediately from the heat and plunge the base of the pan into a bowl of cold water to stop the cooking. Carefully stir in the 2 fluid ounces/¼ cup water. Set the caramel syrup aside to cool completely.

2 Preheat the oven to 350°F/Gas 4. Put all the cookie ingredients, except the egg yolks and vanilla, into a food processor then process until the mixture resembles fine breadcrumbs. Add the egg yolks and vanilla and blend until the mixture just begins to come together as a firm dough. Form into a ball, put in plastic wrap, then chill in the refrigerator for 15 minutes.

3 Roll the dough out on baking parchment to a thickness of just under ¼ inch. Using a 3-inch fluted cookie cutter, stamp out round pieces and place them on two non-stick baking sheets. (If you do not have non-stick baking sheets, line two ordinary sheets with baking parchment.)

4 In a small bowl, beat the egg yolk together with 1 tablespoon of the caramel glaze. Use this to brush sparingly over the cookies. Leave this coating to dry, then apply a second thin layer. Using a fork, prick the cookies, then mark in a neat checked pattern by dragging the tines of the fork over the glaze.

5 Bake for about 10–15 minutes, or until crisp and golden brown. Transfer to a wire rack to cool.

Cook's Tip
If the caramel does not dissolve evenly when the water is added, place the pan over a gentle heat and stir until it is completely dissolved.

Almond Fingers

Sweet and crunchy, and packed with lightly spiced nuts, these very simple Middle
Eastern sweetmeats are hugely popular in their native lands. Serve with fruit salad.

Makes 48

7 ounces/1¾ cups ground almonds
2 ounces/½ cup ground pistachio nuts
2 ounces/¼ cup granulated sugar
1 tablespoon rose water
½ teaspoon ground cinnamon
12 sheets of phyllo pastry
4 ounces/½ cup butter, melted
confectioners' sugar, for dusting

Variation
*You could substitute orange-flower water,
which is also a popular Middle Eastern
flavoring, for the rose water.*

1 Preheat the oven to 325°F/Gas 3.
Grease a large baking sheet with a
little butter. Mix together the nuts,
sugar, rose water and cinnamon.

2 Cut each sheet of phyllo pastry
into four rectangles. Work with one
at a time, and cover the remaining
rectangles with a damp dishtowel
to prevent them from drying out.

3 Brush one rectangle of phyllo
pastry with a little of the melted
butter, place a teaspoonful of the
nut filling in the center.

4 Fold in the sides of the pastry
and roll into a thick finger shape.
Continue until all the phyllo pastry
and nut filling have been used up.

5 Place the almond fingers on
the baking sheet and bake for
30 minutes. Transfer to a wire
rack to cool, then dust with
confectioners' sugar.

Basbousa

These delicious Middle Eastern coconut sweetmeats can be served either hot as a dessert or cold
with tea. To be really authentic, serve them with a glass of sweet mint tea.

Makes 12

4 ounces/½ cup sweet butter
6 ounces/scant 1 cup
   superfine sugar
2 ounces/½ cup all-purpose flour
5 ounces/1¼ cups semolina
3 ounces/1 cup grated
   fresh coconut
6 fluid ounces/¾ cup milk
1 teaspoon baking powder
1 teaspoon vanilla extract
almonds, to decorate

For the syrup
4 ounces/generous ½ cup
   superfine sugar
¼ pint/⅔ cup water
1 tablespoon lemon juice

1 To make the syrup, place the sugar,
water and lemon juice in a heavy
pan, bring to the boil, stirring until
the sugar has dissolved. Lower the
heat and simmer for 6–8 minutes.
Remove the pan from the heat,
leave the syrup to cool, then chill in
the refrigerator.

2 Preheat the oven to 350°F/Gas 4.
Melt the butter in a pan. Add the
sugar, flour, semolina, coconut, milk,
baking powder and vanilla and
mix thoroughly.

3 Pour the mixture into a shallow
cake pan, flatten and smooth the
top with a metal spatula and bake
for 30–35 minutes.

4 Remove the basbousa from the
oven and cut into diamond-shaped
lozenges. Pour the cold syrup evenly
over the top and place an almond
in the center of each diamond
shape to decorate.

Cook's Tip
*Once the sugar has dissolved, do not stir
the syrup while it is simmering. Keep
the heat low so that the syrup thickens
without changing color. If you plan to
serve the basbousa hot, make the
syrup while the mixture is baking and
pour it over the diamond shapes without
chilling it first.*

Italian Glazed Lemon Rings

These delicately flavored, pretty cookies look almost too good to eat. The icing is flavored with Italian liqueur, so they are strictly for adult parties.

Makes about 16

7 ounces/1¾ cups self-rising flour

2 ounces/¼ cup sweet butter, at room temperature, diced

1½ tablespoons milk

2 ounces/¼ cup superfine sugar

finely grated rind of ½ lemon

1 egg, beaten

For the topping

5 ounces/1¼ cups confectioners' sugar, sifted

2 tablespoons Limoncello liqueur

1 tablespoon chopped candied angelica

Variation

If you are baking for children, use lemon syrup instead of liqueur.

1 Preheat the oven to 350°F/Gas 4. Line two large baking sheets with baking parchment. Put the flour into a bowl and rub in the butter. Put the milk, sugar and lemon rind in a small pan and stir over a low heat until the sugar has dissolved. Add to the flour mixture, together with the egg, and mix well. Knead lightly until smooth.

2 Roll walnut-size pieces of dough into strands 6 inches long. Twist two strands together, and join the ends to make a circle. Place on the prepared baking sheets and bake for 15–20 minutes, or until golden.

3 To make the topping, stir the confectioners' sugar and liqueur together. Dip the top of each cookie into the topping; sprinkle with angelica.

Mini Fudge Bites

These cute little cookies have the flavor of butterscotch and fudge and are topped with chopped pecan nuts for a delicious crunch – just the right size for a special little treat with ice cream.

Makes 30

7 ounces/1¾ cups self-rising
   flour

4 ounces/½ cup butter, at room
   temperature, diced

4 ounces/generous ½ cup dark
   molasses sugar

3 ounces vanilla cream fudge, diced

1 egg, beaten

1 ounce/¼ cup pecan nut halves,
   sliced widthwise

1 Preheat the oven to 375°F/Gas 5. Line two or three baking sheets with baking parchment. Put the flour in a bowl and rub in the butter until the mixture resembles fine breadcrumbs.

2 Add the molasses sugar and diced vanilla fudge to the flour mixture and stir well until combined. Add the beaten egg and mix in well. Bring the dough together with your hands, then knead gently on a lightly floured surface. It will be soft yet firm.

3 Roll the dough into two cylinders, 9 inches long. Cut into ½-inch slices and place on the baking sheets. Sprinkle over the pecan nuts and press in lightly. Bake for about 12 minutes, until browned at the edges. Transfer to a wire rack to cool.

Semolina and Nut Halva

Semolina is a popular ingredient in many desserts and pastries in the Eastern Mediterranean. Here it provides a spongy base for soaking up a deliciously fragrant spicy syrup.

Makes 20–24

4 ounces/½ cup sweet butter at room
   temperature, diced

4 ounces/generous ½ cup
   superfine sugar

finely grated rind of 1 orange

2 tablespoons orange juice

3 eggs

6 ounces/1 cup semolina

2 teaspoons baking powder

4 ounces/1 cup ground hazelnuts

2 ounces/½ cup unblanched
   hazelnuts, toasted and chopped

2 ounces/½ cup blanched almonds,
   toasted and chopped

shredded rind of 1 orange

whipped cream, to serve
   (optional)

For the syrup

12 ounces/1¾ cups superfine sugar

18 fluid ounces/2¼ cups water

2 cinnamon sticks, halved

juice of 1 lemon

4 tablespoons orange-flower water

1 Preheat the oven to 425°F/Gas 7. Grease and line the base of a deep 9-inch square heavy cake pan.

2 Lightly cream the butter in a large bowl. Add the sugar, orange rind and juice, the eggs, semolina, baking powder and ground hazelnuts and beat the ingredients together until combined and smooth.

3 Tip the mixture into the prepared pan and level the surface with a spatula. Bake for 20–25 minutes, or until just firm and golden on top. Remove from the oven and place the pan on a wire rack. Leave to cool.

4 To make the syrup, put the sugar in a heavy pan with the water and cinnamon sticks. Heat gently, stirring until the sugar has dissolved.

5 Bring the syrup to the boil and continue to boil hard for 5 minutes without stirring. The syrup should thicken, but not color.

6 Measure half the syrup in a cup and add the lemon juice and orange-flower water to it. Pour this mixture over the halva. Reserve the remainder of the syrup in the pan.

7 Leave the halva in the pan until the syrup has been absorbed, then turn it out onto a plate and cut diagonally into diamond-shaped portions. Sprinkle with the chopped hazelnuts and almonds.

8 Boil the remaining syrup until slightly thickened, then pour it over the halva. Sprinkle the shredded orange rind over the top and serve the halva with lightly whipped cream, if you like.

Cook's Tip

You can make the halva up to two days in advance. At the end of step 6, leave the halva to cool in the pan, then cover with plastic wrap and store in the refrigerator. Pour the remaining syrup into a pitcher, cover and chill. Bring to room temperature to serve. Cut into diamond shapes, sprinkle with the chopped nuts, pour over the reserved syrup and decorate with the shredded orange rind.

Lace Cookies

Very pretty, delicate and crisp, these lacy cookies are ideal for serving with elegant creamy or iced desserts at the end of a dinner party. Don't be tempted to bake more than four on a sheet.

Makes about 14

3 ounces/6 tablespoons butter, diced

3 ounces/¾ cup rolled oats

4 ounces/generous ½ cup golden superfine sugar

1 egg, beaten

2 teaspoons all-purpose flour

1 teaspoon baking powder

½ teaspoon apple pie spice

1 Preheat the oven to 350°F/Gas 4. Line three or four baking sheets with baking parchment. Put the butter in a pan and set over a low heat until just melted. Remove the pan from the heat.

2 Stir the rolled oats into the melted butter. Add the remaining ingredients and mix well.

3 Place only three or four heaped teaspoonfuls of the mixture, spaced far apart, on each of the lined baking sheets.

4 Bake for about 5–7 minutes, or until a deepish golden brown all over. Leave the cookies on the baking sheets for a few minutes. Carefully cut the parchment so you can lift each cookie singly. Invert onto a wire rack and carefully remove the parchment. Leave to cool.

Bittersweet Chocolate Fingers

With their understated elegance and distinctly grown-up flavor, these deliciously decadent chocolate fingers are ideal for serving with a special dinner part dessert.

Makes about 26

4 ounces/1 cup all-purpose flour

½ teaspoon baking powder

2 tablespoons cocoa powder (unsweetened)

2 ounces/¼ cup sweet butter, softened

2 ounces/¼ cup superfine sugar

4 teaspoons light corn syrup

5 ounces bittersweet chocolate

chocolate-flavor mini flakes, for sprinkling

I Preheat the oven to 325°F/ Gas 3. Line two baking sheets with baking parchment. Put the flour, baking powder, cocoa powder, butter, sugar and syrup in a large mixing bowl.

2 Work the ingredients together with your hands to combine and form into a dough.

3 Roll the dough out between sheets of baking parchment to a 7 x 9½ inch rectangle. Remove the top sheet. Cut in half lengthwise, then into bars ¾ of an inch wide. Place on the baking sheets.

4 Bake for about 15 minutes, taking care not to allow the bars to brown, or they will taste bitter. Transfer to a wire rack to cool.

5 Melt the chocolate in a heatproof bowl set over a pan of hot water. Half-dip the cookies, place on baking parchment, sprinkle with chocolate flakes, then leave to set.

Strawberry Shortcakes

More of a dessert than a cookie, shortcake is as American as apple pie – only slightly more popular. It's a favorite summer dessert that is served here with sweet, fresh strawberries.

Makes 6

8 ounces/2 cups all-purpose flour
3 ounces/⅓ cup superfine sugar
1 tablespoon baking powder
pinch of salt
8 fluid ounces/1 cup whipping cream
fresh mint leaves, to decorate

For the filling

1 pound strawberries, hulled and halved
   or quartered, depending on size
3 tablespoons confectioners' sugar
8 fluid ounces/1 cup whipping cream

1 Preheat the oven to 400°F/Gas 6. Grease a baking sheet.

2 To make the shortcakes, sift the flour into a mixing bowl. Add 2 ounces/¼ cup of the superfine sugar, the baking powder and salt. Stir well.

3 Gradually add the cream, tossing with a fork until clumps form.

4 Gather the clumps together, but do not knead the dough. Shape the dough into a 6-inch log. Cut into six slices and place the slices on the prepared baking sheet.

5 Sprinkle with the remaining superfine sugar, then bake for about 15 minutes, until light golden brown. Leave to cool on a wire rack.

6 Meanwhile, mash a quarter of the strawberries with the confectioners' sugar. Stir in the remaining strawberries.

7 Just before serving, whip the cream until soft peaks form.

8 Slice each shortcake in half horizontally. Put the lower halves on individual serving plates and top with some of the cream. Divide the strawberries among the six shortcake halves. Replace the tops and decorate with mint leaves. Serve with the remaining cream.

Cook's Tip

Mix the strawberries with the confectioners' sugar and leave to stand in a cool place for an hour before serving. To achieve the best results when whipping cream, chill both the bowl and beaters until thoroughly cold. If using an electric mixer, increase the speed gradually, and turn the bowl while beating to incorporate as much air as possible.

Raspberry and Rose Petal Shortcakes

Rose-water-scented cream and fresh raspberries form the filling for this delectable dessert. Although they look impressive, these shortcakes are easy to make.

Makes 6

4 ounces/½ cup sweet
  butter, softened
2 ounces/¼ cup superfine sugar
½ vanilla bean, split and
  seeds reserved
4 ounces/1 cup all-purpose flour,
  plus extra for dusting
2 ounces/⅓ cup semolina
confectioners' sugar, for dusting

For the filling

½ pint/1¼ cups heavy cream
1 tablespoon confectioners'
  sugar
½ teaspoon rose water
1 pound/4 cups raspberries

For the decoration

12 miniature roses, unsprayed
6 mint sprigs
1 egg white, beaten
superfine sugar, for dusting

1 Cream the butter, superfine sugar and vanilla seeds in a bowl until pale and fluffy. Sift the flour and semolina together, then gradually work the dry ingredients into the creamed mixture to make a dough.

2 Gently knead the dough on a lightly floured surface until smooth. Roll out quite thinly and prick all over with a fork. Using a 3-inch fluted cutter, stamp out 12 round pieces. Place these on a baking sheet and chill for 30 minutes.

3 Meanwhile, make the filling. Whisk the cream with the confectioners' sugar until soft peaks form. Gently fold in the rose water with a metal spoon, cover with plastic wrap and chill until required.

4 Preheat the oven to 350°F/Gas 4. To make the decoration, paint the roses and leaves with the egg white. Dust with sugar, then dry on a wire rack.

5 Bake the shortcakes for about 15 minutes, or until lightly golden. Lift them off the baking sheet with a metal spatula and cool on a wire rack.

6 To assemble the shortcakes, spoon the rose water cream onto half the cookies. Add a layer of raspberries, then top with a second shortcake. Dust with confectioners' sugar. Decorate with the frosted roses and mint sprigs.

Cook's Tip

For best results, serve the shortcakes as soon as possible after assembling them. Otherwise, they are likely to turn soggy from the berries' liquid. However, unfilled shortcakes can be stored.

Florentine Bites

Very sweet and rich, these little mouthfuls are great with iced desserts, and you can continue serving them with after-dinner coffee and liqueurs.

Makes 36

7 ounces good quality semisweet chocolate (minimum 70 percent cocoa solids)

2 ounces/2½ cups cornflakes

2 ounces/scant ½ cup golden raisins

4 ounces/1 cup toasted sliced almonds

4 ounces/½ cup candied cherries, halved

2 ounces/⅓ cup cut candied peel

7 fluid ounces/scant 1 cup can sweetened condensed milk

1 Preheat the oven to 350°F/Gas 4. Line the base of a shallow 8-inch cake pan with baking parchment. Lightly grease the sides. Melt the chocolate in a heatproof bowl set over a pan of hot water. Spread evenly over the base of the pan. Put in the refrigerator to set.

2 Meanwhile, put the cornflakes, raisins, almonds, cherries and mixed peel in a large bowl. Pour over the condensed milk and toss the mixture gently, using a fork.

3 Spread the mixture evenly over the chocolate base and bake for 12–15 minutes, until golden brown. Cool in the pan, then chill for 20 minutes. Cut into tiny squares.

Chocolate and Pistachio Wedges

These cookies are rich and grainy textured, with a bitter chocolate flavor. They go extremely well with vanilla ice cream and are especially delicious with bananas and custard.

Makes 16

7 ounces/scant 1 cup sweet butter,
   at room temperature, diced

3½ ounces/½ cup golden superfine
   sugar

9 ounces/2¼ cups all-purpose flour

2 ounces/½ cup cocoa powder
   (unsweetened)

1 ounce/¼ cup shelled pistachio nuts,
   finely chopped

cocoa powder (unsweetened),
   for dusting

1 Preheat the oven to 350°F/ Gas 4 and line a shallow 9-inch round sandwich pan with baking parchment.

2 Beat the butter and sugar until light and creamy. Sift the flour and cocoa powder, then add the flour mixture to the butter and work in with your hands until the mixture is smooth. Knead until soft and pliable then press into the prepared pan.

3 Using the back of a tablespoon, spread the mixture evenly in the pan. Sprinkle the pistachio nuts over the top and press in gently. Prick with a fork, then mark into 16 segments using a round-bladed knife.

4 Bake for about 15–20 minutes. Do not allow to brown at all, or the cookies will taste bitter.

5 Remove the pan from the oven and dust the cookies with cocoa powder. Cut through the marked sections with a round-bladed knife and leave to cool completely before removing from the pan.

Almond and Vanilla Cookies with Praline Coating

These short-textured almond cookies, filled with vanilla cream and coated in praline, are just the thing to have with a light dessert, such as fresh fruit salad or compote.

Makes 17–18

5 ounces/1¼ cups all-purpose flour

3 ounces/¾ cup ground almonds

3 ounces/6 tablespoons sweet butter, at room temperature, diced

1 egg yolk

1 teaspoon vanilla extract

confectioners' sugar, sifted, for dusting

For the praline

1 ounce/¼ cup whole blanched almonds

2 ounces/¼ cup superfine sugar

For the filling

5 ounces/1¼ cups confectioners' sugar, sifted

3 ounces/6 tablespoons sweet butter, at room temperature, diced

1 teaspoon vanilla extract

1 First make the praline. Lightly oil a baking sheet and place the almonds on it, fairly close together. Melt the sugar in a small pan over a very low heat. Heat until it turns dark golden brown and pour immediately over the almonds. Cool then crush finely in a food processor.

2 Preheat the oven to 325°F/ Gas 3. Line three baking sheets with baking parchment.

3 Put the flour, ground almonds and butter in a bowl. Rub together until the mixture starts to cling together. Add the egg and vanilla, and work together using your hands to make a soft dough. Roll out to a thickness of about ¼ inch on baking parchment. Stamp out round pieces using a 2-inch cookie cutter, and place on the prepared baking sheets.

4 Bake the cookies for about 15 minutes, or until light golden brown. Leave on the baking sheets for 5 minutes to firm up slightly, then transfer to a wire rack to cool.

5 To make the filling, beat together the confectioners' sugar, butter and vanilla until creamy. Use this mixture to sandwich the cookies in pairs. Be generous with the filling, spreading right to the edges. Press the cookies gently so the filling oozes out of the sides and, using your finger, smooth around the sides of the cookie.

6 Put the praline on a plate and roll the edges of each cookie in the praline until thickly coated. Dust the tops of the cookies with confectioners' sugar.

Cook's Tip
These cookies should be made on the day of serving, or the filling will cause them to become soggy and unpleasant.

Louisiana Pralines

These classic cookies are a sweet combination of sugar, cream and milk. They resemble puddles of nut fudge and are deliciously indulgent with ice cream.

Makes 30

8 ounces/2 cups pecan nut halves

1 pound/2 well-packed cups soft light brown sugar

7 ounces/scant 1 cup granulated sugar

½ pint/1¼ cups heavy cream

6 fluid ounces/¾ cup milk

1 teaspoon vanilla extract

1 Line two or three large baking sheets with baking parchment. Coarsely chop half the pecan nuts and set both the whole and chopped nuts aside.

2 Place both the sugars, the cream and milk together in a heavy pan and stir over a medium heat until the sugar has dissolved. Stir until the mixture reaches 238°F (soft ball stage).

Cook's Tip

Praline is traditionally made with almonds and has a characteristically granulated appearance. Named after the French aristocrat whose chef invented the recipe, Comte du Plessis-Praslin, they quickly became popular and were widely sold in fairgrounds. Peanuts were sometimes substituted for the almonds and when the recipe crossed the Atlantic, indigenous American pecans got their turn.

3 Remove the pan from the heat immediately and beat with an electric mixer or balloon whisk until the mixture loses its sheen and becomes creamy in texture and grainy looking. This could take as long as 15 minutes whisking by hand, or about 5 minutes if you are using an electric mixer.

4 Stir in the vanilla extract and nuts. Drop tablespoonfuls of the mixture onto the prepared baking sheets, allowing it to spread of its own accord. Leave to cool and set at room temperature. Store stacked between layers of waxed paper in an airtight container until required.

Mexican Almond Cookies

Light and crisp, these sugar-dusted cookies make a lively accompaniment to plain ice cream at the end of a family supper and also make a good accompaniment to fruit salads.

Makes 24

4 ounces/1 cup all-purpose flour

6 ounces/1½ cups confectioners' sugar, plus extra for dusting

pinch of salt

2 ounces/½ cup almonds, finely chopped

½ teaspoon vanilla extract

4 ounces/½ cup sweet butter at room temperature, diced

3 Roll out the dough on a lightly floured surface until it is ⅛ of an inch thick. Using a round, fluted cutter, stamp out 24 round pieces, re-rolling the trimmings as necessary.

4 Carefully transfer the cookies to non-stick baking sheets and bake for 30 minutes until browned. Transfer to wire racks to cool, then dust thickly with confectioners' sugar.

1 Preheat the oven to 350°F/Gas 4. Sift the flour, confectioners' sugar and salt into a bowl. Add the almonds and mix well. Stir in the vanilla extract.

2 Using your fingertips, work the butter into the mixture to make a dough. Form it into a ball.

Variation
Try using other nuts such as walnuts, peanuts or pecan nuts.

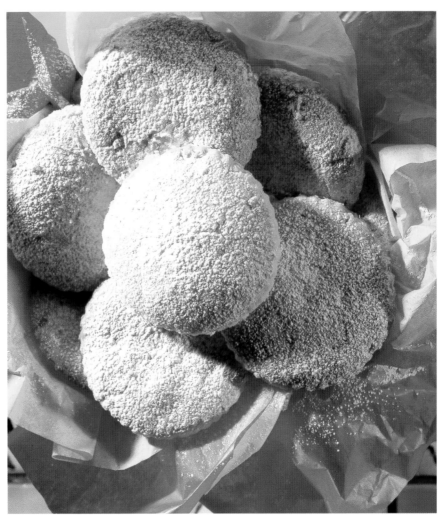

Peppermint and Coconut Chocolate Sticks

Coconut gives these chocolate-mint sticks a unique flavor and texture. The mixture makes lots, so is perfect party fare when you are throwing a big dinner or buffet party.

Makes 80

4 ounces/½ cup granulated sugar

¼ pint/⅔ cup water

½ teaspoon peppermint extract

7 ounces bittersweet
  chocolate, chopped

4 tablespoons toasted dried
  unsweetened shredded coconut

1 Lightly oil a large baking sheet. Place the sugar and water in a small, heavy pan and heat gently, stirring occasionally, until the sugar has dissolved completely.

2 Bring to the boil and boil rapidly, without stirring, until the syrup registers 280°F on a sugar thermometer (hard ball stage).

3 Remove the pan from the heat and add the peppermint extract, then carefully pour onto the prepared baking sheet and leave until set and completely cold.

4 Break the peppermint mixture into a bowl with your hands and then use the end of a rolling pin to crush it into pieces.

5 Melt the bittersweet chocolate in a medium-size heatproof bowl set over a pan of simmering water. Remove the bowl from the heat, add the crushed peppermint pieces and dried coconut and stir well until thoroughly combined.

6 Place a 12 x 10 inch sheet of baking parchment on the work surface. Spread the mixture over the paper, leaving a narrow border all around. Leave to set. When firm, use a sharp knife to cut into thin sticks.

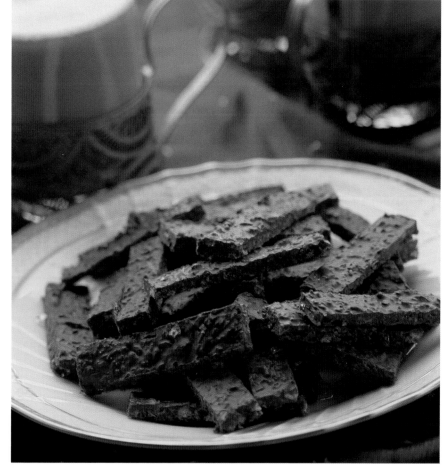

Semisweet Chocolate and Peppermint Crisps

Crunchy peppermint caramel is crushed then stirred into chocolate to make these pretty swirls – choose good quality chocolate for the best result.

Makes 30

2 ounces/¼ cup granulated sugar

2 fluid ounces/¼ cup water

1 teaspoon peppermint extract

8 ounces semisweet chocolate,
   chopped

1 Lightly brush a large baking sheet with unflavored oil. In a pan over a medium heat, heat the sugar and water, swirling the pan gently until the sugar dissolves. Boil rapidly until the temperature registers 280°F on a sugar thermometer (hard ball stage).

2 Remove from the heat and add the peppermint extract; swirl gently to mix. Pour onto the baking sheet and leave to set and cool.

3 When cold, break into pieces. Place in a food processor fitted with a metal blade until fine crumbs form.

Cook's Tip
You can test cooked sugar for "hard ball stage" by spooning a few drops into a bowl of cold water; it should form a hard ball when rolled between your fingers.

4 Line two baking sheets with non-stick baking parchment. Place the chocolate in a heatproof bowl over a small pan of hot water. Place over a very low heat until the chocolate has melted, stirring frequently until smooth. Remove from the heat and stir in the peppermint mixture.

5 Using a teaspoon, drop small mounds onto the prepared baking sheets. Using the back of the spoon, spread to 1½-inch round shapes. Cool, then chill for about 1 hour, until set. Peel off the parchment and store in airtight containers with baking parchment between the layers.

Vanilla Crescents

These attractively shaped cookies are sweet and delicate, ideal to serve with ice cream or a light and fluffy fruit fool for dessert. Kids love them with chocolate ice cream.

Makes 36

6 ounces/1¼ cups unblanched almonds

4 ounces/1 cup all-purpose flour

pinch of salt

8 ounces/1 cup sweet butter at room temperature, diced

4 ounces/½ cup granulated sugar

1 teaspoon vanilla extract

confectioners' sugar, for dusting

1 Grind the almonds with a few tablespoons of the flour in a food processor, blender or nut grinder and process in short pulses until finely ground.

2 Sift the remaining flour with the salt into a bowl. Set aside.

3 With an electric mixer, cream together the butter and sugar until light and fluffy.

4 Add the almonds, vanilla extract and the flour mixture. Stir to mix well. Gather the dough into a ball, wrap in waxed paper, and chill for at least 30 minutes. Preheat the oven to 325°F/Gas 3. Lightly grease two baking sheets.

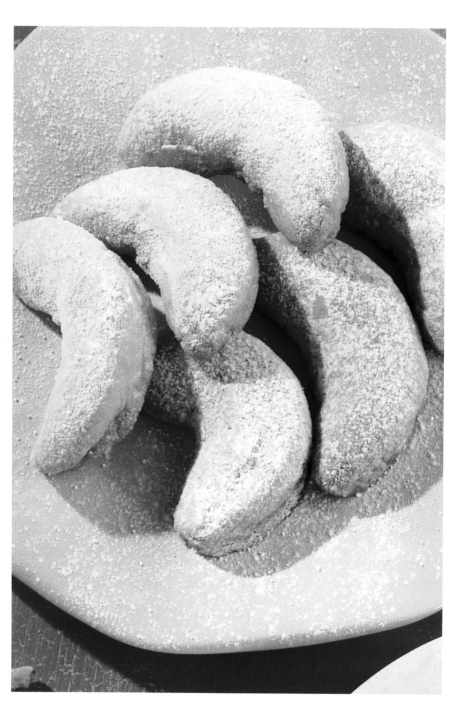

5 Break off walnut-size pieces of dough and roll them into small cylinders about ½ inch in diameter. Bend them into crescent shapes and place on the baking sheets, spaced well apart.

6 Bake for about 20 minutes until dry but not brown. Transfer to a wire rack to cool only slightly. Set the rack over a baking sheet and dust with an even layer of confectioners' sugar. Leave to cool completely.

Black Russian Cookies

The ingredients of the famous cocktail – coffee and vodka – flavor these fabulous cookies. These are strictly for the adults in the family, so why not go the extra mile and serve with vodka jelly?

Makes 16

2 tablespoons ground espresso coffee

4 tablespoons near-boiling milk

4 ounces/½ cup butter

4 ounces/½ cup soft light
  brown sugar

1 egg

8 ounces/2 cups all-purpose flour

1 teaspoon baking powder

pinch of salt

For the icing

4 ounces/1 cup confectioners' sugar

about 1½ tablespoons vodka

1 Preheat the oven to 350°F/Gas 4. Put the coffee in a small bowl and pour the hot milk over it. Leave to steep for 4 minutes, then strain through a fine sieve and leave to cool.

2 Cream the butter and sugar until light and fluffy. Gradually beat in the egg. Sift the flour, baking powder and salt together and fold in with the coffee-flavored milk to make a fairly stiff mixture.

3 Place dessertspoonfuls of the mixture on greased baking sheets, spacing them slightly apart. Bake the cookies for about 15 minutes until lightly browned. Cool on a wire rack.

4 To make the icing, mix the confectioners' sugar and enough vodka together to make a thick icing. Spoon into a small waxed paper pastry bag.

5 Snip off the end of the pastry bag and lightly drizzle the icing over the top of each cookie. Leave the icing to set before serving.

Variations

You could adapt this recipe to re-create other classic and contemporary cocktails. For Black Magic Cookies, add a dash of lemon juice to the vodka when making the icing. For Blackout Cookies, substitute white rum for the vodka in the icing. For Brave Bull Cookies, substitute silver tequila for the vodka in the icing. For Moon Landing Cookies, substitute 1 tablespoon amaretto liqueur for the same quantity of milk. Don't heat it, simply stir it in after straining the coffee.

Nut Lace Cookies

These cookies look so pretty, it almost seems a shame to eat them, but if you didn't, you would certainly be missing out on a treat. Serve them with smooth and creamy desserts.

Makes 18

2 ounces/½ cup blanched almonds

2 ounces/¼ cup butter

3 tablespoons all-purpose flour

4 ounces/½ cup granulated sugar

2 tablespoons heavy cream

½ teaspoon vanilla extract

Variation

Add 1½ ounces/¼ cup finely chopped candied orange peel to the mixture with the almonds in step 3.

1 Preheat the oven to 375°F/Gas 5. Thoroughly grease one or two baking sheets.

2 With a sharp knife, chop the almonds as finely as possible. Alternatively, use a food processor to chop the nuts very finely.

3 Melt the butter in a small pan over a low heat. Remove from the heat and stir in the remaining ingredients, including the almonds.

4 Drop teaspoonfuls of the mixture 2½ inches apart on the prepared baking sheets. Bake for about 5 minutes, or until golden. Cool on the sheets briefly, until the cookies are just firm enough to lift off.

5 With a metal spatula, transfer the cookies to a wire rack to cool.

Oat Lace Cookies

These thin, crisp cookies have quite a different texture from other oat cookie recipes, but they are just as tasty. Use unsalted butter for the best flavor.

Makes 36

5½ ounces/⅔ cup sweet butter
   or margarine

6 ounces/1⅔ cups rolled oats

6 ounces/¾ cup soft dark brown sugar

6 ounces/¾ cup granulated sugar

3 tablespoons all-purpose flour

pinch of salt

1 egg, lightly beaten

1 teaspoon vanilla extract

2 ounces/½ cup pecan nuts or walnuts,
   finely chopped

1 Preheat the oven to 350°F/Gas 4. Thoroughly grease two large baking sheets.

2 Melt the butter or margarine in a small pan over a low heat. Set aside.

3 Mix the oats, sugars, flour and salt. Add the butter or margarine, the egg and vanilla. Mix until blended, then stir in the nuts.

4 Drop rounded teaspoonfuls of the batter about 2 inches apart on the prepared baking sheets. Bake for 5–8 minutes, until lightly browned on the edges and bubbling. Leave to cool slightly on the baking sheets for about 2 minutes, then, using a metal spatula, transfer to a wire rack to cool completely.

Cook's Tip

Walnuts and pecan nuts are quite closely related and, when fresh, have a similar sweetness. Pecans tend to have a slightly softer texture than walnuts. Chop them with a large sharp knife.

Brownies and Bars

Cookies with attitude, brownies and bars make filling snacks, lunchtime treats, perfect picnic fare and a marvelous morale and energy boost at any time of day. There are probably more variations on the basic brownie than on any other cookie in the world, and when you try some of the recipes here, you will understand why. As for bars and slices, the sky's the limit – crisp and nutty, chewy and succulent, sweet and fruity. You choose.

Fruity Lemon Drizzle Bars

These tangy iced, spongy bars are great for kids to snack on after school. This fruit and lemon mixture is lovely but you can easily experiment with other flavors such as orange or lime.

Makes 16

9 ounces ready-made sweet
  shortcrust pastry

3¼ ounces/¾ cup self-rising
  flour

3 ounces/¾ cup fine or
  medium oatmeal

1 teaspoon baking powder

4½ ounces/generous ½ cup light
  brown sugar

2 eggs

5 ounces/10 tablespoons sweet
  butter, at room
  temperature, diced

finely grated rind of 1 lemon

3½ ounces/¾ cup golden
  raisins

5 ounces/1¼ cups confectioners'
  sugar

3–4 teaspoons lemon juice

1 Preheat the oven to 375°F/ Gas 5 and place a baking sheet in the oven to heat through. Generously grease an 11 x 7 inch shallow baking pan.

2 Roll out the pastry thinly on a lightly floured, clean surface. Use to line the base of the baking pan, pressing the pastry up the sides. (Don't worry about rough edges.)

3 Put the flour, oatmeal, baking powder, sugar, eggs, butter and lemon rind in a mixing bowl. Beat with a hand-held electric whisk for about 2 minutes, until pale and creamy. Stir in the raisins.

4 Tip the filling into the pastry case and spread evenly into the corners, using the back of a spoon.

5 Place the pan on the heated baking sheet in the oven and bake for about 30 minutes until pale golden, when the surface feels firm to the touch.

6 Put the confectioners' sugar in a small bowl with enough lemon juice to mix to a thin paste, about the consistency of half-and-half cream.

7 Using a teaspoon, drizzle the icing diagonally across the warm cake in thin lines. Leave to cool in the pan.

8 When the icing has set, use a sharp knife to cut the cake in half lengthwise. Cut each half across into eight even-size bars.

Luscious Lemon Bars

A crisp cookie base is covered with a tangy lemon topping. The bars make a delightful addition to the tea table on a warm summer's day in the garden.

Makes 12

5 ounces/1¼ cups all-purpose
  flour
3½ ounces/7 tablespoons sweet butter,
  chilled and diced
2 ounces/½ cup confectioners'
  sugar, sifted

For the topping

2 eggs
6 ounces/scant 1 cup superfine
  sugar
finely grated rind and juice of
  1 large lemon
1 tablespoon all-purpose flour
½ teaspoon baking soda
confectioners' sugar,
  for dusting

3 To make the topping, whisk the eggs in a bowl until frothy. Add the superfine sugar, a little at a time, whisking well between each addition. Whisk in the lemon rind and juice, flour and soda. Pour over the cookie base. Bake for 20–25 minutes, until set and golden.

4 Leave to cool slightly. Cut into twelve bars and dust lightly with sugar. Leave to cool completely.

1 Preheat the oven to 350°F/Gas 4. Line the base of an 8-inch square shallow cake pan with baking parchment and lightly grease the sides of the pan.

2 Process the flour, butter and confectioners' sugar in a food processor until the mixture comes together as a firm dough. Press evenly into the base of the pan and spread smoothly using the back of a tablespoon. Bake for 12–15 minutes until lightly golden. Cool in the pan.

Lemon Cheese Bars

Using a really creamy cheese for the topping makes these bars suitable for any celebration.

Makes 24

4 ounces/1 cup all-purpose flour

2 ounces/½ cup chopped walnuts

3 ounces/⅓ cup soft light brown sugar

3 ounces/⅓ cup sweet butter,
  softened

grated rind and juice of 1 small lemon

8 ounces/1 cup full-fat cream cheese

2 ounces/¼ cup granulated sugar

1 tablespoon milk

½ teaspoon vanilla extract

1 extra large egg

1 Preheat the oven to 350°F/Gas 4. Grease a 9-inch square cake pan.

2 Beat together the flour, walnuts, brown sugar and butter. Divide the mixture in half. Press half of the mixture into the prepared cake pan. Bake for 12–15 minutes, until lightly browned. Remove from the oven.

3 Beat together the lemon rind and juice, the cheese and sugar, then beat in the milk, vanilla extract and egg. Spoon over the partly cooked pastry and crumble the remaining mixture evenly over the top. Bake for a further 25 minutes, until the top is golden. Transfer to a wire rack to cool, then chill. Cut into bars.

Citrus Spice Bars

These iced bars have a delicious rum-flavored fruit mixture at the base, so they're strictly adults only.

Makes 50

4 ounces/¾ cup candied orange
  peel, chopped

2 ounces/⅓ cup seedless raisins

5 tablespoons rum

2 ounces/¼ cup clear honey

3 tablespoons black molasses

1 egg

4 ounces/1 cup ground almonds

6 ounces/1½ cups whole-wheat flour

½ teaspoon baking powder

large pinch of baking soda

1 teaspoon ground cinnamon

½ teaspoon ground ginger

4 ounces/1 cup almonds, chopped

2 ounces/½ cup sifted confectioners'
  sugar

about 3 tablespoons orange juice

1 Preheat the oven to 400°F/Gas 6. Lightly grease a 13 x 9 inch cake pan. Place the orange peel, raisins and rum in a bowl, cover and set aside for 1 hour.

2 Bring the honey and molasses to the boil in a pan. Cool, then beat in the egg. Combine the ground almonds, flour, baking powder, baking soda and spices, and stir into the mixture. Stir in the chopped almonds and the rum mixture, and form into a dough.

3 Bake for 20 minutes. Transfer to a wire rack to cool. Sift the confectioners' sugar into a bowl and stir in just enough orange juice to make a spreading consistency. Set aside for 1 hour.

4 Spread with the icing. Decorate, if you like, and cut into generous bars.

Lemon Squares

Perfect for when you crave something sweet but don't want the richness of chocolate.

Makes 12

8 ounces/2 cups all-purpose flour

2 ounces/½ cup confectioners' sugar

pinch of salt

6 ounces/¾ cup butter or margarine, diced

For the lemon layer

4 eggs

1 pound/2¼ cups superfine sugar

1 ounce/¼ cup all-purpose flour

½ teaspoon baking powder

1 teaspoon grated lemon rind

2 fluid ounces/¼ cup fresh lemon juice

confectioners' sugar, for sprinkling

1 Preheat the oven to 350°F/Gas 4. Sift the flour, confectioners' sugar and salt into a mixing bowl.

2 Rub in the butter or margarine until the mixture resembles coarse breadcrumbs. Stir in 1 teaspoon water with a fork until the mixture forms a ball.

3 Press the mixture evenly into an ungreased 13 x 9 inch ovenproof dish. Bake for 15–20 minutes, until light golden brown. Remove from the oven and leave to cool slightly.

4 Meanwhile, to make the lemon layer, beat together the eggs, superfine sugar, flour, baking powder and lemon rind and juice in a bowl until smooth and combined.

5 Pour the lemon mixture over the cooked base. Return to the oven and bake for 25 minutes.

6 Leave to cool in the ovenproof dish, placed on a wire rack. Before serving, sprinkle the top with confectioners' sugar. Cut into squares with a knife.

Variation

To make Orange Squares, substitute grated orange rind and orange juice for the lemon rind and juice.

Apricot and Almond Bars

What an utterly perfect combination. If they aren't eaten immediately, these fruity bars will stay moist for several days if stored in an airtight container.

Makes 18

8 ounces/2 cups self-rising flour

4 ounces/½ cup light brown
   sugar

2 ounces/⅓ cup semolina

6 ounces/¾ cup ready-to-eat
   dried apricots, chopped

2 eggs

2 tablespoons malt extract

2 tablespoons clear honey

4 tablespoons skimmed milk

4 tablespoons sunflower oil

a few drops of almond
   extract

2 tablespoons sliced almonds

1 Lightly grease and line an 11 x 7 inch shallow cake pan and line with waxed paper.

2 Preheat the oven to 325°F/Gas 3. Sift the flour into a bowl and add the brown sugar, semolina, dried apricots and eggs. Add the malt extract, clear honey, milk, sunflower oil and almond extract. Mix well until smooth.

3 Turn the mixture into the prepared cake pan and spread to the edges and corner with a metal spatula. Smooth the top. Sprinkle the sliced almonds all over the surface in as even a layer as possible.

4 Bake for 30–35 minutes, until the center of the cake springs back when lightly pressed. Transfer to a wire rack to cool. Remove and discard the lining paper, place the cake on a board and cut it into 18 slices with a sharp knife.

Variation
You can substitute dried peaches or nectarines for the apricots; they all have an affinity with almonds.

Apricot and Walnut Bars

These traditional bars remain firm favorites and are still irresistible. For a truly fabulous flavor, use Hunza apricots and soak them first before poaching.

Makes 12

3 ounces/⅓ cup soft light
   brown sugar

3 ounces/⅔ cup all-purpose
   flour

3 ounces/⅓ cup cold sweet
   butter, diced

For the topping

6 ounces/¾ cup dried apricots

8 fluid ounces/1 cup water

grated rind of 1 lemon

3 ounces/⅓ cup granulated sugar

2 teaspoons cornstarch

2 ounces/½ cup walnuts,
   coarsely chopped

1 Preheat the oven to 350°F/
Gas 4. Grease an 8-inch square
cake pan.

2 In a bowl, combine the sugar and flour. Add the butter, cut it in, then rub it in with your fingers until the mixture resembles coarse breadcrumbs.

3 Press into the prepared cake pan. Bake for 15 minutes. Remove from the oven, but leave the oven on.

4 To make the topping, combine the apricots and water in a pan and simmer for about 10 minutes, until soft. Strain the liquid and reserve. Chop the apricots.

5 Return the apricots to the pan and add the lemon rind, granulated sugar, cornstarch, and 4 tablespoons of the reserved cooking liquid. Cook for 1 minute.

6 Remove the pan from the heat and cool slightly before spreading the topping over the base. Sprinkle over the walnuts and bake for a further 20 minutes. Leave to cool in the pan before cutting into bars.

Spiced Fig Bars

The dried fruit gives these bars a deliciously chewy texture and natural sweetness, while the spices add aroma and warmth to the flavor. Sprinkle with confectioners' sugar just before serving.

Makes 48

12 ounces/2 cups dried figs
3 eggs
6 ounces/¾ cup granulated sugar
3 ounces/⅔ cup all-purpose flour
1 teaspoon baking powder
½ teaspoon ground cinnamon
¼ teaspoon ground cloves
¼ teaspoon grated nutmeg
pinch of salt
3 ounces/¾ cup walnuts, finely chopped
2 tablespoons brandy or cognac
confectioners' sugar, for dusting

1 Preheat the oven to 325°F/Gas 3. Grease and line a 12 x 8 x 1½ inch cake pan with waxed paper.

2 With a sharp knife, chop the figs coarsely. Set aside.

3 Whisk the eggs and sugar in a bowl until well blended. Sift together the flour, baking powder, spices and salt into another bowl, then gently fold into the egg mixture in several batches.

4 Stir the figs, walnuts and brandy or cognac into the mixture until evenly combined.

5 Scrape the mixture into the prepared cake pan and spread out evenly. Bake for 35–40 minutes, until the top is firm and brown. It should still be soft underneath.

6 Leave to cool in the pan for about 5 minutes, then unmold and transfer to a sheet of waxed paper lightly sprinkled with confectioners' sugar. Cut into bars and leave to cool completely.

Creamy Lemon Bars

These delicious bars topped with a rich, creamy custard flavored with lemon are a real treat, ideal for accompanying a cup of coffee.

Makes 36

2 ounces/½ cup confectioners' sugar
6 ounces/1½ cups all-purpose flour
pinch of salt
6 ounces/¾ cup butter, diced

For the topping

4 eggs
12 ounces/1½ cups granulated sugar
grated rind of 1 lemon
4 fluid ounces/½ cup fresh lemon juice
6 fluid ounces/¾ cup whipping cream
confectioners' sugar, for dusting

1 Preheat the oven to 325°F/Gas 3. Grease a 13 x 9 inch cake pan. Sift the sugar, flour and salt into a bowl. Rub in the butter.

2 Press the mixture into the pan.

3 Bake for about 20 minutes, until golden brown.

4 Meanwhile, to make the topping, whisk together the eggs and sugar in a bowl until blended. Add the lemon rind and juice, and mix well.

5 Lightly whip the cream in another bowl and fold into the egg mixture. Pour the topping over the warm crust, return to the oven, and bake for about 40 minutes, until set. Cool completely in the pan, set on a wire rack, before cutting into bars. Dust with confectioners' sugar.

Blueberry Streusel Slices

A pastry base, a crumbly topping and, sandwiched in between, a fruity filling that is both sweet and sharp at the same time makes these moist slices very good, indeed.

Makes 30

2 ounces/½ cup all-purpose flour
¼ teaspoon baking powder
1 ounce/½ cup fresh white breadcrumbs
2 ounces/¼ cup soft light brown sugar
pinch of salt
1½ ounces/3 tablespoons butter or
   margarine, diced
2 ounces/4 tablespoons sliced or
   chopped almonds
8 ounces ready-made shortcrust pastry,
   thawed if frozen
4 tablespoons blackberry or
   bramble jelly
4 ounces/scant 1 cup blueberries,
   fresh or frozen

1 Preheat the oven to 350°F/ Gas 4. Grease a 7 x 11 inch jelly roll pan.

2 Sift the flour into a large bowl and then add the baking powder, bread, sugar and salt. Rub in the butter or margarine, until the mixture resembles breadcrumbs, then mix in the almonds.

3 Roll out the shortcrust pastry and use to line the base and sides of the prepared pan, trimming off any excess.

4 Spread the pastry evenly with the blackberry or bramble jelly, sprinkle with the blueberries, spreading them out well, then cover evenly with the streusel topping, pressing down lightly with the back of the spoon.

5 Bake for 20 minutes, then lower the oven temperature to 325°F/ Gas 3. Bake for a further 10–20 minutes, until firm.

6 Remove from the oven. Using a sharp knife, cut into slices while still hot, then transfer the slices to a wire rack to cool completely. Store in an airtight container.

Sticky Date and Apple Squares

Sometimes the simplest things are the nicest – and these squares, with their combination of fresh and dried fruit, couldn't be easier to make or more delicious to eat.

Makes 16

4 ounces/½ cup margarine
2 ounces/¼ cup soft dark brown sugar
2 ounces/4 tablespoons light corn syrup
4 ounces/⅔ cup chopped dates
4 ounces/generous 1 cup rolled oats
4 ounces/1 cup whole-wheat
   self-rising flour
2 eating apples, peeled, cored
   and grated
1–2 teaspoons lemon juice
walnut halves, to decorate

1 Preheat the oven to 375°F/ Gas 5. Line a 7–8-inch square or rectangular loose-based cake pan.

2 Gently heat the margarine, sugar and syrup together in a large pan, stirring occasionally, until the margarine has melted completely.

3 Add the dates and cook until softened. Gradually work in the oats, flour, apples and lemon juice until well mixed.

4 Spoon the mixture into the prepared pan and spread out evenly. Top with the walnut halves. Bake for 30 minutes, then reduce the oven temperature to 325°F/ Gas 3 and bake for a further 10–12 minutes, until firm to the touch and golden.

5 Cut into squares or bars while still warm, if you are going to eat them right away, or wrap in foil when nearly cold and keep for 1–2 days before eating.

Mincemeat Wedges

The flour used in these wedge-shaped cookies gives a nutty flavor that combines well with the mincemeat. These are great for winter tea parties around a blazing fire.

Makes 12

8 ounces/2 cups self-rising
   whole-wheat flour

3 ounces/6 tablespoons sweet
   butter, diced

3 ounces/⅓ cup raw sugar

1 egg, beaten

4 ounces/⅓ cup good-quality mincemeat

about 4 tablespoons milk

crushed brown or white sugar cubes
   or a mixture, for sprinkling

Cook's Tip

*If you can't find self-rising flour, add
2 teaspoons baking powder to the plain
whole-wheat flour.*

1 Preheat the oven to 400°F/Gas 6. Line the base of an 8-inch round layer pan and lightly grease the sides. Put the flour in a bowl, add the diced butter and rub in with your fingertips just until the mixture resembles coarse breadcrumbs.

2 Stir in the raw sugar, egg and mincemeat. Add enough milk to mix to a soft dough. Spread evenly in the prepared pan and sprinkle generously with the crushed sugar. Bake for about 20 minutes, until firm and golden. Cool in the pan, then cut into wedges to serve.

Sour-cream Streusel Bars

The German word "Streuselkuchen" simply means a cake with a crumbly topping. These tasty bars have a cinnamon-flavored filling and topping and make a deliciously different tea-time treat.

Makes 12–14

4 ounces/½ cup butter, diced

5 ounces/⅔ cup granulated sugar

3 eggs, at room temperature

6 ounces/1½ cups all-purpose
    flour

1 teaspoon baking soda

1 teaspoon baking powder

8 fluid ounces/1 cup sour cream

For the topping

6 ounces/¾ cup dark brown sugar

2 teaspoons ground cinnamon

4 ounces/1 cup walnuts,
    finely chopped

2 ounces/¼ cup butter, chopped

1 Preheat the oven to 350°F/ Gas 4. Line the base of a 9-inch square cake pan with waxed paper, and then grease the paper.

2 To make the topping, place the brown sugar, cinnamon and walnuts in a bowl. Mix with your fingertips, then add the butter and continue working until the mixture resembles coarse breadcrumbs.

3 Cream the butter with an electric mixer until soft. Add the sugar and beat until light and fluffy.

4 Add the eggs, one at a time, beating well after each addition.

5 In another bowl, sift together the flour, baking soda and baking powder three times.

6 Gently fold the dry ingredients into the butter mixture in three batches, alternating with the sour cream. Fold, using a rubber spatula, until all the ingredients are blended after each addition.

7 Pour half of the batter into the prepared pan and sprinkle over half of the topping.

8 Pour the remaining batter on top and then sprinkle over the remaining topping. Bake for 60–70 minutes, until browned. Leave to stand for about 5 minutes, then unmold. Transfer to a wire rack to cool. then cut into squares.

Almond-topped Squares

Sweet and crunchy with a slightly chewy nut topping, these are just the cookies you want when you need to put your feet up and have a cup of tea or coffee and a well-earned break.

Makes 18

3 ounces/⅓ cup butter
2 ounces/¼ cup granulated sugar
1 egg yolk
grated rind and juice of ½ lemon
½ teaspoon vanilla extract
2 tablespoons whipping cream
4 ounces/1 cup all-purpose flour

For the topping

8 ounces/1 cup granulated sugar
3 ounces/¾ cup sliced almonds
4 egg whites
½ teaspoon ground ginger
½ teaspoon ground cinnamon

1 Preheat the oven to 375°F/Gas 5. Line a 13 x 9 inch jelly roll pan with waxed paper and grease the paper.

2 With an electric mixer, cream the butter and sugar until light and fluffy. Beat in the egg yolk, lemon rind and juice, the vanilla extract and cream.

3 Gradually stir in the flour. Gather the dough into a ball. With lightly floured fingers, press the dough into the prepared pan. Bake for 15 minutes. Remove from the oven but leave the oven switched on.

4 To make the topping, combine all the ingredients in a heavy pan. Cook, stirring constantly, until the mixture comes to the boil. Boil for 1 minute. Pour the topping over the base, spreading it evenly.

5 Return to the oven and bake for about 45 minutes. Remove and score into squares or bars with a sharp knife and leave to cool and set completely before serving.

Hazelnut and Raspberry Bars

The hazelnuts are ground and used to make a superb sweet pastry which is then baked with a
layer of raspberry jam in the middle and sprinkled with sliced almonds.

Makes 30

9 ounces/2¼ cups hazelnuts

10 ounces/2½ cups all-purpose
   flour

1 teaspoon apple pie spice

½ teaspoon ground cinnamon

5 ounces/1¼ cups golden confectioners'
   sugar

1 tablespoon grated lemon rind

10 ounces/1¼ cups sweet
   butter, softened

3 egg yolks

12 ounces/1¼ cups seedless
   raspberry jam

For the topping

1 egg, beaten

1 tablespoon clear honey

2 ounces/½ cup sliced almonds

1 Grind the hazelnuts in a food
processor and then put in a bowl.
Sift in the flour, spices and
confectioners' sugar. Add the lemon
rind and mix well, then add the
butter and the egg yolks and, using
your hands, knead until a smooth
dough is formed. Put in plastic
wrap and chill for 30 minutes.
Meanwhile, preheat the oven to
400°F/Gas 6 and lightly grease
a 13 x 9 inch jelly roll pan.

2 Roll out half the dough to fit the
base of the prepared pan and place
in the pan. Spread the jam all over
the dough base. Roll out the
remaining dough and place on top
of the jam.

3 To make the topping, beat the egg
and honey together and brush over
the dough. Sprinkle the almonds
evenly over the top.

4 Bake for 10 minutes, then
lower the oven temperature to
350°F/Gas 4 and bake for another
20–30 minutes, until golden brown.
Cool then cut into bars.

Cook's Tip
*Don't use ready-ground hazelnuts for
these bars, as they lose their flavor
very quickly.*

Walnut and Honey Bars

A sweet, custard-like filling brimming with nuts sits on a crisp pastry base. These scrumptious bars are pure heaven to bite into at any time of day.

Makes 12–14

6 ounces/1½ cups all-purpose
    flour
2 tablespoons confectioners'
    sugar, sifted
4 ounces/½ cup sweet butter,
    diced

For the filling

11 ounces/scant 3 cups walnut halves
2 eggs, beaten
2 ounces/¼ cup sweet butter,
    melted
2 ounces/¼ cup light brown
    sugar
6 tablespoons dark clear honey
2 tablespoons light cream

1 Preheat the oven to 375°F/Gas 5. Lightly grease an 11 x 7 inch shallow pan.

2 Put the flour, confectioners' sugar and butter in a food processor and process until the mixture forms crumbs. Using the pulse button, add 1–2 tablespoons water – enough to make a firm dough.

3 Roll the dough out on baking parchment and line the base and sides of the pan. Trim and fold the top edge inwards.

4 Prick the base, line with foil and baking beans and bake blind for 10 minutes. Remove the foil and beans. Return the base to the oven for about 5 minutes, until cooked but not browned. Reduce the temperature to 350°F/Gas 4.

5 For the filling, sprinkle the walnuts over the base. Whisk the remaining ingredients together. Pour over the walnuts and bake for 25 minutes.

Pecan Nut Squares

A rich, buttery, pastry-like base is topped with a fabulous nutty, toffee-like mixture to make cookies with a tempting crunch and crispness. These cookies are equally good made with walnuts.

Makes 36

8 ounces/2 cups all-purpose flour

pinch of salt

4 ounces/½ cup granulated sugar

8 ounces/1 cup cold butter or
     margarine, diced

1 egg

finely grated rind of 1 lemon

For the topping

6 ounces/¾ cup butter

3 ounces/⅓ cup clear honey

2 ounces/¼ cup granulated sugar

4 ounces/½ cup soft dark
     brown sugar

5 tablespoons whipping cream

1 pound/4 cups pecan nut halves

1 Preheat the oven to 375°F/Gas 5. Lightly grease a 15½ x 10½ x 1 inch jelly roll pan.

2 Sift together the flour and salt into a large mixing bowl. Stir in the sugar. Add the butter or margarine, cut in and then rub in with your fingertips until the mixture resembles coarse breadcrumbs.

3 Add the egg and lemon rind and blend with a fork until the mixture just holds together.

4 Spoon the mixture into the prepared pan. With floured fingertips, press the mixture into an even layer. Prick the pastry all over with a fork and chill for 10 minutes.

5 Bake the pastry for 15 minutes. Remove the pan from the oven and leave to cool. Leave the oven switched on.

6 To make the topping, melt the butter, honey and both sugars in a small saucepan. Bring to the boil. Boil, without stirring, for 2 minutes. Remove from the heat and stir in the cream and pecan nuts.

7 Pour the topping over the crust, return the pan to the oven and bake for 25 minutes. Leave to cool and set completely.

8 When cool, run a knife around the edge of the pan. Invert onto a baking sheet, place another sheet on top and invert again. Dip a sharp knife into very hot water and cut into squares.

Rainbow Gingerbread Squares

These gingerbread squares have a more spongy texture than traditional gingerbread cookies and look stunning decorated with vibrantly colored sprinkles. Ground and preserved stem ginger gives a really spicy flavor, but can easily be left out for younger children.

Makes 16

8 ounces/2 cups all-purpose
   flour

1 teaspoon baking powder

2 teaspoons ground ginger

2 pieces preserved stem ginger from
   a jar, finely chopped

3½ ounces/¾ cup raisins

2 ounces/¼ cup candied
   cherries, chopped

4 ounces/½ cup sweet butter,
   diced

4 ounces/⅓ cup light corn
   syrup

2 tablespoons black molasses

3 ounces/⅓ cup dark molasses
   sugar

2 eggs, beaten

For the decoration

7 ounces/1¾ cups confectioners'
   sugar

2 ounces/¼ cup sweet butter,
   at room temperature, diced

multi-colored sprinkles

1 Preheat the oven to 325°F/Gas 3. Grease an 8-inch square shallow baking or cake pan and line with baking parchment.

2 Sift the flour, baking powder and ground ginger into a bowl. Add the stem ginger, raisins and cherries and stir together well.

3 Put the butter, syrup, molasses and molasses sugar in a small pan and heat gently until the butter melts. Pour the mixture into the dry ingredients. Add the eggs and stir well until evenly combined.

4 Tip the mixture into the baking pan and spread in an even layer, using the back of a wooden spoon. Bake for about 55 minutes, or until risen and firm in the center. Leave to cool in the pan.

5 To make the topping, put the confectioners' sugar and butter in a bowl with 4 teaspoons hot water and beat together until smooth and creamy.

6 Turn the gingerbread out of the baking pan onto a board. Using a large, sharp knife, carefully cut the gingerbread into 16 squares.

7 Using a teaspoon, drizzle a thick line of icing around the top edge of each gingerbread square. Don't worry if it falls down the sides. (If the icing is too stiff and doesn't come off the spoon easily, stir a little more hot water into the icing: about 1 teaspoon.)

8 Scatter the colored sprinkles over the icing to finish and leave to set before serving.

Hermits

How these cookies gained their intriguing name is a matter of guesswork, although it is interesting that both convents and monasteries are thought to have created many original cookie recipes.

Makes 30

3 ounces/⅔ cup all-purpose flour

1½ teaspoons baking powder

1 teaspoon ground cinnamon

½ teaspoon grated nutmeg

¼ teaspoon ground cloves

¼ teaspoon ground allspice

9 ounces/1½ cups raisins

4 ounces/½ cup butter or margarine
   at room temperature, diced

4 ounces/generous ½ cup superfine
   sugar

2 eggs

6 ounces/scant ½ cup black
   molasses

2 ounces/½ cup walnuts, chopped

1 Preheat the oven to 350°F/Gas 4. Grease and line a 13 x 9 inch pan with waxed paper.

2 Sift together the flour, baking powder and spices into a bowl.

3 Place the raisins in another bowl and toss with a few tablespoons of the flour mixture.

Cook's Tip
Don't confuse allspice and apple pie spice. Allspice tastes like a mixture of spices, but comes from a single berry.

4 Cream the butter or margarine and sugar until light and fluffy. Beat in the eggs, one at a time, then the black molasses. Stir in the flour mixture, raisins and walnuts.

5 Spread the mixture evenly in the prepared cake pan. Bake for about 15 minutes, or until just set. Leave to cool in the pan before cutting into squares or bars.

Butterscotch Meringue Bars

Walnuts add a nutty crunch to the sweet meringue topping on these sumptuous bars.

Makes 12

2 ounces/¼ cup butter

6 ounces/¾ cup cup dark brown sugar

1 egg

½ teaspoon vanilla extract

2 ounces/½ cup all-purpose flour

pinch of salt

¼ teaspoon grated nutmeg

For the topping

1 egg white

pinch of salt

1 tablespoon light corn syrup

4 ounces/½ cup granulated sugar

2 ounces/½ cup walnuts, chopped

1 Place the butter and brown sugar in a pan and heat until melted and bubbling. Set aside to cool.

2 Preheat the oven to 350°F/Gas 4. Grease and line an 8-inch square cake pan with waxed paper.

3 Beat the egg and vanilla extract into the cooled sugar mixture. Sift over the flour, salt and nutmeg and fold in. Spread over the base of the prepared cake pan.

4 Beat the egg white with the salt to soft peaks. Beat in the syrup, then the sugar and beat until stiff. Fold in the nuts and spread on top of the base. Bake for 30 minutes. Cut into bars when cool.

Parkin Squares

The flavor of these squares will improve if they are stored in an airtight container for several days or up to a week before serving.

Makes 16–20

½ pint/1¼ cups milk

8 ounces/1 cup light corn syrup

8 ounces/⅔ cup black molasses

4 ounces/½ cup butter or
   margarine, diced

2 ounces/¼ cup soft dark
   brown sugar

1 pound/4 cups all-purpose flour

½ tsp baking soda

1¼ teaspoons ground ginger

12 ounces/scant 3½ cups medium
   rolled oats

1 egg, beaten

confectioners' sugar, for dusting

1 Preheat the oven to 350°F/Gas 4. Grease and line the base of an 8-inch square cake pan. Gently heat together the milk, syrup, molasses, butter or margarine and sugar, stirring until smooth.

2 Stir the flour, baking soda, ginger and rolled oats together in a bowl. Make a well in the center, pour in the egg, then gradually pour in the warmed milk mixture, stirring to make a smooth batter.

3 Pour the batter into the pan and bake for about 45 minutes, or until firm to the touch. Cool slightly in the pan, then turn out onto a wire rack and cool completely. Cut into squares and dust with confectioners' sugar.

Cook's Tip
These are nutritious, energy-giving squares that are a really good choice for school lunches and picnics, as they don't break up too easily.

Banana Ginger Parkin

Parkin is a moist, spicy cake that keeps well and actually improves with keeping. Store in a covered container for up to two months – that is, if you can bear to wait that long.

Makes 26

7 ounces/1⅔ cups all-purpose
 flour
2 teaspoons baking soda
2 teaspoons ground ginger
5 ounces/scant 1½ cups medium
 rolled oats
4 tablespoons dark molasses
 sugar
3 ounces/⅓ cup butter or
 margarine, diced
5 ounces/⅔ cup light corn
 syrup
1 egg, beaten
3 ripe bananas, mashed
3 ounces/¾ cup confectioners'
 sugar
preserved stem ginger,
 to decorate

1 Preheat the oven to 325°F/Gas 3. Grease and line a 7 x 11 inch cake pan.

2 Sift together the all-purpose flour, baking soda and ground ginger into a mixing bowl, then stir in the rolled oats.

3 Melt the sugar, margarine and syrup in a pan over a low heat, then stir into the flour mixture. Beat in the egg and mashed bananas.

4 Spoon the mixture into the prepared pan and bake for about 1 hour, until firm to the touch. Leave to cool in the pan, then turn out and cut into squares.

5 Sift the confectioners' sugar into a bowl and stir in just enough water to make a smooth, runny icing. Drizzle the icing over each square and top with a piece of stem ginger.

Sticky Treacle Slices

This three-layered treat of buttery cookie base, covered with a sticky dried fruit filling, followed by an oaty flapjack-style topping, is utterly delicious and unbelievably easy to make.

Makes 14

6 ounces/1½ cups all-purpose flour

3½ ounces/7 tablespoons sweet
   butter, diced

2 ounces/¼ cup superfine sugar

9 ounces/generous 1 cup mixed dried
   fruit, such as prunes, apricots,
   peaches, pears and apples

½ pint/1¼ cups apple or
   orange juice

8 ounces/⅔ cup light corn syrup

finely grated rind of 1 small orange,
   plus 3 tablespoons juice

3½ ounces/1 cup rolled oats

1 Preheat the oven to 350°F/Gas 4. Grease an 11 x 7 inch shallow baking pan.

2 Put the flour and butter in a food processor and process until the mixture begins to resemble fine breadcrumbs. Add the sugar and mix until the dough starts to cling together in a ball.

3 Tip the mixture into the baking pan and press down in an even layer with the back of a fork. Bake for about 15 minutes until the surface is just beginning to color.

4 Meanwhile, prepare the filling. Remove the pits from any of the dried fruits, if not already done. Chop the fruit fairly finely and put in a pan with the fruit juice. Bring to the boil, reduce the heat and cover with a lid. Simmer gently for about 15 minutes, or until all the juice has been absorbed.

5 Leaving the base in the pan, tip the dried fruit filling on top and spread out in an even layer with the back of a spoon.

6 Put the light corn syrup in a bowl with the orange rind and juice and oats and mix together. Spoon the mixture over the fruits, spreading it out evenly. Return to the oven for 25 minutes. Leave to cool in the pan for several hours before cutting into squares or bars.

Butterscotch Brownies

These gorgeous treats are made with brown sugar, white chocolate chips and walnuts. Who could possibly have the will power to resist? You might want to make two batches at a time.

Makes 12

1 pound white chocolate chips

3 ounces/6 tablespoons sweet butter

3 eggs

6 ounces/¾ cup light brown
sugar

6 ounces/1½ cups self-rising flour

6 ounces/1½ cups walnuts,
chopped

1 teaspoon vanilla extract

1 Preheat the oven to 375°F/Gas 5. Line the base of an 11 x 7 inch shallow pan with baking parchment. Lightly grease the sides. Melt 3½ ounces of the chocolate chips with the butter in a bowl set over a pan of hot water. Leave to cool slightly.

2 Put the eggs and light brown sugar into a large bowl and whisk well, then whisk in the melted chocolate mixture.

3 Sift the flour into the bowl and gently fold in along with the chopped walnuts, vanilla extract and the remaining chocolate chips. Be careful not to overmix.

4 Spread the mixture out in the prepared pan and bake for about 30 minutes, or until risen and golden brown. The center should be firm to the touch but will be slightly soft until it cools down.

5 Leave to cool in the pan, then cut into twelve bars when the brownie is completely cool.

Toffee Bars

It takes no time at all to whip up a batch of these ever-popular cookies, but, equally, it takes no time at all for the family to demolish them.

Makes 32

12 ounces/1½ cups soft light
  brown sugar

1 pound/2 cups butter

2 egg yolks

1½ teaspoons vanilla extract

1 pound/4 cups all-purpose or
  whole-wheat flour

pinch of salt

8 ounces milk chocolate, chopped

4 ounces/1 cup walnuts or pecan nuts or
  a mixture of both, chopped

1 Preheat the oven to 350°F/Gas 4. Lightly grease a 13 x 9 x 2 inch rectangular cake pan.

2 Beat together the sugar and butter until light and fluffy. Beat in the egg yolks and vanilla. Stir in the flour and salt.

3 Spread the dough in the prepared cake pan. Bake for about 25–30 minutes, until lightly browned. The texture will be soft.

4 Remove from the oven and immediately place the chocolate pieces on the hot cookie base. Leave to stand until the chocolate softens, then spread evenly over the top with a spatula. Sprinkle with the chopped nuts. While still warm, cut into 2 x 1½ inch bars. Leave to cool.

Sticky Marmalade Squares

These baked treats have a plain lower layer supporting a scrumptious nutty upper layer flavored with orange and chunky marmalade. Cut into squares or bars – whichever you prefer.

Makes 24

12 ounces/3 cups all-purpose
   flour
7 ounces/scant 1 cup sweet
   butter, diced
5 ounces/⅔ cup light brown
   sugar
½ teaspoon baking soda
1 egg, beaten
4 fluid ounces/½ cup light
   cream
2 ounces/½ cup pecan nuts,
   chopped
2 ounces/⅓ cup candied peel
6 tablespoons chunky marmalade
1–2 tablespoons orange juice

1 Preheat the oven to 375°F/Gas 5. Line the base of an 11 x 7 inch pan with baking parchment.

2 Put the flour in a bowl and rub in the butter. Stir in the sugar and then spread half the mixture over the base of the prepared pan. Press down firmly. Bake for 10–15 minutes, until lightly browned. Leave to cool.

3 To make the filling, put the remaining flour mixture into a bowl. Stir in the baking soda. Mix in the egg and cream, pecan nuts, peel and half the marmalade.

4 Pour the mixture over the cooled base, return to the oven and bake for 20–25 minutes, or until the filling is just firm and golden brown.

5 Put the remaining marmalade into a small pan and heat gently. Add just enough orange juice to make a spreadable glaze. Brush the glaze over the baked cookie mixture while it is still warm. Leave to cool before cutting into bars or squares.

Variation
These bars would be just as delicious made with lemon, lime, grapefruit or mixed fruit marmalade instead of orange. However, do not substitute a sharper juice, such as lemon, for the orange juice, as this would spoil the flavor.

Jeweled Shortbread Fingers

These shortbread fingers are made using a classic, buttery shortbread base, drizzled with icing and decorated with sparkling, crushed candies and glistening gold or silver balls.

Makes 14

3½ounces/7 tablespoons sweet
 butter, diced
6 ounces/1½ cups all-purpose
 flour
2 ounces/¼ cup superfine sugar

To decorate

5 ounces/1¼ cups confectioners'
 sugar
2–3 teaspoons lemon juice
colored hard candies
gold or silver balls

1 Preheat the oven to 325°F/Gas 3. Grease a 7-inch square shallow baking pan.

2 Put the butter and flour in a food processor and process until the mixture resembles breadcrumbs. Add the sugar and process until the ingredients cling together.

3 Put the dough in the baking pan and press down in an even layer using the back of a spoon. Bake for 35 minutes, or until just beginning to color. Leave to cool in the pan.

4 To make the topping, put the confectioners' sugar in a bowl and add enough lemon juice to make a thick paste that only just holds its shape.

5 Tap the hard candies (in their wrappers) gently with a rolling pin to break them into small pieces. Unwrap the candies and mix them together in a bowl.

Cook's Tip
Use a serrated knife and a sawing action to cut the shortbread into neat fingers.

6 Turn out the shortbread base onto a board. Cut in half, then across into fingers. Drizzle with the icing, then sprinkle with the candies and gold or silver balls. Leave to set.

Creamed Coconut Macaroons

These soft-centered cookies are very rich and gooey. Cook them on baking parchment so that they can be easily removed from the baking sheet.

Makes 16–18

2 ounces/1 cup creamed coconut, chilled

2 extra large egg whites

3½ ounces/½ cup superfine sugar

3 ounces/1 cup dried unsweetened shredded coconut

1 Preheat the oven to 350°F/Gas 4. Line one or two large baking sheets with baking parchment. Finely grate the creamed coconut.

2 Use an electric beater to whisk the egg whites in a large, grease-free bowl until they are holding stiff peaks. Whisk in the superfine sugar, a spoonful at a time, to make a stiff and glossy meringue.

3 Gently fold the grated creamed and dried coconut into the whisked egg whites, using a rubber spatula or a large metal spoon until evenly combined.

4 Place dessertspoonfuls of the mixture, spaced far apart, on the baking sheet. Bake for about 15 minutes, or until slightly risen and golden brown.

5 Leave the macaroons to cool on the baking parchment, then transfer to an airtight container.

Chocolate Pecan Nut Squares

These moist and flavorsome cookies look as good as they taste. Serve to adults with tea or coffee and to children with a glass of milk or a creamy milkshake.

Makes 16

2 eggs

2 teaspoons vanilla extract

pinch of salt

6 ounces/1½ cups pecan nuts, coarsely chopped

2 ounces/½ cup all-purpose flour

2 ounces/¼ cup granulated sugar

6 ounces/scant ½ cup molasses

3 ounces semisweet chocolate, finely chopped

1½ ounces/3 tablespoons butter

16 pecan nut halves, to decorate

1 Preheat the oven to 325°F/Gas 3. Line the base and sides of an 8-inch square baking pan with waxed paper, and grease the paper lightly.

2 Whisk together the eggs, vanilla extract and salt in a bowl, using a balloon whisk. In another bowl, mix together the pecan nuts and flour. Set both bowls aside.

3 Place the sugar and molasses in a heavy pan and bring to the boil, stirring constantly.

4 Remove the pan from the heat, stir in the chopped chocolate and butter and blend thoroughly with a wooden spoon.

5 Mix in the beaten eggs, then fold in the pecan nut and flour mixture with a metal spoon. Pour the mixture into the prepared pan and bake for about 35 minutes until set.

6 Cool in the pan for 10 minutes turning out onto a board. Cut into 2-inch squares and press pecan nut halves into the top of each square while still warm. Transfer to a wire rack to cool completely.

Raisin Brownies

Adding dried fruit makes brownies a little more substantial, although no less moist and delicious. Try to find Californian or Spanish raisins for the best flavor and texture.

Makes 16

4 ounces/½ cup butter or margarine, diced

2 ounces/½ cup cocoa powder (unsweetened)

2 eggs

8 ounces/generous 1 cup superfine sugar

1 teaspoon vanilla extract

1½ ounces/⅓ cup all-purpose flour

3 ounces/¾ cup walnuts, chopped

2½ ounces/½ cup raisins

confectioners' sugar, for dusting

1 Preheat the oven to 350°F/Gas 4. Line an 8-inch square baking pan with waxed paper and grease the paper lightly.

2 Melt the butter or margarine in a small pan over a low heat. Remove from the heat and stir in the cocoa.

3 In a bowl, beat together the eggs, sugar and vanilla extract with an electric mixer until light and fluffy. Add the cocoa mixture and stir to blend.

4 Sift the flour over the cocoa mixture and fold in gently with a metal spoon. Add the walnuts and raisins, mixing them in gently, then scrape the mixture into the prepared pan. Bake for about 30 minutes, until firm to the touch, being careful not to overbake.

5 Leave in the pan on a rack to cool completely before cutting into 2-inch squares and removing from the pan. The brownies should be soft and moist. Dust with sifted confectioners' sugar before serving.

White Nut Brownies

Two kinds of chocolate and a topping of sweet melted chocolate and chopped macadamia nuts make these fabulous brownies irresistible to adults and children alike.

Makes 16

5 ounces/1¼ cups all-purpose flour

½ teaspoon baking powder

pinch of salt

6 ounces fine-quality white
   chocolate, chopped

3½ ounces/½ cup superfine
   sugar

4 ounces/½ cup sweet
   butter, chopped

2 eggs, lightly beaten

1 teaspoon vanilla extract

6 ounces semisweet chocolate,
   chopped, or semisweet
   chocolate chips

For the topping

7 ounces milk chocolate, chopped

7½ ounces/scant 2 cups
   unsalted macadamia nuts,
   chopped

1 Preheat the oven to 350°F/ Gas 4. Thoroughly grease a 9-inch springform cake pan. Sift together the flour, baking powder and salt into a small bowl and set aside.

2 Place the white chocolate, sugar and butter in a heavy pan and melt over a medium heat, stirring constantly until smooth.

3 Cool slightly, then beat in the eggs and vanilla extract. Stir in the flour mixture until well blended, then stir in the chopped chocolate or chocolate chips. Spread evenly in the prepared pan, smoothing the top.

4 Bake for 20–25 minutes, until a skewer inserted 5 inches from the side comes out clean. Remove from the oven. Sprinkle the milk chocolate over the surface. Return to the oven for 1 minute.

5 Remove from the oven. Spread the softened chocolate evenly over the top with the back of a spoon. Sprinkle with the nuts and gently press into the chocolate. Cool on a wire rack for 30 minutes, then chill until set. Run a knife around the side of the pan to loosen, unclip the side and remove. Cut into thin wedges.

Chocolate Brownies

Traditional American brownies are usually rich in butter. This version uses sunflower oil in place of butter. It still tastes rich and gooey, but is best eaten on the day it is made.

Makes 20

4 fluid ounces/½ cup sunflower oil

5 ounces semisweet chocolate, chopped

2 eggs

4 ounces/1 cup self-rising flour

4 ounces/generous ½ cup superfine sugar

1 teaspoon vanilla extract

3 ounces/¾ cup halved pecan nuts

1 Preheat the oven to 400°F/Gas 6. Use a little of the oil to grease a 9-inch square shallow cake pan, and then line it with lightly oiled waxed paper.

2 Melt the chocolate with the remaining oil in a heatproof bowl over a pan of simmering water, stirring until smooth.

Cook's Tip

Ingredients can be melted easily in a microwave oven. To soften chocolate, butter, sugar or syrup, microwave on high for a few seconds, until soft. Remember that chocolate and butter may not look melted, so check them carefully by stirring before returning them to the microwave for a few seconds more.

3 Beat the eggs lightly and add them to the melted chocolate, stirring vigorously. Beat in the flour, superfine sugar and vanilla extract and pour the mixture into the prepared pan. Arrange the pecan nut halves over the top.

4 Bake for 10–15 minutes. If you like chewy brownies, take them out of the oven now. If you want a more cake-like finish, leave for a further 5 minutes. Cut into squares and leave to cool before removing from the pan.

Hazelnut Squares

Adding a topping of hazelnuts part of the way through the baking time gives the cookies a lovely toasted flavor and makes them irresistible. Cut them into chunky squares for serving.

Makes 9

2 ounces semisweet chocolate, chopped

2½ ounces/5 tablespoons butter or margarine

8 ounces/generous 1 cup superfine sugar

2 ounces/½ cup all-purpose flour

½ teaspoon baking powder

2 eggs, beaten

½ teaspoon vanilla extract

4 ounces/1 cup skinned hazelnuts, coarsely chopped

1 Preheat the oven to 350°F/ Gas 4. Grease an 8-inch square cake pan.

2 Melt the chocolate and butter or margarine in a heatproof bowl set over a pan of hot water, stirring.

3 Stir the sugar, flour, baking powder, eggs, vanilla extract and half of the hazelnuts into the mixture.

4 Pour the mixture into the prepared cake pan, smoothing the top. Bake for 10 minutes, then sprinkle the remaining hazelnuts over the top. Bake for a further 25 minutes, until firm.

5 Leave to cool in the pan, set on a wire rack, for about 10 minutes, then remove from the pan, transfer to the rack and leave to cool completely. Using a sharp knife, cut into squares to serve.

Chocolate Walnut Bars

Although cookies like these are widely available in supermarkets, once you have tasted this delicious home-made version, you will never want to eat the ready-made bars again.

Makes 24

2 ounces/½ cup walnuts

3 ounces/⅓ cup granulated sugar

3 ounces/⅔ cup all-purpose flour, sifted

3 ounces/6 tablespoons cold sweet butter, diced

confectioners' sugar, for dusting

For the topping

1 ounce/2 tablespoons sweet butter

5 tablespoons water

1½ ounces/⅓ cup cocoa powder (unsweetened)

4 ounces/½ cup granulated sugar

1 teaspoon vanilla extract

pinch of salt

2 eggs

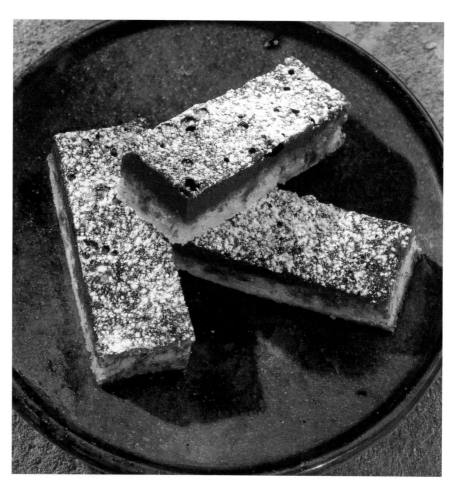

1 Preheat the oven to 350°F/ Gas 4. Grease an 8-inch square cake pan.

2 Grind the walnuts with a few tablespoons of the sugar in a food processor, blender or nut grinder.

3 Mix the ground walnuts, the remaining sugar and the flour in a bowl. Rub in the butter until the mixture resembles breadcrumbs. Alternatively, process all the ingredients in a food processor.

4 Pat the walnut mixture into the base of the prepared pan in an even layer. Bake for 25 minutes.

5 Meanwhile, to make the topping, melt the butter with the water in a small pan over a low heat. Whisk in the cocoa and sugar.

6 Remove the pan from the heat, stir in the vanilla extract and salt and leave to cool for 5 minutes.

7 Whisk in the eggs, one at a time, until thoroughly blended. Remove the cake pan from the oven and pour the topping evenly over the cooked walnut mixture.

8 Return the pan to the oven and bake for about 20 minutes, until set. Set the pan on a wire rack to cool. Once cooled, cut into 2½ x 1 inch bars and dust with sifted confectioners' sugar. Store the bars in the refrigerator.

Chocolate Cheesecake Brownies

A very dense chocolate brownie mixture is swirled with creamy cheese to give a marbled effect. Cut into tiny squares for little mouthfuls of absolute heaven.

Makes 16

For the cheesecake mixture

1 egg

8 ounces/1 cup full-fat
  cream cheese

2 ounces/¼ cup superfine sugar

1 teaspoon vanilla extract

For the brownie mixture

4 ounces bittersweet chocolate
  (minimum 70 percent
  cocoa solids)

4 ounces/½ cup sweet butter

5 ounces/¾ cup light brown sugar

2 eggs, beaten

2 ounces/½ cup all-purpose flour

1 Preheat the oven to 325°F/Gas 3. Line the base and sides of an 8-inch cake pan with baking parchment.

2 To make the cheesecake mixture, beat the egg in a mixing bowl, then add the cream cheese, superfine sugar and vanilla extract. Beat together until smooth and creamy.

3 To make the brownie mixture, melt the chocolate and butter together in the microwave or in a heatproof bowl set over a pan of gently simmering water. When the mixture is melted, remove from the heat, stir well, then add the sugar. Add the eggs, a little at a time, and beat well. Gently stir in the flour.

4 Spread two-thirds of the brownie mixture over the base of the pan. Spread the cheesecake mixture on top, then spoon on the remaining brownie mixture in heaps. Using a skewer, swirl the mixtures together.

5 Bake for 30–35 minutes, or until just set in the center. Leave to cool in the pan, then cut into squares.

Fudge-nut Bars

Although your kids will be desperate to tuck into these fudgy treats, it's well worth chilling them for a few hours before slicing so that they can be cut into neat pieces.

Makes 16

5 ounces/10 tablespoons sweet butter, chilled and diced

9 ounces/2¼ cups all-purpose flour

3 ounces/scant ½ cup superfine sugar

For the topping

5 ounces milk chocolate, broken into pieces

1½ ounces/3 tablespoons sweet butter

14¼-ounce can sweetened condensed milk

2 ounces/½ cup chopped nuts

1 Preheat the oven to 325°F/ Gas 3. Grease an 11 x 7 inch shallow baking pan.

2 Put the butter and flour in a food processor and process until the mixture resembles breadcrumbs. Add the sugar and blend again until the mixture starts to cling together.

3 Tip the mixture into the baking pan and spread out with the back of a wooden spoon to fill the base in an even layer. Bake for 35–40 minutes, until the surface is very lightly colored.

4 To make the topping, put the chocolate in a heavy pan with the butter and condensed milk. Heat gently until the chocolate and butter have melted, then increase the heat and cook, stirring, for 3–5 minutes, until the mixture starts to thicken.

5 Add the chopped nuts to the pan and pour the mixture over the cookie base, spreading it in an even layer. Leave to cool, then chill for at least 2 hours until firm. Serve cut into bars.

Fudgy Glazed Chocolate Slices

These wonderfully flavored treats will delight the hearts of those with a really sweet tooth – they are very rich, so cut them into relatively small bars or squares.

Makes 8–10

11 ounces semisweet chocolate, chopped

4 ounces/½ cup sweet butter, diced

3½ ounces/scant ½ cup soft light brown sugar

2 ounces/¼ cup granulated sugar

2 eggs

1 tablespoon vanilla extract

2½ ounces/generous ½ cup all-purpose flour

4 ounces/1 cup pecan nuts or walnuts, toasted and chopped

5 ounces fine-quality white chocolate, chopped

For the fudgy chocolate glaze

6 ounces semisweet chocolate, chopped

2 ounces/¼ cup sweet butter, chopped

2 tablespoons light corn syrup

2 teaspoons vanilla extract

1 teaspoon instant coffee powder

pecan nut halves, to decorate (optional)

1 Preheat the oven to 350°F/Gas 4. Invert an 8-inch square baking pan and mold a piece of foil over the base. Turn the pan over and line with molded foil. Lightly grease the foil.

2 Place the semisweet chocolate and butter in a heavy pan and melt over a very low heat, stirring until combined and smooth.

3 Stir in the brown and granulated sugars and continue stirring for about 2 minutes, until the sugar has completely dissolved.

4 Remove the pan from the heat and beat in the eggs and vanilla extract. Stir in the flour, nuts and white chocolate. Pour the batter into the prepared pan.

5 Bake for about 20–25 minutes, until a skewer inserted 2 inches from the center comes out clean. Transfer the pan to a wire rack to cool for about 30 minutes. Using the foil to help, lift from the pan, place on the wire rack and leave for 2 hours to cool completely.

6 To make the glaze, melt the chocolate, butter, syrup, vanilla extract and coffee powder in a pan over a medium heat, stirring frequently, until smooth. Remove from the heat. Chill for 1 hour, until thickened and spreadable.

7 Invert the cake onto the wire rack, and remove the foil from the base. Turn the cake top side up. Using a metal spatula, spread a thick layer of fudgy glaze over the top of the cake just to the edges. Chill for 1 hour until set. Cut into bars or squares. If you like, top each slice with a pecan nut half.

Nut and Chocolate Chip Brownies

These chunky chocolate brownies are moist, dark and deeply satisfying. They are delicious with a morning cup of coffee and will definitely boost morale on a dreary day.

Makes 16

5 ounces semisweet chocolate, chopped

4 fluid ounces/½ cup sunflower oil

7½ ounces/scant 1 cup light
   brown sugar

2 eggs

1 teaspoon vanilla extract

2½ ounces/scant ⅔ cup self-rising
   flour

4 tablespoons cocoa powder
   (unsweetened)

3 ounces/¾ cup chopped walnuts

4 tablespoons milk chocolate chips

Variation

Substitute chopped pecan nuts for the walnuts, if you like.

1 Preheat the oven to 350°F/ Gas 4. Lightly grease a shallow 7½-inch square cake pan. Melt the semisweet chocolate in a heatproof bowl over a pan of simmering water.

2 Beat together the oil, sugar, eggs and vanilla extract.

3 Stir in the melted chocolate, then beat well until evenly mixed.

4 Sift the flour and cocoa powder into the bowl and fold in thoroughly. Stir in the chopped nuts and milk-chocolate chips, then tip the mixture into the prepared pan and spread evenly to the edges.

5 Bake for about 30–35 minutes, until the top is firm and crusty. Cool in the pan before cutting into squares.

Cook's Tip

These brownies freeze well and can be stored in the freezer for 3 months in an airtight container.

Chocolate and Coconut Slices

Very simple to make, these slices are deliciously moist and sweet. They look very tempting, too, with their sweet coconut filling and attractive, nutty topping.

Makes 24

4 ounces/½ cup butter or
   margarine, diced
6 ounces/scant 2½ cups crushed
   graham crackers
2 ounces/¼ cup superfine sugar
pinch of salt
3 ounces/1 cup dried unsweetened
   shredded coconut
9 ounces/1½ cups semisweet
   chocolate chips
8 fluid ounces/1 cup sweetened
   condensed milk
4 ounces/1 cup chopped walnuts,
   to decorate

1 Preheat the oven to 350°F/Gas 4. Melt the butter or margarine in a pan over a low heat.

2 Combine the crushed biscuits, sugar, salt and butter or margarine. Press the mixture evenly over the base of an ungreased 13 x 9 inch ovenproof dish.

3 Sprinkle the coconut, then the chocolate chips over the base. Pour the condensed milk evenly over the chocolate. Sprinkle the walnuts on top. Bake for 30 minutes. Transfer to a wire rack and leave to cool, preferably overnight. When cooled, cut into slices.

Chocolate Raspberry Macaroon Bars

Any seedless preserve, such as strawberry or apricot, can be used instead of the raspberry in the topping for these flavor-packed, moist little bars.

Makes 16–18 bars

4 ounces/½ cup sweet butter

2 ounces/½ cup confectioners' sugar

1 ounces/¼ cup cocoa powder (unsweetened)

pinch of salt

1 teaspoon almond extract

5 ounces/1¼ cups all-purpose flour

For the topping

5 ounces/scant ½ cup seedless raspberry preserve

1 tablespoon raspberry-flavor liqueur

6 ounces/1 cup mini chocolate chips

6 ounces/1½ cups finely ground almonds

4 egg whites

pinch of salt

7 ounces/1 cup superfine sugar

½ teaspoon almond extract

2 ounces/½ cup sliced almonds

1 Preheat the oven to 325°F/Gas 3. Invert a 9 x 13 inch cake pan. Mold a sheet of foil over the pan and evenly around the corners. Lift off the foil and turn the pan right side up; line with the molded foil and grease.

2 In a bowl, using an electric mixer, beat together the butter, sugar, cocoa and salt until well blended. Add the almond extract and the flour and mix until the ingredients form a crumbly dough.

3 Turn the dough into the prepared pan and pat firmly over the base to make an even layer. Prick the dough with a fork.

4 Bake for about 20 minutes, until just set. Remove from the oven and increase the oven temperature to 375°F/Gas 5.

5 To make the topping, combine the raspberry preserve and liqueur in a small bowl, mixing well.

6 Spread the topping evenly over the top of the chocolate crust with a narrow metal spatula, then sprinkle evenly with the chocolate chips.

7 In a food processor fitted with a metal blade, process the almonds, egg whites, salt, sugar and almond extract until well blended and foamy. Gently pour the mixture over the raspberry layer, spreading evenly to the edges of the pan. Sprinkle with the sliced almonds.

8 Bake for a further 20–25 minutes, until the top is golden and puffed. Transfer to a wire rack to cool in the pan for 20 minutes, until firm and cool enough to handle.

9 Using the edges of the foil to help, carefully remove the cake from the pan and place on the wire rack to cool completely. Peel off and discard the foil and, using a sharp knife, cut into bars.

Chocolate Butterscotch Bars

Wonderfully sticky with their sweet toffee and chocolate double topping, these rich, nutty cookie bars are very popular with children.

Makes 24

8 ounces/2 cups all-purpose flour

½ teaspoon baking powder

4 ounces/½ cup sweet butter, diced

2 ounces/¼ cup light brown sugar

5 ounces semisweet chocolate, melted

2 tablespoons ground almonds

For the topping

6 ounces/¾ cup sweet butter

4 ounces/generous ½ cup superfine sugar

2 tablespoons light corn syrup

6 fluid ounces/¾ cup condensed milk

5 ounces/1¼ cups toasted hazelnuts

8 ounces semisweet chocolate, chopped

1 Preheat the oven to 325°F/ Gas 3. Grease a shallow 12 x 8 inch cake pan.

2 Sift together the flour and baking powder into a large bowl. Add the butter and rub it in with your fingertips until the mixture resembles fine breadcrumbs.

3 Stir in the brown sugar. Gradually, work in the melted chocolate and ground almonds until they are thoroughly combined.

4 Press the mixture into the prepared cake pan, prick the surface all over with a fork and bake for 25–30 minutes until firm. Place the pan on a wire rack and leave to cool.

5 To make the topping, mix the butter, sugar, syrup and condensed milk in a pan. Heat gently until the butter and sugar have melted. Simmer, stirring occasionally, until golden, then stir in the hazelnuts.

6 Pour the topping over the cooked base and spread it out evenly with a spatula. Leave in a cool place to set.

7 Melt the chocolate in a heatproof bowl set over a pan of hot water. Spread the chocolate over the butterscotch layer. Leave to set before cutting into bars.

Cook's Tip

As these bars are incredibly rich and sticky, cut them in half if serving at a children's party.

Marbled Brownies

These are the perfect brownies for people who like chocolate, but are not complete chocoholics, as they are made from a mixture of flavors swirled together before baking.

Makes 24

8 ounces semisweet chocolate, chopped

3 ounces/⅓ cup butter, diced

4 eggs

12 ounces/1¾ cups superfine sugar

4 ounces/1 cup all-purpose flour

pinch of salt

1 teaspoon baking powder

2 teaspoons vanilla extract

4 ounces/1 cup walnuts, chopped

For the plain batter

2 ounces/¼ cup butter

6 ounces/⅔ cup cream cheese

4 ounces/generous ½ cup superfine sugar

2 eggs

2 tablespoons all-purpose flour

1 teaspoon vanilla extract

1 Preheat the oven to 350°F/Gas 4. Line a 13 x 9 inch pan with waxed paper and lightly grease the paper.

2 Melt the semisweet chocolate and butter in a small, heavy pan over a very low heat, stirring occasionally until smooth and combined, then remove the pan from the heat, and leave to cool slightly.

3 Meanwhile, beat the eggs with an electric mixer until they are light and fluffy. Gradually add the superfine sugar and continue beating well after each addition until thoroughly blended and smooth. Sift over the flour, salt and baking powder and gently fold in with a metal spoon.

4 Stir in the cooled chocolate mixture, the vanilla extract and walnuts. Set aside 16 fluid ounces/ 2 cups of the chocolate batter.

5 To make the plain batter, cream the butter and cream cheese with an electric mixer.

6 Add the sugar and continue beating until blended. Beat in the eggs, flour and vanilla extract.

7 Spread the chocolate batter into the pan. Pour over the plain batter. Drop spoonfuls of the reserved chocolate batter on top.

8 With a metal spatula, swirl the mixtures to marble. Do not blend completely. Bake for 35–40 minutes, until just set. Unmold when cool, and cut into squares for serving.

Muffins and Scones

Marvelous muffins and scones are so quick
and easy to make, you can serve them at any
time of day. When you fancy a muffin, there
are dozens of different flavorings to choose
from, from fresh fruity blueberries, cranberries
and raspberries to rich chocolate and nuts and
tangy citrus. If you're looking for a wholesome
healthy start to the day, go for scones. Try
delicious sweet combinations such as yogurt
and honey, or orange and raisin, or opt for
savory flavors such as bacon and cornmeal or
cheese and chives.

Oat and Buttermilk Muffins

In this traditional recipe, the natural acid of buttermilk activates the raising agent to produce lovely light and airy muffins. Raisins add a sweet contrast.

Makes 12

4 ounces/generous 1 cup
  rolled oats
8 fluid ounces/1 cup buttermilk
4 ounces/½ cup butter, softened
3 ounces/scant ½ cup soft dark
  brown sugar
1 egg
4 ounces/1 cup all-purpose flour
1 teaspoon baking powder
½ teaspoon baking soda
pinch of salt
1 ounce/¼ cup raisins

1 Place the oats in a bowl, stir in the buttermilk and set aside to soak for about 1 hour.

2 Grease 12 muffin pans, or use paper liners. Preheat the oven to 400°F/Gas 6.

3 Put the butter and sugar in a large bowl and, with an electric mixer or wooden spoon, beat together until light and fluffy. Beat in the egg.

4 Sift together the flour, baking powder, baking soda and salt. Stir into the butter mixture, alternating with the oat mixture. Fold in the raisins.

5 Fill the muffin pans two-thirds full. Bake for 20–25 minutes. Transfer to a wire rack to cool.

Cook's Tip
Nowadays, buttermilk is made from pasteurized skimmed milk treated with a special culture and is much more stable than traditional buttermilk.

Pumpkin Muffins

Wonderfully moist, richly colored and packed with flavor, these lightly spiced muffins are delicious whether served still warm from the oven or cold.

Makes 14

4 ounces/½ cup butter or margarine
6 ounces/¾ cup firmly packed
  brown sugar
4 ounces/⅓ cup black molasses
1 egg, beaten
8 ounces/1 cup cooked or
  canned pumpkin
7 ounces/¾ cup all-purpose flour
pinch of salt
1 teaspoon baking soda
1½ teaspoons ground cinnamon
1 teaspoon grated nutmeg
2 ounces/¼ cup currants or raisins

1 Preheat the oven to 400°F/Gas 6. Grease 14 muffin pans, or use paper liners.

2 With an electric mixer, cream the butter or margarine until soft. Add the sugar and black molasses and beat until light and fluffy.

3 Add the egg and pumpkin, and stir until well blended.

4 Sift over the flour, a pinch of salt, the baking soda, cinnamon and grated nutmeg. Fold in with a metal spoon until just blended, but do not overmix.

5 Fold the currants or raisins into the pumpkin mixture.

6 Spoon the batter into the muffin pans, filling them two-thirds full. Bake for 12–15 minutes, until the tops spring back when touched lightly.

Pan Dulce

These "sweet breads" of various shapes are made throughout Mexico, and are eaten as a snack or with jam or marmalade for breakfast – a great way to start the day.

Makes 12

4 fluid ounces/½ cup lukewarm milk

2 teaspoons active dry yeast

1 pound/4 cups strong
* all-purpose flour*

3 ounces/6 tablespoons superfine sugar

1 ounce/2 tablespoons butter, softened

4 extra large eggs, beaten

oil, for greasing

For the topping

3 ounces/6 tablespoons butter, softened

4 ounces/½ cup granulated sugar

1 egg yolk

1 teaspoon ground cinnamon

4 ounces/1 cup all-purpose flour

1 Pour the milk into a small bowl, stir in the dry yeast and leave in a warm place until frothy.

2 Put the flour and sugar in a mixing bowl, add the butter and eggs and mix to a soft, sticky dough.

3 Place the dough on a lightly floured surface and dredge it with a little more flour. Using floured hands, turn the dough over and over until it is completely covered in a light coating of flour. Cover it with lightly oiled plastic wrap and leave to rest for 20 minutes.

4 Meanwhile, make the topping. Cream the butter and sugar together in a bowl, then gently mix in the egg yolk, ground cinnamon and flour. The mixture should have a slightly crumbly texture.

5 Divide the dough into 12 equal pieces and shape each of them into a round form. Space far apart on greased baking sheets. Sprinkle the topping over the breads, dividing it more or less equally among them, then press it lightly into the surface.

6 Leave the rolls in a warm place to stand for about 30 minutes, until they are about one and a half times their previous size. Preheat the oven to 400°F/Gas 6 and bake the breads for about 15 minutes. Leave to cool slightly before serving.

Orange and Pecan Scones

Serve these nutty orange scones with satiny orange or lemon curd or, for a simple, unsweetened snack, fresh and warm with sweet butter.

Makes 10

8 ounces/2 cups self-rising
   flour
2 ounces/¼ cup sweet butter,
   chilled and diced
granted rind and juice of
   1 orange
4 ounces/1 cup pecan nuts,
   coarsely chopped

1 Preheat the oven to 425°F/ Gas 7. Lightly grease a large baking sheet.

2 Put the flour in a food processor with a pinch of salt and add the butter. Process the mixture until it resembles coarse breadcrumbs. Do not overprocess.

3 Add the orange rind. Reserve 2 tablespoons of the orange juice and make the remainder up to 4 fluid ounces/½ cup with water. Add the pecan nuts and the orange juice mixture to the food processor, and process very briefly to a firm dough, adding a little water if the dough seems to be dry.

4 Turn the dough out onto a lightly floured surface and roll out to ¾ inch thick. Cut out scones using a round cutter and transfer them to the baking sheet. Re-roll the trimmings and cut more scones. Brush the scones with the reserved juice and bake for 15–20 minutes, until golden. Transfer to a wire rack to cool.

Banana Muffins

Make sure that you use really ripe bananas for these muffins, not just because they are the sweetest, but also because they are easy to mash to a smooth consistency.

Makes 12

8 ounces/2 cups all-purpose flour

1 teaspoon baking powder

1 teaspoon baking soda

pinch of salt

½ teaspoon ground cinnamon

¼ teaspoon grated nutmeg

3 large ripe bananas

1 egg

2 ounces/¼ cup soft dark
  brown sugar

2 fluid ounces/¼ cup vegetable oil

1½ ounces/⅓ cup raisins

1 Preheat the oven to 375°F/Gas 5. Grease 12 muffin pans, or use paper liners.

2 Sift together the flour, baking powder, baking soda, salt, cinnamon and nutmeg. Set aside.

3 With an electric mixer, mash the peeled bananas at medium speed.

4 Beat the egg, sugar and oil into the mashed bananas.

5 Add the dry ingredients and beat in gradually, on low speed. Mix until just blended. With a wooden spoon, stir in the raisins until just combined. Spoon the mixture into the muffin pans, filling them two-thirds full.

6 Bake for 20–25 minutes, until the tops spring back when touched lightly with your finger. Transfer the muffins to a wire rack to cool completely before serving.

Maple Pecan Nut Muffins

The smooth, rich and distinctive flavor of maple syrup complements the nuts superbly. Make sure you buy the pure syrup, as blended varieties are disappointing.

Makes 20

5 ounces/1¼ cups pecan nuts

11 ounces/2⅔ cups all-purpose
 flour

1 teaspoon baking powder

1 teaspoon baking soda

pinch of salt

¼ teaspoon ground cinnamon

4 ounces/½ cup granulated sugar

2 ounces/¼ cup soft light
 brown sugar

3 tablespoons maple syrup

5 ounces/⅔ cup butter, softened

3 eggs

½ pint/1¼ cups buttermilk

60 pecan nut halves,
 to decorate

1 Preheat the oven to 350°F/Gas 4. Grease 20 muffin pans, or use paper liners.

2 Spread the pecan nuts on a baking sheet and toast in the oven for 5 minutes. Leave to cool, then chop coarsely and set aside.

3 In a bowl, sift together the flour, baking powder, baking soda, salt and cinnamon. Set aside.

4 Combine the granulated sugar, light brown sugar, maple syrup and butter in a bowl. Beat with an electric mixer until light and fluffy. Add the eggs, one at a time, beating well to combine thoroughly after each addition.

5 Pour half of the buttermilk and half of the dry ingredients into the butter mixture, then stir until blended. Repeat with the remaining buttermilk and dry ingredients. Fold the chopped pecan nuts into the batter. Spoon the mixture into the muffin pans, filling them about two-thirds full. Top with the pecan nut halves.

6 Bake for 20–25 minutes, until puffed up and golden brown. Leave to stand in the pans for about 5 minutes before transferring the muffins to a wire rack to cool completely before serving.

Cranberry Muffins

These delicious muffins are perfect to eat at any time of day and are a real energy boost for breakfast or as a lunch box treat. Use fresh or frozen cranberries.

Makes 10–12

12 ounces/3 cups all-purpose flour

1 tablespoon baking powder

pinch of salt

4 ounces/generous ½ cup superfine sugar

2 eggs

¼ pint/⅔ cup milk

2 fluid ounces/¼ cup corn oil

finely grated rind of 1 orange

5 ounces/1¼ cups cranberries, thawed
    if frozen

Variation

Replace half the cranberries with blueberries or raspberries.

1 Preheat the oven to 375°F/Gas 5. Line 10–12 deep muffin pans with paper cases.

2 Mix the flour, baking powder, salt and sugar together. Lightly beat the eggs with the milk and oil.

3 Add the egg mixture to the dry ingredients and blend to a smooth batter. Fold in the orange rind and cranberries. Divide the mixture among the cases and bake for 25 minutes, or until risen and golden. Serve warm or cold.

Raspberry Muffins

Low-fat buttermilk gives these muffins a light and spongy texture. Make them in the summer when fresh raspberries are at their seasonal best.

Makes 10–12

11 ounces/2⅔ cups all-purpose
    flour

1 tablespoon baking powder

4 ounces/generous ½ cup
    superfine sugar

1 egg

8 fluid ounces/1 cup buttermilk

4 tablespoons sunflower oil

5 ounces/1 cup raspberries

1 Preheat the oven to 400°F/ Gas 6. Arrange 10–12 paper cases in deep muffin pans. Sift the flour and baking powder into a mixing bowl.

2 Stir in the sugar, then make a well in the center.

3 Mix the egg, buttermilk and sunflower oil together in a bowl, pour into the flour mixture and mix quickly until just combined.

4 Add the raspberries and lightly fold them into the mixture with a metal spoon until just combined. Spoon the mixture into the prepared paper cases, filling them about two-thirds full.

5 Bake for 20–25 minutes, until golden brown and firm in the center. Transfer to a wire rack and serve warm or cold.

Cook's Tip

Raspberry muffins make a delicious tea-time treat when served warm with cream, preferably clotted.

Double Chocolate-chip Muffins

These marvellous muffins are flavored with cocoa and packed with chunky chips of semisweet and white chocolate, so they are sure to be a success with children. Serve them on their own or with cherry or raspberry jam for a terrific after-school snack or tea-time treat.

Makes 16

14 ounces/3½ cups all-purpose flour

1 tablespoon baking powder

2 tablespoons cocoa powder
(unsweetened), plus extra
for dusting

4 ounces/½ cup dark molasses
sugar

2 eggs

¼ pint/⅔ cup sour cream

¼ pint/⅔ cup milk

4 tablespoons sunflower oil

6 ounces white chocolate

6 ounces semisweet chocolate

1 Preheat the oven to 375°F/Gas 5. Place 16 paper muffin cases in muffin pans, or lightly grease the muffin pans.

2 Sift the flour, baking powder and cocoa into a bowl and stir in the sugar. Make a well in the center.

3 Beat the eggs with the sour cream, milk and sunflower oil in a separate bowl.

4 Add the egg mixture to the well in the dry ingredients. Beat thoroughly with a wooden spoon, gradually incorporating the flour mixture to make a thick and creamy batter. Do not overmix the batter – it's best if it's still slightly lumpy.

5 Finely chop both the white and semisweet chocolate, using a large sharp knife, and stir into the batter mixture until just mixed.

6 Spoon the mixture into the muffin cases, filling them almost to the top. Bake for 25–30 minutes, until well risen and firm to the touch. Transfer to a wire rack to cool, then dust lightly with cocoa powder before serving.

Variations
• *Make sure you use good quality semisweet chocolate with a high cocoa content. Vary the proportions of semisweet and white chocolate, or add milk chocolate, if you prefer.*
• *To make Chocolate Chip and Apple Muffins, sift ½ teaspoon ground cinnamon, a pinch of grated nutmeg and ¼ teaspoon apple pie spice with the dry ingredients in step 1. Halve the quantity of chocolate. Peel, core and grate two eating apples and stir into the batter with the chopped chocolate in step 3. Bake as given in the recipe, but check that the muffins are cooked by inserting a skewer into the center of one of them. If it comes out clean, then they are ready. Cool in the pans for 4–5 minutes, then serve warm or transfer to a wire rack to cool completely.*

Cook's Tip
If sour cream is not available, sour ¼ pint/⅔ cup light cream by stirring in 1 teaspoon lemon juice and letting the mixture stand until thickened.

Chocolate Chip Muffins

Nothing could be easier – or nicer – than these classic muffins. The muffin mixture is plain, with a surprise layer of chocolate chips in the middle.

Makes 10

4 ounces/½ cup butter or
*   margarine, softened*
3 ounces/⅓ cup granulated sugar
2 tablespoons soft dark
*   brown sugar*
2 eggs
6 ounces/1½ cups all-purpose
*   flour*
1 teaspoon baking powder
4 fluid ounces/½ cup milk
6 ounces/1 cup semisweet
*   chocolate chips*

1 Preheat the oven to 375°F/Gas 5. Grease ten muffin pans, or use paper liners.

2 With an electric mixer, cream the butter or margarine until soft. Add both sugars and beat until light and fluffy. Beat in the eggs, one at a time, beating well after each addition.

3 Sift the flour and baking powder, twice. Fold into the butter mixture, alternating with the milk.

4 Divide half of the mixture among the muffin pans. Sprinkle the chocolate chips on top, dividing them equally among the muffins, then cover with the remaining mixture.

5 Bake for about 25 minutes, until lightly colored. Leave to stand for 5 minutes before transferring to a wire rack to cool.

Chocolate Walnut Muffins

Walnuts and chocolate are a delicious combination and provide both smoothness and crunch while vanilla and almond extracts provide extra flavor.

Makes 12

6 ounces/¾ cup sweet butter, diced
5 ounces semisweet chocolate,
*   chopped*
8 ounces/1 cup granulated sugar
2 ounces/¼ cup soft dark
*   brown sugar*
4 eggs
1 teaspoon vanilla extract
¼ teaspoon almond extract
3 ounces/⅔ cup all-purpose flour
4 ounces/1 cup walnuts,
*   coarsely chopped*

1 Preheat the oven to 350°F/Gas 4. Grease 12 muffin pans, or use paper liners.

2 Melt the butter with the chocolate in a heatproof bowl set over a pan of hot water. Transfer to a large mixing bowl.

3 Stir both the sugars into the chocolate mixture. Mix in the eggs, one at a time, beating well after each addition, then add the vanilla and almond extract.

4 Sift the flour over the chocolate mixture and fold in until evenly combined. Stir the walnuts evenly into the mixture.

5 Fill the muffin pans almost to the top and bake for 30–35 minutes. Leave to stand for 5 minutes before transferring to a wire rack to cool.

Banana and Nut Muffins

Sweet, moist and full of flavor, these are bound to become family favorites. Use bananas that are ripe and soft, but not brown, and serve the muffins warm.

Makes 8

5 ounces/1¼ cups all-purpose flour

1½ teaspoons baking powder

2 ounces/¼ cup butter
  or margarine

6 ounces/scant 1 cup superfine
  sugar

1 egg

1 teaspoon vanilla extract

3 bananas, mashed

2 ounces/½ cup coarsely chopped
  pecan nuts

5 tablespoons milk

1 Preheat the oven to 375°F/Gas 5. Thoroughly grease eight muffin pans, or use paper liners.

2 Sift the flour and baking powder into a small bowl. Set aside.

3 With an electric mixer, cream the butter or margarine and the sugar. Add the egg and vanilla extract and beat until fluffy. Mix in the bananas. Add the pecan nuts.

4 With the mixer on low speed, beat in the flour mixture alternately with the milk. Spoon into the pans. Bake for 20–25 minutes, until golden brown.

5 Leave to cool in the pans for 10 minutes. Transfer to a wire rack.

Blueberry Muffins

Lightly spiced with ground cinnamon, these classic sweet muffins are extremely easy to make – and quite astonishingly delicious to eat.

Makes 8

4 ounces/1 cup all-purpose flour

1 tablespoon baking powder

pinch of salt

2½ ounces/generous ¼ cup soft
  light brown sugar

1 egg

6 fluid ounces/¾ cup milk

3 tablespoons vegetable oil

2 teaspoons ground cinnamon

5 ounces/1¼ cups fresh or
  thawed frozen blueberries
  or blackcurrants

1 Preheat the oven to 375°F/ Gas 5. Thoroughly grease eight muffin pans.

2 With an electric mixer, beat together the flour, baking powder, salt, sugar, egg, milk, vegetable oil and cinnamon until smooth.

3 Fold the blueberries or blackcurrants into the flour mixture until just evenly combined.

4 Spoon the mixture into the prepared pans, filling them about two-thirds full. Bake for 25 minutes, or until golden brown.

5 Leave to cool in the pans for 10 minutes, then transfer the muffins to a wire rack to cool completely.

Carrot Muffins

Carrots have a natural sweetness and moistness that makes them an ideal ingredient for cakes and muffins. If you haven't used them when baking before, you will be pleasantly surprised.

Makes 12

6 ounces/¾ cup margarine at room
   temperature, diced
3 ounces/⅓ cup soft dark
   brown sugar
1 egg
1 tablespoon water
10 ounces/2 cups grated carrots
5 ounces/1¼ cups all-purpose
   flour
1 teaspoon baking powder
½ teaspoon baking soda
1 teaspoon ground cinnamon
¼ teaspoon grated nutmeg
pinch of salt

1 Preheat the oven to 350°F/ Gas 4. Grease 12 muffin pans, or use paper liners.

2 With an electric mixer, cream the margarine and sugar until light and fluffy. Beat in the egg and water.

3 Stir the grated carrots into the creamed mixture until evenly combined. Sift over the flour, baking powder, baking soda, cinnamon, nutmeg and salt. Stir to blend evenly.

4 Spoon the batter into the prepared muffin pans, filling them almost to the top.

5 Bake for about 35 minutes, until the tops spring back when touched lightly with your fingers. Leave to stand in the pans for 10 minutes before transferring to a wire rack to cool completely.

Dried Cherry Muffins

Both sweet and sour cherries are available dried. These muffins are traditionally made with a sour variety, which is, in any case, something of a misnomer, as they are sharp rather than sour.

Makes 16

8 fluid ounces/1 cup plain yogurt
8 ounces/1 cup dried cherries
4 ounces/½ cup butter, softened
6 ounces/scant 1 cup superfine sugar
2 eggs
1 teaspoon vanilla extract
7 ounces/1⅔ cups all-purpose flour
2 teaspoons baking powder
1 teaspoon baking soda
pinch of salt

1 In a mixing bowl, combine the yogurt and dried cherries. Cover with plastic wrap and leave to stand for 30 minutes.

2 Preheat the oven to 350°F/Gas 4. Grease 16 muffin pans, or use paper liners.

3 Dice the butter and place in a bowl with the sugar. Cream together until light and fluffy. Add the eggs, one at a time, beating well after each addition.

4 Add the vanilla extract and the cherry mixture and stir to blend. Set aside.

5 In another bowl, sift together the flour, baking powder, baking soda and salt. Gently fold into the cherry mixture in three batches.

6 Spoon the mixture into the prepared muffin pans, filling them about two-thirds full. Bake for 20 minutes, or until the tops spring back when touched lightly. Transfer to a wire rack to cool.

Blueberry and Lemon Muffins

Blueberries grow wild all over the United States, which is where this traditional recipe comes from. If you cannot obtain blueberries, use raspberries or bilberries instead.

Makes 12

6 ounces/1¼ cups all-purpose
   flour
3 ounces/scant ½ cup superfine
   sugar
2 teaspoons baking powder
pinch of salt
2 eggs
2 ounces/¼ cup butter, melted
6 fluid ounces/¾ cup milk
1 teaspoon vanilla extract
1 teaspoon grated lemon rind
5 ounces/1¼ cups fresh blueberries

Cook's Tip
Rinse the blueberries in cold water, drain well and pat dry with kitchen paper before adding them to the batter.

1 Preheat the oven to 400°F/Gas 6. Grease 12 muffin pans, or use paper liners.

2 Sift the flour, sugar, baking powder and salt into a bowl and set aside.

3 In another bowl, lightly whisk the eggs until blended. Add the melted butter, milk, vanilla extract and lemon rind and stir well until thoroughly combined.

4 Make a well in the dry ingredients and pour in the egg mixture. Using a large metal spoon, stir until the flour is just moistened and incorporated, but not until the mixture is smooth.

5 Gently fold the blueberries into the mixture with a metal spoon until they are evenly distributed.

6 Spoon the mixture into the pans, leaving room for the muffins to rise. Bake for 20–25 minutes. Leave to cool for 5 minutes before transferring to a wire rack.

Date and Apple Muffins

These spiced muffins are delicious and very filling. If possible, use fresh medjool dates from Egypt, as they have sweet, dense flesh and a truly opulent flavor.

Makes 12

5 ounces/1¼ cups self-rising
  whole-wheat flour
5 ounces/1¼ cups self-rising
  white flour
1 teaspoon ground cinnamon
1 teaspoon baking powder
1 ounce/2 tbsp margarine
3 ounces/⅓ cup light brown sugar
1 eating apple
8 fluid ounces/1 cup apple juice
2 tablespoons pear and apple
  spread
1 egg, lightly beaten
3 ounces/½ cup chopped dates
1 tablespoon chopped pecan nuts

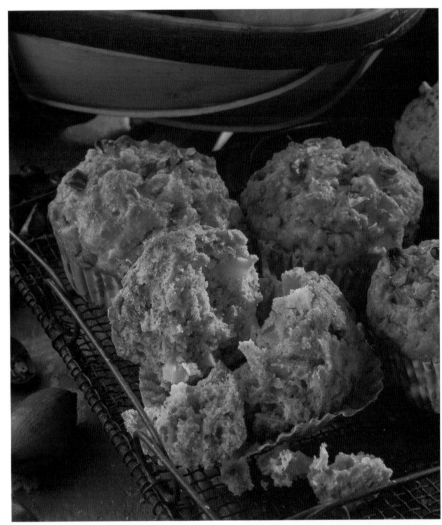

1 Preheat the oven to 400°F/Gas 6. Arrange 12 paper cases in a deep muffin pan.

2 Sift both flours with the cinnamon and baking powder into a bowl. Rub in the margarine until the mixture resembles breadcrumbs.

3 Stir in the brown sugar. Quarter and core the apple, chop the flesh finely and set aside. Stir a little of the apple juice with the pear and apple spread until smooth. Mix in the remaining apple juice, then add to the rubbed-in mixture with the beaten egg.

4 Add the chopped apple to the bowl and stir in the dates. Mix quickly until just combined. Divide the mixture among the prepared muffin cases.

5 Sprinkle the chopped pecans on top. Bake for 20–25 minutes, until golden brown and firm in the middle. Transfer to a wire rack and serve while still warm.

Cook's Tip
If self-rising whole-wheat flour is not available, use more self-rising white flour instead.

Blackberry Muffins

Blackberries are deliciously succulent with a slightly sharp flavor, but other similar berries, such as elderberries or blueberries, can be used instead.

Makes 12

10 ounces/2½ cups all-purpose flour

2 ounces/¼ cup soft light brown sugar

4 teaspoons baking powder

pinch of salt

2½ ounces/generous ½ cup chopped
   blanched almonds

3½ ounces/generous ¾ cup
   fresh blackberries

2 eggs

7 fluid ounces/scant 1 cup milk

2½ ounces/5 tablespoons butter,
   melted

1 tablespoon blackberry liqueur

1 tablespoon rose water

1 Preheat the oven to 400°F/Gas 6. Grease 12 muffin pans, or use paper liners.

2 Mix the flour, sugar, baking powder and salt in a bowl and stir in the almonds and blackberries, mixing them well to coat all over with the flour mixture.

3 In another bowl, mix the eggs with the milk, then gradually add the butter, liqueur and rose water.

4 Make a well in the center of the bowl of dry ingredients and add the egg and milk mixture. Stir well until the mixture is smooth.

5 Spoon the mixture into the prepared muffin pans or cases. Bake for 20–25 minutes, until browned. Transfer to a wire rack to cool slightly, if you want to serve them warm, or cool completely.

Variation

If you can't find blackberries, substitute a different berry, of your choice, or chocolate chips or nuts. All are excellent replacements.

Chocolate Blueberry Muffins

Blueberries are one of the many fruits that combine deliciously with the richness of chocolate, while still retaining their own distinctive flavor. These muffins are best served warm.

Makes 12

4 ounces/½ cup butter

3 ounces semisweet chocolate, chopped

7 ounces/1 cup granulated sugar

1 egg, lightly beaten

8 fluid ounces/1 cup buttermilk

2 teaspoons vanilla extract

10 ounces/2½ cups all-purpose flour

1 teaspoon baking soda

6 ounces/generous 1 cup fresh or thawed frozen blueberries

1 ounce semisweet chocolate, melted, to decorate

1 Preheat the oven to 375°F/Gas 5. Grease 12 deep muffin pans, or use paper liners.

2 Melt the butter and chocolate in a medium pan over a medium heat, stirring frequently until smooth. Remove the pan from the heat and leave to cool slightly.

Cook's Tip

Do not keep the batter waiting once you have folded in the blueberries. Bake the muffins immediately, or they won't rise very well during cooking.

3 Stir the sugar, egg, buttermilk and vanilla extract into the melted chocolate mixture. Gently fold in the flour and baking soda until just blended. (Be careful not to overblend; the mixture is best slightly lumpy.) Gently fold in the blueberries.

4 Spoon the batter into the prepared pans or paper cases. Bake for 25–30 minutes, until a skewer inserted in the center comes out with just a few crumbs attached. Transfer the muffins to a wire rack. (If left in the pan, they will go soggy.) To decorate, drizzle with the melted chocolate and serve warm or at room temperature.

Prune Muffins

Muffins with prunes are nutritious as well as delicious and perfect as a weekend breakfast treat. These are made with oil rather than butter, so are marvelously quick to mix.

Makes 12

1 egg

8 fluid ounces/1 cup milk

2 fluid ounces/¼ cup vegetable oil

2 ounces/¼ cup granulated sugar

2 tablespoons soft dark
   brown sugar

8 ounces/2 cups all-purpose flour

2 teaspoons baking powder

pinch of salt

¼ teaspoon grated nutmeg

5 ounces/¾ cup cooked prunes, or
   ready-to-eat prunes, chopped

1 Preheat the oven to 400°F/Gas 6. Grease 12 muffin pans, or use paper liners.

2 Break the egg into a mixing bowl and beat with a fork. Beat in the milk and oil.

3 Stir the sugars into the egg mixture. Set aside. Sift the flour, baking powder, salt and nutmeg into a mixing bowl. Make a well in the center, pour in the egg mixture and stir. The batter should be slightly lumpy.

4 Gently fold the prunes into the batter until just evenly distributed. Spoon into the prepared muffin pans, filling them two-thirds full.

5 Bake for about 20 minutes, until golden brown. Leave to stand for 10 minutes before transferring to a wire rack. Serve warm or cold.

Yogurt Honey Muffins

Yogurt and honey are known to boost energy levels, so these muffins go well in lunch boxes.

Makes 12

2 ounces/4 tablespoons butter

5 tablespoons clear honey

8 fluid ounces/1 cup plain
   yogurt

1 egg

grated rind of 1 lemon

2 fluid onces/¼ cup lemon juice

4 ounces/1 cup all-purpose flour

4 ounces/1 cup whole-wheat
   flour

1½ teaspoon baking soda

pinch of grated nutmeg

1 Preheat the oven to 375°F/Gas 5. Grease 12 muffin pans.

2 In a pan, melt the butter and honey. Remove from the heat and set aside to cool slightly.

3 In a bowl, whisk together the yogurt, egg, lemon rind and juice. Add the butter and honey mixture.

4 In another bowl, sift together the flours, baking soda and nutmeg. Fold the dry ingredients into the yogurt mixture just enough to blend them.

5 Fill the prepared muffin pans two-thirds full. Bake for 20–25 minutes, then leave to cool in the pans for about 5 minutes before transferring to a wire rack.

Variation
To make Walnut Yogurt Honey Muffins, add 2 ounces/½ cup chopped walnuts, folded in with the flour.

Raisin Bran Muffins

These traditional muffins remain hugely popular. This is hardly surprising, as they are delicious, served warm and spread with butter and honey.

Makes 15

2 ounces/¼ cup butter
  or margarine
3 ounces/⅔ cup all-purpose
  flour
2 ounces/½ cup whole-wheat
  flour
1½ teaspoons baking soda
pinch of salt
1 teaspoon ground cinnamon
1 ounce/½ cup bran
3 ounces/generous ½ cup raisins
2 ounces/¼ cup soft dark
  brown sugar
2 ounces/¼ cup granulated sugar
1 egg
8 fluid ounces/1 cup buttermilk
juice of ½ lemon

1 Preheat the oven to 400°F/Gas 6. Grease 15 muffin pans, or use paper liners.

2 Place the butter or margarine in a pan and melt over a low heat. Set aside to cool slightly. In a mixing bowl, sift together the plain flour, wholemeal flour, baking soda, salt and ground cinnamon.

3 Add the bran, raisins and sugars and stir until blended. In another bowl, mix together the egg, buttermilk, lemon juice and melted butter or margarine.

4 Add the buttermilk mixture to the dry ingredients and stir lightly and quickly until just moistened; do not mix until smooth.

5 Spoon the batter into the prepared muffin pans, filling them almost to the top. Bake for about 15 minutes, or until golden. Serve warm or at room temperature.

Cook's Tip
Bran is the outer husk of cereal grains, removed during milling. Wheat bran is the most widely available and popular variety, but other cereal brans are available from health food stores.

Raspberry Crumble Muffins

Make these stylish muffins for a special occasion in the summer when raspberries are bursting with flavor. For total luxury, serve like scones, with raspberry jam and cream.

Makes 12

6 ounces/1½ cups all-purpose flour

2 teaspoons baking powder

pinch of salt

1 teaspoon ground cinnamon

2 ounces/¼ cup granulated sugar

2 ounces/¼ cup soft light
   brown sugar

4 ounces/½ cup butter, melted

1 egg

4 fluid ounces/½ cup milk

8 ounces/1⅓ cups fresh raspberries

grated rind of 1 lemon

For the crumble topping

2 ounces/½ cup pecan nuts,
   finely chopped

2 ounces/¼ cup soft dark
   brown sugar

3 tablespoons all-purpose flour

1 teaspoon ground cinnamon

1½ ounces/3 tablespoons butter,
   melted

1 Preheat the oven to 350°F/Gas 4. Grease 12 muffin pans.

2 Sift the flour, baking powder, salt and cinnamon into a bowl. Stir in the sugars. Make a well in the center, add the butter, egg and milk and mix until just combined. Stir in the raspberries and lemon rind.

3 Spoon the batter into the muffin pans, filling them almost to the top.

4 To make the topping, mix the pecans, sugar, flour and cinnamon in a bowl. Stir in the melted butter.

5 Spoon a little of the crumble topping over the top of each muffin. Bake for about 25 minutes. Transfer to a wire rack to cool slightly. Serve the muffins warm.

Nutty Muffins with Walnut Liqueur

These are slightly spicy and topped with a delicious crunchy sugar and nut mixture. If you're making them for children, simply omit the walnut liqueur and add more milk.

Makes 12

8 ounces/2 cups all-purpose flour

4 teaspoons baking powder

½ teaspoon apple pie spice

pinch of salt

4 ounces/½ cup soft light brown sugar

3 ounces/¾ cup chopped walnuts

2 ounces/¼ cup butter, melted

2 eggs

6 fluid ounces/¾ cup milk

2 tablespoons walnut liqueur

For the topping

2 tablespoons soft dark brown sugar

1 ounce/¼ cup chopped walnuts

1 Preheat the oven to 400°F/Gas 6. Line a muffin pan with 12 paper cases. Sift the flour, baking powder, apple pie spice and salt into a bowl. Stir in the sugar and walnuts.

2 Combine the melted butter, eggs, milk and liqueur in a pitcher.

3 Pour the butter mixture into the dry mixture and stir for just long enough to combine the ingredients. The batter should be lumpy.

4 Fill the pans two-thirds full, then top with a sprinkling of sugar and walnuts. Bake for 15 minutes until the muffins are golden brown. Leave in the pans for a few minutes, then transfer to a wire rack to cool.

Cook's Tip
Probably the best-known walnut liqueur is brou de noix from France, which is made from green walnut husks and flavored with cinnamon and nutmeg. Other versions are also produced.

Apple and Cinnamon Muffins

These fruity, spicy muffins are quick and easy to make and are perfect for serving for breakfast or tea. The appetizing aroma as they bake is out of this world.

Makes 6

1 egg, beaten

1½ ounces/3 tablespoons superfine sugar

4 fluid ounces/½ cup milk

2 ounces/¼ cup butter, melted

5 ounces/1¼ cups all-purpose flour

1½ teaspoon baking powder

pinch of salt

½ teaspoon ground cinnamon

2 small eating apples, peeled, cored and finely chopped

For the topping

12 brown sugar cubes, coarsely crushed

1 teaspoon ground cinnamon

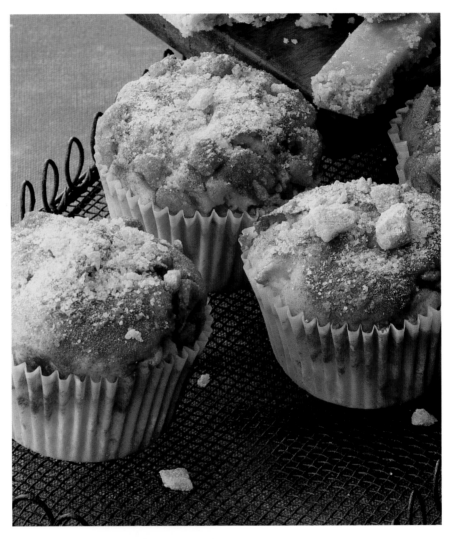

1 Preheat the oven to 400°F/Gas 6. Line a large muffin pan with six paper cases.

2 Mix the egg, sugar, milk and melted butter in a large bowl. Sift in the flour, baking powder, salt and cinnamon. Add the chopped apple and mix roughly.

Variation

You can also make these muffins with pears, which also go well with cinnamon.

3 Spoon the mixture into the prepared muffin cases. To make the topping, mix the crushed sugar cubes with the cinnamon. Sprinkle over the uncooked muffins.

4 Bake for 30–35 minutes, until well risen and golden brown on top. Transfer the muffins to a wire rack to cool. Serve them warm or at room temperature.

Cook's Tip

Do not overmix the muffin mixture – it should be slightly lumpy.

Pineapple and Cinnamon Drop Scones

Making the batter with pineapple juice instead of milk cuts down on the amount of fat and adds a delicious piquancy to the flavor of these delicious drop scones.

Makes 24

4 ounces/1 cup self-rising
   whole-wheat flour

4 ounces/1 cup self-rising
   white flour

1 teaspoon ground cinnamon

1 tablespoon superfine sugar

1 egg

½ pint/1¼ cups pineapple juice

3 ounces/½ cup semi-dried
   pineapple, chopped

1 Put the wholemeal flour in a mixing bowl. Sift in the white flour, add the cinnamon and sugar and make a well in the center. Add the egg with half of the pineapple juice.

2 Gradually incorporate the flour, then beat in the remaining pineapple juice with the chopped pineapple.

3 Heat a griddle or electric frying pan, then lightly grease it. Drop tablespoons of the batter onto the surface, spacing them apart, and leave them until they bubble and the bubbles begin to burst.

Cook's Tips
• *Drop scones do not keep well and are best eaten freshly cooked. In any case, they are especially delicious served hot.*
• *If self-rising wholewheat flour is not readily available, use self-rising white flour instead.*

4 Turn over the drop scones with a metal spatula and cook until the underside is golden brown. Continue to cook in successive batches.

Chocolate-chip Banana Drop Scones

These scrumptious, moist scones are topped with whipped cream and toasted almonds. You may find it difficult to keep up with the speed the family can eat them.

Makes 16

2 ripe bananas

7 fluid ounces/scant 1 cup milk

2 eggs

5 ounces/1¼ cups self-rising
    flour

1 ounce/¼ cup ground
    almonds

1 tablespoon superfine sugar

pinch of salt

1 ounce/2½ tablespoons semisweet
    chocolate chips

butter, for frying

For the topping

¼ pint/⅔ cup heavy cream

1 tablespoon confectioners' sugar

2 ounces/½ cup toasted sliced almonds,
    to decorate

1 In a bowl, mash the bananas with a fork, combine with half the milk and beat in the eggs. Sift in the flour, ground almonds, sugar and salt.

2 Make a well in the center of the dry ingredients and pour in the remaining milk. Add the chocolate chips and stir with a wooden spoon to produce a thick batter.

3 Heat a pat of butter in a non-stick frying pan. Spoon the drop scone mixture into heaps, allowing room for them to spread. When the mixture starts to bubble, turn the drop scones over and cook briefly on the other side.

4 When all the batches of scones have been cooked, lightly whip the cream with the confectioners' sugar to sweeten it slightly. Spoon the cream onto the drop scones and decorate with sliced almonds. Serve immediately, while still warm.

Teatime Scones

Although the great British institution of tea time is fast becoming a memory, there are occasions when reviving the tradition is worthwhile – and making these scones is one of them.

Makes 16

8 ounces/2 cups all-purpose
    flour
pinch of salt
½ teaspoon baking soda
1 teaspoon cream of tartar
1 ounce/2 tablespoons butter
about ¼ pint/⅔ cup milk
    or buttermilk

1 Preheat the oven to 425°F/ Gas 7. Flour a baking sheet. Sift the flour, salt, baking soda and cream of tartar into a large mixing bowl.

2 Rub in the butter until the mixture resembles breadcrumbs. Gradually stir in just enough milk to make a light, spongy dough.

3 Turn out the dough onto a lightly floured surface and knead until smooth. Roll to 1 inch thick. Stamp out round pieces with a floured 2-inch cutter.

4 Place the scones on the prepared baking sheet and brush the tops with milk. Bake for 7–10 minutes, until the scones are well risen and golden brown.

Lavender Scones

These scented scones are literally a taste of the summer and are delicious served warm with jam.

Makes 12

8 ounces/2 cups all-purpose flour
1 tablespoon baking powder
2 ounces/¼ cup butter
1½ ounces/3 tablespoons superfine sugar
2 teaspoons fresh lavender florets, chopped
about 6 fluid ounces/¾ cup milk

1 Preheat the oven to 425°F/Gas 7. Grease a baking sheet.

2 Sift together the flour and baking powder into a bowl. Rub the butter into the dry ingredients until the mixture resembles breadcrumbs.

3 Stir in the sugar and lavender, reserving a pinch of lavender to sprinkle on the top of the scones.

4 Add enough milk to make a soft, sticky dough. Bind the mixture together and then turn the dough out onto a well-floured surface.

5 Roll out the dough to a round shape about 1 inch thick. Stamp out 12 scones with a floured cutter and place them on the baking sheet. Brush the tops with a little milk and sprinkle with the reserved lavender.

6 Bake for 10–12 minutes, until golden brown.

Sunflower Raisin Scones

Baking a batch of fruit scones takes very little time and is extremely easy, but it is both satisfying and rewarding. They make the perfect snack for both morning and afternoon breaks.

Makes 10–12

8 ounces/2 cups self-rising flour

1 teaspoon baking powder

1 ounce/2 tablespoons margarine

2 tablespoons golden superfine
  sugar

2 ounces/⅓ cup golden raisins

2 tablespoons sunflower seeds

¼ pint/⅔ cup plain yogurt

about 2–3 tablespoons milk

Cook's Tip

These scones would be perfect served with sunflower honey, which has a wonderful floral fragrance.

1 Preheat the oven to 450°F/Gas 8. Grease a baking sheet. Sift the flour and baking powder into a bowl, add the margarine and rub in. Stir in the sugar, raisins and half of the sunflower seeds, then mix in the yogurt.

2 Add just enough milk to the mixture to make a soft dough.

3 Roll out on a lightly floured surface to about ¾ of an inch thick. Stamp out 2½-inch round pieces with a floured cookie cutter and lift onto the baking sheet.

4 Brush the tops of the scones with milk, and sprinkle with the reserved sunflower seeds.

5 Bake for 10–12 minutes until well risen and golden brown. Transfer to a wire rack to cool slightly. Serve while still warm, spread with a little butter and jam.

Whole-wheat Scones

These scones make a delicious and healthy option. As you would expect, they taste great spread with jam, but they are also surprisingly good with cheese – either soft or hard.

Makes 16

6 ounces/¾ cup cold butter
8 ounces/2 cups whole-wheat
   flour
4 ounces/1 cup all-purpose
   flour
2 tablespoons superfine sugar
pinch of salt
2½ teaspoons baking soda
2 eggs
6 fluid ounces/¾ cup buttermilk
1½ ounces/⅓ cup raisins

1 Preheat the oven to 400°F/ Gas 6. Grease and flour a large baking sheet.

2 Dice the butter. Mix the dry ingredients in a bowl, then add the butter and rub in. Set aside. In another bowl, whisk together the eggs and buttermilk. Set aside 2 tablespoons for glazing.

3 Stir the remaining egg mixture into the dry ingredients to form a dough. Stir in the raisins.

4 Roll out the dough on a lightly floured surface to about ¾ of an inch thick. Stamp out round pieces with a floured cutter. Place on the prepared baking sheet and brush with the reserved egg mixture.

5 Bake for 12–15 minutes, until golden brown. Leave to cool slightly before serving. Split the scones in half while they are still warm, and spread with whatever you like.

Orange Raisin Scones

These sweet, tangy scones are really at their best served warm, in the traditional British way, with thick cream and home-made jam.

Makes 16

8 ounces/2 cups all-purpose flour
1½ tablespoons baking powder
3 ounces/scant ½ cup superfine sugar
pinch of salt
2½ ounces/5 tablespoons butter,
   chopped
grated rind of 1 large orange
2 ounces/⅓ cup raisins
4 ounces/½ cup buttermilk
milk, for glazing

1 Preheat the oven to 425°F/ Gas 7. Grease and flour a large baking sheet.

2 Combine the dry ingredients in a large bowl. Rub in the butter.

3 Add the orange rind and raisins and mix well. Gradually stir in the buttermilk to form a soft dough.

4 Roll out the dough on a lightly floured surface to about ¾ inch thick. Stamp out round pieces with a floured cookie cutter.

5 Place on the prepared baking sheet and brush the tops with milk to glaze. Bake for 12–15 minutes, until golden brown. Serve hot or warm, with butter or whipped cream and jam.

Cook's Tips
• *For light, delicate scones, handle the dough as little as possible.*
• *If you wish, split the scones when cool and toast them under a preheated broiler. Butter them while they are still hot.*

Ham and Tomato Scones

These savory scones make an ideal accompaniment for soup. Choose a strong-flavored ham and chop it fairly finely, so that a little goes a long way.

Makes 12

8 ounces/2 cups self-rising flour
1 teaspoon mustard powder
1 teaspoon paprika, plus extra
  for sprinkling
pinch of salt
1 ounce/2 tablespoons margarine,
  diced
1 tablespoon chopped fresh basil
2 ounces/½ cup sun-dried tomatoes in oil,
  drained and chopped
2 ounces strong-flavored ham, chopped
3–4 fluid ounces/⅓–½ cup skimmed milk,
  plus extra for brushing

1 Preheat the oven to 400°F/Gas 6. Flour a large baking sheet. Sift the flour, mustard, paprika and salt into a bowl. Rub in the margarine with your fingertips.

2 Stir the basil, sun-dried tomatoes and ham into the bowl. Pour in enough milk to make a soft dough.

3 Turn the dough out onto a lightly floured surface, knead lightly and roll out to an 8 x 6 inch rectangle. Cut into 2-inch squares and arrange on the baking sheet.

4 Brush the tops of the scones with milk, sprinkle lightly with paprika and bake for 12–15 minutes, until risen and golden brown. Transfer to a wire rack to cool.

Bacon Corn-meal Muffins

Serve these tasty muffins fresh from the oven for an extra special breakfast. They would also be ideal as part of a weekend brunch menu, served with scrambled eggs or an omelette.

Makes 14

8 bacon strips

2 ounces/¼ cup butter

2 ounces/¼ cup margarine

4 ounces/1 cup all-purpose
    flour

1 tablespoon baking powder

1 teaspoon superfine sugar

pinch of salt

6 ounces/1½ cups corn meal

8 fluid ounces/1 cup milk

2 eggs

1 Preheat the oven to 400°F/Gas 6. Grease 14 muffin pans, or use paper liners.

2 Remove the bacon rind, if necessary, then fry the bacon over a medium heat until crisp. Drain on kitchen paper, then chop into small pieces. Set aside. Melt the butter and margarine in a pan over a low heat and set aside.

3 Sift the flour, baking powder, sugar and salt into a large mixing bowl. Stir in the corn meal, then make a well in the center. In another pan, heat the milk to lukewarm. In a small bowl, lightly whisk the eggs, then add to the milk. Stir in the melted butter and margarine.

4 Pour the milk and egg mixture into the center of the well and stir in the dry ingredients until smooth and well blended.

5 Fold in the bacon. Spoon the batter into the prepared pans, filling them halfway. Bake for about 20 minutes, until risen and golden.

Savory Cheese Whirls

These make a tasty – and healthy – after-school snack for children, and you may be surprised to discover that adults like them, too. Serve them with carrot and cucumber sticks.

Makes 16

9 ounces frozen puff pastry, thawed
about 1 tablespoon Vegemite
1 egg, beaten
2 ounces/½ cup grated
   Cheddar cheese

1 Preheat the oven to 425°F/ Gas 7. Lightly grease a large baking sheet. Roll out the pastry on a lightly floured surface to a large rectangle, measuring about 14 x 10 inches.

2 Spread the pastry with Vegemite, leaving a ½-inch border. Brush the edges of the pastry with egg and sprinkle over the cheese to cover the Vegemite.

3 Roll the pastry up quite tightly like a jelly roll, starting from a long edge. Brush the outside of the pastry with beaten egg.

4 Cut the pastry roll into thick slices and place on the prepared baking sheet.

5 Bake for 12–15 minutes, until the pastry is well risen and golden. Arrange on a serving plate and serve warm or cold with carrot and cucumber sticks.

Cook's Tip
If the shapes become a little squashed when sliced, re-form them into round shapes by opening out the layers slightly with the tip of a knife.

Variation
Omit the Vegemite and use peanut butter, if you like.

Cheese Muffins

These muffins would be terrific served straight from the oven at a brunch party, or wonderfully restorative and warming after a brisk walk on a cold winter's afternoon.

Makes 9

2 ounces/¼ cup butter

6 ounces/1½ cups all-purpose flour

2 teaspoons baking powder

2 tablespoons superfine sugar

pinch of salt

1 teaspoon paprika

2 eggs

4 fluid ounces/½ cup milk

1 teaspoon dried thyme

2 ounces sharp Cheddar cheese, cut into ½ inch dice

1 Preheat the oven to 375°F/ Gas 5. Grease nine muffin pans, or use paper liners. Melt the butter in a small pan.

2 Sift the flour, baking powder, sugar, salt and paprika into a bowl.

3 Combine the eggs, milk, melted butter and thyme and whisk well.

4 Add the milk mixture to the dry ingredients and stir until just moistened. Do not mix until smooth.

5 Place a mounded spoonful of batter into each of the prepared pans. Drop a few pieces of cheese over each, then top with another spoonful of batter.

6 Bake the muffins for about 25 minutes, until puffed and golden brown. Leave to stand in the pans for about 5 minutes before unmolding them onto a wire rack to cool slightly. These muffins are best served while still warm from the oven, or at room temperature.

Feta Cheese and Chive Scones

Salty feta cheese makes an excellent substitute for butter in these tangy savory scones. They not only go well with hot soup, but also make a delicious snack at any time of day.

Makes 9

4 ounces/1 cup self-rising flour

5 ounces/1¼ cup self-rising
   whole-wheat flour

pinch of salt

3 ounces feta cheese

1 tablespoon chopped fresh chives

¼ pint/⅔ cup skimmed milk, plus extra
   for glazing

¼ teaspoon cayenne pepper

1 Preheat the oven to 400°F/Gas 6. Sift together both the flours and the salt into a mixing bowl, adding any bran left over from the flour in the sieve.

2 Crumble the feta cheese roughly and rub it into the dry ingredients. Stir in the chives, then add the milk and mix lightly to form a soft, not sticky dough.

3 Turn out the dough onto a floured surface and knead lightly until smooth. Roll out to ¾ of an inch thick and stamp out nine scones with a floured 2½-inch cookie cutter.

4 Transfer to a non-stick baking sheet. Brush with skimmed milk, then sprinkle over the cayenne pepper. Bake for 15 minutes, until golden brown. Serve warm or cold.

Cook's Tip
Try to obtain genuine sheep's milk feta, as it has the best flavor. Much modern feta is made from cow's milk, but some Greek and, surprisingly, Bulgarian feta is still made in the traditional manner.

Variation
If self-rising whole-wheat flour is not readily available, use self-rising white flour instead.

Chive and Potato Scones

These little scones should be fairly thin, soft inside and crisp on the outside. Traditionally served for what was once known as "high tea," they are also excellent for breakfast.

Makes 20

1 pound potatoes

4 ounces/1 cup all-purpose flour

2 tablespoons olive oil, plus extra
   for greasing

2 tablespoons chopped fresh chives

salt and ground black pepper

1 Cook the potatoes in a pan of lightly salted, boiling water for about 20 minutes, until tender, then drain thoroughly. Return the potatoes to the clean pan and mash them with a masher or a fork. Preheat a griddle or heavy frying pan.

2 Add the flour, olive oil and chives to the mashed potato. Season to taste with salt and pepper. Mix to a soft dough.

3 Roll out the dough on a well-floured surface to a thickness of about ¼ of an inch, and stamp out round pieces with a floured 2-inch plain cookie cutter. Lightly grease the griddle or frying pan with a little olive oil.

4 Cook the scones in batches for about 10 minutes, turning once halfway through cooking.

Cook's Tip

Cook over a low heat to avoid burning the outsides before the insides are cooked.

No-bake Cookies

The recipes in this chapter require even less time and effort to mix than traveling to the supermarket to buy a packet of cookies – and they taste a lot better, too. Some are not just no-bake but even no-cook, making them great for kids to prepare as well. None of them requires anything more demanding than melting some chocolate, but you may have to be patient to allow the cookies enough time to set in the refrigerator before sampling them.

Fruit and Nut Clusters

This is a fun, no-cook recipe that children will like, although if they are making it themselves, adult supervision for melting the chocolate is required.

Makes 24

8 ounces white chocolate

2 ounces/⅓ cup sunflower seeds

2 ounces/½ cup sliced almonds

2 ounces/¼ cup sesame seeds

2 ounces/⅓ cup seedless raisins

I teaspoon ground cinnamon

I Break the white chocolate into small pieces. Put the chocolate in a microwave-proof container and cook in a microwave on medium for 2–3 minutes.

2 Alternatively, melt the chocolate by putting it into a heatproof bowl set over a pan of hot water on a low heat. Do not allow the water to touch the base of the bowl, or the chocolate may become too hot.

3 Stir the melted chocolate until it is smooth and glossy.

4 Mix the remaining ingredients together, pour on the melted chocolate and stir well.

5 Using a teaspoon, spoon the mixture into paper cases and leave in a cool place to set, but do not put the clusters in the refrigerator.

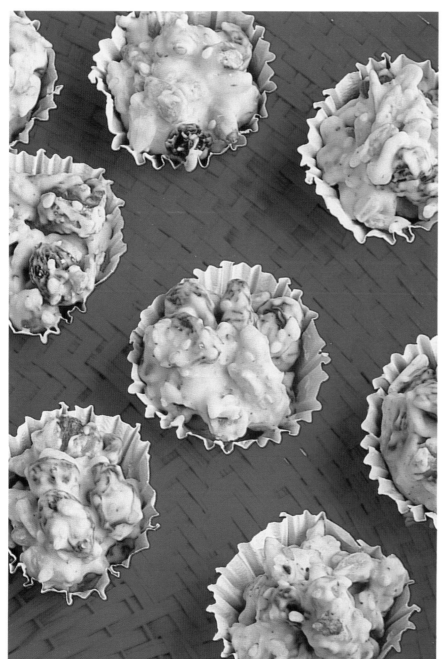

Cook's Tip

As for any recipe that contains nuts, always check that those who will be eating the cookies do not have nut allergies. You could always substitute other dried fruit, such as dates, in place of the nuts.

Oat and Apricot Clusters

Here is a variation on an old favorite, which children can easily make themselves, so have plenty of the dried fruits and nuts ready for them to add.

Makes 12

2 ounces/¼ cup butter or margarine

2 ounces/¼ cup clear honey

2 ounces/½ cup medium rolled oats

2 ounces/½ cup chopped ready-to-eat dried apricots

1 tablespoon dried banana chips

1 tablespoon dried shreds of coconut or dried unsweetened coconut

2–3 ounces/2–3 cups cornflakes or crisped rice cereal

1 Place the butter or margarine and honey in a small pan and warm over a low heat, stirring.

2 Remove the pan from the heat and add the oats, apricots, banana chips, coconut and cornflakes or crisped rice cereal and stir well with a wooden spoon until combined.

3 Spoon the mixture into 12 paper cake cases, piling it up roughly. Transfer to a baking sheet or place on a tray and chill in the refrigerator until set and firm.

Variations

• To make Oat and Cherry Clusters, use rinsed and chopped glacé (candied) cherries in place of the apricots.

• To make Chocolate Chip Clusters, substitute 75g/3oz/½ cup chocolate chips.

Cook's Tip

The ingredients can be changed according to what you have in your pantry – try peanuts, pecan nuts, raisins or dried dates.

Apricot and Coconut Kisses

These tangy, fruity treats make a colorful addition to the tea table. Although they are easy to make, remember to allow plenty of time for the apricots to soak.

Makes 12

4½ ounces/generous ½ cup ready-to-eat dried apricots

3½ fluid ounces/scant ½ cup freshly squeezed orange juice

1½ ounces/3 tablespoons sweet butter, at room temperature, diced

3 ounces/¾ cup confectioners' sugar, plus extra for dusting

3½ ounces/generous 1 cup dried unsweetened shredded coconut, lightly toasted

2 candied cherries, cut into wedges

1 Finely chop the dried apricots, then tip them into a bowl. Pour in the orange juice and leave to soak for about 1 hour until all the juice has been absorbed.

2 In a large bowl, beat together the butter and sugar with a wooden spoon until pale and creamy.

3 Gradually add the soaked apricots to the creamed butter and sugar mixture, beating well after each addition, then stir in the toasted coconut.

4 Line a small baking tray with waxed paper.

5 Place teaspoonfuls of the coconut mixture onto the paper, piling them up into little pyramid shapes. Gently press the mixture together with your fingers to form neat shapes.

6 Top each kiss with a tiny wedge of cherry, gently pressing it into the mixture. Chill the kisses for about 1 hour, until firm, then serve lightly dusted with a little confectioners' sugar.

Cook's Tip

It is essential that all the orange juice has been absorbed by the apricots before adding them to the butter mixture, otherwise the kisses will be too moist to set properly.

Date Crunch

A tasty mixture of dried fruit, syrup and chocolate is guaranteed to be a success with the younger members of the family – and they will need to keep an eye on the adults, too.

Makes 24

8 ounces graham crackers

3 ounces/⅓ cup butter

2 tablespoons light corn
   syrup

3 ounces/½ cup finely chopped
   pitted dried dates

3 ounces/⅔ cup golden raisins

5 ounces milk or semisweet
   chocolate, chopped

1 Line a 7-inch square shallow cake pan with foil. Put the graham crackers in a plastic bag and crush coarsely with a rolling pin.

2 Gently heat the butter and syrup together in a small pan until the butter has melted.

Variation
You could drizzle 3 ounces each of melted white and bittersweet chocolate.

3 Stir the crushed graham crackers, dates and raisins into the butter and syrup mixture and mix well with a wooden spoon until evenly combined. Spoon into the prepared pan, spreading it out evenly, press flat with the back of the spoon and chill for 1 hour.

4 Melt the chocolate in a heatproof bowl set over a pan of hot water, stirring until smooth. Spoon over the cookie mixture, spreading evenly with a metal spatula. Chill until set. Lift the foil out of the cake pan and peel away. Cut the crunch into 24 pieces to serve.

Chocolate Nut Clusters

These delightful chocolate-coated cookies are packed with chunky nuts and are an ideal way to end a dinner party, or the perfect gift for a special friend.

Makes 30

18 fluid ounces/2¼ cups
   heavy cream
1 ounce/2 tablespoons sweet
   butter, diced
12 fluid ounces/1½ cups light
   corn syrup
7 ounces/scant 1 cup granulated sugar
3½ ounces/scant ½ packed cup soft
   light brown sugar
pinch of salt
1 tablespoon vanilla extract
15 ounces/3¾ cups hazelnuts, pecan
   nuts, walnuts, brazil nuts or unsalted
   peanuts, or a combination
14 ounces semisweet
   chocolate, chopped
1 ounce/2 tablespoons shortening

1 Lightly oil two baking sheets. Put the cream, butter, syrup, both kinds of sugar and the salt in a heavy pan and cook over a medium heat, stirring constantly until the sugars dissolve and the butter melts. Bring to the boil and cook, stirring frequently, for about 1 hour, until the caramel reaches 238°F (soft ball stage) on a sugar thermometer.

2 Place the base of the pan in a pan of cold water to stop further cooking, or transfer the caramel to a smaller pan. Cool slightly, then stir in the vanilla extract.

3 Stir the nuts into the caramel until well-coated. Using an oiled tablespoon, drop spoonfuls of the mixture onto the baking sheets, about 1 inch apart. If the mixture hardens, return to the heat.

4 Chill the clusters for 30 minutes, until firm and cold, or leave in a cool place until hardened.

Cook's Tip

You can test cooked sugar for "soft ball stage" by spooning a small amount into a bowl of cold water: when taken out it should form a soft ball when rolled between finger and thumb.

5 Using a metal spatula, transfer the clusters to a wire rack placed over a baking sheet to catch drips.

6 Melt the chocolate with the shortening in a pan over a low heat, stirring until smooth. Remove the pan from the heat and leave to cool slightly.

7 Spoon the melted chocolate mixture over each cluster, being sure to cover completely. Alternatively, using a fork, dip each cluster, one at a time, into the chocolate mixture and lift out, tapping the fork on the edge of the pan to shake off the excess chocolate.

8 Place the nut clusters on the wire rack over the baking sheet. Leave to set for about 2 hours until hardened.

Nutty Marshmallow and Chocolate Squares

Unashamedly sweet, with chocolate, marshmallows, cherries, nuts and coconut, this recipe is a favorite with children of all ages, and sweet-toothed adults, too.

Makes 9

7 ounces graham crackers

3½ ounces semisweet chocolate

7 ounces mini colored marshmallows

5 ounces/1¼ cups chopped walnuts

3½ ounces/scant ½ cup candied cherries, halved

2 ounces/⅔ cup sweetened shredded dried coconut

12 ounces milk chocolate

1 Put the graham crackers in a plastic bag and, using a rolling pin, crush them until they are fairly small. Place them in a bowl. Melt the semisweet chocolate in the microwave or in a heatproof bowl set over a pan of hot water. Pour the melted semisweet chocolate over the broken graham crackers and stir well. Spread the mixture in the base of an 8-inch square shallow cake pan.

2 Put the marshmallows, walnuts, cherries and coconut in a large bowl. Melt the milk chocolate in the microwave or in a heatproof bowl set over a pan of hot water.

3 Pour the melted milk chocolate over the marshmallow and nut mixture and toss gently together until almost everything is coated. Spread the mixture over the chocolate base, but leave in chunky lumps – do not spread flat.

4 Chill until set, then cut into squares or bars.

Variation
Other nuts can be used instead of the walnuts – the choice is yours.

Almond-scented Chocolate Cherry Wedges

These cookies are a chocoholic's dream, and they use the very best quality chocolate. Erratically shaped, they are packed with crunchy cookies, juicy raisins and munchy nuts.

Makes about 15

2 ounces almond macaroons
   or small amaretti

3½ ounces shortcake cookies

5 ounces/1 cup jumbo raisins

2 ounces/¼ cup undyed candied
   cherries, quartered

1 pound bittersweet chocolate
   (minimum 70 percent cocoa solids)

3½ ounces/scant ½ cup sweet
   butter, diced

2 tablespoons amaretto liqueur
   (optional)

1 ounce/¼ cup toasted sliced almonds

1 Line a baking sheet with baking parchment. Put the almond macaroons or amaretti in a large bowl. Leave half whole and break the remainder into coarse pieces. Break each of the shortcake cookies into three or four jagged pieces and add to the bowl. Add the raisins and cherries and toss lightly together.

Cook's Tip
If you cannot find undyed candied cherries in the supermarket, look for them in your local delicatessen instead.

2 Melt the chocolate and butter with the liqueur, if using, in the microwave or in a heatproof bowl set over a pan of hot water. When the chocolate has melted, remove from the heat and stir the mixture until combined and smooth. Set aside to cool slightly.

3 Pour the chocolate over the cookie mixture and toss lightly together until everything is coated in chocolate. Spread out over the prepared baking sheet. Sprinkle over the almonds and push them in at angles so they stick well to the chocolate-coated biscuits.

4 When the mixture is completely cold and set, cut or break into crazy shapes, as you wish, such as long thin triangles, short stumpy squares or irregular shapes.

Chocolate Crispy Cookies

These little chocolate-coated cornflake cakes are always a hit with kids. They couldn't be easier to make – and they are great for young aspiring cooks who want to get involved in the kitchen. The only problem is giving the mixture time to set before they've been gobbled up by hungry helpers.

4 Remove the bowl from the heat and tip in the cornflakes. Mix well until the cornflakes are thoroughly coated in the chocolate mixture.

5 Place a 2½-inch round cutter on the paper and put a spoonful of the chocolate mixture in the center. Pack down firmly with the back of the spoon to make a thick cookie.

6 Gently ease away the cutter, using the spoon to help keep the mixture in place. Continue making cookies in this way until all the mixture has been used up. Chill for 1 hour.

7 Put a little confectioners' sugar in a small bowl. Lift each cookie from the paper and roll the edges in the confectioners' sugar to finish.

Makes 10

3½ ounces milk chocolate
1 tablespoon light corn syrup
3½ ounces/4½ cups cornflakes
confectioners' sugar, for dusting

1 Line a large baking sheet with baking parchment.

2 Break the chocolate into a heatproof bowl and add the syrup. Rest the bowl over a pan of gently simmering water and leave until melted, stirring frequently.

3 Put the cornflakes in a plastic bag and, using a rolling pin, lightly crush the cornflakes, breaking them into fairly small pieces.

Chocolate Nut Slice

Children of all ages will love this combination of broken cookies, chocolate and nuts. Although the unsliced bar looks small, it's very rich so is best sliced very thinly. You can use any kind of plain cookie in the cupboard, with equally good results.

Makes 10 slices

8 ounces milk chocolate

1½ ounces/3 tablespoons sweet butter, diced

3 ounces plain cookies

2 ounces/½ cup sliced almonds

3 ounces semisweet or white chocolate, roughly chopped

confectioners' sugar, for dusting

1 Break the milk chocolate into pieces and place in a heatproof bowl with the butter. Rest the bowl over a pan of simmering water and stir frequently until melted.

2 Meanwhile, dampen a 1-pound loaf pan and line the base and sides with plastic wrap. Don't worry about smoothing out the creases in the film.

3 When the chocolate has melted, remove it from the heat and leave for 5 minutes until slightly cooled.

4 Break the cookies into small pieces, then stir into the melted chocolate with the almonds. Add the chopped chocolate to the bowl and fold in quickly and lightly.

5 Turn the mixture into the pan and pack down with a fork. Tap the base of the pan gently on the work surface. Chill for 2 hours, until set.

6 To serve, turn the chocolate loaf onto a board and peel away the plastic wrap. Dust lightly with confectioners' sugar and slice thinly.

Chocolate Birds' Nests

These delightful crispy chocolate nests make a perfect Easter tea-time treat and are a real favorite with kids. They're so quick and easy to make, and young children can have great fun shaping the chocolate mixture inside the paper cases and tucking the pastel-colored eggs inside.

Makes 12

7 ounces milk chocolate

1 ounce/2 tablespoons sweet
  butter, diced

3½ ounces Shredded Wheat cereal

36 small pastel-colored, sugar-coated
  chocolate eggs

Cook's Tip

*Bags of sugar-coated chocolate eggs
are widely available in supermarkets at
Easter time. However, if you have trouble
finding them out of season, try an old-
fashioned candy store. Often they have
large jars of this type of candy, which
they sell all year round.*

1 Line the sections of a muffin
pan with 12 decorative paper
cake cases.

2 Break the milk chocolate into
pieces and put in a bowl with the
butter. Rest the bowl over a pan
of gently simmering water and stir
frequently until melted. Remove the
bowl from the heat and leave to
cool for a few minutes.

3 Using your fingers, crumble the
Shredded Wheat into the melted
chocolate. Stir well until the cereal is
completely coated in chocolate.

4 Divide the mixture among the
paper cases, pressing it down gently
with the back of a spoon, and make
a slight indentation in the center.
Tuck three eggs into each nest
and leave to set for about 2 hours.

White Chocolate Snowballs

These little spherical cookies are particularly popular during the Christmas season. They're simple to make, yet utterly delicious and bursting with creamy, buttery flavors. If you like, make them in advance of a special tea, as they will keep well in the refrigerator for a few days.

Makes 16

7 ounces white chocolate

1 ounce/2 tablespoons butter, diced

3½ ounces/generous 1 cup dried unsweetened shredded coconut

3½ ounces syrup sponge

confectioners' sugar, for dusting

1 Break the chocolate into pieces and put in a heatproof bowl with the butter. Rest the bowl over a pan of gently simmering water and stir frequently until melted. Remove the bowl from the heat and set aside for a few minutes.

2 Meanwhile, put 2 ounces/⅔ cup of the coconut on a plate and set aside. Crumble the cake and add to the melted chocolate with the remaining coconut. Mix well to form a chunky paste.

3 Take spoonfuls of the mixture and roll into balls, about 1 inch in diameter, and immediately roll them in the reserved coconut. Place the balls on waxed paper and leave to set.

4 To serve, dust the snowballs with plenty of confectioners' sugar.

Cook's Tip
You'll need to shape the mixture into balls as soon as you've mixed in the coconut and cake; the mixture sets very quickly, and you won't be able to shape it once it hardens.

Ice Mountain

To create an alternative shape to round forms, and squares, this refrigerator cookie is set in the corner of a cake pan, giving it a "pyramid" shape for slicing into triangles.

Makes 12

3 ounces malted milk cookies

3½ ounces milk chocolate

3 ounces white chocolate mint sticks

9 ounces white chocolate

4 tablespoons heavy cream

several hard mint candies,
* to decorate*

1 Break the cookies into small pieces, chop the milk chocolate into small dice and break the chocolate mint sticks into short lengths. Keep these ingredients separate.

2 Reserve 2 ounces of the white chocolate. Break up the remainder and put in a small heatproof bowl with the cream. Set the bowl over a pan of gently simmering water and leave until melted, stirring the chocolate frequently. Remove the bowl from the heat and scrape the melted chocolate into a clean bowl.

Cook's Tip

It is important to avoid overheating white chocolate when you are melting it. It is less robust than other types of chocolate, as it contains no cocoa solids. Do make sure that the base of the bowl is not touching the surface of the water.

3 Cut out a 9-inch square piece of baking parchment. Grease one side and 2 inches of the base of a 7-inch square cake pan. Fold the paper in half and fit the crease line into the greased corner of the pan so that the side and part of the base and ends are lined. Make sure the ends are greased under the lining paper, too.

4 Stir the cookies into the white chocolate mixture, followed by the chocolate mint sticks. Add the milk chocolate, stir quickly to combine then turn the mixture into the lined section of the pan. Hold the pan at an angle, then smooth the surface of the chocolate level. Place in the refrigerator, propping the pan up with another container to maintain the angle to form the pyramid shape. Leave for about 2 hours, until set.

5 Remove the cake from the pan, place on a flat plate and peel off the paper. In their wrappers, crush the mints with a rolling pin. Melt the reserved white chocolate in a heatproof bowl set over a pan of hot water.

6 Spread the white chocolate over the top sloping side of the pyramid, sprinkle with the crushed mints and press in lightly.

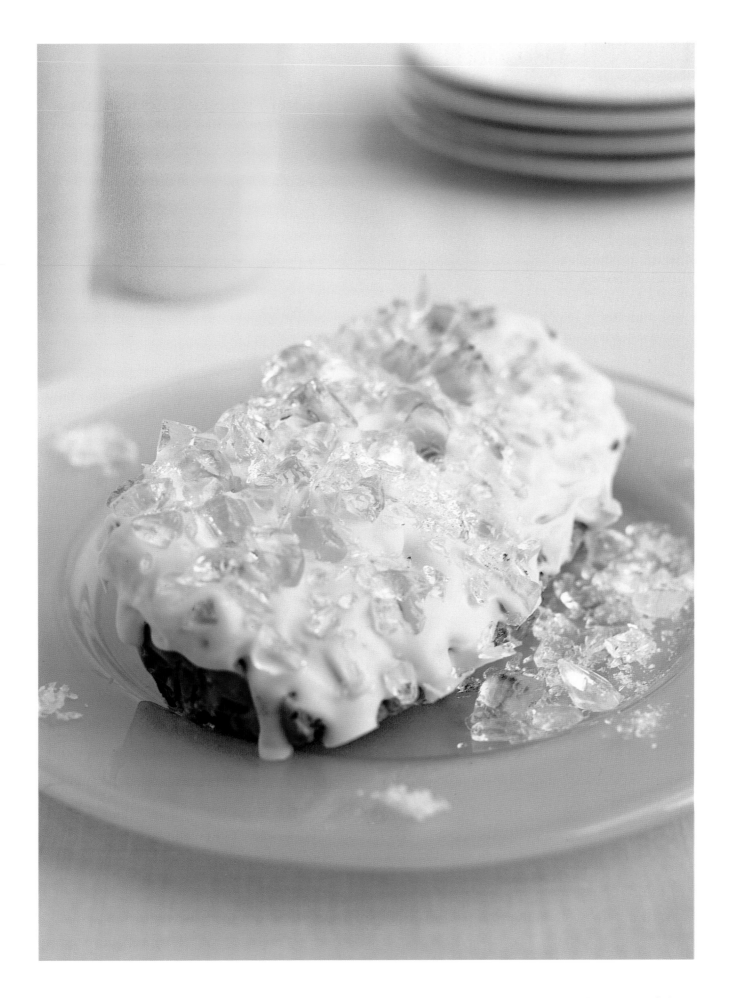

Pink Piggies

These are what you could call rainy-day cookies. They are fun to make and thoroughly absorbing when the family is stuck indoors. You might want to make up icings in other colors and experiment with your own animal variations. Children's books are a great source of inspiration.

Makes 10

3½ ounces/scant I cup
   confectioners' sugar, plus extra
   for dusting
2 ounces/¼ cup sweet butter,
   at room temperature, diced
10 plain cookies or
   graham crackers
7 ounces white ready-to-roll
   icing
pink food coloring
small, pink soft candies
tube of black writer icing

1 To make the buttercream, put the confectioners' sugar and butter in a bowl and beat with a hand-held electric whisk until smooth, pale and creamy.

2 Using a small metal spatula spread the plain cookies or graham crackers almost to the edges with the buttercream.

3 Reserve I ounce of the ready-to-roll icing and add a few drops of the pink food coloring to the remainder. Knead on a clean work surface that has been lightly dusted with confectioners' sugar, until the pink coloring is evenly distributed.

4 Reserve about I ounce of the pink icing. If necessary, lightly dust your work surface with more confectioners' sugar and roll out the remaining pink icing very thinly.

5 Using a cookie cutter that is just slightly smaller than the plain cookies or graham crackers, cut out round pieces of pink icing. Lay a piece over each cookie and press it down gently onto the buttercream.

6 Halve five of the pink candies and press into an oval shape. Make two small holes in each one with a wooden skewer or toothpick to make a nose.

7 Using a little of the buttercream, attach a halved candy to the center of each cookie.

8 Using the black writer icing, pipe two small dots of icing above the nose to resemble eyes, then pipe a small, curved mouth.

9 Thinly roll out the reserved pink icing and the reserved white icing. Dampen the white icing with a little water and press the pink icing gently on top. Using a small sharp knife, cut out triangles for ears.

10 Dampen one edge of the ears with a little water and secure, pink side up, to the cookies. Gently curl the ears out at the ends.

Cook's Tip
If you cannot get black writer icing, use any dark food coloring, such as black, blue or brown, and paint on the features with a fine brush.

Savory Crackers

Cheese and crackers is a classic combination, but there are many other occasions when a savory crunch is just what is needed. Crackers go well with home-made soup and salads for a light lunch and make delicious snacks when you want something with a little bite to it. This superb collection of tasty recipes offers something for all occasions, from sophisticated Wheat Thins to rustic Herbed Seeded Oatcakes.

Polenta Chip Dippers

These tasty Parmesan-flavored batons are best served warm from the oven with a spicy, tangy dip. A bowl of Thai chili dipping sauce or a creamy, chili-spiked guacamole are perfect.

2 Remove the pan from the heat and add the cheese, butter, pepper and salt to taste. Stir well until the butter has completely melted and the mixture is smooth.

3 Pour onto a smooth surface, such as a marble slab or a baking sheet. Spread the polenta out using a metal spatula to a thickness of ¾ of an inch and shape into a rectangle. Leave for at least 30 minutes to become quite cold. Meanwhile preheat the oven to 400°F/Gas 6 and lightly oil two or three baking sheets with some olive oil.

4 Cut the polenta slab in half, then carefully cut into even-size strips using a sharp knife.

5 Bake the polenta chips for about 40–50 minutes, until they are dark golden brown and crunchy. Turn them over from time to time during cooking. Serve warm.

Cook's Tip
The unbaked dough can be made a day ahead, then wrapped in plastic wrap and kept in the refrigerator until ready to bake.

Makes about 80

2½ pints/6¼ cups water
2 teaspoons salt
13 ounces/3¼ cups instant polenta
5 ounces/1½ cups freshly grated
   Parmesan cheese
3½ ounces/scant ½ cup butter
2 teaspoons cracked black pepper
olive oil, for brushing
salt

I Put the water in a large heavy pan and bring to the boil over a high heat. Reduce the heat, add the salt and pour in the polenta in a steady stream, stirring constantly with a wooden spoon. Cook over a low heat, stirring constantly, until the mixture thickens and starts to come away from the sides of the pan — this will take about 5 minutes.

Corn-meal Crackers

These are delicious served hot, straight from the oven and spread with butter. They are great for breakfast and also go well with soup for a light lunch.

Makes 12

2 ounces/½ cup corn meal, plus extra
  for sprinkling
6 ounces/1¼ cups all-purpose
  flour
2½ teaspoons baking powder
pinch of salt
6 ounces/¾ cup shortening or
  butter, diced
6 fluid ounces/¾ cup milk

1 Preheat the oven to 450°F/ Gas 8. Sprinkle a large ungreased baking sheet lightly with a little corn meal.

2 Sift together the flour, baking powder and salt into a bowl. Stir in the corn meal. Add the shortening or butter and rub into the dry ingredients with your fingertips until the mixture resembles coarse breadcrumbs.

3 Make a well in the center and pour in the milk. Stir in quickly with a wooden spoon until the dough begins to pull away from the sides of the bowl.

4 Turn the dough out onto a lightly floured surface and knead lightly 8–10 times only. Roll it out to a thickness of ½ inch. Stamp out into round pieces with a floured 2-inch cookie cutter.

5 Arrange the round dough pieces on the prepared baking sheet, spacing them about 1 inch apart. Sprinkle with a little corn meal, then bake for about 10–12 minutes, until golden brown.

Cocktail Shapes

Tiny savory crackers are always a welcome treat and make lovely party nibbles. Try making a range of shapes and flavoring them with different cheeses and spices.

Makes 80

12 ounces/3 cups all-purpose
   flour
pinch of salt
½ teaspoon ground black pepper
1 teaspoon wholegrain mustard
6 ounces/¾ cup sweet butter,
   chopped
4 ounces Cheddar cheese
1 egg, beaten
1 teaspoon chopped nuts
2 teaspoons dill seeds
2 teaspoons curry paste
2 teaspoons chili sauce

1 Line several large baking sheets with non-stick baking parchment and set aside.

2 Sift the flour into a large mixing bowl and add the salt, pepper and wholegrain mustard. Mix well.

3 Add the butter and rub it into the flour mixture with your fingertips until it resembles fine breadcrumbs. Grate the cheese then, with a fork, stir it into the butter and flour mixture until thoroughly incorporated. Add the beaten egg and mix together to form a soft dough.

4 Turn out the dough onto a floured surface, knead lightly until smooth, then divide it into four equal pieces.

5 Knead chopped nuts into one piece, dill seeds into another, and curry paste and chili sauce into the remaining pieces. Put each piece in plastic wrap and chill for at least 1 hour.

6 Preheat the oven to 400°F/Gas 6. Roll out each piece of dough in turn. Use a floured heart-shaped cutter to stamp out about 20 shapes from the curry-flavored dough. Use a club-shaped cutter to cut out the chili-flavored dough. Arrange the shapes spaced enough apart on the baking sheets and bake for 6–8 minutes, until slightly puffed and pale gold. Cool on wire racks.

7 Repeat with the remaining dough using spade- and diamond-shaped cutters. Knead any trimmings together, and make more shapes.

Spiced Cocktail Crackers

These prettily specked savory crackers are ideal for serving with pre-dinner drinks. Each of the spice seeds contributes to the flavor and makes them very irresistible, indeed.

Makes 20–30

5 ounces/1¼ cups all-purpose flour

2 teaspoons curry powder

4 ounces/½ cup butter, chopped

3 ounces/¾ cup grated
    Cheddar cheese

2 teaspoons poppy seeds

1 teaspoon black onion seeds

1 egg yolk

1 tablespoon cumin seeds

1 Grease two baking sheets. Sift the flour and curry powder into a large bowl. Add the butter and rub it in with your fingertips until the mixture resembles breadcrumbs.

2 Stir in the grated cheese, poppy seeds and black onion seeds until thoroughly combined. Stir in the egg yolk and mix to a firm dough. Put the dough in plastic wrap and chill for 30 minutes.

Cook's Tip

You can make these well in advance and freeze them until almost ready to serve. Spread out on baking sheets and reheat in a moderate oven.

Variation

Use caraway or sesame seeds instead of the poppy seeds, if you like.

3 Roll out the dough on a floured surface to a thickness of about ⅛ of an inch. Stamp out round pieces with a floured cookie cutter.

4 Arrange the dough pieces on the prepared baking sheets, spaced far apart, and sprinkle with the cumin seeds. Allow to chill for 15 minutes.

5 Meanwhile, preheat the oven to 375°F/Gas 5. Bake the crackers for about 20 minutes, until crisp and golden. Serve warm, or transfer to wire racks and leave to cool, and serve cold.

Cheese Scones

These delicious, old-fashioned scones make a good teatime treat. They are best served fresh and still slightly warm from the oven and are delicious served with soup.

Makes 12

8 ounces/2 cups all-purpose flour

2½ teaspoons baking powder

½ teaspoon mustard powder

½ teaspoon salt

2 ounces/¼ cup cold butter, chopped

3 ounces/¾ cup grated sharp
   Cheddar cheese

¼ pint/⅔ cup milk

1 egg, beaten

1 Preheat the oven to 450°F/Gas 8. Sift the flour, baking powder, mustard powder and salt into a mixing bowl. Add the butter and rub it in until the mixture resembles coarse breadcrumbs.

2 Stir 2 ounces/½ cup of the grated Cheddar cheese into the butter and flour mixture. Make a well in the center and pour in the milk and beaten egg. Stir gently using a wooden spoon until the mixture forms a soft, only slightly sticky dough.

3 Turn the dough out onto a lightly floured surface.

4 Roll out the dough and cut into triangles or squares. Place them on a baking sheet, brush lightly with milk and sprinkle with the remaining grated cheese. Leave to rest for about 15 minutes, then bake for 15 minutes, until well risen.

Cook's Tip
Don't overwork the dough, or roll it out too thinly, or the scones will be hard and not rise well.

Oatcakes

These are very simple to make and are an excellent addition to any cheese board. They also make a delicious snack spread with pâté and topped with slices of hard-boiled egg.

Makes 24

8 ounces/2¼ cups medium
   rolled oats, plus extra
   for sprinkling

3 ounces/⅔ cup all-purpose flour

¼ teaspoon baking soda

1 teaspoon salt

1 ounce/2 tablespoons shortening

1 ounce/2 tablespoons butter

Cook's Tip
You can store the oatcakes in an airtight container in a cool place for up to 1 week, but they are best eaten when freshly baked.

1 Preheat the oven to 425°F/Gas 7. Place the rolled oats, flour, baking soda and salt in a large bowl and mix well. Melt the shortening and the butter together in a small pan over a low heat.

2 Add the melted shortening and enough boiling water to the dry ingredients to make a dough. Turn out onto a surface sprinkled with rolled oats. Roll out thinly and stamp out 24 round pieces. Bake on ungreased baking sheets for 15 minutes.

Curry Crackers

Crisp curry-flavored crackers are very good with creamy cheese or yogurt dips and make an unusual nibble with pre-dinner drinks. Add a pinch of cayenne pepper for an extra kick.

Makes about 30

6 ounces/1½ cups self-rising flour

pinch of salt

2 teaspoons garam masala

3 ounces/6 tablespoons butter, diced

1 teaspoon finely chopped
  fresh cilantro

1 egg, beaten

For the topping

beaten egg

black onion seeds

garam masala

1 Preheat the oven to 400°F/Gas 6. Put the flour, salt and garam masala into a bowl. Rub in the butter until the mixture resembles fine breadcrumbs. Stir in the cilantro, add the egg and mix to a soft dough.

Cook's Tip

Garam masala is a mixture of Indian spices and usually contains a blend of cinnamon, cloves, peppercorns, cardamom seeds and cumin seeds. You can buy it ready-made, or make your own.

2 Turn out onto a lightly floured surface and knead gently until smooth. Roll out to a thickness of about ⅛ of an inch.

3 Using a fluted cookie wheel, knife or pizza wheel, cut the dough into neat rectangles measuring about 3 x 1 inches. Brush with a little beaten egg and sprinkle each cracker with a few black onion seeds. Place on non-stick baking sheets and bake in the oven for about 12 minutes, until the crackers are light golden brown all over.

4 Remove from the oven and transfer to a wire rack using a metal spatula. Put a little garam masala in a saucer and, using a dry pastry brush, dust each cracker with a little of the spice mixture. Leave to cool before serving.

Chili and Herb Crackers

These spicy, crisp little crackers are ideal for serving as a nibble with drinks and would also be an interesting alternative to bread or rolls, served with a seafood appetizer.

Makes 12

2 ounces/½ cup all-purpose
   flour
pinch of salt
1 teaspoon curry powder
¼ teaspoon chili powder
1 tablespoon chopped fresh
   cilantro
2 tablespoons water

1 Preheat the oven to 350°F/ Gas 4. Sift the flour and salt into a mixing bowl, then add the curry powder and chili powder and mix well. Make a well in the center and add the chopped fresh cilantro and water. Gradually incorporate the flour and mix to a firm dough.

2 Turn the dough out onto a lightly floured surface, knead until smooth, then cover and leave to rest for about 5 minutes.

3 Cut the dough into 12 even-size pieces and knead into small balls. Roll each ball out very thinly to a 4-inch round shape, sprinkling more flour over the dough, if necessary, to prevent it from sticking to the rolling pin.

4 Arrange the round forms on two ungreased baking sheets, spaced apart, then bake for 15 minutes, turning the crackers over once during cooking. Using a metal spatula, transfer the crackers to a wire rack to cool.

Dill and Potato Cakes

Serve these light savory cakes topped with thinly sliced smoked salmon and a spoonful of sour cream for a superb light lunch or dinner party appetizer.

Makes 10

8 ounces/2 cups self-rising flour
1½ ounces/3 tablespoons butter
pinch of salt
1 tablespoon finely chopped fresh dill
6 ounces/2 cups mashed potato,
   freshly made
2–3 tablespoons milk

Variation

For extra flavor, sift ½ teaspoon mustard powder with flour and add ½ finely chopped onion or 2 finely chopped scallions with the potato.

1 Preheat the oven to 450°F/ Gas 8. Grease a baking sheet. Sift the flour into a bowl and add the butter, salt and dill. Stir in the potato and add enough milk to mix to a soft dough.

2 Roll out the dough until fairly thin. Cut into neat round pieces with a floured 3-inch cookie cutter. Place the cakes on the prepared baking sheet and bake for 20–25 minutes.

Whole-wheat Herb Triangles

These make a good lunchtime snack when filled with chicken and salad, and are also an ideal accompaniment to a bowl of steaming soup.

Makes 8

8 ounces/2 cups whole-wheat flour

4 ounces/1 cup strong white
    bread flour

pinch of salt

½ teaspoon baking soda

1 teaspoon cream of tartar

½ teaspoon chili powder

2 ounces/¼ cup margarine, diced

4 tablespoons chopped mixed
    fresh herbs

8 fluid ounces/1 cup skimmed milk

1 tablespoon sesame seeds

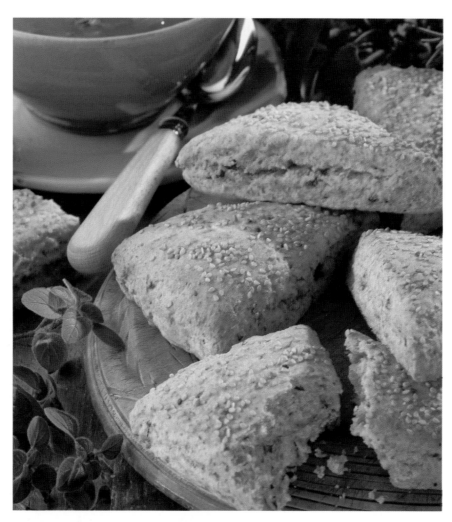

1 Preheat the oven to 425°F/Gas 7. Lightly flour a baking sheet. Put the flours into a mixing bowl. Sift together the salt, baking soda, cream of tartar and chili powder into the bowl, then rub in the margarine with your fingertips until the mixture resembles coarse breadcrumbs.

Variation

To make Sun-dried Tomato Triangles, replace the fresh mixed herbs with 2 tablespoons drained, chopped sun-dried tomatoes in oil, and add 1 tablespoon each mild paprika, chopped fresh parsley and chopped fresh marjoram. Add to the mixture in step 2.

2 Add the mixed fresh herbs and milk and mix quickly but thoroughly to a soft dough. Turn out onto a lightly floured surface. Knead only very briefly, or the dough will become tough.

3 Roll the dough out to a 9-inch round shape and place on the prepared baking sheet. Brush lightly with water and sprinkle the top evenly with the sesame seeds.

4 Carefully cut the round-shaped dough into eight wedges, separate them slightly and bake for 15–20 minutes, until golden brown. Using a metal spatula, transfer to a wire rack to cool. Serve warm or cold.

Herb and Garlic Twists

These twists are very short and crumbly, made with garlic-flavored dough sandwiched with fresh herbs, and some chili flakes for an extra kick. A very popular party nibble.

Makes about 20

3½ ounces/scant ½ cup butter,
   at room temperature, diced
2 large garlic cloves, crushed
1 egg
1 egg yolk
6 ounces/1½ cups self-rising flour
large pinch of salt
2 tablespoons chopped fresh mixed
   herbs, such as basil, thyme,
   marjoram and flat
   leaf parsley
½–1 teaspoon dried chili flakes
paprika or cayenne pepper,
   for sprinkling

1 Preheat the oven to 400°F/Gas 6. Put the butter and garlic into a bowl and beat well. Add the egg and yolk and beat in thoroughly. Stir in the flour and salt and mix to a soft but not sticky dough.

2 Roll the dough out on a sheet of baking parchment to an 11-inch square. Using a sharp knife, cut it in half to make two rectangles.

3 Sprinkle the herbs and chili flakes over one of the rectangles, then place the other rectangle on top. Gently roll the rolling pin over the herbs and chili flakes to press them into the dough.

4 Using a sharp knife, cut the dough into ½ inch sticks. Make two twists in the center of each one and place on a non-stick baking sheet.

5 Bake the twists for 15 minutes, or until crisp and golden brown. Leave on the baking sheet to cool slightly, then carefully transfer to a wire rack to cool completely. To serve, sprinkle with a little paprika or cayenne pepper, according to taste.

Cook's Tip

If the dough seems a little too soft to handle, put it in plastic wrap and chill in the refrigerator for about 15 minutes to firm up. It will be much easier to roll it out.

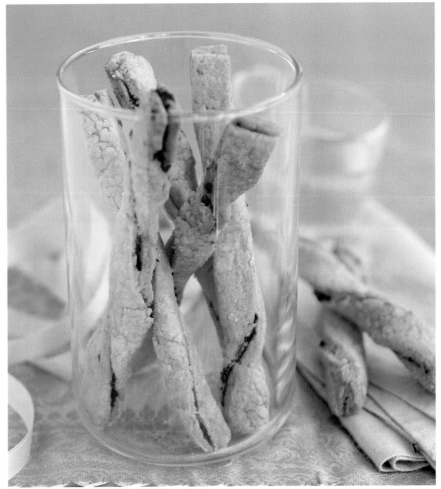

Fennel and Chili Rings

Based on an Italian recipe, these savory bakes are made with yeast and are dry and crumbly. Try them with drinks, dips or with antipasti.

Makes about 30

1 pound 2 ounces/4½ cups type 00 flour

4 ounces/½ cup shortening

1 teaspoon rapid-rise yeast

1 tablespoon fennel seeds

2 teaspoons crushed chili flakes

1 tablespoon olive oil

14–18 fluid ounces/1⅔–2½ cups
　lukewarm water

olive oil, for brushing

1 Put the flour in a bowl and rub in the shortening until the mixture resembles fine breadcrumbs. Add the yeast, fennel and chili and mix well. Add the oil and enough water to make a soft but not sticky dough. Turn out onto a floured surface and knead lightly.

2 Take small pieces of dough and shape into sausages about 6 inches long. Shape into rings and pinch the ends together.

3 Place the rings on a non-stick baking sheet and brush lightly with olive oil. Cover with a dishtowel and set aside at room temperature for 1 hour to rise slightly.

4 Meanwhile, preheat the oven to 300°F/Gas 2. Bake the rings for 1 hour, until they are dry and only slightly browned. Leave on the baking sheet to cool completely.

Cook's Tip

Type 00 is an Italian grade of flour used for pasta. It is milled from the center part of the endosperm so that the resulting flour is much whiter than all-purpose flour. It contains 70 percent of the wheat grain. It is available from Italian delicatessens and some large supermarkets. If you cannot find it, try using strong white bread flour instead.

Bacon Twists

Making bread is always good fun, so try this simple savory version and add that extra twist to breakfast or brunch. Choose good quality bacon, or try Italian pancetta or prosciutto for a change. Serve hot or warm with farmer's cheese with herbs for dipping or spreading.

Makes 12

1 pound/4 cups strong white
   bread flour
1 tablespoon rapid-rise
   dried yeast
pinch of salt
14 fluid ounces/1¾ cups
   lukewarm water
12 fatty bacon strips
1 egg, beaten

1 Place the flour, yeast and salt in a large bowl and stir them together until well combined.

2 Add a little of the lukewarm water to the flour mixture and mix with a round-bladed knife. Add the remaining water and use the knife and then one of your hands to pull the mixture together, to make a soft, slightly sticky dough.

3 Turn the dough out onto a lightly floured surface and knead for about 5 minutes, or until the dough is smooth and stretchy.

4 Divide the dough into 12 even-size pieces and roll each one into a fat sausage shape. Lightly brush a baking sheet with oil.

5 Place each bacon rasher on a chopping board and run the back of the knife along its length to stretch it slightly. Wind a rasher of bacon round each dough "sausage".

6 Brush the "sausages" with beaten egg and arrange them on the prepared baking sheet. Leave in a warm place for 30 minutes, or until doubled in size.

7 Preheat the oven to 400°F/Gas 6. Bake for 20–25 minutes, until cooked and browned. Serve hot or warm with farmer's cheese.

Cook's Tips
The same basic dough mix can be used to make plain rolls or a loaf of bread. At the end of the cooking time, tap the base of the loaf with your knuckles – if it sounds hollow, it's cooked.

Variations
Make some meat-free versions of these twists for vegetarians by twisting the dough by hand and sprinkling with poppy or sesame seeds before baking.

Walnut Biscotti

These light crunchy cookies with toasted walnuts are flavored with orange and coriander seeds.

Makes about 40

4 ounces/½ cup sweet butter, diced

7 ounces/1 cup granulated sugar

2 eggs

1 tablespoon walnut or olive oil

finely grated rind of 1 large orange

12 ounces/3 cups all-purpose flour

1½ teaspoons baking powder

3 ounces/¾ cup corn meal

4 ounces/1 cup toasted walnuts, chopped

2 teaspoons coriander seeds, crushed

Cook's Tip

To toast the nuts, spread them on a baking sheet and place in the oven at 325°F/Gas 3 for 5–7 minutes, until just beginning to brown.

1 Preheat the oven to 325°F/Gas 3. Put the butter and sugar into a bowl and beat together well. Add the eggs, walnut or olive oil and orange rind and mix well. Sift the flour and baking powder over the mixture and add the corn meal, walnuts and coriander seeds. Mix thoroughly and bring together to form a soft but not sticky dough.

2 Shape the dough into four logs, about 7 inches long and 2 inches in diameter. Place slightly apart on non-stick baking sheets. Bake for 35 minutes until lightly golden.

3 Leave the logs for 10 minutes on wire racks, then slice diagonally into ½-inch slices. Place on the baking sheets and bake for 10 minutes.

Sun-dried Tomato Butter Cookies

These buttery cookies have all the flavors of classic pizza – cheese, tomato, oregano and olives.

Makes about 25

6 ounces/1½ cups all-purpose flour

5 ounces/10 tablespoons sweet butter, chilled and diced

5 ounces/1¼ cups grated sharp Cheddar cheese

1 tablespoon sun-dried tomato paste

1 ounce semi-dried sun-dried tomatoes, coarsely chopped

1 tablespoon oregano

½ ounce/2 tablespoons pitted black olives, drained

1–2 tablespoons cold water

2 ounces sesame seeds

1 Put all the ingredients, except the water and sesame seeds, into a food processor. Process until the mixture forms fine crumbs.

2 Add enough water to mix to a soft dough, then shape it into a neat log about 10 inches long. Spread out the sesame seeds over a sheet of baking parchment or on a large plate. Roll the dough log in the seeds until the sides are thoroughly coated. Put in plastic wrap and chill for about 2 hours.

3 Preheat the oven to 350°F/Gas 4. Remove the plastic wrap from the dough log. Using a long, sharp knife, slice the log into ¼-inch slices and place on non-stick baking sheets, spaced slightly apart. Bake for 15–20 minutes, or until golden brown. Transfer the cookies to a wire rack to cool.

Malted Wheat and Mixed Seed Crackers

These large crackers have plenty of crunch and flavor provided by the selection of different seeds that are used. They taste fabulous with robust farmhouse cheeses.

Makes 12–14

9 ounces/2¼ cups whole-wheat or
   malted wheat flour
½ teaspoon salt
½ teaspoon baking powder
4 ounces/½ cup butter, chilled and diced
1 egg, beaten
2 tablespoons milk, plus extra for brushing
1 tablespoon pumpkin seeds
1 tablespoon sunflower seeds
1 tablespoon sesame seeds
½ teaspoon celery salt

1 Preheat the oven to 350°F/Gas 4. Put the flour, salt, baking powder and butter in a bowl. Rub together until well combined.

2 Add the egg and milk and mix to a stiff dough. Roll out on a floured surface to about ¼ inch thick.

3 Using a pastry brush, brush a little milk over the rolled dough. Sprinkle all the pumpkin, sunflower and sesame seeds over the top in an even layer, then sprinkle the celery salt over the top.

4 Very gently, roll the rolling pin back and forth over the seeds to press them into the dough.

5 Stamp out round pieces using a 4-inch plain cookie cutter, and place on a non-stick baking sheet, spacing them slightly apart. Alternatively, use a sharp knife to trim off the rough edges of the rolled out dough, then cut the dough into equal-size squares, rectangles or triangles.

6 Bake the crackers for about 15 minutes, or until just beginning to brown. Carefully transfer the crackers to a wire rack to cool completely.

Cook's Tips
• *To make your own celery salt, grind five parts lightly toasted celery seeds with one part sea salt. Transfer to an airtight container and store in a cool, dark place.*
• *You can also use other seeds, if you prefer. Try using poppy seeds in place of the sesame seeds.*

Poppy Seed and Sea Salt Crackers

These attractive little crackers are ideal to use as the base of drinks party canapés, or they can be served plain as tasty nibbles in their own right.

Makes 20

4 ounces/1 cup all-purpose flour

¼ teaspoon salt

1 teaspoon superfine sugar

½ ounce/1 tablespoon butter

1 tablespoon poppy seeds

about 6 tablespoons light cream

For the topping

a little milk

sea salt flakes

Variation

You can use black or white poppy seeds – or a mixture of the two – for these crackers, or substitute sesame, caraway or celery seeds, if you like.

1 Preheat the oven to 300°F/Gas 2. Put the flour, salt and sugar in a bowl and rub in the butter. Stir in the poppy seeds. Add enough cream to mix to a stiff dough. Roll out on a lightly floured surface to an 8 x 10 inch rectangle. Cut into 20 squares.

2 Place the dough squares on an ungreased baking sheet and brush sparingly with milk. Sprinkle a few sea salt flakes over each cracker.

3 Bake in the oven for 30 minutes until crisp but still pale. Transfer to a wire rack to cool.

Rye and Caraway Seed Sticks

Wonderful with cocktails or pre-dinner drinks and a great addition to the cheese board, these long sticks are made with rye flour and have crunchy caraway seeds inside and out.

Makes 18–20

3½ ounces/¾ cup all-purpose flour

3 ounces/⅔ cup rye flour

½ teaspoon salt

½ teaspoon baking powder

3½ ounces/7 tablespoons sweet
  butter, diced

2 teaspoons caraway seeds

4 tablespoons boiling water

1 Preheat the oven to 350°F/Gas 4. Put the flours, salt and baking powder in a bowl and mix together. Add the butter and rub in until the mixture resembles fine breadcrumbs. Stir in 1 teaspoon of the caraway seeds. Add the water and mix well to form a soft dough.

2 Divide the dough into about 18 even-size pieces and, using your fingers, gently roll each one out to a long thin stick about 10 inches long. Do not use any flour when rolling out the sticks, unless the mixture is a little too moist, and try to make the sticks as uniform as possible.

3 Place the sticks on a non-stick baking sheet. Sprinkle over the remaining caraway seeds, rolling the sticks in any spilled seeds.

4 Bake the sticks in the oven for about 20 minutes, until crisp. Remove from the oven and transfer carefully to a wire rack to cool.

Thyme and Mustard Crackers

These aromatic crackers are delicious served with herbed cheese as a light, savory last course. Wrap them in cellophane and tie with string for a pretty gift.

Makes 40

6 ounces/1½ cups whole-wheat flour

2 ounces/⅔ cup rolled oats

1 ounce/2 tablespoons superfine sugar

2 teaspoons baking powder

2 tablespoons fresh thyme leaves

2 ounces/¼ cup butter, diced

1 ounce/2 tablespoons shortening, diced

3 tablespoons milk

2 teaspoons Dijon mustard

2 tablespoons sesame seeds

salt and ground black pepper

1 Preheat the oven to 400°F/Gas 6. Grease two baking sheets. Put the flour, oats, sugar, baking powder, thyme leaves and seasoning into a bowl and mix together. Rub in the butter and shortening.

2 Mix the milk and mustard together and stir into the flour mixture until you have a soft dough.

3 Knead lightly on a floured surface then roll out to a thickness of ¼ inch. Stamp out 2-inch round pieces with a floured fluted cookie cutter, and arrange them, spaced slightly apart to allow room for spreading, on the baking sheets.

4 Re-roll the trimmings and continue stamping out round pieces until all the dough is used. Prick the crackers with a fork and sprinkle them with sesame seeds. Cook for 10–12 minutes, until golden.

5 Leave to cool completely on the baking sheets, then pack the crackers into a small airtight container. Store in a cool place for up to 5 days.

Wheat Thins

These classic wheat biscuits are especially delicious with rich-tasting creamy cheeses, and they also make a quick snack simply spread with butter when you are in a hurry.

Makes 18

6 ounces/1½ cups fine stoneground
   whole-wheat flour

pinch of salt

1 teaspoon baking powder

2 ounces/½ cup coarse oatmeal

1½ ounces/3 tablespoons granulated sugar

4 ounces/½ cup sweet butter, chilled
   and diced

Cook's Tip

These cookies are perfect for serving with a cheeseboard and look very pretty cut into different shapes. You could make star-shaped cookies for Christmas, or heart-shaped ones for Valentine's Day.

1 Preheat the oven to 375°F/Gas 5. Put all the ingredients into a food processor and process until the mixture starts to clump. Tip out onto a floured surface, gather the dough together with your hands and roll out.

2 Stamp out 18 round pieces with a 3-inch round cookie cutter. Place on an ungreased baking sheet. Bake for 12 minutes, until just beginning to color at the edges. Leave to cool slightly, then transfer to a wire rack to cool completely.

Herbed Seeded Oatcakes

The addition of thyme and sunflower seeds to this traditional recipe makes these oatcakes an especially good accompaniment to cheese – try them spread with chèvre cheese or ripe Brie.

Makes 32

6 ounces/1½ cups plain whole-wheat flour
6 ounces/1½ cups fine oatmeal
1 teaspoon salt
¼ teaspoon baking soda
3 ounces/6 tablespoons shortening
1 tablespoon fresh thyme leaves, chopped
2 tablespoons sunflower seeds
rolled oats, for sprinkling

1 Preheat the oven to 300°F/Gas 2. Sprinkle two ungreased, non-stick baking sheets with rolled oats and set aside.

2 Put the flour, oats, salt and soda in a bowl and rub in the shortening until the mixture resembles fine breadcrumbs. Stir in the thyme.

3 Add just enough cold water (about 6–7 tablespoons) to the dry ingredients to mix to a stiff but not sticky dough.

4 Gently knead the dough on a lightly floured surface until smooth, then cut roughly in half and roll out one piece on a lightly floured surface to make a 9–10-inch round shape.

5 Sprinkle sunflower seeds over the dough and press them in with the rolling pin. Cut into triangles and arrange on one of the baking sheets. Repeat with the remaining dough. Bake for 45–60 minutes, until crisp but not brown. Cool on wire racks.

Cream-cheese Spirals

Not totally savory, yet not a sweet snack either, these attractive little spirals make delightfully adult canapés and are much easier to prepare than they look.

Makes 32

8 ounces/1 cup butter

8 ounces/1 cup cream cheese

2 teaspoons granulated sugar

8 ounces/2 cups all-purpose flour

1 egg white beaten with 1 tablespoon water, for glazing

granulated sugar, for sprinkling

For the filling

4 ounces/1 cup walnuts or pecan nuts, finely chopped

3 ounces/⅓ cup soft light brown sugar

1 teaspoon ground cinnamon

1 With an electric mixer, cream the butter, cream cheese and sugar until soft. Sift over the flour and mix to form a dough. Gather into a ball and divide in half. Flatten each piece, wrap in waxed paper and chill for at least 30 minutes.

2 To make the filling, mix together the chopped walnuts or pecan nuts, brown sugar and cinnamon. Preheat the oven to 375°F/Gas 5. Grease two baking sheets.

3 Roll out each half of dough thinly into a round shape about 11 inches in diameter. Trim the edges with a knife, using a dinner plate as a guide.

4 Brush the surface with the egg white glaze and sprinkle each round shape evenly with half the filling.

5 With a sharp knife, cut each round shape into quarters, and then cut each quarter into four sections, to form 32 triangles.

6 Starting from the base of the triangles, roll up to form spirals.

7 Place on the prepared baking sheets and brush with the remaining glaze. Sprinkle with granulated sugar. Bake for 15–20 minutes, until golden. Cool on a wire rack.

Herb Popovers

These tasty puffs are really easy to prepare and cook. Serve as an imaginative alternative to garlic bread to accompany salads, soups and stews.

Makes 12

1 ounce/2 tablespoons butter

3 eggs

8 fluid ounces/1 cup milk

6 ounces/1½ cups all-purpose flour

pinch of salt

1 small sprig each of fresh herbs, such as chives, tarragon, dill and parsley

1 Preheat the oven to 425°F/Gas 7. Grease 12 small ramekins or popover pans. Melt the butter in a small pan over a low heat.

2 Beat the eggs in a bowl until well blended. Beat in the milk, then beat in the melted butter.

3 Sift together the flour and salt into another bowl, then gradually beat the flour and salt into the egg mixture.

4 Strip the herb leaves from the stems and chop finely. Stir 2 tablespoons of the herbs into the batter.

5 Pour the batter into the prepared dishes or pans so they are half-full. Bake for 25–30 minutes, until golden. Do not open the oven door during baking time, or the popovers may fall. For slightly drier popovers, pierce each one with a knife after 30 minutes baking time and bake for a further 5 minutes. Serve hot.

Cheese Popovers

Light-as-air and full of flavor, these irresistible puffs are guaranteed to become a family favorite. Serve them as they are – fresh from the oven.

Makes 12

½ tablespoon butter

3 eggs

8 fluid ounces/1 cup milk

3 ounces/⅔ cup all-purpose flour

pinch of salt

¼ teaspoon paprika

3 ounces/1 cup freshly grated Parmesan cheese

1 Preheat the oven to 425°F/Gas 7. Grease 12 small ramekins or popover pans. Melt the butter in a small pan over a low heat.

2 Beat the eggs until blended, then beat in the milk and melted butter.

3 Sift together the flour, salt, and paprika, then beat into the egg mixture. Stir in the cheese.

4 Fill the prepared ramekins or popover pans so they are half-full. Bake for 25–30 minutes, until golden. Do not open the oven door during baking, or the popovers will fall. For drier popovers, pierce each one with a knife after 30 minutes baking time and bake for a further 5 minutes. Serve hot.

Cook's Tip

Use an electric mixer to beat the batter to make sure that it is thoroughly blended and incorporates plenty of air.

Salted Peanut Crackers

The combination of salt and sweet flavors in these little crackers is delicious. The texture is delightfully crunchy and will appeal particularly to adult tastes.

Makes 70

9 ounces/generous 1 cup soft
   light brown sugar, plus extra
   for dipping
12 ounces/3 cups all-purpose flour
½ teaspoon baking soda
4 ounces/½ cup butter at room
   temperature, diced
4 ounces/½ cup margarine
2 eggs
2 teaspoons vanilla extract
8 ounces/2 cups salted peanuts

1 Preheat the oven to 375°F/Gas 5. Lightly grease two baking sheets. Grease the base of a glass and dip in sugar.

2 Sift together the flour and baking soda and set aside.

3 With an electric mixer, cream the butter, margarine and sugar until light and fluffy. Beat in the eggs, one at a time, and then the vanilla extract. Gently fold in the flour mixture with a metal spoon.

4 Add the peanuts and gently stir them into the butter mixture until evenly combined.

5 Drop teaspoonfuls of the mixture, spaced 2 inches apart, onto the prepared baking sheets. Flatten with the prepared glass.

6 Bake for about 10 minutes, until lightly colored. With a metal spatula, carefully transfer to a wire rack to cool.

Cheddar Pennies

Serve these tasty snacks with pre-dinner drinks. Choose a strong-flavored Cheddar, or substitute Parmesan, Pecorino or a farmhouse Lancashire cheese.

Makes 20

2 ounces/4 tablespoons butter
   at room temperature, diced
4 ounces/1 cup freshly grated
   Cheddar cheese
1½ ounces/⅓ cup all-purpose
   flour
pinch of salt
pinch of chili powder

1 With an electric mixer, cream the butter until soft. Stir in the cheese, flour, salt and chili powder. Gather to form a dough.

2 Transfer the dough to a lightly floured work surface. Shape into a long cylinder about 1¼ inches in diameter. Wrap in waxed paper and chill for 1–2 hours.

3 Preheat the oven to 350°F/Gas 4. Grease one large or two medium-size baking sheets.

4 Cut the dough into ¼-inch thick slices and place on the prepared baking sheets. Bake for about 15 minutes.

Parmesan Tuiles

These lacy tuiles look very impressive, but they couldn't be easier to make. Believe it or not, they use only a single ingredient – Parmesan cheese.

Makes 8–10

4 ounces Parmesan cheese

❙ Preheat the oven to 400°F/Gas 6. Line two baking sheets with baking parchment. Grate the cheese using a fine grater, pulling it down slowly to make long strands.

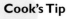

Cook's Tip

Tuiles can be made into little cup shapes by draping over an upturned egg cup. These little cups can be filled to make tasty treats to serve with drinks. Try a little cream cheese flavored with herbs.

2 Spread the grated cheese out in 3–3½-inch round shapes. Do not spread the cheese too thickly; it should just cover the parchment. Bake for 5–7 minutes until bubbling and golden brown.

3 Leave on the baking sheet for about 30 seconds and then carefully transfer, using a metal spatula to a wire rack. Alternatively, drape over a rolling pin to make a curved shape.

Savory Parmesan Puffs

Serve these tasty popovers with home-made soup or salad for a sustaining lunch or to accompany an appetizer for an impressive start to a dinner party menu.

Makes 6

4 ounces/1¼ cups freshly grated
   Parmesan cheese
4 ounces/1 cup all-purpose flour
pinch of salt
1 tablespoon butter or margarine
2 eggs
8 fluid ounces/1 cup milk

1 Preheat the oven to 450°F/Gas 8. Grease six individual baking pans. Sprinkle each pan with 1 tablespoon of the grated Parmesan. Alternatively, you can use ramekins, in which case, heat them on a baking sheet in the oven, then grease and sprinkle with Parmesan just before filling.

2 Sift the flour and salt into a small bowl. Set aside. Melt the butter or margarine in a small pan.

3 Beat together the eggs, milk and melted butter or margarine in a mixing bowl. Add the flour mixture and stir until smoothly blended.

Variation
You could also use another hard or semi-hard cheese, such as Pecorino, Gruyère or Emmenthal.

4 Divide the batter evenly among the containers, filling each one about half-full. Bake for 15 minutes, then sprinkle the tops of the puffs with the remaining Parmesan.

5 Reduce the oven temperature to 350°F/Gas 4 and continue baking for 20–25 minutes, or until the puffs are firm and golden brown.

6 Remove the puffs from the oven. To unmold, run a thin knife around the inside of each container to loosen them. Gently ease out, then transfer to a wire rack to cool.

Tiny Cheese Puffs

These bite-size portions of choux pastry are the ideal accompaniment to a glass of chilled white wine or to cocktails before dinner. They are delicious on their own, but are also good split and filled with garlic-flavored farmer's cheese, or mascarpone flavored with fresh parsley.

Makes 45

4 ounces/1 cup all-purpose flour

pinch of salt

1 teaspoon mustard powder

pinch of cayenne pepper

8 fluid ounces/1 cup water

4 ounces/½ cup butter, diced

4 eggs

3 ounces Gruyère cheese, finely diced

1 tablespoon finely chopped fresh chives

1 Preheat the oven to 400°F/ Gas 6. Lightly grease two large baking sheets.

2 Sift together the flour, salt, mustard powder and cayenne pepper.

Variations

To make Ham and Cheese Puffs, add 2 ounces/⅓ cup finely diced ham or prosciutto with the cheese. For Cheese Herb Puffs, stir in 2 tablespoons chopped fresh herbs or scallions with the cheese.

Cook's Tip

The puffs can be prepared ahead and are suitable for freezing. Thaw at room temperature for an hour or so, then reheat them in a hot oven for about 5 minutes, until crisp, before serving.

3 In a pan, bring the water and butter to the boil over a medium-high heat. Remove the pan from the heat and add the flour mixture all at once, beating with a wooden spoon until the dough forms a ball.

4 Return the pan to the heat and beat constantly for 1–2 minutes to dry out. Remove the pan from the heat and cool for 3–5 minutes.

5 Beat three of the eggs into the dough, one at a time, beating well after each addition.

6 Beat the fourth egg in a separate small bowl and add to the dough a teaspoon at a time, beating until the dough is smooth and shiny and falls slowly when dropped from a spoon. (You may not need all of the fourth egg; reserve any remaining egg for glazing.)

7 Stir the diced cheese and chives into the dough.

8 Using two teaspoons, drop small mounds of dough, spaced about 2 inches apart, onto the prepared baking sheets.

9 Beat any remaining egg with 1 tablespoon water and brush the tops of the choux puffs with the glaze.

10 Bake for 8 minutes, then reduce the oven temperature to 350°F/ Gas 4 and bake the puffs for a further 7–8 minutes, until puffed and golden. Transfer to a wire rack to cool. Serve warm.

Three-cheese Crumble Cookies

A delicious combination of mozzarella, Red Leicester and Parmesan cheese and the fresh taste of pesto make these cookies totally irresistible. Make mini ones to serve with drinks.

Makes 10

8 ounces/2 cups self-rising flour

2 ounces/¼ cup butter, diced

2 ounces mozzarella cheese, diced

2 ounces Red Leicester cheese, diced

1 tablespoon fresh pesto

1 egg

4 tablespoons milk

½ ounce/2 tablespoons grated
    Parmesan cheese

1 tablespoon mixed chopped nuts

▌ Preheat the oven to 400°F/Gas 6. Put the flour in a bowl and rub in the butter until the mixture resembles fine breadcrumbs.

2 Add the diced mozzarella and Red Leicester cheeses to the bowl and stir to mix well. In a separate bowl, beat together the pesto, egg and milk, then pour into the flour and cheese mixture. Stir together quickly until well combined.

3 Using a tablespoon, place in rocky piles on non-stick baking sheets. Sprinkle over the Parmesan cheese and chopped nuts. Bake for 12–15 minutes, until well risen and golden brown. Transfer to a wire rack to cool.

Blue Cheese and Chive Crisps

A classic combination and one that never fails to please – serve these tasty crackers with a selection of dips and spreads as part of a party buffet.

Makes 48

8 ounces/2 cups crumbled blue cheese

4 ounces/½ cup sweet butter at room
   temperature, diced

1 egg

1 egg yolk

2 teaspoons chopped fresh chives

8 ounces/2 cups all-purpose
   flour, sifted

ground black pepper

1 The day before serving, beat together the cheese and butter until well blended. Add the egg, egg yolk, chives and a little pepper and beat until just blended.

2 Add the flour in three batches, folding in between each addition.

3 Divide the dough in half and then shape each half into a log about 2 inches in diameter. Wrap in waxed paper and chill overnight. Preheat the oven to 375°F/Gas 5. Lightly grease two baking sheets.

4 Using a sharp knife, cut the dough logs across into slices about ⅛ inch thick. Place on the prepared baking sheets. Bake for about 10 minutes, until just golden around the edges. With a metal spatula, transfer to a wire rack to cool.

Cook's Tip

The cheese crisps will keep for up to 10 days in an airtight container.

Wisconsin Cheddar and Chive Crackers

These soft-textured crackers are almost like scones. They are delicious warm, split and spread with butter. Serve with soup or to accompany a rich-flavored stew.

Makes 20

7 ounces/1¾ cups all-purpose
   flour
2 teaspoons baking powder
½ teaspoon baking soda
pinch of salt
¼ teaspoon ground black pepper
2½ ounces/5 tablespoons sweet
   butter, diced
2 ounces/½ cup grated sharp
   Cheddar cheese
2 tablespoons chopped
   fresh chives
6 fluid ounces/¾ cup
   buttermilk

1 Preheat the oven to 400°F/Gas 6. Grease a baking sheet.

2 Sift the flour, baking powder, baking soda, salt and pepper into a large bowl. Add the butter and rub it into the dry ingredients with your fingertips until the mixture resembles coarse breadcrumbs. Add the cheese and chives and stir to mix.

3 Make a well in the center of the mixture. Add the buttermilk and stir vigorously until the mixture comes away from the sides of the bowl.

4 Drop in 2-tablespoon mounds spaced 2–3 inches apart on the prepared baking sheet. Bake for 12–15 minutes until golden brown.

Corn Oysters

Fried rather than baked, these savory snacks are best served hot by themselves or as an accompaniment to meat or chicken dishes.

Makes about 8

5 ounces/1 cup grated fresh
   corn kernels
1 egg, separated
2 tablespoons all-purpose flour
pinch of salt
¼ teaspoon ground black pepper
1–2 ounces/2–4 tablespoons butter
   or margarine
2–4 tablespoons vegetable oil

1 Combine the grated corn kernels, egg yolk and flour in a bowl. Mix well. Add the salt and black pepper.

2 In a separate, grease-free bowl, whisk the egg white until it forms stiff peaks. Carefully fold it into the corn mixture with a metal spoon.

3 Heat 2 tablespoons butter or margarine with 2 tablespoons of the oil in a heavy frying pan.

4 When the fats are very hot and almost smoking, drop tablespoonfuls of the corn mixture into the pan. Cook over a medium heat until crisp and brown on the undersides.

5 Turn the "oysters" over with a spatula and cook for 1–2 minutes on the other side. Drain well on kitchen paper and keep hot. Continue frying the remaining "oysters", adding more fat as necessary.

Cheese Straws

Everyone loves these crisp, cheesy sticks, so it is fortunate that they are so quick and easy to make. They are perfect for serving with pre-dinner drinks or as party snacks.

Makes 50 straws and 8 rings

4 ounces/1 cup all-purpose flour,
    plus extra for dusting
1 teaspoon mustard powder
pinch of salt
4 ounces/½ cup butter
3 ounces/¾ cup grated Cheddar cheese
pinch of cayenne pepper
2 tablespoons water
1 egg, beaten

1 Preheat the oven to 400°F/Gas 6. Grease two baking sheets. Sift the flour, mustard powder and salt into a bowl and rub in the butter until the mixture resembles fine breadcrumbs.

2 Stir in the grated cheese and cayenne pepper and sprinkle on the water. Add half the beaten egg, mix to a firm dough and knead lightly until smooth.

3 Roll out the dough pastry on a lightly floured surface and cut into strips about 4 inches long and ¼ inch wide.

4 Gather up the trimmings, roll them out and stamp out round pieces using two cookie cutters of different sizes, a 2½-inch one to cut out the round piece and a 2-inch diameter one to stamp out the center to make rings.

5 Arrange the straws and rings on the baking sheets, brush with egg and bake for 8–10 minutes.

6 Leave on the baking sheets to cool slightly for about 2 minutes, then transfer to wire racks to cool completely. To serve, push six or seven straws through each ring.

Variation
You can use other types of cheese for making the pastry. Try Parmesan, Pecorino, Emmenthal, Mahon or, for extra color, Red Leicester. For a less spicy flavor, substitute sweet paprika for the cayenne pepper.

Cook's Tip
Some or all of the cheese straws can be sprinkled with poppy, sunflower and/or sesame seeds before baking. A mixture of plain and coated straws looks attractive.

Festive Nibbles

Shape these spicy cheese snacks in any way you wish – stars, crescent moons, triangles, squares, hearts, or round shapes. Serve them with drinks, from ice-cold cocktails to hot and spicy mulls.

Makes 60

4 ounces/1 cup all-purpose flour, plus
    extra for dusting
1 teaspoon mustard powder
pinch of salt
4 ounces/½ cup butter
3 ounces/¾ cup grated Cheddar cheese
pinch of cayenne pepper
2 tablespoons water
1 egg, beaten
poppy seeds, sunflower seeds or sesame
    seeds, to decorate

1 Preheat the oven to 400°F/Gas 6. Grease two baking sheets. Sift the flour, mustard powder and salt into a bowl and rub in the butter until the mixture resembles fine breadcrumbs.

2 Stir in the grated cheese and cayenne pepper and sprinkle on the water. Add half the beaten egg, mix to a firm dough and knead lightly until smooth.

3 Roll out the dough on a lightly floured surface and cut out a variety of shapes with cutters, or freehand with a sharp knife. Re-roll the trimmings and cut out more shapes.

4 Place on the prepared baking sheets and brush with the remaining egg. Sprinkle on the seeds. Bake for 8–10 minutes, until golden. Transfer to wire racks to cool completely before serving.

Wholesome Bites

When anyone is trying to lose weight or eat a healthier diet, the first items to be scrapped are almost always cookies, but this doesn't have to be the case. The recipes in this chapter are nutritious and delicious, packed with fruit, fiber and flavor. Many are low in fat and use natural sweeteners rather than refined sugars. You don't even have to sacrifice "chocolate" cookies. They are the perfect pick-me-up for adults and ideal for after-school snacks.

Coconut Oat Cookies

Toasting the oats and coconut before mixing them with the other ingredients is the secret of both the delicious flavor and the lovely crunchy texture of these cookies. You'll need to keep an eye on the oats and coconut, as they will burn if cooked too long.

Makes 18

4 ounces/½ cup granulated sugar

6 ounces/2 cups quick-cooking oats

3 ounces/1 cup shredded coconut

8 ounces/1 cup butter or margarine at room temperature, diced

1½ ounces/¼ cup firmly packed dark brown soft sugar

2 eggs

4 tablespoons milk

1½ teaspoons vanilla extract

4 ounces/1 cup all-purpose flour

½ teaspoon baking soda

pinch of salt

1 teaspoon ground cinnamon

1 Preheat the oven to 400°F/Gas 6. Lightly grease two baking sheets. Grease the base of a glass and dip in some granulated sugar.

2 Spread the oats and coconut on an ungreased baking sheet. Bake for 8–10 minutes, until golden brown, stirring occasionally.

3 Cream the fat and both sugars. Beat in the eggs, then add the milk and vanilla. Sift the dry ingredients and fold in. Stir in the oat mixture.

4 Drop spoonfuls of the dough onto the baking sheets and flatten with the sugared glass. Bake for 8–10 minutes. Cool on a wire rack.

Crunchy Jumbles

Making up your mind about whether you prefer milk or semisweet chocolate chips is the perfect excuse for baking another batch of these tasty cookies.

Makes 36

4 ounces/½ cup butter or margarine at room temperature, diced

8 ounces/1 cup granulated sugar

1 egg

1 teaspoon vanilla extract

6 ounces/1¼ cups all-purpose flour

½ teaspoon baking soda

pinch of salt

4 ounces/2 cups crisped rice cereal

6 ounces/1 cup chocolate chips

1 Preheat the oven to 350°F/Gas 4. Lightly grease two or three large baking sheets.

2 With an electric mixer, cream the butter or margarine and sugar until light and fluffy. Beat in the egg and vanilla extract. Sift over the flour, baking soda and salt and fold in until just mixed.

Variation

To make Crunchy Walnut Jumbles, add 2 ounces/½ cup walnuts, coarsely chopped, with the cereal and chocolate.

3 Add the cereal and chocolate chips and stir thoroughly to mix. Drop spoonfuls of the dough onto the baking sheets. Bake for 10–12 minutes, until golden and cooked. Transfer to a wire rack to cool.

Crunchy Oatmeal Cookies

Any-time-of-day cookies, these are delicious with morning coffee or as a great after-school treat for hungry children. The combination of crunchy cereal and oats is highly nutritious, providing protein, carbohydrates, vitamins and minerals – and the cookies taste wonderful.

Makes 14

6 ounces/¾ cup butter or margarine
   at room temperature, diced

4½ ounces/¾ cup superfine
   sugar

1 egg yolk

6 ounces/1½ cups all-purpose flour,
   plus extra for dusting

1 teaspoon baking soda

pinch of salt

1½ ounces/½ cup rolled oats

1½ ounces/½ cup crunchy nugget
   cereal

1 Cream the butter or margarine and sugar together until light and fluffy. Mix in the egg yolk.

2 Sift over the flour, baking soda and salt, then stir into the butter mixture. Add the oats and cereal and stir to blend. Chill for at least 20 minutes.

3 Preheat the oven to 375°F/Gas 5. Grease a baking sheet. Flour the base of a wide, heavy glass.

4 Using two spoons, drop teaspoons of the dough onto the prepared baking sheet, spaced far apart. Gently flatten them with the floured base of the glass, dusting it with more flour if necessary.

5 Bake for 10–12 minutes, until golden. With a metal spatula, transfer the cookies to a wire rack. Allow to cool completely before serving or storing.

Variation
To make nutty oatmeal cookies, substitute an equal quantity of chopped walnuts or pecan nuts for the cereal, and prepare as described in the recipe.

Cook's Tip
These cookies will store for a week in an airtight container.

Granola Cookies

These are popular American cookies, which are packed with flavor. Use almonds, peanuts or pistachios in place of the walnuts, if you prefer.

Makes 18

4 ounces/½ cup butter or margarine
   at room temperature, diced
3 ounces/½ cup soft light brown sugar
3 ounces/⅓ cup crunchy peanut butter
1 egg
2 ounces/½ cup all-purpose flour
½ teaspoon baking powder
½ teaspoon ground cinnamon
pinch of salt
8 ounces/2 cups granola
2 ounces/⅓ cup raisins
2 ounces/½ cup walnuts, chopped

1 Preheat the oven to 350°F/Gas 4. Lightly grease two baking sheets. Put the butter or margarine in a large bowl.

2 With an electric mixer, cream the butter or margarine and sugar until light and fluffy. Beat in the peanut butter, then beat in the egg.

3 Sift together the flour, baking powder, cinnamon and salt over the peanut butter mixture and stir with a wooden spoon to blend well.

4 Add the granola, raisins and chopped walnuts and stir well.

5 Drop rounded tablespoonfuls of the dough onto the prepared baking sheets, spacing them about 1 inch apart. Press gently with the back of a spoon to spread each mound into a round shape.

6 Bake the cookies for about 15 minutes, until lightly colored. Remove the baking sheets from the oven and, with a metal spatula, transfer the cookies to a wire rack. Leave to cool completely.

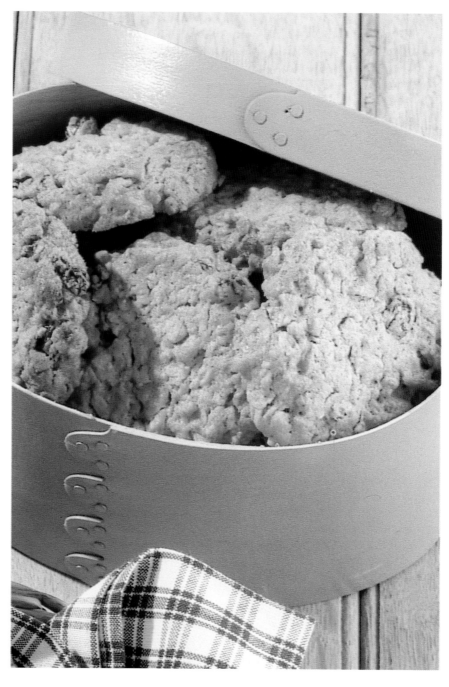

Low-fat Orange Oaties

These are so delicious that it is difficult to believe that they are healthy, too. As they are packed with flavor and wonderfully crunchy, the whole family will love them.

Makes about 16

6 ounces/¾ cup clear honey

4 fluid ounces/½ cup orange juice

3½ ounces/1 cup rolled oats, lightly toasted

4 ounces/1 cup all-purpose flour

4 ounces/generous ½ cup golden superfine sugar

finely grated rind of 1 orange

1 teaspoon baking soda

1 Preheat the oven to 350°F/ Gas 4. Line two baking sheets with baking parchment.

2 Put the honey and orange juice in a small pan and simmer over a low heat for 8–10 minutes, stirring occasionally, until the mixture is thick and syrupy.

3 Put the oats, flour, sugar and orange rind into a bowl. Mix the baking soda with 1 tablespoon of boiling water and add to the flour mixture, together with the honey and orange syrup. Mix well with a wooden spoon.

4 Place spoonfuls of the mixture onto the prepared baking sheets, spaced slightly apart, and bake for 10–12 minutes, or until golden brown. Leave to cool on the sheets for 5 minutes before transferring to a wire rack to cool completely.

Apricot Yogurt Cookies

These soft cookies are very quick to make and are perfect for children's school lunches, as they taste great and are low in fat, not too sweet and full of natural goodness.

Makes about 16

6 ounces/1½ cups all-purpose
   flour
1 teaspoon baking powder
1 teaspoon ground cinnamon
3 ounces/scant 1 cup
   rolled oats
3 ounces/⅓ cup light
   brown sugar
4 ounces/¾ cup chopped ready-to-eat
   dried apricots
1 tablespoon sliced hazelnuts
   or almonds
5 ounces/⅔ cup plain yogurt
3 tablespoons sunflower oil
raw sugar,
   for sprinkling

1 Preheat the oven to 375°F/ Gas 5. Lightly grease a large baking sheet.

2 Sift together the flour, baking powder and cinnamon. Stir in the oats, sugar, apricots and nuts.

Cook's Tip
These moist cookies do not keep well, so it is best to eat them within 2 days, or to freeze them. Pack the cookies into plastic bags and freeze for up to 4 months.

3 Beat together the yogurt and sunflower oil, then stir evenly into the flour mixture to make a firm dough. If necessary, add a little more yogurt. Use the palms of your hands to roll the mixture into about 16 small balls.

4 Place the balls on the prepared baking sheet and flatten gently with a fork. Sprinkle with raw sugar. Bake for 15–20 minutes, until firm and golden brown. With a spatula, transfer to a wire rack and leave to cool completely.

Chewy Flapjacks

Flapjacks are about the easiest cookies to make and, with a little guidance, can be put together in minutes by even the youngest cooks. This chunky, chewy version is flavored with orange rind.

Makes 18

9 ounces/generous 1 cup
  sweet butter
finely grated rind of 1 large orange
8 ounces/⅔ cup light corn syrup
3 ounces/⅓ cup light brown
  sugar
3 ounces/3¾ cups rolled oats

1 Preheat the oven to 350°F/Gas 4. Line the base and sides of an 11 x 8 inch shallow baking pan with baking parchment.

2 Put the butter, orange rind, syrup and sugar in a large pan and heat gently until the butter has melted.

3 Add the oats to the pan and stir to mix thoroughly. Tip the mixture into the pan and spread into the corners in an even layer.

4 Bake for 15–20 minutes, until just beginning to color around the edges. (The mixture will still be very soft but will harden as it cools.) Leave to cool in the pan.

5 Lift the flapjack out of the tin in one piece and cut into fingers.

Cook's Tip
Don't be tempted to overcook flapjacks; they'll turn crisp and dry, and lose their lovely chewy texture.

Apricot and Pecan Flapjack

A tried-and-tested favorite made even more delicious by the addition of maple syrup, fruit and nuts. This is a real energy booster at any time of day – great for kids and adults alike.

Makes 10

5 ounces/⅔ cup sweet butter, diced

5 ounces/⅔ cup light brown sugar

2 tablespoons maple syrup

7 ounces/2 cups rolled oats

2 ounces/½ cup pecan nuts, chopped

2 ounces/¼ cup ready-to-eat dried
  apricots, chopped

Variations

• *You can substitute walnuts for the pecan nuts, if you like, although the nutty flavor won't be so intense.*

• *Use different dried fruits instead of the apricots, if you like. Let children choose their own.*

1 Preheat the oven to 325°F/Gas 3. Lightly grease a 7-inch square shallow baking pan. Put the butter, sugar and maple syrup in a large heavy pan and heat gently until the butter has melted. Remove from the heat and stir in the oats, nuts and apricots until well combined.

2 Spread evenly in the prepared pan and, using a knife, score the mixture into ten bars. Bake for about 25–30 minutes, or until golden.

3 Remove from the oven and cut through the scored lines. Leave until completely cold before removing from the pan.

Ker-runch Cookies

An unusual coating of bran flakes covers these small cookies – a painless way of making sure that you have plenty of fiber in your diet. They are fun to make, too.

Makes about 18

6 ounces/¾ cup vegetable
   margarine

6 ounces/¾ cup light brown sugar

I egg

6 ounces/1½ cups self-rising
   whole-wheat flour

4 ounces/generous I cup
   rolled oats

4 ounces/⅔ cup mixed dried fruit

2 ounces/2 cups bran flakes
   breakfast cereal

I Preheat the oven to 325°F/Gas 3. Line two baking sheets with baking parchment. Put the margarine and sugar in a bowl and beat until pale and creamy.

2 Add the egg to the margarine mixture and beat in until thoroughly combined. Stir in the flour, oats and fruit. Roll into walnut-size balls between the palms of your hands. Spread out the bran flakes on a shallow plate and roll the balls in them to coat.

3 Place on the prepared baking sheets and flatten each one gently with your hand.

4 Bake for about 20 minutes, until firm and golden brown. Remove from the baking sheets while still hot, as these cookies firm up very quickly. Place on a wire rack to cool.

Fruity Breakfast Bars

Instead of buying fruit and cereal bars from the supermarket, try making this quick and easy version – they are tastier and more nutritious than most of the commercially-made ones.

Makes 12

10-ounce jar apple sauce

4 ounces/1½ cup ready-to-eat dried apricots, chopped

4 ounces/¾ cup raisins

2 ounces/¼ cup raw sugar

2 ounces/⅓ cup sunflower seeds

1 ounce/2 tablespoons sesame seeds

1 ounce/¼ cup pumpkin seeds

3 ounces/scant 1 cup rolled oats

3 ounces/⅔ cup self-rising whole-wheat flour

2 ounces/⅔ cup dried unsweetened shredded coconut

2 eggs

Cook's Tip

Allow the baking parchment to hang over the edges of the pan; this makes baked bars easier to remove.

1 Preheat the oven to 400°F/ Gas 6. Grease an 8-inch square shallow baking pan and line with baking parchment.

2 Put the apple sauce in a large bowl with the apricots, raisins, sugar and the sunflower, sesame and pumpkin seeds, and stir together with a wooden spoon until thoroughly mixed.

3 Add the oats, flour, coconut and eggs to the fruit mixture and gently stir together until evenly combined.

4 Turn the mixture into the pan and spread to the edges in an even layer. Bake for about 25 minutes, or until golden and just firm to the touch.

5 Leave to cool in the pan, then lift out onto a board and cut into bars.

Chewy Fruit Granola Slice

An easy recipe that just needs measuring out, mixing together, pressing into a cake pan and baking. The only other instruction is to eat it – and you will find that it tastes delicious.

Makes 8

3 ounces/¾ cup ready-to-eat dried
  apricots, chopped

1 eating apple, cored and grated

5 ounces/1¼ cups Swiss-style
  granola

¼ pint/⅔ cup apple juice

½ ounce/1 tablespoon soft
  sunflower margarine

1 Preheat the oven to 375°F/Gas 5. Place all five of the ingredients in a large bowl and mix well with a wooden spoon.

2 Press the mixture into an 8-inch non-stick layer pan, and bake for 35–40 minutes, or until lightly browned and firm.

3 Mark the granola slice into eight equal wedges with the blade of a knife and leave to cool completely in the pan.

Malted Oaty Crisps

These sweet cookies are made with rolled oats and flavored with malt. They are very crisp and crunchy and are ideal to serve with morning coffee or a cup of tea in the afternoon.

Makes 18

6 ounces/1½ cups rolled oats

3 ounces/⅓ cup light brown sugar

1 egg

4 tablespoons sunflower oil

2 tablespoons malt syrup

Variation

To give these crisp cookies a coarser texture, substitute jumbo oats for some or all of the rolled oats.

1 Preheat the oven to 375°F/Gas 5. Lightly grease two baking sheets. Mix the rolled oats and brown sugar in a bowl, breaking up any lumps in the sugar. Add the egg, sunflower oil and malt syrup, mix well, then leave to soak for about 15 minutes.

2 Using a teaspoon, place small heaps of the mixture far apart on the baking sheets. Press the heaps into 3-inch round shapes with the back of a dampened fork.

3 Bake for 10–15 minutes, until golden brown. Leave to cool for 1 minute, then remove to cool on a wire rack.

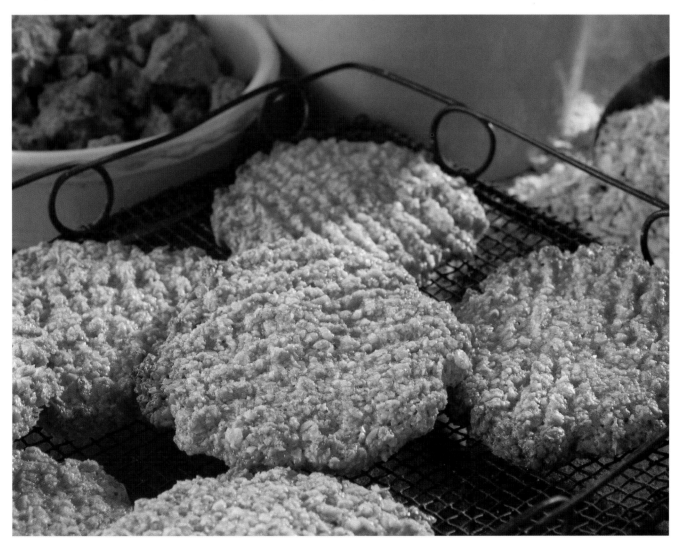

Almond, Orange and Carrot Bars

An out-of-this-world cookie version of the ever-popular carrot cake, these flavorsome, moist bars are best eaten fresh or stored in the refrigerator after making.

Makes 16

3 ounces/6 tablespoons sweet
  butter, softened
2 ounces/¼ cup superfine sugar
5 ounces/1¼ cups all-purpose flour
finely grated rind of 1 orange

For the filling

3½ ounces/7 tablespoons sweet
  butter, diced
3 ounces/scant ½ cup superfine sugar
2 eggs
½ teaspoon almond extract
6 ounces/1½ cups ground almonds
1 cooked carrot, coarsely grated

For the topping

6 ounces/¾ cup cream cheese
2–3 tablespoons chopped walnuts

1 Preheat the oven to 375°F/Gas 5. Lightly grease an 11 x 7-inch shallow baking pan. Put the butter, superfine sugar, flour and orange rind into a bowl and rub together until the mixture resembles coarse breadcrumbs. Add water, a teaspoon at a time, to mix to a firm but not sticky dough. Roll out on a lightly floured surface and use to line the base of the pan.

2 To make the filling, cream the butter and sugar together. Beat in the eggs and almond extract. Stir in the ground almonds and the grated carrot. Spread the mixture over the dough base and bake for about 25 minutes, until firm in the center and golden brown. Leave to cool in the pan.

3 To make the topping, beat the cream cheese until smooth and spread it over the cooled, cooked filling. Swirl with a small metal spatula and sprinkle with the chopped walnuts. Cut into bars with a sharp knife.

Tropical Fruit Slice

Densely packed dried exotic fruits make the filling for these deliciously moist bars. They make a popular after-school snack for hungry kids, or you could pop one into their lunch box as a surprise.

Makes 12–16

6 ounces/1½ cups all-purpose flour

3½ ounces/generous ½ cup
   shortening

4 tablespoons apricot jam, sieved, or
   ready-made apricot glaze

For the filling

4 ounces/½ cup sweet
   butter, softened

4 ounces/generous ½ cup
   superfine sugar

1 egg, beaten

1 ounce/¼ cup ground almonds

1 ounce/2½ tablespoons ground rice

11 ounces/scant 2 cups
   ready-to-eat mixed dried tropical
   fruits, chopped

1 Preheat the oven to 350°F/ Gas 4. Lightly grease an 11 x 7 inch pan. Put the flour and shortening in a bowl and rub in with your fingers until the mixture resembles fine breadcrumbs. Add enough water to mix to a firm dough.

2 Roll out on a lightly floured surface and use to line the base of the prepared pan. Spread 2 tablespoons of the jam or glaze over the dough.

3 To make the filling, cream together the butter and sugar until light and creamy. Beat in the egg, then stir in the almonds, rice and mixed fruits. Spread the mixture evenly in the pan.

4 Bake for about 35 minutes. Remove from the oven and brush with the remaining jam or glaze. Leave to cool completely in the pan before cutting into bars.

Cook's Tip

If you cannot find a ready-mixed packet of dried tropical fruits, make your own fruit mixture, choosing from the following: mangoes, apricots, guavas, dates, apples, pears, nectarines, peaches, figs and whatever else takes your fancy.

Spicy Fruit Slice

A double-layered sweet cookie in which the topping combines dried fruit, with grated carrot to keep it moist. An indulgent tea-time treat.

Makes 12–16

3½ ounces/7 tablespoons vegetable margarine

3 ounces/scant ½ cup superfine sugar

1 egg yolk

4 ounces/1 cup all-purpose flour

2 tablespoons self-rising flour

2 tablespoons dried unsweetened shredded coconut

confectioners' sugar, for dusting

For the topping

2 tablespoons ready-to-eat prunes, chopped

2 tablespoons golden raisins

2 ounces/½ cup ready-to-eat dried pears, chopped

1 ounce/¼ cup walnuts, chopped

3 ounces/⅔ cup self-rising flour

1 teaspoon ground cinnamon

½ teaspoon ground ginger

6 ounces/generous 1 cup grated carrots

1 egg, beaten

5 tablespoons vegetable oil

½ teaspoon baking soda

3½ ounces/scant ½ cup dark molasses sugar

1 Preheat the oven to 350°F/Gas 4. Line an 11 x 7 inch shallow baking pan with baking parchment. In a large mixing bowl, beat together the margarine, sugar and egg yolk until smooth and creamy.

Cook's Tip

There is no need to peel the carrots before grating them. Just give them a good scrub to remove any dirt.

2 Stir in the plain flour, self-rising flour and coconut and mix together well. Press into the base of the prepared pan, using your fingers to spread the dough evenly. Bake for about 15 minutes, or until firm and light brown.

3 To make the topping, mix together all the ingredients and spread over the cooked base. Bake for about 35 minutes, or until firm. Cool completely in the pan before cutting into bars or squares. Dust with confectioners' sugar.

Granola Bar Cookies

A gloriously dense fruity, nutty and oaty mixture, packed with goodness and delicious, too, these bars are an ideal snack and perfect to pack for a school lunch.

Makes 12

6 ounces/¾ cup sweet butter, diced

5 ounces/⅔ cup clear honey

9 ounces/generous 1 cup raw sugar

12 ounces/3 cups jumbo oats

1 teaspoon ground cinnamon

3 ounces/¾ cup pecan nut halves

3 ounces/generous ½ cup raisins

3 ounces/¾ cup ready-to-eat dried papaya, chopped

3 ounces/¾ cup ready-to-eat dried apricots, chopped

2 ounces/scant ½ cup pumpkin seeds

2 ounces/scant ½ cup sunflower seeds

2 ounces/2 tablespoons sesame seeds

2 ounces/½ cup ground almonds

1 Preheat the oven to 375°F/ Gas 5. Line a 9-inch square cake pan with baking parchment. Put the butter and honey in a large heavy pan and heat gently until the butter has melted and the mixture is completely smooth.

2 Add the raw sugar to the pan and heat very gently, stirring constantly, until the sugar has completely dissolved. Bring the butter mixture to the boil and continue to boil for 1–2 minutes, stirring the mixture constantly until it has formed a smooth caramel sauce.

3 Add the remaining ingredients and mix together. Transfer the mixture to the pan and press down with a spoon. Bake for 15 minutes, until the edges turn brown.

4 Place in the refrigerator and chill well. Turn out of the pan, peel off the parchment and cut into bars.

Luxury Granola Cookies

It is best to use a "luxury" granola for this recipe, preferably one with 50 percent mixed cereal and 50 percent fruit, nuts and seeds. These buttery, crunchy cookies are ideal for a snack at any time.

Makes about 20

4 ounces/½ cup sweet butter

3 tablespoons light corn syrup

*4 ounces/generous ½ cup
  raw sugar*

6 ounces/1½ cups "luxury" granola

3½ ounces/¾ cup self-rising flour

1 teaspoon ground cinnamon

1 Preheat the oven to 325°F/Gas 3. Line two or three baking sheets with baking parchment.

Variation

Tropical granola containing coconut and dried tropical fruits makes an interesting alternative to regular luxury granola.

2 Put the butter, syrup and sugar in a large pan and heat gently. Stir constantly until the butter has completely melted. Remove the pan from the heat, then stir in the granola, flour and cinnamon and mix together well. Set aside to cool slightly.

3 Place spoonfuls of the mixture, slightly apart, on the baking sheets. Bake for 15 minutes, until the cookies are just beginning to brown around the edges. Leave to cool for a few minutes on the baking sheets, then carefully transfer to a wire rack to cool completely.

Date Slice

Lemon-flavored icing tops these scrumptious, low-fat bars, which are full of succulent fruit and crunchy seeds – the perfect mid-morning pick-me-up with a cup of decaf.

Makes 12–16

6 ounces/¾ cup light brown sugar

6 ounces/1 cup ready-to-eat dried dates, chopped

4 ounces/1 cup self-rising flour

2 ounces/½ cup granola

2 tablespoons sunflower seeds

1 tablespoon poppy seeds

2 tablespoons golden raisins

¼ pint/⅔ cup natural low-fat yogurt

1 egg, beaten

7 ounces/1¾ cups confectioners' sugar, sifted

lemon juice

1–2 tablespoons pumpkin seeds

1 Preheat the oven to 350°F/Gas 4. Line an 11 x 7 inch shallow pan with baking parchment. Mix together all the ingredients, except the confectioners' sugar, lemon juice and pumpkin seeds.

2 Spread in the pan and bake for about 25 minutes, until golden brown. Cool.

3 To make the topping, put the confectioners' sugar in a bowl and stir in just enough lemon juice to make a spreading consistency.

4 Spread over the baked date mixture and sprinkle generously with pumpkin seeds. Leave to set before cutting into squares or bars.

Iced Carob Cookies

If you are unable to eat chocolate but still crave it, these heavenly cookies, with their creamy topping, provide the answer to your prayers.

Makes 12–16

4 ounces/½ cup butter

2 teaspoons carob powder

4 ounces/1 cup whole-wheat flour

1 teaspoon baking powder

3 ounces/⅓ cup molasses sugar

2 ounces/generous ½ cup rolled oats

For the topping

2 ounces carob bar, coarsely chopped

3 tablespoons heavy cream

1 tablespoon chopped ready-to-eat dried apricots

Cook's Tip

Carob is derived from the carob bean, which has a nutritious, flavorsome pulp.

1 Preheat the oven to 375°F/Gas 5. Line the base and sides of a 7-inch square shallow cake pan with baking parchment. Put the butter in a large pan and add the carob powder. Stir over a low heat until the mixture is smooth and combined. Stir in the remaining ingredients and mix well.

2 Press the mixture into the prepared pan and bake for about 20–25 minutes, until just set. Mark into squares or bars while still hot. Leave to cool in the pan.

3 To make the topping, stir the carob and cream in a small pan over a low heat. Spread over the cookies and sprinkle the apricots on top.

Carob and Cherry Cookies

Simplicity itself to make, these little cookies are given a chocolate-like flavor by the addition of carob and are deliciously crisp and crunchy.

Makes about 20

3½ ounces/7 tablespoons sweet butter, at room temperature, diced

3 ounces/scant ½ cup superfine sugar

3 ounces/⅓ cup light brown sugar

1 egg

5 ounces/1¼ cups self-rising flour

1 ounce/2 tablespoons carob powder

2 ounces/¼ cup candied cherries, quartered

2 ounces carob bar, chopped

1 Preheat the oven to 350°F/ Gas 4. Line two large baking sheets with baking parchment. Put the sweet butter, superfine sugar, brown sugar and the egg in a large mixing bowl and beat well together until the mixture is smooth and creamy.

2 Add the flour, carob powder, cherries and chopped carob bar to the mixture and mix well with a wooden spoon until thoroughly combined, making sure the carob powder is completely blended in.

3 Shape the mixture into walnut-size balls and place, spaced slightly apart to allow for spreading, on the prepared baking sheets.

4 Bake for about 15 minutes. Leave on the baking sheets for 5 minutes before transferring to a wire rack to cool completely.

Variations
• *If you aren't on a diet, use unsweetened cocoa powder and a bar of chocolate instead of the carob.*
• *Use raisins instead of cherries, if you like.*

Cookies for Special Diets

Food intolerances, allergies and health problems need not deprive you of the pleasures of baking and eating home-made cookies. You will be amazed by the range of low-fat, dairy-free, reduced-sugar or gluten-free sweet treats you can make – and what's more, they're so scrumptious, the whole family will be clamoring for them. Whether layered slices or fabulous brownies, the cookies in this chapter are special in every way.

Very Low-fat Brownies

If you ever need proof that you can still enjoy sweet treats even when you are on a low-fat diet, here it is. These brownies are not just tasty, but also very quick and easy to make.

Makes 16

3½ ounces/scant 1 cup
  all-purpose flour
½ teaspoon baking powder
3 tablespoons cocoa powder
  (unsweetened)
7 ounces/1 cup superfine sugar
3½ fluid ounces/scant ½ cup plain
  low-fat yogurt
2 eggs, beaten
1 teaspoon vanilla extract
½ tablespoon vegetable oil

1 Preheat the oven to 350°F/Gas 4. Line an 8-inch square cake pan with baking parchment.

2 Sift the flour, baking powder and cocoa powder into a bowl. Stir in the superfine sugar, then beat in the yogurt, eggs, vanilla, and vegetable oil until thoroughly combined. Put the mixture into the prepared pan.

3 Bake for about 25 minutes, until just firm to the touch. Leave in the pan until cooled completely.

4 Using a sharp knife, cut into 16 squares, then remove from the pan using a spatula.

Carob Chip Shorties

Perfect for anyone on a gluten-free or cow's-milk-free diet, these lovely cookies are best eaten freshly made, preferably while still slightly warm from the oven.

Makes 12

6 ounces/1½ cups gluten-free flour

1 ounce/2 tablespoons soft light
    brown sugar

3 ounces/6 tablespoons vegetable
    margarine

2 ounces/⅓ cup carob chips

1–1½ tablespoons clear honey, warmed

raw or superfine sugar, for sprinkling

1 Preheat the oven to 325°F/
Gas 3. Line two baking sheets with
baking parchment.

Cook's Tip
*Gluten-free flour can be bought at most
health-food stores.*

2 Put the flour and brown sugar
in a mixing bowl and rub in the
margarine. Add the carob chips,
then stir in just enough honey to
bring the mixture together but not
make it sticky. Roll the dough out
between two sheets of baking
parchment to about ⅓ inch.

3 Stamp out round pieces using a
plain 2-inch round cookie cutter.
Place on the baking sheets. Prick
each cookie once with a fork and
sprinkle with sugar.

4 Bake for about 15–20 minutes, or
until firm. Cool on a wire rack.

Rocky Road Wedges

Free from gluten and wheat, these crumbly chocolate wedges contain home-made popcorn in place of broken cookies, which are the classic ingredient in no-bake cookies such as this. This recipe uses an orange-flavored chocolate bar, but any gluten-free chocolate can be used.

Makes 8

1 tablespoon vegetable oil

1 ounce/2½ tablespoons popping corn

5 ounces orange-flavored semisweet chocolate

1 ounce/2 tablespoons sweet butter, diced

3 ounces soft vanilla fudge, diced

confectioners' sugar, for dusting

Cook's Tip

When buying products such as chocolate or fudge, always check the label to make sure they are gluten-free.

1 Heat the oil in a heavy pan. Add the popping corn, cover with a lid and heat, shaking the pan once or twice, until the popping noises die down. (It is important not to lift the lid until the popping stops.)

2 Remove the pan from the heat and leave for about 30 seconds before removing the lid. Be careful, as there may be quite a lot of steam trapped inside. Transfer the popcorn to a bowl and leave to cool for about 5 minutes.

3 Meanwhile, line the base of a 7-inch sandwich pan.

4 Once cooled, tip the corn into a plastic bag and tap with a rolling pin to break up into small pieces.

5 Break the chocolate into a heatproof bowl. Add the butter and rest the bowl over a pan of gently simmering water. Stir frequently until melted. Remove the bowl from the heat and leave to cool for 2 minutes.

6 Stir the popcorn and fudge into the chocolate until well coated, then turn the mixture into the pan and press down firmly in an even layer. Leave to set for about 30 minutes.

7 Turn the cookie out onto a board and cut into eight wedges. Serve lightly dusted with sugar.

Meringue Squiggles

Free from gluten, wheat and cow's milk, these wiggly wands are great for children's parties. They are fun to shape and eat, and kids of all ages love making and decorating them. Be sure to check that the multi-colored sprinkles are free from gluten and cow's milk.

Makes 14–16

2 egg whites

3½ ounces/ ½ cup superfine sugar

3 tablespoons confectioners'
   sugar

multi-colored sugar sprinkles,
   to decorate

1 Preheat the oven to 300°F/ Gas 2. Line a large baking sheet with baking parchment.

2 Put the egg whites in a large, clean bowl and whisk with a hand-held electric whisk until they form firm peaks.

3 Add a spoonful of superfine sugar to the whisked egg whites and whisk for about 15 seconds to combine. Add another spoonful and whisk again. Continue in this way until all the sugar has been added.

4 Spoon the meringue mixture into a large pastry bag fitted with a large plain nozzle. Alternatively, spoon the mixture into a plastic bag, gently push it into one corner and snip off the tip so that the meringue can be pushed out in a ¾-inch-thick line.

5 Pipe wavy lines of meringue, about 5 inches long, onto the baking sheet and bake for about 1 hour, until dry and crisp.

6 Carefully peel the meringues off the baking parchment and transfer to a wire rack to cool.

7 Put the confectioners' sugar in a small bowl and mix in a few drops of water to make a smooth paste.

8 Using a fine pastry brush, brush the tops of the meringues with a little of the sugar paste, then scatter over the multi-colored sugar sprinkles to decorate.

Cashew-nut Button Cookies

These light little cookies, flavored with ground cashew nuts, are coated in toasted hazelnuts. They are suitable for people on gluten-free and cow's-milk-free diets.

Makes about 20

1 egg white

1 ounce/2 tablespoons superfine sugar

5 ounces/1¼ cups unroasted cashew nuts, ground

2 ounces/⅓ cup dates, finely chopped

1 teaspoon finely grated orange rind

2 tablespoons pure maple or maple-flavored syrup

3½ ounces/scant 1 cup toasted hazelnuts, chopped

1 Preheat the oven to 375°F/ Gas 5. Line two baking sheets with baking parchment.

2 In a bowl, whisk the egg white until stiff. Whisk in the sugar. Stir in the cashews, dates, orange rind and syrup. Mix well. Put the chopped hazelnuts in a small bowl.

3 Drop small spoonfuls of the cookie mixture into the hazelnuts and toss until well coated.

4 Place on the prepared baking sheets and bake for about 10 minutes, until lightly browned. Leave to cool on the baking sheets.

Fruit and Millet Molasses Cookies

These little cookies are quick to make, and will no doubt disappear just as quickly when they come out of the oven. They are gluten- and cow's milk-free.

Makes about 25–30

3½ ounces/7 tablespoons vegetable margarine

5 ounces/⅔ cup light brown sugar

2 tablespoons black molasses

1 egg

5 ounces/1¼ cups gluten-free flour

2 ounces/½ cup millet flakes

2 ounces/½ cup almonds, chopped

7 ounces/generous 1 cup luxury mixed dried fruit

Cook's Tip

Make sure that you use millet flakes for these cookies, rather than millet grains. The grains will swell too much during cooking and spoil the cookies.

1 Preheat the oven to 375°F/Gas 5. Line two large baking sheets with baking parchment.

2 Put the margarine, brown sugar, molasses and egg in a large bowl and beat together until well combined. (The mixture should be light and fluffy.)

3 Stir in the flour and millet flakes, the almonds and dried fruit. Put tablespoonfuls of the mixture onto the prepared baking sheets.

4 Bake for about 15 minutes, until brown. Leave on the baking sheets for a few minutes, then transfer to a wire rack to cool completely.

Big Macaroons

These giant macaroons are crisp on the outside, chewy in the middle and naturally free from gluten and cow's milk. Ground almonds can be a great alternative to the wheat flour used in most cookies, and macaroons don't need butter for their deliciously moist, rich taste.

Makes 9

2 egg whites

1 teaspoon almond extract

4 ounces/1 cup ground almonds

4½ ounces/generous 1 cup light
  brown sugar

Cook's Tips

• *These macaroons will store well in an airtight container; do not store in the refrigerator, because they'll turn soft and lose their lovely crisp and chewy texture.*

• *To make a macaroon with a milder flavor, use superfine sugar in place of the light brown sugar.*

1 Preheat the oven to 350°F/Gas 4. Line a large baking sheet with baking parchment. Put the egg whites in a large, clean bowl and whisk until they form stiff peaks.

2 Add the almond extract to the egg whites and whisk to combine. Sprinkle over the ground almonds and sugar, and gently fold in using a large metal spoon.

3 Place nine spoonfuls of the mixture, spacing them far apart, onto the baking sheet and flatten slightly. Bake for 15 minutes until risen, deep golden and beginning to turn crisp.

4 Leave the macaroons on the baking sheets for 5 minutes, then transfer to a wire rack to cool.

Shortbread Ring Cookies

Decorated with colorful chopped candies, these little gluten- and dairy-free cookies are great for younger kids. They make delicious lunchbox fillers or snacks during the day. Don't forget to check the ingredients on the jellied fruit candies, as some varieties could contain gluten.

Makes 8–10

5 ounces/1¼ cups gluten-free flour

3½ ounces/½ cup rice flour

finely grated rind of 1 lemon

3 ounces/6 tablespoons dairy-free
  margarine

2 ounces/¼ cup superfine sugar

1 egg yolk

2 teaspoons water

For the topping

3½ ounces/scant 1 cup confectioners' sugar

2 ounces/½ cup dairy-free margarine

small jellied fruit candies

1 Put the gluten-free flour, rice flour, lemon rind and margarine in a food processor and process briefly to combine. Add the sugar, egg yolk and water, and mix to a dough.

2 Turn the dough onto a lightly floured surface and knead. Put in plastic wrap and chill for about 30 minutes.

3 Preheat the oven to 350°F/Gas 4. Grease a baking sheet.

4 Roll out the dough on a lightly floured surface to a thickness of about ¼ inch.

5 Using a 2½-inch plain or fluted cutter, cut out round pieces and place on the baking sheet. Using a 1½-inch round cutter, cut out and remove the center of each round.

6 Bake for about 20 minutes, until beginning to turn pale golden. Leave on the baking sheet for 2 minutes, then transfer to a wire rack to cool.

7 To make the topping, put the confectioners' sugar, and margarine in a bowl and beat together until creamy.

8 Pipe or spoon the topping onto the ring cookies. Chop the jellied candies into small pieces with a pair of scissors and gently press them into the cream to decorate.

Cornflake Caramel Slice

A wickedly decadent caramel layer nestles between the gluten-free base and the crispy cornflake topping. These cookies are simply irresistible – and fun to make, too.

Makes 12

6 ounces/¾ cup butter

5 ounces/¾ cup superfine sugar

10 ounces/2½ cups gluten-free
   flour

1 egg, beaten

For the topping

2 tablespoons light corn syrup

14-ounce can sweetened
   condensed milk

2 ounces/¼ cup butter

6 tablespoons sour cream

about 1½ ounces/2 cups cornflakes

confectioners' sugar (optional)

1 Preheat the oven to 375°F/ Gas 5. And proceed to line an 11 x 7 inch shallow cake pan with baking parchment.

2 Melt the butter in a pan, then remove from the heat. Put the sugar and flour in a bowl. Add the beaten egg and melted butter, and mix well. Press the mixture evenly into the base of the prepared pan.

3 Bake for about 20 minutes, until golden brown. Leave the base to cool completely in the pan.

4 For the topping, heat the syrup, condensed milk and butter over a low heat for 10–15 minutes, stirring occasionally, until the mixture is thick and turns a caramel color.

5 Remove from the heat and stir in the sour cream. Spread over the base. Sprinkle over the cornflakes and leave to set. Sprinkle with confectioners' sugar, if using, and cut into bars.

Double Chocolate Slices

These delicious gluten-free cookies have a smooth chocolate base, topped with a mint-flavored cream and drizzles of melted chocolate. Perfect for a tea-time treat – or at any time of day.

Makes 12

7 ounces/1¾ cups gluten-free flour

1 ounce/2 tablespoons cocoa powder
  (unsweetened)

5 ounces/⅔ cup sweet butter,
  cut into small pieces

3 ounces/¾ cup confectioners'
  sugar

For the topping

3 ounces white chocolate mint crisps

2 ounces/¼ cup sweet butter,
  softened

3½ ounces/scant 1 cup confectioners'
  sugar

2 ounces milk chocolate

1 Preheat the oven to 350°F/ Gas 4. Grease a 7-inch square shallow baking pan, and line with a strip of baking parchment that comes up over two opposite sides. This will make it easier to remove the cookie base from the pan after baking.

2 Put the flour and cocoa powder into a food processor and add the pieces of butter. Process briefly until the mixture resembles fine breadcrumbs. Add the confectioners' sugar and mix briefly again to form a smooth soft dough.

3 Turn the flour mixture into the prepared pan and gently press out to the edges with your fingers to make an even layer. Bake for 25 minutes, then remove from the oven and leave the base to cool completely in the pan.

4 To make the topping, put the chocolate mint crisps in a plastic bag and tap firmly with a rolling pin until they are crushed. Beat the butter and sugar together until creamy, then beat in the crushed chocolate mint crisps. Spread the mixture evenly over the cookie base.

5 Melt the milk chocolate in a small heatproof bowl set over a pan of hot water. Lift the cookie base out of the pan, and remove the paper. Using a teaspoon, drizzle the melted chocolate over the topping. Leave to set, then cut into squares.

Chocolate-chip Cookies

This gluten-free version of these perennially popular cookies is bound to be a big hit with all the family because of their lovely, light texture.

Makes 16

3 ounces/6 tablespoons soft margarine
2 ounces/¼ cup soft light brown sugar
2 ounces/¼ cup superfine sugar
1 egg, beaten
few drops of vanilla extract
3 ounces/¾ cup rice flour
3 ounces/¾ cup gluten-free cornmeal
1 teaspoon gluten-free baking powder
pinch of salt
4 ounces/⅔ cup semisweet chocolate
　chips, or a mixture of milk and white
　chocolate chips

1 Preheat the oven to 375°F/Gas 5. Lightly grease two baking sheets. Place the margarine and sugars in a bowl and cream together until light and fluffy.

2 Beat in the egg and vanilla extract. Fold in the rice flour, cornmeal, baking powder and salt, then fold in the chocolate chips.

3 Place spoonfuls of the mixture on the prepared baking sheets, leaving space for spreading between each one. Bake for 10–15 minutes, until the cookies are lightly browned.

4 Remove the cookies from the oven and leave on the baking sheets for a few minutes to cool slightly, then carefully transfer to a wire rack, using a metal spatula, and leave them to cool completely before serving.

Cook's Tip
Once the cookies are cold, they can be stored in an airtight container for up to a week. Alternatively, pack them into plastic bags and freeze.

Cherry Coconut Munchies

You'll find it hard to stop at just one of these gluten-free munchies, which make a wonderful morning or afternoon treat. If you like, drizzle 1–2 ounces of melted chocolate over the cold munchies and leave to set before serving.

Makes 20

2 egg whites
4 ounces/1 cup confectioners' sugar, sifted
4 ounces/1 cup ground almonds
4 ounces/generous 1 cup dried
　unsweetened shredded coconut
few drops of almond extract
3 ounces/½ cup candied cherries,
　finely chopped

Variation
Use ground hazelnuts in place of the almonds, and omit the almond essence.

1 Preheat the oven to 300°F/Gas 2. Line two baking sheets with non-stick baking parchment. Place the egg whites in a grease-free bowl and whisk until stiff.

2 Gently fold in the confectioners' sugar, then fold in the ground almonds, coconut and almond extract to form a sticky dough. Finally, fold in the chopped candied cherries.

3 Place mounds on the baking sheets. Bake for 25 minutes. Cool briefly on the baking sheets, then transfer to a wire rack.

Phyllo and Apricot Purses

Phyllo pastry is very easy to use. Keep a packet in the freezer ready for rustling up a speedy dairy-free tea-time treat that looks as good as it tastes.

Makes 12

4 ounces/½ cup ready-to-eat dried apricots

3 tablespoons apricot compote
or conserve

3 macaroons, crushed

3 phyllo pastry sheets

4 teaspoons soya margarine, melted,
plus extra for greasing

confectioners' sugar, for dusting

1 Preheat the oven to 350°F/Gas 4. Lightly grease two baking sheets with soya margarine.

2 Chop the apricots fairly finely, put them in a bowl and stir in the apricot compote or conserve. Add the crushed macaroons and mix together well.

3 Cut the phyllo pastry into 24 × 5-inch squares, pile the squares on top of each other and cover with a clean dishtowel to prevent the pastry from drying out and becoming hard and brittle.

4 Lay one pastry square on a flat surface, brush lightly with melted soya margarine and lay another square on top. Brush the top square with melted margarine. Spoon a small amount of apricot mixture in the center of the pastry, bring up the edges and pinch together in a money-bag shape. Repeat with the remaining pastry squares and filling to make 12 purses in all.

5 Arrange on the baking sheets and bake for 5–8 minutes, until golden. Transfer to a wire rack and dust lightly with confectioners' sugar. Serve warm.

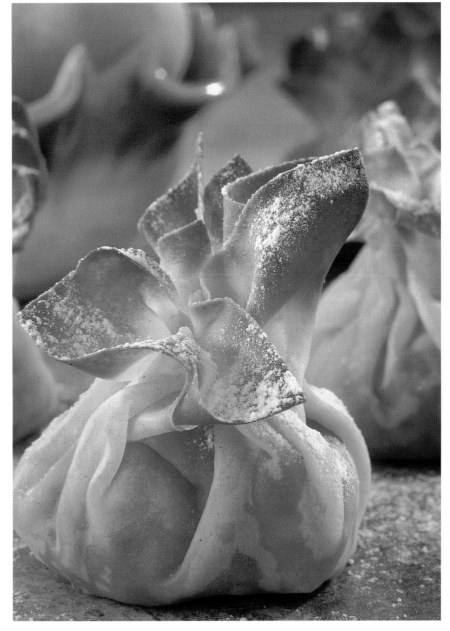

Tomato Breadsticks

Once you've tried this simple recipe you'll never buy manufactured breadsticks again. Serve as a gluten-free snack, or with aperitifs and a dip at the beginning of a meal.

Makes 16

8 ounces/2 cups gluten-free
  all-purpose flour

½ teaspoon salt

½ teaspoon rapid-rise
  dry yeast

1 teaspoon clear honey

1 teaspoon olive oil

¼ pint/⅔ cup warm water

6 halves sun-dried tomatoes in olive oil,
  rinsed, drained and chopped

1 tablespoon skimmed milk

2 teaspoons poppy seeds

1 Place the flour, salt and yeast in a food processor. Add the honey and oil and, with the machine running, gradually pour in the water – stop adding water as soon as the dough starts to cling together. Process for 1 minute more.

2 Turn out the dough onto a floured board and knead for about 3–4 minutes until it is springy, smooth and elastic.

3 Knead in the chopped sun-dried tomatoes until evenly distributed. Form the dough into a ball and place in a lightly oiled bowl. Cover with oiled plastic wrap and leave to rise for 5 minutes.

4 Divide the dough into 16 pieces and roll each into an 11 × ½ inch stick. Place on a lightly oiled baking sheet and leave to rise in a warm place for 15 minutes.

5 Preheat the oven to 300°F/Gas 2. Brush the sticks with milk and sprinkle with poppy seeds. Bake for 30 minutes. Leave to cool on a wire cooling rack.

Sunflower and Yogurt Scones

For those who have to watch their gluten intake, these golden scones, with their lovely crunchy topping, are a treat indeed.

Makes 10–12

8 ounces/2 cups gluten-free
  self-rising flour
1 teaspoon baking powder
1 ounce/2 tablespoons soft sunflower
  margarine
2 tablespoons light brown sugar
2 ounces/⅓ cup raisins
4 tablespoons sunflower seeds
5 fluid ounces/⅔ cup plain yogurt
about 2 tablespoons skimmed milk

1 Preheat the oven to 450°F/ Gas 8. Lightly oil a baking sheet. Sift the flour and baking powder into a bowl and rub in the margarine evenly.

2 Stir in the superfine sugar, raisins and about half the sunflower seeds, then mix in the yogurt, adding just enough milk to make a fairly soft, but not sticky dough.

3 Roll out the dough on a lightly floured surface to about ¾ of an inch thickness. Cut into 2½-inch flower shapes, or stamp out round pieces with a fluted cutter and lift them onto the prepared baking sheet.

4 Brush with milk and sprinkle with the reserved sunflower seeds, then bake for 10–12 minutes, until well risen and golden brown.

5 Cool the scones on a wire rack. Serve split and spread with jam.

Prune and Peel Rock Buns

These gluten-free buns are quick and easy to make, and they taste absolutely wonderful.

Makes 12

8 ounces/2 cups gluten-free
  all-purpose flour
2 teaspoons baking powder
3 ounces/⅔ cup raw sugar
2 ounces/1½ cup chopped ready-to-eat
  dried prunes
2 ounces/⅓ cup chopped
  candied peel
finely grated rind of 1 lemon
4 tablespoons sunflower oil
5 tablespoons skimmed milk

1 Preheat the oven to 400°F/Gas 6. Lightly oil a large baking sheet. Sift the flour and baking powder, then stir in the sugar, prunes, peel and lemon rind.

2 Mix the oil and milk, then stir into the mixture, to make a dough which just binds together.

Variation

For a dairy-free version of these rock buns, you can substitute soya milk for the skimmed milk.

3 Spoon into rocky heaps on the baking sheet and bake for about 20 minutes, until golden. Transfer to a wire rack to cool.